Green Development of Asia-Pacific Cities

Building Better Cities Towards 2030

Green Development of Asia-Pacific Cities
Building Better Cities Towards 2030

Zheng Zhao
*Development Research Center
of the State Council, PRC*

NEW JERSEY · LONDON · SINGAPORE · BEIJING · SHANGHAI · HONG KONG · TAIPEI · CHENNAI · TOKYO

Published by

World Scientific Publishing Co. Pte. Ltd.

5 Toh Tuck Link, Singapore 596224

USA office: 27 Warren Street, Suite 401-402, Hackensack, NJ 07601

UK office: 57 Shelton Street, Covent Garden, London WC2H 9HE

Library of Congress Cataloging-in-Publication Data
Names: Zhao, Zheng, 1979– editor.
Title: Green development of Asia-Pacific cities : building better cities towards 2030 /
edited by: Zheng Zhao (Development Research Center of the State Council, PRC).
Description: New Jersey : World Scientific, 2018. | Includes bibliographical references and indexes.
Identifiers: LCCN 2018006458 | ISBN 9789813236813 (hc : alk. paper)
Subjects: LCSH: Sustainable urban development--Pacific Area--Case studies. |
Sustainable urban development--Asia--Case studies. | City planning--
Pacific Area--Case studies. | City planning--Asia--Case studies.
Classification: LCC HT243.A78 G74 2018 | DDC 307.1/416095--dc23
LC record available at https://lccn.loc.gov/2018006458

British Library Cataloguing-in-Publication Data
A catalogue record for this book is available from the British Library.

亚太城市绿色发展报告
Originally published in Chinese by China Social Sciences Press.
Copyright © China Social Sciences Press, 2016

Copyright © 2019 by World Scientific Publishing Co. Pte. Ltd.

All rights reserved. This book, or parts thereof, may not be reproduced in any form or by any means, electronic or mechanical, including photocopying, recording or any information storage and retrieval system now known or to be invented, without written permission from the publisher.

For photocopying of material in this volume, please pay a copying fee through the Copyright Clearance Center, Inc., 222 Rosewood Drive, Danvers, MA 01923, USA. In this case permission to photocopy is not required from the publisher.

For any available supplementary material, please visit
https://www.worldscientific.com/worldscibooks/10.1142/10897#t=suppl

Desk Editors: Dr. Sree Meenakshi Sajani/Sylvia Koh

Typeset by Stallion Press
Email: enquiries@stallionpress.com

Printed in Singapore

Preface

City is the greatest invention of humanity and carries our most beautiful hope. The history of city has a far-reaching impact on the progress of human civilization. It can be said that the future of cities determines the future of humanity. Technological and industrial revolutions have brought more and more countries into "urban societies". Growing at an unprecedented pace, cities are creating enormous material and spiritual wealth, nurturing and unleashing the vitality of innovation and changes, and influencing the future and destiny of human development. The Asia-Pacific region, which covers a vast territory with a large population, boasts the world's fastest growing economy, greatest development potential and most active cooperation. Moreover, the region is also an important engine driving the economic recovery and development worldwide. Cities in the Asia-Pacific region are distinctively characterized by diversified economic development and their vital role in the global city network. However, while the traditional urbanization pattern of the Asia-Pacific region has facilitated the rapid economic growth, it has also caused many problems, such as environmental pollution and disruption; excessive consumption of energy and resources; social fragmentation and inequality and other "urban diseases". In addition, the aftermath of the financial crisis has not yet been completely eliminated. Therefore, urban development and transformation in the Asia-Pacific region are confronted with huge pressure and challenges.

vi *Preface*

Cities in the Asia-Pacific region are at the crossroad of transformation and development. In order to create better cities, more beautiful environment, more vigorous economy, more affluent and happier life, we need to think about the future, invest in our future, and more importantly, make decisions and take actions today. On 25 September 2015, the United Nations Sustainable Development Summit approved *Transforming Our World: The 2030 Agenda for Sustainable Development*, a programmatic document that has outlined the blueprint for global development for the next 15 years. In this new century, we need to rethink the development pattern of cities in the Asia-Pacific region and fully understand the diversity and complexity of urban green development. Moreover, we need to explore ways to promote the exchange of our experience in pursuing the post-2015 sustainable development goals, so as to better share the achievements made in facilitating urban development.

This report provides an analytical framework for urban green development. According to the report, urban green development is not only a sustainable development pattern that serves to create wealth more efficiently and benefit more people while protecting the environment, but it also contributes to a balanced development between man and nature, economy and society, government and market, and city and nation. The report proposes the urban green development philosophy that features livability, prosperity, inclusiveness, governance and partnership. Moreover, the report introduces an evaluation indicator system for urban green development. It evaluates and analyzes the green development level of 100 major cities in the Asia-Pacific region; studies urban green development cases, especially the urban green development in China; summarizes the experience of China and foreign countries in pursuing urban green development; analyzes the major problems in Chinese urban green development; provides advice on urban green development.

Preparing this report was a daunting and challenging job. Over 50 young experts and scholars from international organizations and renowned universities and think tanks of the United States, Russia, Australia, Singapore, Thailand, Britain and China, such as Chinese Academy of Social Sciences, Development Research Center of the

State Council and Beijing Normal University, had jointly established a research team. This report is an achievement made by the joint team based on their research, discussion, exchange of ideas and refinement over nearly one year and a half. We sincerely hope that through international cooperation in research, we can obtain insights from far-sighted people, so as to contribute to the urban green development of the Asia-Pacific region and beyond to jointly build better cities in accordance with the *2030 Agenda for Sustainable Development*.

Zheng Zhao

About the Editor

Zheng Zhao is a researcher in Development Research Center of the State Council of PRC and a Vice President at Capital Institute of Science and Technology Development Strategy. He studies region and urban development. He is a China expert on the Global Outlook Project, a China expert on the China–EU Policy Dialogue Project, a standing member of Discipline Construction Committee of China Urban Economics Association, a guest researcher at the Urban and Competitiveness Research Center of Chinese Academy of Social Sciences, and a guest researcher at the Tourism Research Center of Chinese Academy of Social Sciences. He acquired his Ph.D. in Economics from Beijing Normal University and has served as Associate Professor in Economics for 8 years. He also held the position of Vice President of Asia-Pacific Green Development Research Center of Beijing Normal University.

He has published several books as author and chief editor such as *Green Development and Green Finance: Theory, Policy and Cases, China City Marketing Development Report, China's Urbanization and Financial Support, Industrial Upgrading and National Competitive Advantage, Beijing Urban Industrial System Selection Research.* And he participated in the preparation of more than 10 research reports, such as *China's Urban Competitiveness Report, China's Market Economic Development Report and China Green Development Index Report.*

Contents

Preface   v

About the Editor   ix

*Research Group of the Asia-Pacific Urban Green
Development Report*   xix

Part I. Theoretical Framework   **1**

**Chapter 1. Background and Theoretical
Interpretation of Urban Green
Development**   **3**

Zheng Zhao

I.   Green Development: Direction of Sustainable
Development for 2030   4
II.   Why Green Development for Cities?   9
III. Theoretical Model and Realization Mechanism
of Urban Green Development   14
References   21

**Chapter 2. Basic Connotations and Analysis
Framework of Urban Green
Development**   **23**

Zheng Zhao

xii   *Contents*

I.   Basic Connotations of Urban Green Development:
Four Important Relations 23
II.   Five-Dimensional Analysis Framework of Urban
Green Development 30
References 52

Part II. Evaluation Chapters   55

Chapter 3. Urban Green Development Index
and Evaluation Index System   57

Zheng Zhao

I.   Urban Green Development Index 57
II.   Design Principles of Asia-Pacific UGDI 58
III. UGDI System 60
IV. Samples of Cities 61
V.   Sources of Data 62
VI. Evaluation Methods 63

Chapter 4. Evaluation Results and Main
Research Findings of Asia-Pacific
Urban Green Development   67

Zheng Zhao

I.   Overall Ranking and Sub-ranking
of Asia-Pacific UGDI 67
II.   Main Findings 92
Reference 103

Part III. International Chapters   105

Chapter 5. Clean Technology and Sustainable
Urban Solutions in Singapore   107

Chen Gang

I.   Low-Carbon City Planning 108

Contents

II. Wide Use of Renewable Energy, Energy-Saving
Building Materials and Technology 109

III. Conservation and Recycling of Water Resources
in Urban Areas 111

IV. Sustainable Transport 112

V. Power Generation 115

References 116

**Chapter 6. Air Governance in London:
Experiences and Strategies**   **119**

Frank Birkin

I. A Persistent Problem 119

II. London's Transport Strategy 123

III. Raising Air Pollution Awareness 124

IV. More Air Pollution Knowledge 125

V. Engaging Communication 128

VI. Some Recent Proposals for Cleaning London's Air 132

References 138

**Chapter 7. Urban Green Energy Development
in Russia: Vladivostok City**   **141**

Pavel Luzin

I. Russian Political Economy Frameworks
for the Green Energy 141

II. The Definition of "Flexible City" 144

III. Vladivostok: Possible Green Energy Scenarios 147

IV. Conclusion 149

References 150

**Chapter 8. Green Urban Development in Asia
and the Pacific — Water Issues
for Tourism**   **153**

Susanne Becken and Noel Scott

I. Introduction 153

II. Water Usage 154

Contents

III. The Cost of Water 156
IV. Availability and Quality 158
V. Measures to Reduce Water Usage 160
VI. Conclusion 162
References 163

Chapter 9. Current Practice on Resource Efficiency in Southeast Asian Cities   167

Li Liang and Alice Sharp

I. Introduction 167
II. Trends in Resource Consumption 169
III. Resource Efficiency and Environmental Issues 174
IV. Resource Efficiency Initiatives in South East
    Asian Cities 185
V. Parameters for Gauging Resource Efficiency
    Implementation 188
VI. Conclusion 189
Acknowledgments 190
References 190

Chapter 10. Case Study: Portland Urban Growth Management   193

Shiming Yang and Jefferey M. Sellers

I. Introduction 194
II. Politics, Institutions and Policies 196
III. Conclusion 203

Chapter 11. Urban Green Growth in Japan: The Case of Kitakyushu   205

Haibo Zhao and Sho Haneda

I. Introduction 205
II. Economy and Environment in Kitakyushu 206
III. Green Growth Strategy in Kitakyushu 209
IV. Technology Exporting to Asian Cities 213
V. Conclusion 216
References 217

Chapter 12. Malaysia Urban Green Development: A Case Study of Penang
219

Stuart MacDonald and Tong Yee Siong

I.   Introduction 219
II. Physical Planning 222
III. Transportation 224
IV. Housing 227
V.   Public Spaces 230
VI. Environment 232
VII. Conclusion 235
References 236

Chapter 13. Seoul's Experience and Inspiration from the Governance of Cheonggyecheon
237

Zheng Zhao

I.   Innovative Governance of Urban Inland Rivers 237
II. Inclusive Participation 238
III. Integrated Renovation of Water and Transport 239
IV. Urban Fabrics Interwoven by Ancient Bridges 240
V.   City Revitalization through Concentrated
     Investments 240
VI. Inspirations 241
Acknowledgments 242

Chapter 14. Taiwan China: A Green City Underpinned by YouBike
243

Chin-Hsien Yu and Chin-Hsiu Ting

Chapter 15. Hong Kong's Inspiring Severe Weather Pre-warning and Response Mechanism for Beijing
251

Chia-Kuan Han

xvi   *Contents*

I.   Hong Kong's Severe Weather Pre-warning and
Response Mechanism 252
II.   Characteristics and Successful Experiences
of Hong Kong's Natural Disaster Emergency
Response Mechanism 256
III. Beijing's Existing Mechanism for Inclement Weather ... 260
IV. Inspiration from Hong Kong's Experience
for Establishing Early-warning Mechanism
for Weather Crisis in Beijing 262

Chapter 16. Contributing and Creating Attractiveness through the Development of a Sustainable and Smart City District — Stockholm Royal Seaport   265

Emma Björner

I.   Introduction 265
II.   The Sustainable, Smart City 266
III. Branding a City — to Contribute 268
IV. Stockholm Royal Seaport: A Sustainable City Area 269
V.   Conclusion 272
References 273

Part IV. China Chapters   277

Chapter 17. Green Space and Peoples' Leisure Life: Overseas Experience and China's Reality   279

Song Rui

I.   Urban Green Space: Benefits, Classification
and Standards 279
II.   Experience of Urban Green Space from Overseas: Oxford,
Britain 281

III. Urban Green Space in China: Supply–Demand Imbalance
and Solutions 284
References 289

Chapter 18. China's Regional Development Strategy and Urban Green Development Efficiency Based on Urban Data Analysis of the Silk Road Economic Belt 291

Zheng Zhao

I. Introduction 291
II. Measurement of Green Development Efficiency
of Cities in the Silk Road Economic Belt 293
III. Analysis of Factors Affecting Urban
Green Development Efficiency of the Silk
Road Economic Belt 299
IV. Main Suggestions 303
Reference 305

Part V. Strategy Chapters 307

Chapter 19. Green Development Strategy of Asia-Pacific Cities 309

Zheng Zhao

I. Strategic Goals of Green Development in Cities
in the Asia-Pacific Region 310
II. Strategic Path of Green Development in Asia-Pacific
Cities 312
Reference 320

Chapter 20. Urban Green Development Strategy in China 321

Zheng Zhao

I. Livability Strategy 322
II. Prosperity Strategy 326

III.	Inclusiveness Strategy	332
IV.	Governance Strategy	336
V.	Partnership Strategy	341
References		346

Appendix I. Literature Review of Relevant Studies on Urban Green Development Evaluation · · · 347

I.	Green Accounting Evaluation	347
II.	Ecological Footprint Assessment	352
III.	Green Economic Assessment	355
IV.	Green Index Evaluation	359
V.	Governance Performance Evaluation	361
VI.	Comprehensive Welfare Assessment	361
VII.	Green City Assessment	366
VIII.	Green Development Evaluation in China	369
References		371

Appendix II. Interpretation and Data Sources of Urban Green Development Indexes · · · 373

Appendix III. Analysis on Urban Green Development Index Rankings of Main Cities in Asia-Pacific Region · · · 377

I.	China	377
II.	United States	377
III.	Japan	379
IV.	South Korea	381
V.	Australia	381
VI.	Canada	382
VII.	Russia	382
VIII.	India	383
IX.	New Zealand	384

Index · · · 385

Research Group of the Asia-Pacific Urban Green Development Report

Consultants

Zhongyuan Lu (Former Deputy Director, Development Research Center, State Council)

Xiaoxi Li (Deputy Director, Academic Committee, Beijing Normal University; Convener, Faculty of Economics, Committee of Social Sciences, Ministry of Education)

Yongnian Zheng (Director, East Asia Institute, National University of Singapore)

Chenghua Guan (Dean, Institute of Economics and Resource Management, Beijing Normal University)

Osamu Mizuno (Director, Regional Resource Centre for Asia and the Pacific, Asian Institute of Technology)

Mu Yang (Executive Dean, Institute of Public Policy, South China University of Technology)

Pengfei Ni (Director, Center for City and Competitiveness, Chinese Academy of Social Sciences)

Editor-in-Chief: Zheng Zhao

Associate Editor-in-Chief: Gang Chen, Li Liang

Assistant to Editor-in-Chief: Xiangfei Yuan

Members of Editorial Board

Gang Chen, Researcher, East Asian Institute, National University of Singapore

Frank Birkin, Professor, Sheffield University Management School

Pavel Luzin, PhD in International Relations/Researcher, Institute of World Economy and International Relations, Perm State National Research University

Susanne Becken, Professor, School of Tourism, Griffith University

Noel Scott, Professor, School of Tourism, Griffith University

Li Liang, Project Officer, Regional Resource Centre for Asia and the Pacific, Asian Institute of Technology

Alice Sharp, Associate Professor, Sirindhorn International Institute of Technology, Thammasat University

Shiming Yang, Doctor, Department of Political Science, University of Southern California

Jefferey M. Sellers, Professor, Department of Political Science, University of Southern California

Sho Haneda, PhD in Economics, University of Edinburgh

Stuart MacDonald, Research/Director, Department of Urban Studies, Penang College

Tong Yee Siong, Doctor, Centre of Development Studies, University of Cambridge

Emma Björner, Doctor, Business School, Stockholm University

Jinxian Yu, Associate Professor, Institute of Development Studies, Southwestern University of Finance and Economics

Jinxiu Ding, Associate Professor, Department of Finance, Xiamen University

Chia-kuan Han, Researcher, Hong Kong General Chamber of Commerce

Rui Song, Director/Researcher, Tourism Research Center, Chinese Academy of Social Sciences

Yanping Liu, Deputy Director/Associate Researcher, Urban and Real Estate Economic Research Office, Chinese Academy of Social Sciences

Tao Liu, Director/Associate Researcher, Service Economy Research Office, Development Research Center of the State Council

Shaokun Wei, Associate Researcher, Urban and Small Town Reform and Development Center, National Development and Reform Commission

Sisi Tang, Deputy Secretary General/Associate Researcher, China Smarter City Development and Research Center, State Information Center

Yudong Yang, Researcher, Research Division, Advisory Committee for State Informatization

Haiyuan Wan, Associate Researcher, Institute for Social Development, National Development and Reform Commission

Haisheng Xie, Associate Researcher, Center for Policy Research, Ministry of Housing and Urban-Rural Development

Hongguang Cheng, Professor, School of Environment, Beijing Normal University

Weibin Lin, Deputy Director/Associate Professor, Research Center for Energy and Strategic Resources, Beijing Normal University

Minghui Qian, Deputy Director/Associate Professor, Smart City Research Center, Renmin University of China

Ran Ren, Post-Doctor, Lecturer, School of Languages and Cultural Communication, Beijing Jiatong University

Boqiang Xiao, General Manager of Project Research, Tianjin Climate Exchange

Data Analysis and Trans-Editing Group

Yang Liu (Tsinghua University), Jie Yang (Ministry of Land and Resources), Henan Wang (Beijing Normal University), Delong Min (China-Africa Development Fund), Qian Wan (Renmin University of China), Huachen Liu (Beijing Normal University), Qi Wang (Beijing Normal University), Yikai Chai (School of Translation Studies, Xi'an International Studies University), Hua Zhong (School of Translation Studies, Xi'an International Studies University, Sa Liu (School of Translation Studies, Xi'an International Studies University), Yin He (School of Translation Studies, Xi'an International Studies University), Yiwei Feng (School of Translation Studies, Xi'an International Studies University)

Research Support

Asia-Pacific Green Development Center

Regional Resource Centre for Asia and the Pacific, Asian Institute of Technology

East Asian Institute, National University of Singapore

Green Industry Platform, China Chapter Office, United Nations Industrial Development Organization

Center for City and Competitiveness, Chinese Academy of Social Sciences

Institute of Economics and Resource Management, Beijing Normal University

Institute of Innovation Development, Beijing Normal University

Institute of Green Economy, Beijing Normal University

Smart City Research Center, Renmin University of China

Institute of Public Policy, South China University of Technology

Capital Institute of Science and Technology Development Strategy

Beijing Key Laboratory of Urban Green Development Science and Technology Strategy Research

Part I

Theoretical Framework

Chapter 1

Background and Theoretical Interpretation of Urban Green Development

Zheng Zhao
Researcher, Development Research Center
of the State Council of PRC
zz_bnu@126.com

Cities are humanity's greatest invention. Urbanization is a process through which humanity not only uses and changes the natural environment but also identifies with and adapts to its self-development support system. Whether in the past, at the present or in the future, the quality of urban development depends largely on the way we understand and build cities. The UN 2030 Agenda for Sustainable Development began amidst the conflicts between prosperity and poverty, progress and decline, and opportunity and challenge; and amidst the impacts of environmental destruction, economic recession, escalating poverty and social imbalances. The Agenda rethinks the relationships between man and nature, man and economy, and man and society; in turn, it redefines the goals, implications and patterns of urban development. Green development is the inevitable direction of urban development.

I. Green Development: Direction of Sustainable Development for 2030

Humanity never stops thinking about its self-development, especially since the mid-20th century after the arrival of industrial civilization. Industrial civilization is the state of civilization following the industrial revolution that is characterized by widespread use of powered machines and the commonly seen chimneys, wastewater and sprawling slums. Since the industrial revolution, various conflicts had been escalating and the issues facing the economy, resources, environment and society had become increasingly salient. This has provoked humanity into thinking seriously about its development pattern. The book *Silent Spring* written by Rachel Carson (an American biologist) and published in 1962 revealed the detrimental impacts of industrial development to the environment, calling for effective actions to reduce environmental pollution and disruption caused by industrialization. The report *The Limits to Growth* published by the Club of Rome in 1972 warned that population and industrial growth will become limited, since the earth's resources are depleted and the ecological environment is disrupted. The report holds that the earth's resources are finite and growth could not continue indefinitely. It also proposed the well-known "zero growth" strategy. In the same year, the first United Nations Conference on the Human Environment was held in Stockholm. At the conference, the slogan "Only One Earth" was proposed and the *Declaration of the United Nations Conference on the Human Environment* (the first international environmental declaration) was adopted. This has not only impacted the conventional perception on relations between society and nature but also helped humanity identify with the sustainable development idea. In 1987, the World Commission on Environment and Development, headed by Mrs. Brundtland, published the report *Our Common Future*. The report formally used the concept of sustainable development and defined sustainable development as "development that meets the needs of the present without compromising the ability of future generations to meet their own needs". In 1992, the *United Nations Conference on Environment and Development* adopted "Agenda 21", which formed an action plan for sustainable development worldwide and received the highest level of political commitment. Since the conference, the concept of sustainable development has been put into practice. In 2000, the United Nations Millennium Summit adopted the *Millennium Declaration* and set the Millennium Development Goals (MDGs), which established indexes and schedules for achieving the development goals at global level for the first time ever. It marks a groundbreaking moment in the history of human development.

On 25 September 2015, the United Nations Sustainable Development Summit was held at UN Headquarters in New York. *Transforming Our World: The 2030 Agenda for Sustainable Development* adopted by the summit maps out the blueprint for global development in the next 15 years (Table 1.1). The 2030 Agenda is a set of 17 "Global Goals" with 169 targets between them, which are clustered into five categories: people, planet, prosperity, peace and partnerships. Ending poverty remains the primary goal of the agenda. The 2030 Agenda remains committed to improving health and education, promoting gender equality and combating climate change. In addition, it sets higher standards for protecting water resources, ensuring energy security, reducing inequality within and among countries and protecting marine resources, in an attempt to build consensus between the developed and developing countries. The agenda serves as a road map for ending poverty and allowing everyone to benefit from sustainable development.

The 2030 Agenda for Sustainable Development is a set of global goals and programs designed to end poverty, protect the earth and ensure prosperity for all, amidst the increasing global problems and challenges. Compared with the MDGs set in 2000, the 2030 Agenda reflects a new global understanding of sustainable development. The SDGs cover a wider scope of targets and fields than the MDGs. The SDGs not only involve the concept of intergenerational equity explored in sustainable development but also cover the ecological, economic, social and governance fields. They are designed for the following purposes: protecting the ecosystems and climate on which all lives rely; developing innovation-based, environmentally friendly economic systems; building peaceful, inclusive and well-governed

Table 1.1. The Sustainable Development Goals (SDGs) of the UN 2030 Agenda for Sustainable Development.

No.	Goals
1	End poverty in all its forms everywhere
2	End hunger, achieve food security and improved nutrition, and promote sustainable agriculture
3	Ensure healthy lives and promote well-being for all at all ages
4	Ensure inclusive and equitable quality education and promote lifelong learning opportunities for all
5	Achieve gender equality and empower all women and girls
6	Ensure availability and sustainable management of water and sanitation for all
7	Ensure access to affordable, reliable, sustainable and modern energy for all
8	Promote sustained, inclusive and sustainable economic growth; full and productive employment; decent work for all
9	Build resilient infrastructure; promote inclusive and sustainable industrialization; foster innovation
10	Reduce inequality within and among countries
11	Make cities and human settlements inclusive, safe, resilient and sustainable
12	Ensure sustainable consumption and production patterns
13	Take urgent action to combat climate change and its impacts
14	Conserve and sustainably use the oceans, seas and marine resources for sustainable development
15	Protect, restore and promote sustainable use of terrestrial ecosystems; sustainably manage forests; combat desertification; halt and reverse land degradation; halt biodiversity loss
16	Promote peaceful and inclusive societies for sustainable development; provide access to justice for all; build effective, accountable and inclusive institutions at all levels
17	Strengthen the means of implementation and revitalize the global partnership for sustainable development

Source: United Nations Environment Programme.

societies; fundamentally changing the development outlook from traditional excessive pursuit of economic growth to a balanced development of the economy, society and the environment by strengthening multilateral cooperation through the revitalization of global partnerships. The SDGs also offer a clear action plan.

The concept of green development is consistent with that of sustainable development, especially the concept of the *2030 Agenda for Sustainable Development.* In 1989, David Pearce, a British environmental economist, first used the term "green economy" in his book *Blueprint for a Green Economy.* He treats the term "green economy" as a synonym of sustainable development and has explored the ways to achieve sustainable development from the perspective of environmental economics. Amidst the increasingly severe international financial crisis, the United Nations Environment Programme (UNEP) launched a "Global Green New Deal" in 2008. The new deal was designed to allow global leaders and policy makers of relevant departments to realize that a green economy is not a burden on economic growth but an engine of growth. The UNEP called on countries to develop green economies by transforming the pattern of economic growth, which has received positive responses from the international community. In 2009, the Organisation for Economic Cooperation and Development (OECD) issued the *Declaration on Green Growth.* In 2010, the EU introduced the *Europe 2020 Strategy.* These documents present green development as a core strategy for promoting regional and national competitiveness. The US, Japan and other developed countries have launched green development strategy plans in an attempt to get out of the financial crisis by transforming their previous development pattern to a green one driven by technology and innovation. Green development has become the trendy pattern of global development. It is widely believed that in the short term, promoting green development not only can boost employment and the economy but also can effectively adjust the economic structure and strike a balance between resources and economic growth; in the long term, it can serve to achieve coordinated, sustainable development in a large number of fields and prevent another round of international financial crisis.[1] Generally, green development is a development pattern that is gradually emerging under the backdrop of sustainable development. Green development starts with the sustainable development of the economy, society, nature and the environment. It is highly consistent with the core value and philosophy upheld by the *2030 Agenda for Sustainable Development.* Both green and sustainable development patterns pursue a balance between economic, ecological and social benefits.

Moreover, emphasizing fairness, sustainability and development, both patterns aim to transform development patterns and enhance human well-being. Like sustainable development, green development is also the result of humanity's self-examination of traditional civilization, especially industrial civilization. It represents a great progress in the development philosophy and the form of human civilization. Moreover, it serves not only as a way to reduce and prevent environmental pollution and ecological disruption so as to achieve sustainable development of the economy and society but also as a new option that humanity has chosen to improve its ways of living, production and development.

Although the concepts of both sustainable and green development are interlinked, their implications are different primarily in the following three aspects:

1. Green development focuses more on development than resource conservation and environmental protection. Based on the philosophy of achieving economic and social development not at the expense of natural resources and environment, green development seeks a balance between environmental protection and development and highlights "sustainable development".

2. Green development emphasizes actions rather than concepts. Green development focuses more on the ways of solving "unsustainability" and the approaches to achieving fair development. It serves as a feasible support and guarantees for achieving the balance between economic and social development and environmental protection.

3. Green development focuses more on overall coordination than local improvement. Green development is a process in which governments, enterprises and the public participate to achieve economic and social development yet not at the expense of the environment. In this process, the ecological environment should be improved. Moreover, natural resources and environment should not be treated as external factors but as an integrated part of the social and economic value. Factoring in the interests of all stakeholders, green development is an overall coordinated development pattern.

The key to green development lies in development. Green development is an effective pattern of sustainable development. In green development, natural resources and environment are treated as internal factors of growth. As a transformed development pattern, green development is efficient and environmentally friendly with regard to the use of intelligence, capital, technology and system. Such efficient development pattern will, in turn, enhance humanity's capability of protecting the environment and balance economic growth, social progress and ecological conservation. Green development serves to improve the quality of human lives and promote the sustainable development pattern that is fair, balanced and shared by all.

II. Why Green Development for Cities?

Cities are the carriers of human civilization. Aristotle, the ancient Greek philosopher, once said, the city "comes into existence, originating in the bare needs of life, and continuing in existence for the sake of a good life". Oswald Spengler, the German historian, once said, "it is a conclusive fact — yet one hitherto never appreciated — that all great Cultures are town-Cultures."[2] Humanity has undergone a long process of evolution from traveling from place to place to settling in walled communities and to living in today's cities. From the perspective of history, people and the economic and social activities concentrate in cities is a phenomenon that commonly seen in global development. In the 21st century, the vast majority of people worldwide will live in cities rather than rural areas, which is unprecedented in human history. For countries worldwide, including low-income countries, the ever faster urbanization may bring numerous benefits.[3] Green development requires close attention to efforts and practices at the city level. Urban green development has irreplaceable influences on the concepts and practices of green development. Cities are the spatial carriers of green development. The industries, geography, population and development pattern of cities have a bearing on the level and quality of green development. The changes of social attitudes and customs in urban development affect the spread of green development concept. Cities have obvious economic advantages in the pursuit of green development strategy.

As the innovation center, cities serve to promote the agglomeration of economies, the knowledge spillover, the overall planning for labor market and the sharing of investments, by gathering skills and businesses. This plays a key role in implementing the strategies designed to cope with climate change and resource scarcity.[4] The cause, process and result of green development are shown through cities. In the past, cities created wealth while also causing brown development issues. At present, more than half of the world's population lives in cities. Accordingly, most of the greenhouse gas emissions and energy consumption occur in cities. Economic wealth is mainly concentrated in urban areas; green development and innovations are mostly seen in cities. Therefore, cities have become key nodes for the economic, social and cultural contact regionally and internationally. With the urban renewal of developed countries and the accelerating urbanization of emerging economies, urban green development will have a far-reaching effect on the green development capabilities and patterns of different countries and the entire world alike. Moreover, it will have a bearing on the future of all countries and humanity.

(I)   Solve the historical issue of urban development

Urban development has created a great deal of material and spiritual wealth. However, since the industrial revolution, driven by the development concept that focuses only on the pursuit of material wealth and economic growth, a large quantity of natural resources, energy and primary products have been consumed to boost the economy and increase material wealth. As a result, natural resources have largely decreased, ecological environment has deteriorated with frequent contamination and pollution incidents, and imbalances between economic growth, ecological conservation and environmental protection have become increasingly salient. In reality, urban brown development issues exist in both developed and developing world but in different forms. Cities in developing countries where industrial development is generally at low level tend to rely on industrial development to boost their economy. Accordingly, these cities have densely distributed heavy industries, which have caused air, noise, and solid waste pollutions. As a result, the health of urban residents is harmed, which in turn negatively affects their work and life. Pollutions caused by heavy industries are particularly severe in smaller cities, where in most cases waste is dumped from one or two factories into a river nearby or a large volume of exhaust gas is emitted from factories to the air. As a result, the water and air environments of these cities are polluted. Moreover, with the urban–rural dual structure, numerous slums in cities have also posed daunting challenges to urban development. Dense population, poor housing, substandard education, worrisome sanitation and public security environment result in various "urban diseases" and their spread. Cities in developed countries where industrial development is generally at high level face the same problems, though not as salient as environment deteriorate, young people and well-educated people tend to migrate, leading to a lack of labor required to drive economic growth. Historical issues cannot be avoided. If we followed the traditional urban development pattern that prioritizes economic growth as its primary goal, how long would natural resources and environment sustain? This is a question worth asking. As a balanced, coordinated and sustainable development concept and pattern, green development is expected to solve the brown development issues in conventional urban development process.

(II) Respond to the existing crises of urban development

With the spread of global sustainable development concept, the international community has reached a consensus on the view that the environment should be protected in the human development process. As a result, the *2030 Agenda for Sustainable Development* has been developed. In the practices of urban development worldwide, an increasing number of leaders and general public realize that what matters most in urban development is not the availability of lucrative investment but its sustainability. Nature is not only generous but also very vulnerable. Natural resources are limited. If they are overused, the integrity of the natural system will suffer and urban life will suffer accordingly. Moreover, the drive for changes also comes from the global financial and economic crises we are facing. The crises make it salient that if the global economy and technological innovation lag behind real economy, and if real economy lags behind virtual economy, the balance of the overall economic development will be disrupted, and the urban development will face huge pressure. Facing the downward pressure on the economy and its lack of vitality, some developing countries suffer from deteriorating economy and mounting debts, which in turn cause these countries to overlook environmental planning and natural resources protection when developing urban and industrial development plans. As a result, many cities cut their budgets on environmental protection programs, hindering the remediation of brown development. Moreover, many of the approaches to brown development remediation have to be redesigned and relevant assistance and cooperation are affected. In this context, urban green development becomes particularly important. It is not only an inevitable choice for the change of urban development pattern but also an important approach to coping with the existing crises in urban development. According to relevant studies, cities that implement green development policies tend to be wealthier, with the incidence of poverty being 11.7% on average, whereas cities that implement non-green development have the poverty incidence of 17% on average.[5] Promoting economic growth in an environmentally friendly way through green development will serve to greatly ease the pressure on cities caused by limited natural resources and energy, and effectively improve the supply and demand structure. In addition, it can create new market demand, stimulate the supply and demand of green products and services, foster new growth poles, increase market capacity and significantly enhance the dynamic growth of cities. It is also worth noting that in response to the crises, we need to turn crises into opportunities. The world is in a period where the fifth technological revolution and the third industrial revolution occur at the same time. Unlike the first and second industrial revolutions, the emerging third industrial revolution is based on renewable energy distributed worldwide. The concentrated business pattern formed in the first and second industrial revolutions will be replaced by the dispersed business pattern formed by the third one.[6] Cities have a large number of talented people and advantages in technological research, development and application, making them the primary carriers of distributed intelligent energy network and cooperative organizations. Promoting urban green development will help cities grasp the opportunities of the third industrial revolution so that they can make technological innovations for using and developing energy and resources. Moreover, it can help create new demand and markets, develop new ways to boost the economy and provide new impetus for the economic recovery of cities.

(III)   Achieve urban development goals

Cities are not only the engine of economic growth but also serve human development and carry humanity's hope for a better life. From remote ancient times when people lived on fishing and hunting and traveled from place to place, to despotic society when "the castle was built to protect the monarch and the outer wall was built to protect the people", to feudal society when the concept of citizens emerged and finally to industrial society when population largely expanded and productivity increased rapidly, the evolution of cities mirrors the development of human civilization. From 2000 B.C. to this day, as cities at the center of human civilization in different times, namely Ur, Thebes, Babylon, Xi'an, Luoyang, Athens, Rome, Constantinople, Kaifeng, Hangzhou, Beijing, London, Paris, New York and Tokyo have achieved the dreams of humanity and created numerous development miracles. In the future, cities will still be the juncture of human ideal and reality. The United Nations Center for Human Settlements (UNCHS) held that cities would provide us with the following: numerous job opportunities; adequate access to good education; access to basic transport services; affordable access to safe water and complete health facilities; affordable access to medical care services; access to housing; clean air and a safe, inclusive and healthy environment; available parks, community gardens and public spaces; recreation and entertainment; opportunities for people to participate in local democratic governance; access to enjoying nature.[7] The *2030 Agenda for Sustainable Development* shifts the focus of development from the pursuit of economic growth to the pursuit of inclusive and green development that "leaves no one behind". The agenda proposes to build inclusive, safe, resilient and sustainable cities, and human settlements. Cities have gone through primitive civilization, agricultural civilization and industrial civilization. Urban green development not only heralds the arrival of ecological civilization for cities but also serves to achieve urban development goals in an environmentally friendly manner. Following the green development pattern, cities will focus on people's all-round development and treat the capacity of ecological environment and the carrying capacity of resources as the internal factors of social and economic development. Moreover, cities will promote sustainable use of natural resources, constant improvement of ecological environment, continuous improvement of the quality of life and sustainable economic growth. In doing so, cities not only will meet people's rising demand for natural resources as population increases but also can integrate the development of economy, society and people with environmental protection, so as to create a better environment for city dwellers, achieve urban development goals and truly realize the urban dream of the humanity.

III. Theoretical Model and Realization Mechanism of Urban Green Development

City is a comprehensive system that includes economic, ecological and social factors.[8] The traditional urban development outlook should be re-examined for urban green development, and the sustainable growth of urban economy, sustainable use of resources and harmonious coexistence of society should be integrated into the system framework of urban green development. On the basis of the classical model of traditional urban economic growth, this report constructs a theoretical model of urban green development, explores the realization mechanism of urban green development and analyzes the urban green development system.

(I) Model construction: Urban growth system under constraints

Urban green development is an improvement process of both quantity and quality. The natural environment factors are assumed as exogenous variables in the traditional urban development model, so they are not discussed in the model. We believe that urban green development is a complex and profound system, and the degree of development is determined by all the state variables within the system. The problems of urban environmental economy stability, social development, environmental protection and resource conservation should be discussed in the form of endogenous variables. Specifically, urban green development pursues overall optimization under certain constraints, i.e. the concept of "$1 + 1 > 2$". It requires the overall system utility to be optimal, rather than requiring the subsystems to be optimal at the same time. The key for achieving optimal overall utility of urban green development is creating balance and coordination among various factors, including the coordination among the various factors within the system, as well as among various systems. Therefore, urban green development is an urban growth system under constraints. According to the theory of maximum effect and relevant models of urban economic development, the report selects variables from the perspective of input, and then constructs urban green development model.

First of all, it is assumed that the urban green development system covers five input factors, i.e. labor, capital, resource, environment and technology. The utility equations of the five factors are as follows: Labor utility function: $U_p(t,s) = f_1(x_{pts}, M_{ts})$; capital utility function: $U_c(t,s) = f_2(x_{cts}, M_{ts})$; resource utility function: $U_r(t,s) = f_3(x_{rts}, M_{ts})$; environment utility function: $U_e(t,s) = f_4(x_{ets}, M_{ts})$; technology utility function: $U_f(t,s) = f_5(x_{fts}, M_{ts})$.

Each of the aforementioned variables has its constraints, which include, labor capacity constraint: $X_{pt} \le X_p^{\max}$, indicating that the labor capacity does not exceed the maximum urban labor capacity; resource carrying capacity constraint: $X_{rt} \le X_r^{\max}$, indicating that the resource usage does not exceed the maximum carrying capacity of urban resources; environmental supporting capacity constraint: $X_{et} \leq X_e^{\max}$, indicating that the environmental usage does not exceed the maximum urban environmental supporting capacity.

There are two additional constraints: the first is the intergenerational development constraint, indicating that the total utility of future generations should be at least no less than the total utility of contemporary people, i.e. $U(t, s) \leq U(t+1, s) \leq U(t+2, s) \leq \cdots \leq U(t+n, s)$; the second is the intercity development constraint: $\partial U^2/\partial t \partial s \geq 0$, indicating that the urban development cannot weaken the total utility of other cities.

Thus, we can construct the conceptual model of urban green development, i.e.

$$\max U = \pi_{pt} U_{pt}(t, s) + \pi_{ct} U_{ct}(t, s) + \pi_{rt} U_{rt}(t, s)$$
$$+ \pi_{et} U_{et}(t, s) + \pi_{ft} U_{ft}(t, s).$$

The variables in the model are described as follows: t is a time variable, representing the stage of urban green development; s is a space variable, representing the cities in different spaces; $U(t, s)$ is the total utility of the t generation of s city; $U_i(t, s)$ is the utility value for the development of the i system factor (p, c, r, e and f represent labor, capital, resources, environment and technical factors, respectively) of the t generation of s city; X_{it} is the horizontal vector of the development of the i factor of the t generation; π_{it} is the weight of development utility of the i system factor of the t generation; $X_p^{\max}$, $X_r^{\max}$ and $X_e^{\max}$, respectively, indicate the threshold of labor, resource carrying capacity and environmental carrying capacity.

According to the principle of system dynamics, the aforementioned formula also satisfies the Bertalanffy equation, i.e.

$$\frac{dX_{pt}}{dt} = g_1(X_{pt}, X_{ct}, X_{rt}, X_{et}, X_{ft}, X \propto_1),$$

$$\frac{dX_{ct}}{dt} = g_2(X_{pt}, X_{ct}, X_{rt}, X_{et}, X_{ft}, X \propto_2),$$

$$\frac{dX_{rt}}{dt} = g_3(X_{pt}, X_{ct}, X_{rt}, X_{et}, X_{ft}, X \propto_3),$$

$$\frac{dX_{et}}{dt} = g_4(X_{pt}, X_{ct}, X_{rt}, X_{et}, X_{ft}, X \propto_4),$$

$$\frac{dX_{ft}}{dt} = g_5(X_{pt}, X_{ct}, X_{rt}, X_{et}, X_{ft}, X \propto_5).$$

The Bertalanffy equation shows that there are pairwise correlations among all factors in the urban green development system, and any factor may cause changes in the overall system on the basis of affecting other factors.

It can be seen that the objective function ($\max U$) representing the goal of urban green development is the maximum overall utility of urban system, which is obtained by weighted average of utility values of each subsystem. The weights of each generation vary according to the preferences of a particular generation. For example, in cities with relatively developed economy and society, people may attach more importance to resources and environment, so the weight of utility may be higher; while cities in developing countries are in urgent need of economic growth, so the weight of utility value for economic growth may be higher. Therefore, weights can also be expressed as functions of the development level of each system, i.e.

$$\overrightarrow{\pi_t} = \theta(X_t).$$

Among them, $\overrightarrow{\pi_t}$ is the weight vector, that is $\overrightarrow{\pi_t} = (\pi_{1t}, \pi_{2t}, \pi_{3t}, \pi_{4t}, \pi_{5t})$; X_t is the vector of the development level of each system; $X_t = (X_{pt}, X_{ct}, X_{rt}, X_{et}, X_{ft})$.

Generally speaking, the weights π_i of labor, resources, environment and technology are the increasing functions of time (t), i.e. $d\pi_{pt}/dt > 0$, $d\pi_{rt}/dt > 0$, $d\pi_{et}/dt > 0$ and $d\pi_{ft}/dt > 0$; while the weight π_i of economic system is a decreasing function of time (t), i.e. $d\pi_{ct}/dt < 0$.

The aforementioned conceptual model of urban green development indicates that urban green development is a developing pattern with stage characteristics, comprehensiveness and multi-dimension. It requires the overall promotion and improvement of various parts in urban development, including improvement of the development level of each system, development potential and coordination. At the same time, the model emphasizes the integrity of urban development which considers that the optimization of the urban system is based on the optimization of each subsystem, and requires attention to the factors, structure and balance among subsystems.

(II)   Realization mechanism: From general development to green development

According to the urban economic theory, the development of urban composite system is affected by two categories of factors: The first category refers to positive factors that support development activities, known as the "guiding factors"; under the guidance of such factors, cities move forward quickly by actively utilizing resources and embracing competition; the development speed of this stage is generally fast. The second category refers to factors that restrict development activities, known as the "limiting factors". With the consumption and continuous usage of guiding factors, some restricting and limiting factors are gradually emerging; at this time, the urban development process is to seek development in the case of overcoming limiting factors, so the development speed is generally limited. The essence of urban development is the continuous improvement of development condition of urban composite system, i.e. the process of constantly promoting guiding factors and overcoming limiting factors.

1.   General mechanism of urban development

In order to analyze the urban development mechanism, X is used to indicate the urban development level, $X(t)$ is used to indicate the urban development process, the urban development speed is expressed as dX/dt, and the relative development speed is expressed as $dX/dt/X$. With the development of the city, the function of the limiting factor will be gradually prominent and the speed of urban development will be slowed down. In this case, the relative development speed is taken as the linear decreasing function of X, i.e.

$$\frac{1}{X} \cdot \frac{dX}{dt} = r - \frac{r}{K} \cdot X.$$

Among them, K represents the highest development level of the city under development and environment conditions, i.e. $X_{max} = K$; r represents the maximum relative development speed promoted by the limiting factors of the city under development and environment conditions.

The aforementioned equation is a first-order ordinary differential equation with separable variables. After the separation of variables, the differential equation of the Logistic curve is as follows:

$$\frac{dX}{dt} = r \cdot X \left(1 - \frac{X}{K}\right).$$

The changes in urban development level (X) and development speed (dX/dt) are further investigated. According to the three points where the second and the third derivative are zero in the Logistic equation, we can divide the urban development curve into four stages, including the initial stage, the development stage, the mature stage and the peak stage. In the initial stage, the urban development speed is slow, gradually rising from 0 to $rK/6$. In the development stage, the city is in a stage of rapid development, and the development speed is continuously increasing, gradually rising from $rK/6$ to $rK/4$. In the mature stage, the urban development level is high, and the development speed declines gradually but is still greater than $rK/6$. In the peak stage, the urban development speed is declining gradually to zero, and the development level is no longer increasing. It can be seen that the urban development level (X) increases rapidly and maintains a high level in the development stage and mature stage, and these two stages can be regarded as the rapid development zone of urban development. Therefore, the urban development should be kept in the two stages as long as possible.

Table 1.2 shows the specific changes in the four stages of urban development. For cities in the initial stage, due to lack of available resources, backward technology, and low production and consumption levels, the whole urban system is growing slowly. For cities in the development stage, due to continuous improvement of scientific and technological means, and continuous increase of available resources and unapparent environmental restriction, cities

Table 1.2. Four Stages of Urban Development.

t	X	dX/dt	$d2X/dt2$	Development Stage
$(0, t_1)$	Rise slowly	Rise	Rise	Initial stage
t_1	$K/2 - K/2^{\sqrt{3}}$	$rK/6$	$r2K/6^{\sqrt{3}}$	
(t_1, t_0)	Rise rapidly	Rise	Decline	Development stage
t_0	Inflection point	$rK/4$	0	
(t_0, t_2)	Continue to rise	Decline	Decline	Mature stage
t_2	$K/2 + K/2^{\sqrt{3}}$	$rK/6$	$-r2K/6^{\sqrt{3}}$	
$(t_2, +\infty)$	Tend to be smooth	Decline	Rise	Peak stage

show a trend of rapid development. In the mature stage, cities are restricted by population, environment capacity and resources. The function of limiting factors is gradually prominent, and urban development begins to be restricted. When urban development reaches its peak, the development speed slowly decreases to 0. If the city cannot overcome the limiting factors of the system, there may be a recession.

2. Mechanism of urban green development

The purpose of green development is to maintain normal operation and sustainable growth of urban composite system, i.e. the urban development level X is increasing constantly, and will not decline from the peak stage. To achieve this goal, we must overcome the limiting factors of urban development and look for opportunities for development starting from the guiding factors, so that the city can transit to a higher development level from a lower level and step into the next round of development. Therefore, the urban green development curve can be expressed as a combined Logistic curve, that is, although there are fluctuations in a short time, it is a smooth and sustainable process in the long run (Figure 1.1).

In order to realize urban green development, it can be considered from two perspectives. The first is to extend the period of

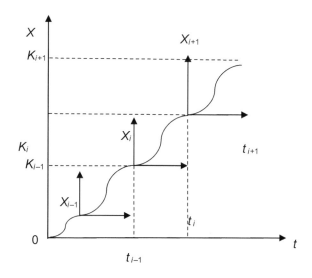

Figure 1.1. Realization Mechanism of Urban Green Development.

development and maturity, i.e. to extend (t_1 and t_2) intervals; the second is to delay the time for entering the recession and to remain in the mature period as much as possible, and to promote urban development from the current equilibrium into a better equilibrium through structure optimization and system configuration. From either perspective, urban green development is a constant process from equilibrium to better equilibrium. It is of vital importance to promote the upgrading and coordination of various subsystems of urban green development, and to drive forward the optimization of economic structure, innovation of science and technology and constant progress of life quality and social welfare. Therefore, in order to promote urban green development, efforts should be made to guide the harmonious development of urban systems, so that they will evolve into a more balanced and complementary state.

References

1. OECD, *Cities and Green Growth: A Conceptual Framework*, OECD Regional Development Working Papers, OECD Publishing, Paris, 2011.
2. Oswald Spengler, *The Decline of the West*, The Commercial Press, New Jersey, 2001, p. 199.

3. Jeffrey D. Sachs, *Common Wealth: Economics for a Crowded Planet*, Beijing, Citic Press, Beijing, 2010, p. 24.
4. Lamia Kamal-Chaoui, Margo Cointreau and Wang Xao, Green cities: Examples of governing for green growth from OECD countries, in Ni Pengfei and Peter Karl Kresl (eds.), *The Global Urban Competitiveness Report (2011–2012)*, Social Sciences Academic Press, Beijing, 2012, pp. 124–131.
5. Matthew E. Kahn, *Green Cities: Urban Growth and the Environment*, Citic Press, Beijing, 2008, pp. 139–140.
6. Jeremy Rifkin, *The Third Industrial Revolution: How Lateral Power is Transforming Energy, Economy and the World*, China Citic Press, Beijing, 2012, pp. 118–119.
7. UNCHS, *Cities in a Globalising World: Global Report on Human Settlements*, Earthscan, London, 2001.
8. Ronan Paddison, *Handbook of Urban Studies*, Shanghai People's Publishing House, Shanghai, 2009, pp. 32–34.

Chapter 2

Basic Connotations and Analysis Framework of Urban Green Development

Zheng Zhao
Researcher, Development Research Center
of the State Council of PRC
zz_bnu@126.com

Green development is inevitable for all cities and is determined by many factors. The components and influencing factors of urban green development are complicated, and the urban green development system is established by joint and mutual actions of many factors and environment systems in different ways. Although in practice, the effect of various green development factors may differ in different cities and at different stages of social and economic development; in the long run, the urban green development will be a balanced system, requiring organic integration and superposition of various factors and thus creating the resultant forces for green development.

I. Basic Connotations of Urban Green Development: Four Important Relations

Centering on improvement of life quality, urban green development is a development mode aiming to further, better, economically and sustainably create economic wealth and improve social welfare on the basis of respective, protective and efficient utilization of resources and environment. The basic connotation of urban green development mainly embodies the following four relations: symbiosis between man and nature, balance between economy and society, cooperation between government and market, and interaction between city and state.

(I) Symbiosis between man and nature

Nature is the foundation for the existence and development of cities. Cities take materials from nature and have great influence on nature, other creatures and their habitats. The discussion of the relationship between man and nature has a long history. The theory of "unity of nature and man" in ancient China put forward the idea of originating from nature, letting nature take its course, benefiting from nature and nurturing nature. However, with the acceleration of urbanization, the increase of population and the progress of productivity, the binary opposition between man and nature has become increasingly prominent. Nature often becomes the means and tools of humans to achieve their goals and the status of nature has been weakened constantly; meanwhile, humans are destroying the earth's ecosystem at an unprecedented speed and in an unexpected manner. Destruction means punishment. There are many tragedies of deterioration of relationship between humans and nature in the history of cities, many of which are caused by the social collapse due to wanton destruction of natural environment. Both the legend of Atlantis and the loss of the ancient city of Loulan clearly indicate that urban activities must be carried out in sound ecological environment; only by doing so, can a city survive and strive in the long term. If a city can't handle the relation between man and nature appropriately and is expanded and developed immoderately, it will be severely punished no matter how brilliant its civilization can be. The current air, water and soil pollution also serve as warnings for modern cities that the destruction of nature has a high price.

At present, half of the population in the world lives in cities and most of the other half depends on cities economically. Urban green development requires a solution to the issue of how to sustain the city without destroying the natural environment, as well as re-examination and reconsideration of the relationship between man and nature. The solutions are as follows: (1) Changing ideas. Today, values are strongly linked to materialism, anthropocentrism and contemporary centralism. The concept of consumption focuses on satisfying human needs by constantly strengthening the purchase of goods and services.[1] In the process of urban development, we shall first change our ideas and correctly and objectively examine the natural environment being created and transformed by us. (2) Attaching great importance to the value of nature. We shall regard the earth itself as a vast life organism instead of just a means for the realization of human purpose.[2] When handling the relationship between city and nature, we shall further respect and protect the natural environment, emphasize the symbiosis, coexistence and common prosperity of city and nature, respond to crisis and challenges including over-exploitation of urban resources, severe environmental pollution and widening gap between the rich and the poor, completely solve the problem of urban development via non-renewable resource consumption and pollutant emission, reduce urban expansion and resource losses restore natural ecology system. (3) Giving full play to the value of nature. Cities shall not destroy natural ecology for the development of economy because the economy relies on the materials and energies from natural environment and can in turn affect the natural environment.[3] But there is no need to pause development to protect the environment. Different from traditional environmental protection, urban green development emphasizes on the greening of development and governance patterns, and is the most fundamental way to solve the problem of environment resources. Urban green development requires to find the balance point between man and nature, properly arrange urban consumption and production based on natural ecological rationality, give full play to the advantages of natural environment and avoid its disadvantages, re-integrate natural, human, physical and technology capital, accumulate ecological capital and ecological wealth of the city.

(II) Balanced between economy and society

Urban green development requires development with growth. In the process of green development, the idea of "growth trumps all" shall be abandoned, but there is no need to decelerate the growth or overemphasize "zero growth". Economic prosperity is a solid foundation for urban green development. Without the increase of material wealth brought by economic growth, we will lack the capital input in environmental management and life improvement. Therefore, economic growth shall be regarded as a mandatory approach for green development. Stable economic growth enables sustainable environmental governance and ecological protection, continuous improvement of living environment of urban residents, suppression of various extremisms, stable popular feelings and social conditions. Therefore, urban green development requires us to correctly understand and handle economic growth, emphasize on quality rather than material expansion, regard material growth as a tool instead of a permanent mission, neither pursue nor oppose economic growth but take differentiated approaches according to the types and goals of growth, and choose those which satisfy social goals and strengthen sustainability as far as possible.[4] To achieve urban green development, we still need to promote economic prosperity and stability, especially encourage urban efforts to achieve economic growth through innovations in product, technology, culture, business models and institutional innovations.

At the same time, we cannot make the mistake of "growth mania", i.e. simply focusing on gross national product (GNP), inflation rate and other economic data, and ignoring the "cost of economic growth" and social welfare loss behind.[5] In the final analysis, urban green development is human development. It is both the driving force and the goal of green development to reduce poverty-stricken population and constantly improve health, safety, life quality and cultural quality of citizens. To achieve urban green development, we shall rethink the basic ideas in the western dominant paradigm, including "market-based economic efficiency", "self-correcting ability of democratic government", "benefits from sustainable economic growth based on fossil fuel", "welfare improved through free trade and globalization", build a long-term materially and spiritually sustainable society and improve the "sustainable welfare".[6] We shall not simply seek for maximization of development increment but continuously enhance the city's ability to resist natural disasters and risks; build a mechanism conducive to the development of vulnerable groups; form stable support system for healthy urban development; improve intellectual and cultural heritage, innovation and communication system; build a democratic, equal and stable social environment; enhance inclusiveness and sharing of urban development process and results; optimize the fairness of urban development chances and welfare.

(III) Coordination between government and market

City is a spatial complex of interests. From the perspective of stakeholders, urban public sectors are responsible for providing public goods and services, enterprises are responsible for manufacturing and providing private goods and services and individuals and families are responsible for providing elements and meanwhile, have demands on products. Under the condition of market economy, all public sectors, enterprises and individuals and families are seeking maximum benefits; urban green development requires comprehensive consideration of demands of different stakeholders and strives to achieve the overall interests of the city on the premise of balancing these interests. The core is to handle the relationship between government and market.

In the process of urban green development, from the perspective of the government, the ecological system has the property of public goods, and there is a large gap between social and private benefits from protection of ecological environment, so the market mechanism does not necessarily encourage people to protect the ecological environment. Thus, we should give full play to the government's strengths in macro-control and administrative organization force and behavior guidance and establish a strict and appropriate environment management system (e.g. emission rights and environmental taxes). These measures can motivate people to participate in environmental protection and to change from being passive to participate actively in the protection process, encourage enterprises to develop innovative production technology and organization mode and improve production efficiency and market competitiveness of enterprises, so that enterprises are willing to carry out green transformation and provide and produce more green products and services.

From the perspective of the market, a well-functioning market will help reduce the adverse influence of urban growth on resources and environment. If environmental protection brings benefits to people, people will be actively engaged and the benefits gained will completely reflect the social cost of environment protection. And, this is the voluntary behavior guided by market, the "invisible hand". Without market transactions, the economic method cannot estimate the overall and partial value of natural ecological system, since the marginal value of ecological system can only be reflected by market transactions and market price.[7] With the development of a city, according to the law of supply and demand, the price of scarce commodities such as land, water and other natural resources will rise. The rise in price will make people reduce the consumption of these resources and thus stimulate enterprises to take the following measures: developing and using greener technology; allocating technology, capital, manpower and other elements properly according to supply and demand information and price signals in the green production and consumption market; including ecological value in the original value system through the economic leverage and producing more green products and services at the same cost by improving the input–output efficiency. Besides, it can stimulate corporate social responsibilities to create premium brand and actual income by promoting urban green development. As the supplier of green production elements and demander of green products, individuals and families can share the benefits in the process of green development of government and enterprises, and affect such benefits through green consumption ideas and behaviors.

(IV)   Interaction between city and state

Urban development is closely related to national development. The success of state often depends on the success of city. City is an irreplaceable engine of national economic growth, a bridgehead for economic exchanges between the state and the world, and a key space for competition among various states. If the state can develop a robust urban system covering metropolises, a large number of medium-sized cities and small towns, produce a "spreading effect" of extending from metropolis areas in the heartland to the regional inland areas, "hierarchical spreading" of extending from the centers at higher level to lower level and "inland spreading" of extending from urban center to its surrounding areas, then the state will have a strong driving force for the national economic and social development.[8] At the same time, an important feature of the city is to produce diverse products for its residents, trade with the hinterland and other cities, and promote national ecological diversity by increasing market variety, and a close relation between city and its hinterland shall be established.[9] Cities are part of the state and the state is the largest hinterland to support urban development. Urban development is deeply affected by the development of the state, national conditions and development strategy. In practice, an open city cannot exist in a closed country. In the early 20th century, Argentina is one of the world's most open countries and Buenos Aires is a vibrant international city with entrepreneurs from Britain, Spain, Italy and Sweden. By the end of the 20th century, Argentina closed its borders and Buenos Aires became an isolated city, though its exquisite historic buildings showcase the more dynamic, more international past to tourists.[10]

However, it is worth noting that economic development levels of different countries differ, and urban and rural development is also unbalanced. If the actual national development level is ignored during urban development, negative effects of unbalanced development will be increased, development gap will be broadened and unfair and unequal development pattern will be intensified. And if the local unfairness is degraded into overall unfairness, it will eventually cause damages to the city's own interests and even to the common interests of the national and even global development. On the one hand, for the whole country, different cities have different development opportunities. The metropolises directly connected to global and national commercial, financial, scientific, cultural and political networks are often the most important participants of green development, while a number of small- and medium-sized cities can hardly share the development opportunities. But in the long term, the development of metropolis still relies on sound urban network relations. It requires cooperation and support of other cities of different scale, at different levels and with different functions with each other and needs contributions of all people to the well-being of the whole city.[11] At the same time, the imbalance between urban and rural development is also very prominent, especially in developing countries. Due to the dual economic and social structure, the division of urban and rural areas is reflected not only in the economic and social development level but also in the ability of seizing green development opportunities and achieving green development. Therefore, in order to promote urban green development, we shall attach great importance to the relationship between the city and the state. In the process of promoting urban green development, we shall embody the driving force and influence of the city itself for national green development, fully consider national resources and environment conditions and the level of economic and social development, give consideration to both intercity and urban–rural development, and achieve common prosperity and progress of the city and the state.

II. Five-Dimensional Analysis Framework of Urban Green Development

A proper framework is needed to describe urban green development system. Based on the understanding of the theory and connotation of urban green development, the analysis framework of urban green development has been established. The framework consists of five aspects, i.e. livability, prosperity, inclusiveness, governance and partnership. Among them, a different level of urban livability has formed the basic environment of natural resources, i.e. the basic resource conditions for urban green development and the actual environment context. The level of prosperity reflects the economic quality of urban green development, i.e. the economic prosperity foundation of urban green development and its economic development model. The level of inclusiveness reflects the degree of social progress of urban green development, i.e. the economic prosperity foundation of urban green development and the degree of its diversity, stability and inclusion. The level of governance embodies the communication rules among various stakeholders, i.e. the governance system of urban green development and the improvement of governance capability. The level of partnership reflects the supply and demand conditions of potential elements of urban green development and reflects the interactive actions and mutual influences mechanism between the city and the state in green development (Figure 2.1)

The analysis framework of urban green development not only considers the actual conditions of urban green development but also pays more attention to the driving force and extensive connection of urban green development. The nature, characteristics and action model of influential factors of urban green development are different in five aspects, i.e. livability, prosperity, inclusiveness, governance and partnership, and also show different effect in various stages of urban green development. But in the long term, all these factors play a critical role in urban green development process. Neglecting any of them will hinder the formation of stable urban green development capacity. To promote urban green development, we need to rely on the overall urban green development system and promote all-round, balanced and coordinated development of these five aspects.

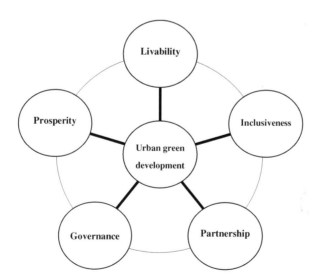

Figure 2.1. Five-Dimensional Analysis Framework of Urban Green Development.

(I) Livability

Livability mainly considers the natural resources and environmental factor endowments of urban green development. Good natural resources and ecological environment are the prerequisites for urban green development and urban green development depends on the natural environment to a great extent. Specifically, natural ecosystem determines the quality of life and even survival in the city. It provides us with air, water and food; it maintains the climate at ·a livable level — neither too hot nor too cold, neither too wet nor too dry; it also protects us from the biological and non-biological threats and from harm of the pests and ultraviolet radiation; another function is to clear the wastes in environment. Natural ecosystems are vital to the maintenance of human life and the promotion of social welfare.[12] For example, according to the studies of Kenneth Kay and Michael Greenstein, air pollution has a direct effect on infant mortality. They concluded that every reduction of 10 micrograms per cubic meter of particles in the air will make the infant mortality decrease by 0.055%.[13] Natural resources which are scare, difficult to flow and reproduce, such as special mineral resources, urban special location and climate environment, play an important role in urban green development. For example, natural geographical conditions directly affect the health of urban residents. According to the test data of 118 monitoring stations in the cities worldwide on suspended particles, Susmita Dasgupta *et al.* explored the relative importance of city population, city governance, national income and geographical factors to the local pollution level. These factors indicate that whether the air pollution degree of a poor, crowded city with poor governance reaches the crisis level or is close to the optimal level of cities in developed countries completely depends on the geographical factors. Similarly, under the circumstance of the same level of economic activity, the unique and advantageous geographical environment can make the city suffer less from public health problems.[14]

At the same time, climate, resources and environment are still the main factors for enhancing urban competitiveness. Although developed cities at present do not rely on their resource endowments in enhancing their competitiveness, easy access to natural resources is still the foundation of development in these cities.[15] This is because maintaining the factor endowments is of great importance in making the region more competitive in relative price, external enterprises, industrial elements, and non-price and non-trade elements. It strengthens the region's capability to absorb further growth. The primary reasons that the tropical areas are relatively backward lie in the local temperature and soil factors.[16] At the same time, the talents influencing the urban development also have higher demands for natural conditions. Higher-end talents and industries require higher quality ecological environment.[17] In practice, the relative scale and scope of natural element endowment of a city will largely affect the competitive and comparative advantages of urban green development. Whether these elements are available or not will decide the monopoly position and roles of cities in green development. Better natural environment endowment will lead to monopolistic advantages and having these elements may bring monopoly profits that are much higher than the cost to cities, thus forming congenital competitive advantages.

Therefore, urban green development requires respecting and protecting the nature, rationally developing and utilizing the nature, maintaining the livability level of cities from the perspective of harmonious coexistence of human and nature, paying particular attention to the natural ecological environment for the survival and development of cities, fully considering the climate characteristics, geological features and resource endowment of the cities in urban planning and layout as well as industry selection, strengthening the suitability of urban population, industry, society and natural ecological system and guaranteeing the green livability of cities through reasonable regional resource and environment allocation and improved resource environment protection and utilization system.

(II) Prosperity

Urban green development requires affluent economic foundation. Urban green development is not against growth. It does not excessively depend on economic growth, especially the scale economic growth at the expense of resource, environment and social welfare. There is great difference between independence on economic growth and no need of economy. Facing up to economic growth, proactively anticipating the problems of economy itself and optimizing our system environment step by step ahead of time are helpful for turning the harmonious coexistence between humans and nature from an envisaged concept into reality. In the long run, economic prosperity and stability and affluent lifestyle of people are the most basic standards of urban green development, and provide the basic guarantee for satisfying physical and safety demands of urban residents. On the basis of affluence, people can then develop the demands for love, sense of belonging, respect and self-fulfilling. At the same time, urban green development shall not only emphasize the outcomes but also the path to realize them. Namely, it shall reflect the economic development scale, income and welfare; it shall have both the affluent development as outcomes and the paths to create such outcomes; it shall pay attention to the growth and interaction of various economic elements influencing the affluence and prosperity of cities.

1. Vigorous innovation vitality

Innovation is the key of urban green development and also the booster of the affluence and prosperity of cities. Reading the urban development history, it can be observed that in the 14th century, less than 100,000 residents lived in Florence, Venice, Genoa, Milan or Bologna of Italy, but great achievements were made in these cities. It can be said that the greatest wealth of the Renaissance cities lies in the strong business spirit and the desire to accept the classical city traditions, and more importantly, the creativity on which their development depends.[18] Among them, scientific and technological innovations are essential. Science and technology is an independent production factor and has spillover effect.[19] Scientific and technological innovation promotes and expands the ability of urban green development through technological progress, scientific and technological outputs and high-tech industries, and plays a crucial and professional role in promoting urban green development. Technological progress is conducive to relieving the stress brought by urban population growth and solving the problems caused by increased urban resource consumption. According to William Nordhaus, concerns about exhaustion of resources were relieved when the magnitude of technological progress overrode that of resource exhaustion during much of the time in the 19th and 20th centuries. New seeds and fertilizers substituted the development of more land; development of exploration and drilling technology replaced the drilling of deeper wells or drilling in the cold zone; investment for reducing pollution enabled sustainable economic development while reducing the concentration of harmful substances. In short, technological progress was undoubtedly the winner in the race of resource consumption and marginal returns diminishing in the past two centuries.[20]

In the era of information network and knowledge economy, the information revolution begins to exert huge impact just as the industrial revolution has done, fundamentally changes the way we live, work, learn and create and highlights the "ecology-technology system" characteristics of cities which become unprecedented complex of biology and technology.[21] In conjunction with rapidly evolving communication means, it can help increase productivity, energy and resource efficiency and improve the organizational structure of industry. Urban green development shall be driven by scientific and technological innovations, and cities shall become the key location of transferring new ideas and discoveries into new products and services. Urban regional regeneration shall be realized through scientific activities, and the innovation output, productivity and growth rate of cities shall be improved. In the future, in the process of promoting urban green development, we need to pay more attention to the role of all-round innovation with technology innovation as the core and including innovation in product, technology, business mode, system and mechanism; form innovation-based economic development mode through continuously releasing the motivation, capacity and energy of human; establish dynamic mechanism that promotes highly efficient and steady urban economy through innovation; get rid of dependence of economy on high emission, high resource consumption, environmental damages and social imbalance and promote prosperous urban development.

2. Reasonable industrial structure

The prosperity of urban economy does not originate from the economic growth itself but depends on the economic growth mode that a city undertakes. We must carefully analyze and prudently choose this model, and integrate the remodeling of natural environment into the model to meet the needs of people's happy life rather than the needs of industrial production (p. 7). In the process of urban green development, economic growth mode is often concentrated in the rationality and high-end nature of industrial structure. Among them, the rationalization of industrial structure reflects the proportional relationship of the production scale among industries and reflects the objective quantity requirements of the industrial structure. The high-level industrial structure reflects the utilization efficiency and output effect of resource elements among industries and the objective quality requirements of the industrial structure. Optimization and upgrading of urban industrial structure can use the intensive, green, cyclic and low-carbon mode and technology to upgrade and improve the energy and resource utilization efficiency of traditional industrial departments and remarkably reduce the resource consumption and environmental loss in economic development process on the one hand, and promote the emerging green industry and service departments including the emerging service industry to develop continuously and offer new driving force for urban economic growth on the other hand. From the perspective of overall urban development, safe and clean modern industrial system with optimized structure, advanced technology, high added value and strong ability to create employment opportunities can effectively realize the green reorganization of industrial structure and the unity of green development of industry and green development, thus providing prosperous and stable economic support to urban green development.

3. Sound infrastructure

Urban green development requires good infrastructure. There are three main types of urban infrastructure: first, the infrastructure that serves work and entrepreneurship. It mainly includes the facilities of communication, transport, water supply, power supply, gas supply, etc. The conditions of such infrastructure directly affect the possibility of urban employment and entrepreneurship. Second, the infrastructure that serves life. It mainly includes the facilities of accommodation, eating, shopping, culture, entertainment, etc. The conditions of such infrastructure directly affect the living costs of cities. Third, the infrastructure that serves development. It mainly includes the facilities of education, health and elderly care service and all kinds of service places for the migrants, such as the talent market and the labor market, etc. This type of facility is beneficial to the formation of strong attraction of a city. For urban development, the dense, quality and improved low-price infrastructure covering a large area is a means to realize the transaction and contact among economic subjects. It can not only enable the city to better take advantage of more external markets and resources but can also improve the city's attraction in talents, technology, investment and trade, improve the production and transaction efficiency, reduce the cost, produce multiplier effect of investment and promote optimization of urban spatial form. Possessing convenient, efficient and high-quality railway, highway, port, airport, telecommunication facilities and other infrastructure will be able to effectively improve the production efficiency and reduce production and service cost of enterprises and will make it more convenient for a city to attract agglomeration of high-end production elements, form high-end industry, produce and provide high value-added products and services. Meanwhile, good infrastructure is also conducive to enhancing urban vitality and creating conditions for the diversification of urban exchanges.[22] In the information era, with rapid rise of information technology and Internet, the role of sound information network infrastructure becomes more prominent. The development of information infrastructure provides not only more convenient platform and tools for urban green development but also strong support for dissemination of sharing, interactive and cooperative development concept. Therefore, in urban green development, we shall attach great importance to improvement of railway, highway, airport, water supply and power supply facilities and other infrastructure and have to further develop and improve the information network infrastructure and give full play to advantages of the Internet and information technology, thus providing strong basis for the urban green development.

4. Outstanding urban enterprises

Urban green development requires support from highly efficient and quality enterprises as competition among cities requires attracting much capital and quality labors as practical as possible to efficiently use the land resources and provide continuous force for urban development.[23] The outstanding enterprise is also the subject of innovation at the same time. New products, new technologies and new business models are often generated in the city's most outstanding enterprises and the spillover effect of innovation is formed, driving development of innovation-based industry cluster. Therefore, outstanding enterprises are the core force for change of urban growth mode. In addition, outstanding enterprises often have a sense of social responsibility and good governance structure, management organization, operation mechanism and enterprise culture, are able to adapt and lead the green development investment and consumption frontier, maintain their competitiveness and provide continuous impetus for urban green development by improving the green technological content and green added value of products and services.

5. Rich human capital

Urban green development requires support of rich human capital, as human capital is the capital of "people" rather than "material". As a form of capital, human capital can not only create its own value but can also change the potential resources into real resources, turn the potential wealth into real wealth, create value that is larger than its own value and realize value increase. This has obvious increase in income and the benefits are far more than that of material investment.[24] The essence of cooperation in the creative process that enhances urban vitality is the combination of the educated people with creative people.[25] Among them, the creative human capital will be more valuable, better improve the productivity and can better realize the optimal allocation of urban resources. Therefore, when it comes to urban green development, we should gather more talents to make the continuous affluence and prosperity of a city no longer purely rely on resource consumption, environmental damages and loss of welfare but mainly rely on talents and innovation and form the pattern that urban development is for the benefits of people and relies on the people.

(III) Inclusiveness

Urban green development is inclusive development. "When economic progress becomes an essential component of development, it is not the only part, and development is not a purely economic phenomenon. Fundamentally, it contains more contents other than materials and money which are necessary for people's life. Therefore, development should be viewed as a multifaceted process of restructuring and reorientation of the entire economic and social system".[26] The city is the center of economy, industry and social activities, and also a friendly place for people to create culture, enjoy civil rights and pursue equity and justice. Not only the sustainable development cannot be maintained but also the equity and justice are violated in a city where the rich get richer and the poor get poorer. "Integrating the merits of its own nation and the merits of other nations" is the loftiest ideal of human beings and also the proper meaning of urban development. Urban green development should reflect humanistic care and humanistic value, should be people-oriented in the development process and results, reflect the equity in opportunity and rights in different regions, genders and groups, eliminate the gap between the rich and the poor, bridge the institutional gap, persist with sharing of development fruits, pay attention to the value, rights and freedom of the people, pay attention to life quality, development

40   *Z. Zhao*

potential and happiness index of residents and let all residents of a city lead a more happier and dignified life.

1. Welfare enhancement

For cities, people are also a creative resource that must be exploited by the society. In order to cultivate and strengthen this precious wealth, it is necessary to improve the people's material welfare by improving nutrition, health care and so on. Education must be provided to enable them to become more capable, creative, skilled and efficient and be able to cope with daily problems better.[27] Urban green development requires a city to provide sufficient basic welfare products and services, clean air and water, that everyone can have the fair and convenient right to receive basic education, health and medical care and social security and that a city can generally increase the welfare of urban residents.

2. Poverty relief

Poverty will not only bring economic difficulties to urban residents but also aggravate the influence of urban brown development. For instance, some researchers found out after studies on daily records of the California smog weather that wealthy residents are more conducive to the collection and dissemination of information about the quality of the local environment while the poor in the city are less likely to enjoy the policy of pollution reduction.[28] The consumption choices of the poor in a city will have greater impact on the sustainability of a developing city. With prosperity of the urban economy, the poor families will also change their consumption patterns along with increase of their income and often choose the consumption patterns that can improve the environmental quality. If a household chooses to improve their consumption quality rather than increase the consumption quantity, income growth will lower the level of pollution.[29] Therefore, it is necessary for a city to reduce the poor population when it intends to realize green development. At the same time, it is worth noting that a city will inevitably have poor people but is not the root cause of poverty. It just attracts the poor people by providing them a good outlook of life. Urban green development should aim at helping the poor population improve their social and economic status and providing more economic opportunities, public services and fun for the poor. The basis for evaluating whether a city is good or bad is not its poverty but should be its achievements in helping poor people improve their social and economic status. "If a city is attracting the poorer population to continue to flow in, help them succeed and watch them leave, and then attract influx of new group of poor people, then the city is successful in the aspect of the most important social function of a city. If a place has become the home of the poor people who have long been poor, then it is a failure".[30]

3. Education improvement

Education plays an important role in urban green development. Urban education not only trains talent but also attracts talent. Rise of some cities is often attributed to its prestigious academic and educational institutions, such as Boston in the United States. While decreased economic status of Detroit and other city also shows the importance of education and talent for maintaining long-term and stable development of a city. Specifically, education can maintain stable economic development of a city. In the United States, the proportion of people who have a bachelor's degree is often used to determine the local skills level. When the proportion of adult population with a bachelor's degree increased by 10%, the income growth rate in a given area in the period from 1980 to 2000 increased by 6% accordingly. When the proportion of population with a bachelor's degree increases by 10%, the per capita output value of a city increases by 22% accordingly.[31] At the same time, education can provide the people with the ability to obtain and process information so as to understand the impact of environmental disaster on their own interests and even the earth. The more educated people are more patient than the less educated people, are more willing to support the high cost investment in coping with long-term environmental threat and are more likely to discover the environmental friendly products and service.[32] In addition, education is also directly linked with the preference of environmental policies. In the past 30 years, California's voters had chances to vote for a series of environmental problems, including increasing the public transportation expenses, raising the gasoline tax, weakening the anti-smoking law and issuing bonds to improve the city water supply quality and local air quality, etc. In the past 30 years, California's voters had chances to vote for a series of environmental problems, including increasing the public transportation expenses, raising the gasoline tax, weakening the anti-smoking law and issuing bonds to improve the city water supply quality, local air quality, etc. When the proportion of adult population receiving college education increases by 10%, the degree of support to environmental protection increases by 11% accordingly.[33] More importantly, education will not only provide high-quality and innovative public groups for urban green development, it will also change a city's economic prospects and help enlighten the people, foster the development concept of contemporary equity and intergenerational equity and build a more equitable and sustainable society.

4. Leisure time

As early as in 1933, the "Athens Charter" defined the four basic functions of the city — life, work, leisure and transportation. The three functions of life, work and leisure are relatively independent. They are the three main aspects of urban life while the transportation function plays a connecting role and enables urban residents to make convenient conversion between life, work and leisure. With continuous development of urban economy, the material wealth is constantly enriched, and the cultural level of citizens is continuously improved. The leisure function of cities has gradually been paid more and more attention. Leisure in the modern sense is accompanied by the establishment of urbanized life mode. The city is the largest provider and demander of leisure and it is the basic function of the city to meet people's leisure needs. Green development of a city makes the large-scale leisure service possible, should create more favorable leisure facilities and rich leisure activities for the city residents to enjoy the leisure time, thus enhancing the city residents' life quality.

Meanwhile, if a city has good leisure facilities, it will help attract large enterprises or government agencies and thus enhance the overall competitiveness of the city. For instance, Barcelona, Baltimore and other cities are representatives of urban regeneration through the key investment in leisure tourism infrastructure, improving the urban landscape and supporting the arts and cultural undertakings. However, some traditional industrial cities, which decline because of capital withdrawal and withering industry, also redesign urban space and rebuild industrial sites into heritage parks and creative fashion bases to improve the urban environment quality and represent the new look of cities. These cities are full of vigor and vitality.

5. Stability and safety

The city represents the people's expectation and pursuit of stability, order and harmony and the city with safe production and living environment is guarantee for development. Urban green development should not only pay attention to the ecological environment and the safety problems caused by natural disasters but also attach importance to social security and stability. From the prospective of city development history, magnificent buildings and basic physical properties of a city, including the location near the river or the sea, adjacent to the trade channel, attractive green space, or highway crossing, all contribute to the generation of a great city or can help a city develop. But it cannot maintain the long-term prosperity of a city and it must depend on a common identity to gather all urban residents. Whether in the traditional urban centers or in the expanding urban areas under new development mode, identity awareness and other issues still largely determine which places will have the final success.[34] This is because, comparing with no income, the feeling of being relatively poor and the sense of loss coupled with the loss of self-awareness will be more likely to lead to violence.[35] Therefore, in the long run, diversity will lead to communication, communication will nurture integration and integration will drive progress. Urban green development requires paying special attention to shaping of common cultural awareness of a city, increasing the social acceptance of a city, providing space for the harmonious coexistence between people of different nationalities, different cultures and different beliefs, promoting mutual respect, learning from each other and harmonious coexistences of urban residents in diversified development and keeping the lasting vitality of the city.

(IV) Governance

Good governance reflects the ideal urban governance. However, whether it is from the source of governance or from its concept and theory, the involvement of multiple subjects is the most essential characteristic of governance. There is no doubt that urban governance is the core of national governance. The city is the place where the country's resources and problems are concentrated, the important resources such as land resources, environmental resources and other resources have become increasingly scarce and a variety of social conflicts and risks frequently happen. It can be said without hesitation that most of the problems facing the future governments will be urban problems. How to achieve good governance in cities is crucial to the development of every city. As to the concept of governance, "Our Global Neighborhood" of the United Nations Commission on Global Governance in 1995 thinks that governance is the sum of multiple methods that various public or private institutions manage their common affairs, is a continuous reconciliation process of the conflicts or different interests and taking joint actions and includes both the right to force people to obey the formal rules and regulations and informal institutional arrangement agreed by people upon consultation. In the practice of urban green development, decision-makers of the city often find themselves in a dilemma. On the one hand, they expect the rapid development of city economy and scale so they formulate preferential policies to promote growth of economy and industry and strive to occupy a greater share in global investment and attract more skillful and creative migrants so as to improve the city's global competitiveness. On the other hand, they must also stabilize the social harmony and cohesion in the face of the serious social problems posed by the rapid economic growth and updated development plan or projects of the expanding cities. In particular, cities in some developing countries have experienced the same division: becoming a westernized modern metropolis and a more impoverished and traditional urban complex. Here, unspeakable poverty, filth, and disease coexist with great wealth and privilege. Moreover, the constraints imposed by many traditional ethical systems no longer work.[36] Therefore, to promote urban green development, we need to face the challenge of interest conflicts and confusion, improve governance mechanism through formal and informal institutional arrangements, increase the consensus and identity of different stakeholders on development goals and ideas, strengthen the cooperation and exchange platform among different departments, enrich the management means and tools and achieve "good development" with "good governance".

1. Modernization of governance capability of city government

"The concept of governance has many ways of development, and its intersection is attributed to the practical guidance of the authority".[37] The city government plays an irreplaceable role in green development. The correct direction of government in economic development, environmental protection, ecological construction and urban development will directly decide the harmony and stability of urban green development system. Meanwhile, the development policy contributing to urban economic welfare, the distribution policy of urban resources and the redistribution policy of services for urban poor groups also rely on the government's governance capacity.[38] We should pay attention to the following aspects in order to promote the modernization of city governments' governance capability. First, give full play to the role of city governments in promoting green development. It includes direct providers of green products and services; public interest coordinators; supporters and purchasers of green services; legislators and regulators of green activities and organizations. Second, promote the governance effectiveness of the city government. The city government actively makes the mechanism reasonable, the procedures scientific and the management flexible, significantly improves the decision-making level, execution ability and work efficiency, and timely responds to citizen's demand for green development through institutional and organizational transformation. Third, implement transparent governance, disclose information timely and enable citizens to better understand and use the information while protecting the privacy right. Fourth, be capable of long-term planning and design. Since there is no market, which can provide future resources and environmental commodities and service in the world, it is impossible for the market to effectively play its role through the supply–demand relationship in the future. In addition, there is no sufficient incentive mechanism in the market, which makes the commodities supplier meet the demands of people for future resource and environmental consumption.[39] Hence, the city government also needs to make a fair and reasonable trade-off between the present and the future and have long-term planning on development, utilization and protection of various urban resources and environment.

2. Public–private cooperative governance

Urban green development itself is a kind of interaction between market power and public policy. The public sector and the private sector have the potential to work together in the process of providing green products and services. The public sector mainly performs its functions of market supervision and public service while the private sector performs its functions of self-governance and mutual supervision. Without the private sectors, green development will be inefficient and the market mechanisms will not be able to function. And without sufficient investment and leadership of the public sectors, the private sector will not be able to function effectively, either. From the point of view of governance, in order to promote urban green development, the intervention by the public sector mainly includes the following six aspects. First, help the poor and ensure their access to basic health care services, adequate nutrition, primary education, safe drinking water and other basic services. Second, the public sector provides critical infrastructure and other public goods such as communicable disease control and environmental management. Third, provide good operating environment, including stable financial system, intellectual

Basic Connotations and Analysis Framework of Urban Green Development   47

property protection, contract enforcement and open international trade. Fourth, provide social security to ensure that all people are able to maintain their economic security and well-being in the face of inevitable economic chaos. Fifth, promote and popularize modern science and technology. Sixth, provide correct management of natural environment.[40] It not only includes the responsibility of maintaining social equity but also has the function of stimulating the market. Of course, more attention should be paid to the boundaries between the functions of the public and private sectors in actual operations.

3. Public participation in governance

The most important reason for occurrence of governance is that the social public affairs are becoming increasingly complex, diverse and dynamic and the traditional government is difficult to cope with them unilaterally. Therefore, the relevant parties concerned are required to participate in decision-making and implementation. Urban green development is not only the development of the government or enterprises but also involves the interests and future development of all urban residents. For each resident, isolated exclusive lifestyle is impossible to obtain a high quality of life in the modern society. The life quality of individuals cannot be realized without active participation of each person in the community and requires each member to have a high sense of responsibility to ensure their involvement in the process of pursuing quality life.[41] Historically, the public opinion often plays a key role in major movement of improving the city environment. In some cities, the stress exerted by the public forced the government to abolish large scale urban development projects in cities, promoted the development of more reasonable residential planning and prevented the behavior of blindly tearing down historical and cultural relics, exerting important influences on the urban environment transform and cultural inheritance. Therefore, we need to listen to the interests and demands of ordinary residents in the process of urban green development, so that urban green development will truly enable the development of most people. Meanwhile, the non-governmental organizations have the advantages of being close to the disadvantaged, professional, good at communication, creative and good in social image. In the process of urban green development, we need to develop non-governmental organizations to undertake some social governance responsibilities, more efficiently integrate and allocate various social resources and make up certain defects of governance purely by city government.

4. Urban community governance

Community is the microscopic node of the concept and practice of urban green development. In his book *City as a Way of Life*, the American sociologist Louis Wirth defined the city as large-scale rallying points of highly dense and heterogeneous residents. And the community "is not only the geographical units, but consists of various relationships which exist in those who share common interest in the social relation network".[42] It reflects the city which is as a lifestyle and social relation in a centralized way. A prosperous city should not only provide all kinds of recreation for the vagrant but also have the people who do their duty responsibly. Their economic and family interests are closely related to the city's fate. A successful city is not only the location of trendy clubs, galleries and hotels but also the location of specialized industries, small businesses, schools and communities where innovation can be made for future generations.[43] For urban green development, we need to view the community as the starting point, cultivate the concept of green development value of individuals and households and their ability to participate in the green development, and make the green development not only become a concept of city development but also the embodiment of urban residents' lifestyle, fully reflecting the vitality of urban green development.

5. E-governance

E-governance neither refers to purely applying information technology to handle governmental and public affairs nor is about how to apply information technology to provide information and electronic service so as to improve administration efficiency. It is about how to reform the government, promote transformation of the government, set up new government governance mode adapting to the needs of information society and promote good governance when facing the challenge of new social pattern brought by information technology.[44] For urban green development, the electronic governance process includes both the application and updating of hardware facilities and design and upgrading of software system and even the innovation and breakthrough of governing ideas of the governments. It is a process where the city government changes its positioning and realizes the changes of its function transformation; it is a process that helps the city government improve its performance and provides quality public services; it is a process that the city government interacts with the public and improves its public images. Most of the industrial cities in the 20th century require agglomeration development, as the interdependent professionals have to frequently or closely contact each other and short distance means lower transportation and communication cost. And with profound development and application of information technology, especially the Internet technology, new urban development in the 21st century is more influenced by the information technology revolution. Development of modern communication technology provides better channel for information dissemination and remote handling of social affairs, enables the people to live and work in locations far away from the activity center and also enables the information user to obtain information of a remote place, forming the city network in the information era. The information network technology has not only changed the spatial and economic form of urban development to some extent, but has also changed urban life and social organization method. This requires us to implement decentralized, transparent, convenient and electronic city governance, change governance concept and model, pursue innovative governance means, improve the utilization of big data, Internet, new media and other modern information technologies and tools with openness, sharing and common development to construct government–enterprise–public interconnected network and to implement e-governance.

6. City brand

Good governance is also reflected in city brand building. Currently, more and more cities have begun to apply the idea of branding, techniques and methods to seek the competitive advantages, enhance people's sense of pride and identity toward the city, attract business and investments, tourists, qualified residents, public institutions and other important activities and expand the export market and so on.[45,46] Successful cases in city brand building continuously emerge with Hi Seoul, Uniquely Singapore, Inspiring Capital and Toronto unlimited as the representatives. From theoretical and practical points of view, urban green development should have the following characteristics: first, the overall city brand image is outstanding and can fully demonstrate the function and characteristics of urban green development; second, the city brand is highly recognized, appreciated and trusted by main target clients like the investors and tourists; third, the city brand is widely recognized by local residents, can build social consensus of green development and form the sense of belonging of local culture and value. It should be noted that the city is not a "growth machine" and it is not through the ways of enterprise-oriented operation, purely service for the growth and rental rise.[47] The city is a complex of interest instead of simple combination of personal interests. Only when the development means are for the benefits of the overall city and for maintaining or improving the overall economic status and social reputation of the city, can they be viewed as means and methods in line with the urban interests. Therefore, city brand building shall fully reflect the overall development interest of the city. We should not regard city brand building as general publicity and promotion activity. Also, we should not achieve the goal of business and investment attraction through operation of urban land and resources. City brand is the accumulation of materials and spiritual in long-term urban development and reflects the orientation, value, concepts and governance model of urban development. It neither strives for short-term benefits for a small number of people at the expense of the long-term benefits of the majority nor focuses on interests of some sectors while neglecting the collective appeal of urban residents and the public.

(V) Partnership

The city and the state are inseparable and need to promote each other and develop together. "When the urbanization of a prosperous economy becomes higher, the rural areas will gradually narrow down".[48] For the state, the urbanization level is often closely related to the development level of the state. The urbanization level reflects the comprehensive national strength and international competitiveness of a state and has become an important symbol to measure the economic and social progress. City is the engine of national development. The national economy is deeply rooted in the city and controlled by the city. The national production is concentrated in the city, the national wealth is generated in the city and most of the national consumption also occurs in the city. They are also a state's economic, political and media center and home to the national green development strategy and practice. But the national development also affects the development of the city at the same time. The destinies of states and cities are always intertwined. Some cities are located in a stagnant or declining region of the continent or state and will encounter development problems no matter how livable and safe they are and whether they have rich cultural atmosphere.[49]

In urban green development, we shall not separate the green development of a city from that of the state. Firstly, national natural resources conditions will affect urban green development. States with good natural resource endowments and ecological environment will provide a broad foundation for urban green development. Secondly, the balanced development between urban and rural areas and between cities directly affects the green development ability and potential of a single city. Meantime, the overall health conditions, life expectancy and educational level of a country will provide high-quality human resources for the city. Finally, the clear and powerful implementation of national green development strategy will reduce cross-regional environmental pollution damage and provide good regional conditions for urban green development. Hence, for urban green development, we should fully consider the overall situation of national green development, consider the overall development level of both the urban and rural areas, intercity and other areas, well deal with the development relations between the center and the hinterland, consider the urban green development strategy and paths in the context of national development and improve the influence and competitiveness of green development of a country through green development of cities.

References

1. James Gustave Speth, *The Bridge at the Edge of the World*, Peking University Press, Beijing, 2014, pp. 50–51.
2. James Lovelock, *Gaia: A New Look at Life on Earth*, Shanghai People's Publishing House, Shanghai, 2007, pp. 11–14.
3. Peter A. Victor, *Managing without Growth*, China Citic Press, Beijing, 2012, p. 61.
4. Donella Meadows, Jorgen Randers and Dennis Meadows, *Limits to Growth* (Collector's Edition), China Machine Press, Beijing, 2013, pp. 238–245.
5. Ezra J. Mishan, *The Cost of Economic Growth*, China Machine Press, Beijing, 2011, pp. 3–17.
6. Jorgen Randers, *2052: A Global Forecast for the Next Forty Years*, Yilin Press, Nanjing, 2013, pp. 7–14.
7. Geoffrey Heal, *Nature and Marketplace* (1st Edition), China Citic Press, Beijing, 2006, pp. 116–122.
8. Brian J.L. Berry, *Comparative Urbanization — Different Roads in 20th Century*, The Commercial Press, Beijing, 2008, pp. 101–104.
9. Richard Register, *Ecocities: Rebuilding Cities in Balance with Nature* (Revised Edition), Social Sciences Academic Press, Beijing, 2010, pp. 76–82.
10. Edward Glaeser, *Triumph of the City: How Our Greatest Invention Makes Us Richer, Smarter, Greener, Healthier and Happier*, Shanghai Academy of Social Sciences Press, Shanghai, 2012, p. 232.
11. P.J. Taylor, On city cooperation and city competition, in B. Derudder, M. Hoyler, P. J. Taylor and F. Witlox (eds.), *International Handbook of Globalization and World Cities*, Edward Elgar, Cheltenham, UK, 2012, pp. 56–63.
12. See Daley, *New Eco-economy: An Exploration Making Environmental Protection Profitable*, Shanghai Science and Technology Education Press, Shanghai, 2005.

Basic Connotations and Analysis Framework of Urban Green Development 53

13. Chay Kenneth and Michael Greenstone, The impact of air pollution on infant mortality: Evidence from geographic variation in pollution shocks induced by a recession, *Quarterly Journal of Economics*, 2003, 118(3), 1121–1167.
14. Susmita Dasgupta, *Air Pollution during Growth: Accounting for Governance and Vulnerability*, Policy Research Working Paper 3383, World Bank (August), Washington, 2004.
15. Michael E. Porter, Location, competition and economic development: Local clusters in a global economy, *Economic Development Quarterly*, 2000, 1, 15–34.
16. D. Bloom and J. Sachs, Geography, demography and economic growth in Africa, *Brookings Papers on Economic Activity*, 1998, 2, 207–273.
17. See R. Florida, *The Rise of the Creative Class*, Basic Books, New York, 2002.
18. Kurt King, *Global City History*, Social Sciences Academic Press, Beijing, 2014, p. 111.
19. P. M. Romer, Endogenous technological change, *Journal of Political Economy*, 1990, 98, 71–102.
20. William D. Nordhaus, Lethal Model 2: The limits to growth revisited, *Brookings Papers on Economic Activity*, 1992, 2, 1–59.
21. Herbert Girardet, *Cities People Planet: Urban Development and Climate Change* (2nd Edition), Publishing House of Electronics Industry, Beijing, 2011, pp. 108–127.
22. J. Jacobs, *The Death and Life of Great American Cities*, Yilin Press, Nanjing, 2006, pp. 341–346.
23. Paul E. Peterson, *City Limits*, Shanghai People's Publishing House, 2012, pp. 27–30.
24. Gary Becker and Casey Mulligan, The endogenous determination of time preference, *Quarterly Journal of Economics*, 1997, 3, 729–758.
25. Arthur O'Sullivan, *Urban Economics* (8th Edition), Peking University Press, Beijing, 2015, pp. 27–29.
26. Michael P. Todar, *Economic Development*, China Economic Publishing House, Beijing, 1999, pp. 61–62.
27. World Commission on Environment and Development, *Our Common Future*, Jilin People's Publishing House, Changchun, 1997, p. 136.
28. Brian Bresnahan, Mark Dickie and Shelby Gerking, Averting behavior and urban air pollution, *Land Economics*, 1997, 3, 340–357.
29. Alexander S.P. Pfaff, Shubham Chaudhuri and H. Nye, Household: Production and environmental kuznets curves: Examining the desirability and feasibility of substitution, *Environmental and Resource Econotnics*, 2004, 2, 187–200.
30. Edward Glaeser, *Triumph of the City: How Our Greatest Invention Makes Us Richer, Smarter, Greener, Healthier and Happier*, Shanghai Academy of Social Sciences Press, Shanghai, 2012, pp. 75–77.
31. Edward Glaeser, *Triumph of the City: How Our Greatest Invention Makes Us Richer, Smarter, Greener, Healthier and Happier*, Shanghai Academy of Social Sciences Press, Shanghai, 2012, p. 26.

32. Gary Becker and Casey Mulligan The endogenous determination of time preference, *Quarterly Journal of Economics*, 1997, 3, 729–758.

33. Matthew Kahn and John Matsusaka, Demand for environmental goods: Evidence from voting patterns on California initiatives, *Journal of Law and Economics*, 1997, 1, 137–173.

34. Kurt King, *Global City History*, Social Sciences Academic Press, Beijing, 2014, pp. 292–293.

35. Luca Pattaroni and E. Pedrazzini, Insecurity and fragmentation: The rejection of frightening urbanization, Reproduced from Pierre Jacquet, Rajendra K. Pachauri and Laurence Tubiana, *Villes: Changer de tracjectoire (Regards sur la terre 2010)*, Social Sciences Academic Press, Beijing, 2010, pp. 155–163.

36. Kurt King, *Global City History*, Social Sciences Academic Press, 2014, p. 233.

37. Jean-Pierre Gaudin, *Pourquol La Gouvernance*, Social Sciences Academic Press, Beijing, 2010, p. 15.

38. Paul E. Peterson, *City Limits*, Shanghai People's Publishing House, Shanghai, 2012, pp. 42–47.

39. Geoffrey Heal, *Nature and Marketplace*, China Citic Press, Beijing, 2006, pp. 116–122.

40. Jeffrey Sachs, *Common Wealth: How Will Sustainable Development Change Human Destiny*, China Citic Press, Beijing, 2010, pp. 211–212.

41. Jeremy Kifkin, *The Third Industrial Revolution: How does the New Economic Model Change the World*, China Citic Press, Beijing, 2012, p. 232.

42. Dilys M. Hill (ed.), *Citizens and Cities*, Harvester Wheatsheaf, New York, 1994, p. 34.

43. Kurt King, *Global City History*, Social Sciences Academic Press, Beijing, 2014, pp. 285–286.

44. OECD, *The E-Government Imperative*, OECD Publishing, Paris, 2003, p. 203.

45. Philip Kotler, Donald Haider and Irving Rein, *Marketing Places, Attracting Investment, Industry and Tourism to Cities, States, and Nations*, Maxwell Macmillan Int., New York, 1993.

46. R. Paddison, City marketing, image reconstruction and urban regeneration, *Urban Studies*, 1993, 2, 339–350.

47. David Harvey, *Rebel Cities: From the Right to the City to the Urban Revolution*, The Commercial Press, Beijing, 2014, pp. 100–113.

48. Jane Jacobs, *Cities and the Wealth of Nations*, China Citic Press, Beijing, 2008, p. 154.

49. Mario Polis, *The Wealth & Poverty of Regions*, Xinhua Publishing House, Beijing, 2011, p. 20.

Part II

Evaluation Chapters

Chapter 3

Urban Green Development Index and Evaluation Index System

Zheng Zhao
Researcher, Development Research Center
of the State Council of PRC
zz_bnu@126.com

I. Urban Green Development Index

The evaluation on urban green development remains an important issue for the theoretical circle and departments of practical affairs. Evaluation enables us to have a better knowledge of a city's pros and cons in green development when compared with other cities. In doing this, it not only is helpful for enterprises and citizens to be informed of the conditions and opportunities of urban green development but also provides a reference for the government to improve urban green development environment.

Urban Green Development Index (UGDI) measures and assesses the comprehensive performance in urban green development. The research group of Asia-Pacific urban green development is responsible for proposing and reasoning specific research methods. During the construction of city, fully learning from academic research at home and abroad, and based on their understanding of green development, the research group, taking into consideration the system analysis framework of urban green development and centering on five aspects, i.e. livability, prosperity, inclusiveness, governance and partnership, constructs Asia-Pacific's UGDI to measure and assess the green development level in the Asia-Pacific region. Specific performance is as follows: urban green development = F (livability, prosperity, inclusiveness, governance, partnership).

1. **Livability:** It demonstrates the basic resource environment of urban green development, i.e. resource and environment endowments, environmental capacity and environmental suitability in urban green development.
2. **Prosperity:** It mirrors economy quality of urban green development, namely, foundation for economic affluence in urban green development and the matching degree between its economic pattern and economy.
3. **Inclusiveness:** It shows the social advances in urban green development: the social support, diversity, stability and inclusion of urban green development.
4. **Governance:** It reflects the communicative and behavioral rule arrangements of interest subjects, namely, governance system and perfect degree of governance capacity.
5. **Partnership:** It showcases the interrelation and influencing mechanism among country factors, cities and the country, i.e. the potential factors, market supply and demand conditions and their spatial coordination degree that urban green development should rely on.

On the whole, urban green development level is codetermined by various aspects, each of which includes a host of specific influencing factors. These factors are part and parcel of urban green development, although their contributions to and actions on urban green development vary from one to another.

II. Design Principles of Asia-Pacific UGDI

1. **Principle of internal logic:** UGDI system refers to a system with strict internal logic instead of a system with a pile of indexes. In addition, indexes at the same level, without influencing each

other, can independently reflect different aspects of Asia-Pacific urban green development.

2. **Principle of data availability:** In order to compare the green development levels of different cities in Asia-Pacific region, we need to know whether the data are available and the standard is consistent to determine the scientificity and reliability of quantification. As a result, we should try utmost to use common indexes or potentially accessible indexes for international cities.

3. **Principle of combining systemic and representative indexes:** Asia-Pacific UGDI system is the joint result of systemic development of relevant elements, so the index system should neither be too numerous nor too simple to influence the value of evaluation. As a result, the selected evaluation indexes should cover the fundamental aspects as much as practical and be representative indexes of key fields so as to better analyze the characteristics of urban green development and carry out regular dynamic monitoring.

4. **Principle of combining guiding and forward-looking indexes:** When selecting indexes, we pay particular attention to the practical guiding significance of indexes and tightly focus on the actual green development of Asian-Pacific cities when having index system design so as to facilitate guidance on practice with the evaluation. At the same time, we pay attention to the green development orientation and future of Asian-Pacific cities when selecting some individual indexes in the evaluation index system, hoping to encourage the forward-looking layout and planning of Asian-Pacific cities through the index system design and evaluation and thus leading the global green development trend.

5. **Principle of combining objective and subjective indexes:** Due to the restrictions from statistical indexes and statistical methods, objective statistical data are far from enough to completely meet the needs of evaluation. Therefore, some appropriate subjective indexes are added to the evaluation index system. In doing this, subjective data and objective data are bound

together, which can reflect the conditions of Asia-Pacific urban green development in a more truthful manner.

III. UGDI System

In compliance with the aforesaid principles as well as the understanding of research group on the global urban green development, we try to build an index system including five level-I indexes and 18 level-II indexes (see Table 3.1). Among these indexes, level-I indexes include livability, prosperity, inclusiveness, governance and partnership. Level-II indexes include climate, environment, population, growth, innovation, enterprise, security, living, education, e-governance, brand, NGO, income, information, health, energy consumption, emission, water purification, etc. UGDI system centers on five aspects of urban green development, namely, livability, prosperity, inclusiveness, governance and partnership, aiming to reflect urban green development level in a comprehensive, concise and truthful way.

Table 3.1. Index System of Asia-Pacific's UGDI.

Level-I Index	Level-II Index	Proportion (%)	Index Nature
Livability environment	Climate	6.67	Objective
	Environment	6.67	Objective
	Population	6.67	Objective
Prosperity	Growth	6.67	Objective
	Innovation	6.67	Objective
	Enterprise	6.67	Objective
Inclusiveness	Security	6.67	Objective
	Living	6.67	Objective
	Education	6.67	Objective
Governance	E-governance	6.67	Objective
	Brand	6.67	Subjective
	Ngo	6.67	Objective
Partnership	Income	3.33	Objective
	Information	3.33	Objective
	Health	3.33	Objective
	Energy consumption	3.33	Objective
	Emission	3.33	Objective
	Water purification	3.33	Objective

IV. Samples of Cities

The universality and typicality of evaluated samples in Asia-Pacific urban green development have a bearing on the accuracy and value of research conclusions. This chapter, on the basis of the availability, accuracy and standard of urban statistical data considered, refers to the suggestions of senior experts and scholars and selects 100 major cities in the Asia-Pacific region[a] for quantitative research. Specific selection standards of city samples are as follows: (1) the influence and popularity of the city; (2) socio-economic status and representativeness of the city in its county and region; (3) the availability, accuracy and standard of urban statistical data; (4) research value of the city.

In accordance with the selection standards of city samples, we chose 160 cities from the Asia-Pacific region as original samples and then selected 100 cities as formal research samples. Among the 100 cities, cities of both developed counties and developing countries are included. Many of them, as the economic, political or cultural center of its country, boast a world-renowned reputation, fully representing the urban conditions of different countries and regions of different development levels in Asia-Pacific region.

Among the 100 sample cities, 43 Chinese cities are included, including 35 cities in 31 provincial capitals and municipalities directly under the State Council and four major cities, i.e. Shenzhen, Dalian, Qingdao and Xiamen, and six cities in Hong Kong SAR China, Macau SAR China and Taiwan. Nineteen American cities are included: Washington, New York, Los Angeles, Chicago, Boston, Philadelphia, Seattle, Detroit, Dallas, Houston, Phoenix,

---

[a] Asia-Pacific region is short for Asian region and Pacific Rim. There are a broad notion and a narrow notion for the Asia-Pacific region. In the broad sense, it refers to the whole Pacific Rim including Canada, America, Mexico, Peru, Chile, and other North and South American countries in the east coast and Russian Far East, Japan, Korea, the Mainland China, Taiwan (China), Hong Kong, ASEAN countries, Australia, and New Zealand and other countries and regions in the west coast. In the narrow sense, Asia-Pacific region refers to western Pacific region, mainly including China (Hong Kong, Macau and Taiwan included), Japan, Russian Far East, ASEAN countries in Southeast Asia, and sometimes including Australia, and New Zealand and other countries in Oceania. This report, based on the broad notion of Asia-Pacific region, selects samples of cities.

Figure 3.1. Distribution of Evaluated City Samples in Asia-Pacific UGDI.

San Francisco, Denver, Las Vegas, Atlanta, Miami, Baltimore, San Jose and San Diego. Nine Japanese cities are included, i.e. Tokyo, Osaka, Kyoto, Sapporo, Yokohama, Fukuoka, Nagoya, Hiroshima, Kobe. Five cities of South Korea are included, i.e. Seoul, Busan, Daejeo, Inchon and Daegu. In addition, the 100 sample cities also include Wellington and Auckland in New Zealand; Canberra, Sydney, Melbourne and Brisbane in Australia; Moscow, St Petersburg and Vladivostok in Russia; Ottawa, Toronto and Vancouver in Canada; Delhi, Mumbai, Bangalore and Calcutta in India; Hanoi in Vietnam; Manila in Philippines; Jakarta in Indonesia; Kuala Lumpur in Malaysia; Singapore; Bangkok in Thailand; Lima in Peru; Mexico City in Mexico (see Figure 3.1).

V. Sources of Data

For quantitative measure of cities of different countries in the Asia-Pacific region, data on each sample city should be complete and reliable, and the data of the same aspect can be compared. Relevant data of this report come from the official websites of city governments and statistical departments, publications of city governments and statistical departments, statistical yearbooks (reports) of countries, regions and cities, etc. In addition to official websites, we also obtain data from famous research institutes, consultancy companies and websites such as the websites of United Nations Statistics Division, the World Bank, OECD, http://www.citymayors.com and http://wikipedia.jaylee.cn/. Moreover, related reports and investigation data of famous media serve as reference. In the course of collecting and organizing data, a host of research institutes and scholars at home and abroad have provided strong support and help. At the same time, because the definition and scopes of city may be different, we use data of metropolitan area and urbanized area of some cities for a more convenient comparison. Besides, due to the restrictions of subjective and objective conditions, some important indexes still remain unrevealed. It is hoped that these indexes can be supplemented and completed in the future research.

VI. Evaluation Methods

This report mainly adopts analytic hierarchy process (AHP) for research. AHP, aiming to carry out quantitative analysis on qualitative issues, is a multi-criteria decision-making method which is convenient, flexible and practical. The method, by classifying all factors in complicated problems into interrelated and orderly hierarchies, enables all factors to be arranged in an orderly manner. The method also, based on subjective judgments on some objective realities, addresses various decision-making factors through the combination of qualitative analysis and quantitative analysis. This report classifies Asia-Pacific UGDI into multiple levels on the basis of framework of logic analysis to determine the original index. Based on the numerical value of the original index, we calculate all indexes one after another, and then put them all together by hierarchy to obtain Asia-Pacific UGDI. The key to measure the method lies in the processing method of original index and the way to constitute higher indexes.

(I) Processing of original indexes

Consistency processing of evaluated indexes is an important procedure in this research. UGDI is a complex index of multiple evaluated indexes. In order to ensure that different dimensional indexes can be combined efficiently, after the collection of data, the indexes should be made dimensionless to enable different indexes to compare with each other. During this process, standardization calculation and the method that returning data ranks intensively among data should be mainly adopted. Due to the different attributes of indexes, we classify them into positive and negative indexes.

Positive indexes: the higher the numerical value of index is, the more beneficial it will be to urban green development, such as per capita GDP, patent numbers, etc. The normalization formula of positive indexes is as follows:

$$\langle M \rangle X_i = \frac{x_i - x_{\min}}{x_{\max} - x_{\min}},$$

where X_i refers to the converted value, $x_{\max}$ refers to the maximum sample value of indexes, $x_{\min}$ refers to the minimum sample value of indexes and x_i refers to the original index value.

Negative indexes: the higher the numerical value of index is, the more unfavorable it will be to urban green development, for example, crime rate. The normalization formula of negative indexes is as follows:

$$X_i = \frac{x_{\max} - x_i}{x_{\max} - x_{\min}},$$

where X_i refers to the converted value, $x_{\max}$ refers to the maximum sample value of indexes, $x_{\min}$ refers to the minimum sample value of indexes and x_i refers to the original index value.

(II) Index combination

The key to index combination lies in the proportion of chosen indexes when combining indexes of the same level. Because the indexes of the same level have been assumed to be of equal importance when designing the index system, this research mainly combines indexes with same proportion by hierarchy to obtain Asia-Pacific's UGDI. In addition, for the sake of comparison, before the indexes are combined into a higher index, all indexes should be made dimensionless to restrict the sample value of indexes to range from 0 to 1.

(III) Index analysis

UGDI includes not only combined index but also sub-index. Specifically speaking, UGDI belongs to combined index while livable environment, economic affluence, social inclusion, good governance and country prosperity belong to the combined index. The evaluation ordering of combined index differs from that of sub-index, which also reflects the overall conditions and structure conditions of each city's urban green development. Therefore, for the evaluation of urban green development, it needs to analyze not only the combined index of urban green development but also each sub-index so as to have a comprehensive understanding of the urban green development level.

Chapter 4

Evaluation Results and Main Research Findings of Asia-Pacific Urban Green Development

Zheng Zhao
Researcher, Development Research Center
of the State Council of PRC
zz_bnu@126.com

I. Overall Ranking and Sub-ranking of Asia-Pacific UGDI

(I) Overall ranking

The top 15 cities of Asia-Pacific's Urban Green Development Index (UGDI) in turn are Tokyo, Seoul, New York, Hong Kong, Washington, Sydney, Singapore, San Jose, Houston, Wellington, Ottawa, San Francisco, Melbourne, Los Angeles and Shanghai.

As shown in Table 4.1, from the perspective of a country, among the top 15 cities of Asia-Pacific UGDI, America ranks the first, with six cities; China and Australia rank the second, each with two cities; Japan, South Korea, Singapore, New Zealand and Canada each has one city included.

The top 16–30 cities in turn are Seattle, Osaka, Kyoto, San Diego, Chicago, Beijing, Nagoya, Kuala Lumpur, Philadelphia, Dallas, Toronto, Phoenix, Moscow, Yokohama and Miami.

Table 4.1. Overall Ranking of Asia-Pacific's UGDI.

City	Score	Ranking	City	Score	Ranking
Tokyo	0.707	1	Sapporo	0.478	41
Seoul	0.669	2	Kobe	0.478	42
New York	0.650	3	Chengdu	0.477	43
Hong Kong	0.611	4	Canberra	0.475	44
Washington	0.611	5	Taipei	0.475	45
Sydney	0.600	6	Bangkok	0.475	46
Singapore	0.599	7	Taichung	0.474	47
San Jose	0.580	8	Denver	0.473	48
Houston	0.578	9	Vancouver	0.471	49
Wellington	0.577	10	Detroit	0.468	50
Ottawa	0.560	11	Hsinchu	0.466	51
San Francisco	0.556	12	Tainan	0.463	52
Melbourne	0.555	13	Baltimore	0.461	53
Los Angeles	0.551	14	Wuhan	0.457	54
Shanghai	0.550	15	Busan	0.457	55
Seattle	0.540	16	Macau	0.451	56
Osaka	0.540	17	Jakarta	0.450	57
Kyoto	0.536	18	Daejeon	0.450	58
San Diego	0.535	19	Guangzhou	0.449	59
Chicago	0.527	20	Kaohsiung	0.448	60
Beijing	0.526	21	Xi'an	0.447	61
Nagoya	0.524	22	Daegu	0.446	62
Kuala Lumpur	0.517	23	Hanoi	0.444	63
Philadelphia	0.507	24	Incheon	0.437	64
Dallas	0.506	25	Xiamen	0.437	65
Toronto	0.506	26	Nanjing	0.436	66
Phoenix	0.504	27	Changchun	0.432	67
Moscow	0.502	28	Manila	0.425	68
Yokohama	0.501	29	Mexico City	0.425	69
Miami	0.496	30	Keelung	0.420	70
Boston	0.494	31	Vladivostok	0.410	71
Auckland, NZ	0.494	32	Qingdao	0.410	72
Hiroshima	0.493	33	Hangzhou	0.410	73
Fukuoka	0.490	34	Bangalore	0.405	74
Brisbane	0.490	35	Tianjin	0.405	75
Changsha	0.487	36	Taiyuan	0.403	76
Atlanta	0.485	37	Ningbo	0.400	77
Las Vegas	0.484	38	Chongqing	0.399	78
Lima	0.480	39	Delhi	0.398	79
Shenzhen	0.480	40	Kunming	0.393	80

(Continued)

Evaluation Results and Main Research Findings　　69

Table 4.1. (*Continued*)

City	Score	Ranking	City	Score	Ranking
Nanchang	0.392	81	Shijiazhuang	0.368	91
Hefei	0.389	82	Zhengzhou	0.365	92
Dalian	0.388	83	Mumbai	0.364	93
Fuzhou	0.386	84	Shenyang	0.364	94
Haikou	0.385	85	Yinchuan	0.361	95
Calcutta	0.385	86	Urumqi	0.355	96
Jinan	0.381	87	Lanzhou	0.346	97
St. Petersburg	0.377	88	Xining	0.343	98
Nanning	0.372	89	Harbin	0.337	99
Hohhot	0.370	90	Guiyang	0.337	100

The top 31–45 cities in turn are Boston, Auckland, Hiroshima, Fukuoka, Brisbane, Changsha, Atlanta, Las Vegas, Lima, Shenzhen, Sapporo, Kobe, Chengdu, Canberra and Taipei.

The top 46–60 cities in turn are Bangkok, Taichung, Denver, Vancouver, Detroit, Hsinchu, Tainan, Baltimore, Wuhan, Busan, Macau, Jakarta, Daejeo, Guangzhou and Kaohsiung.

The top 61–85 cities in turn are Xi'an, Daegu, Hanoi, Incheon, Xiamen, Nanjing, Changchun, Manila, Mexico City, Keelung, Vladivostok, Qingdao, Hangzhou, Bangalore, Tianjin, Taiyuan, Ningbo, Chongqing, Delhi, Kunming, Nanchang, Hefei, Dalian, Fuzhou and Haikou.

The last 15 cities in turn are Kolkata, Jinan, St. Petersburg, Nanning, Hohhot, Shijiazhuang, Zhengzhou, Bombay, Shenyang, Yinchuan, Urumqi, Lanzhou, Xining, Harbin and Guiyang.

(II)　Overall conditions

From the overall UGDI in the Asia-Pacific region, the mean value of indexes is 0.466; the median is 0.467; the standard deviation is 0.08; the coefficient of variation is 0.17. So the data are comparably stable. By fitting with normal curve, we found that data are slightly lean to the right, which is comparatively in accordance with the statistics rule. This suggests that the selected samples shall have certain representativeness (see Figure 4.1).

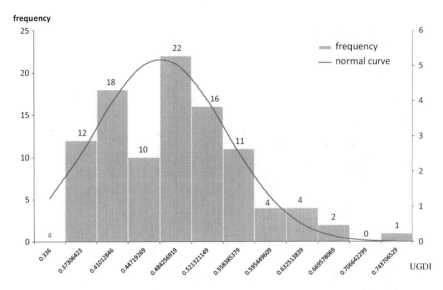

Figure 4.1. Histogram of Score of Green Development Index of Asia-Pacific Cities.

Among the 100 cities in the Asia-Pacific region, most scores of green development index range from 0.41 to 0.52. Xining posts the lowest score, 0.037 while Tokyo ranks the first, 0.707, a difference of 0.371. From the overall conditions of UGDI, there exists a distinct gap between cities with highest scores and lowest scores in terms of their urban green development level, and they also present a distinct gap in various aspects of urban green development.

(III) Ranking and analysis of livability

1. Sub-ranking

In terms of livability, the top 15 cities in turn are Washington, Dallas, Houston, Melbourne, Atlanta, Miami, San Jose, Detroit, Brisbane, San Diego, Phoenix, Canberra, Philadelphia, Seattle and Las Vegas.

As shown in Table 4.2, among the top 15 cities in livability, all cities belong to America (12) and Australia (3). These cities are sparsely populated, with favorable climate and beautiful scenery.

The top 16–30 cities in turn are New York, Ottawa, Boston, Los Angeles, Chicago, Sydney, San Francisco, Baltimore,

Evaluation Results and Main Research Findings 71

Table 4.2. Ranking of Livability.

City	Score	Ranking	City	Score	Ranking
Washington	0.951	1	Bangkok	0.788	40
Dallas	0.941	2	Yinchuan	0.788	41
Houston	0.940	3	Tainan	0.782	42
Melbourne	0.933	4	Shenzhen	0.779	43
Atlanta	0.912	5	Hohhot	0.778	44
Miami	0.909	6	Bangalore	0.771	45
San Jose	0.904	7	Dalian	0.762	46
Detroit	0.903	8	Kunming	0.762	47
Brisbane	0.899	9	Busan	0.762	48
San Diego	0.898	10	Jinan	0.761	49
Phoenix	0.890	11	Hsinchu	0.761	50
Canberra	0.889	12	Kaohsiung	0.759	51
Philadelphia	0.888	13	Mexico City	0.755	52
Seattle	0.887	14	Tianjin	0.753	53
Las Vegas	0.882	15	Lima	0.752	54
New York	0.881	16	Keelung	0.751	55
Ottawa	0.875	17	Nanchang	0.751	56
Boston	0.873	18	Shijiazhuang	0.750	57
Los Angeles	0.871	19	Haikou	0.749	58
Chicago	0.863	20	Sapporo	0.742	59
Sydney	0.861	21	Taipei	0.741	60
San Francisco	0.861	22	Xiamen	0.736	61
Baltimore	0.861	23	Hefei	0.735	62
Nagoya	0.861	24	Jakarta	0.733	63
Wellington	0.861	25	Shanghai	0.732	64
Yokohama	0.860	26	Nanjing	0.731	65
Denver	0.859	27	Taiyuan	0.729	66
Toronto	0.850	28	Daejeon	0.728	67
Auckland, NZ	0.846	29	Shenyang	0.727	68
Hiroshima	0.842	30	Daegu	0.723	69
Kuala Lumpur	0.834	31	Ningbo	0.722	70
Kyoto	0.833	32	Singapore	0.721	71
Tokyo	0.827	33	Hangzhou	0.719	72
Osaka	0.818	34	Wuhan	0.719	73
Fukuoka	0.813	35	Seoul	0.714	74
Kobe	0.813	36	Chengdu	0.713	75
Vancouver	0.808	37	Zhengzhou	0.712	76
Taichung	0.796	38	Qingdao	0.712	77
Guangzhou	0.792	39	Fuzhou	0.712	78

(Continued)

72 Z. Zhao

Table 4.2. (*Continued*)

City	Score	Ranking	City	Score	Ranking
Calcutta	0.707	79	Changchun	0.662	90
Incheon	0.707	80	Xining	0.661	91
Beijing	0.705	81	Vladivostok	0.660	92
Chongqing	0.701	82	Guiyang	0.657	93
Nanning	0.694	83	Harbin	0.614	94
Moscow	0.686	84	Lanzhou	0.601	95
Xi'an	0.686	85	Macau	0.574	96
Changsha	0.683	86	Urumqi	0.554	97
Hanoi	0.682	87	Hong Kong	0.500	98
St. Petersburg	0.682	88	Delhi	0.488	99
Manila	0.663	89	Mumbai	0.410	100

Nagoya, Wellington, Yokohama, Denver, Toronto, Auckland and Hiroshima.

The top 31–45 cities are Kuala Lumpur, Kyoto, Tokyo, Osaka, Fukuoka, Kobe, Vancouver, Taichung, Guangzhou, Bangkok, Yinchuan, Tainan, Shenzhen, Hohhot and Bangalore.

The top 46–60 cities are Dalian, Kunming, Busan, Jinan, Hsinchu, Kaohsiung, Mexico City, Tianjin, Lima, Keelung, Nanchang, Shijiazhuang, Haikou, Sapporo and Taipei.

The top 61–85 cities are Xiamen, Hefei, Jakarta, Shanghai, Nanjing, Taiyuan, Daejeon, Shenyang, Daegu, Ningbo, Singapore, Hangzhou, Wuhan, Seoul, Chengdu, Zhengzhou, Qingdao, Fuzhou, Kolkata, Incheon, Beijing, Chongqing, Nanning Moscow and Xi'an.

The last 15 cities are Changsha, Hanoi, St. Petersburg, Manila, Changchun, Xining, Vladivostok, Guiyang, Harbin, Lanzhou, Macau, Urumqi, Hong Kong, Delhi and Mumbai.

None of the Chinese cities is among the top 15 cities, but many Chinese cities are among the last 10 cities. This suggests that there are some environment problems in China's major cities. Besides, none of the cities in Southeast Asia and India is among the top 30 cities. Instead, cities of developed countries which develop much earlier are among the list. This reflects that developing countries still remain in their primary or middle stage of industrialization and need to transform their economic development modes.

2. Analysis of core indexes

The relative scales and scopes of a city's natural element endowments pose great impact on the competitive advantages and comparative advantages in urban green development. The presence of these factors usually determines city's monopoly position and role in green development and easily forms an inherent competitive advantage. Urban green development needs not only protecting the natural ecological environment which a city depends on for existence and development but also finding a suitable green development path and integrating a city's own climate features, geographical features and resource endowments through reasonable regional resource allocation and perfect resource utilization system.

We mainly adopt three indexes to measure livable environment: population, climate and environment. Population index reflects a city's population scale and density; climate index comprehensively shows a city's livability in light of temperature, humidity and sunshine duration; environment index suggests a city's environment situations especially air quality.

(1) **Population index:** The top 10 cities in population are Atlanta, Boston, Canberra, Brisbane, Detroit, Philadelphia, Dallas, Houston, Seattle and Baltimore, among which eight are American cities and the other two are Australian cities.

The last 10 cities in the population index are Incheon, Lanzhou, Singapore, Lima, Delhi, Calcutta, Manila, Macau, Hong Kong and Mumbai. Most of these cities are from East Asia; three Indian cities (Delhi, Calcutta and Mumbai) are included; three Chinese cities, namely, Lanzhou, Macau and Hong Kong are also included (see Figure 4.2).

(2) **Climate index:** The top 10 cities in climate index are Washington, Bangalore, Houston, Dallas, Melbourne, Mexico City, Delhi, Jinan, Kolkata and Lima. The last 10 cities are Guiyang, Vancouver, Hong Kong, Changchun, Harbin, Sapporo, Urumqi, Vladivostok, Moscow and St. Petersburg (see Figure 4.3). In comparison with other indexes, there exists a slightly smaller gap among cities in climate index because the

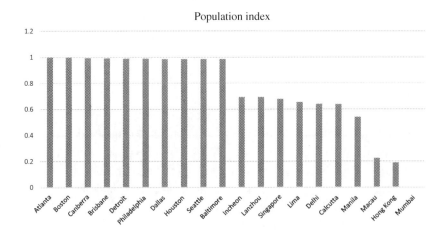

Figure 4.2. Top 10 and Bottom 10 Cities in Population Index.

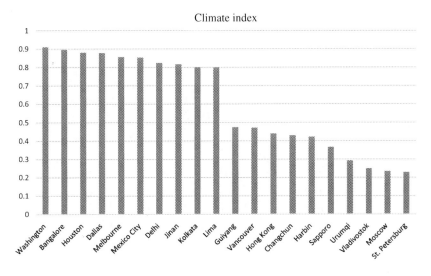

Figure 4.3. Top 10 and Bottom 10 Cities in Climate Index.

chosen cities are typically relatively large- and medium-sized cities. These cities aggregating a large quantity of people throughout the history indicates that these cities enjoy a relatively livable environment.

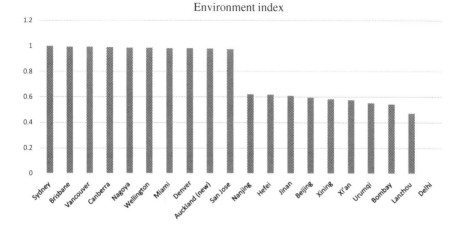

Figure 4.4. Top 10 and Bottom 10 Cities in Environment Index.

(3) **Environment index:** The top 10 cities in environment index are Sydney, Brisbane, Vancouver, Canberra, Nagoya, Wellington, Miami, Denver, Auckland (new) and San Jose. Among the top 10 cities, most cities belong to America and Australia with three cities each, and two cities of New Zealand are included.

The last 10 cities are Nanjing, Hefei, Jinan, Beijing, Xining, Xi'an, Urumqi, Bombay, Lanzhou and Delhi, of which eight are Chinese cities and two are Indian cities (see Figure 4.4). We found that environment index is closely related to urban economic development level and industrialization degree, and all top-ranking cities are cities of developed countries while low-ranking cities are all cities of developing countries as well as countries in their primary and middle industrialization.

(IV) Ranking and analysis of prosperity

1. The Sub-ranking of prosperity

The top 15 cities in prosperity are New York, San Jose, Houston, Tokyo, San Francisco, Seattle, San Diego, Washington, Los Angeles, Seoul, Osaka, Chicago, Dallas, Kyoto and Boston.

As shown in Table 4.3, among the top 15 cities in prosperity, America accounts for the majority with 11 cities included. Japan ranks second with three cities included: Tokyo, Osaka and Kyoto. In addition, Seoul, the capital of South Korea, ranks at 10th place.

The top 16–30 cities are Philadelphia, Shenzhen, Denver, Shanghai, Phoenix, Baltimore, Melbourne, Atlanta, Miami, Nagoya, Wellington, Hiroshima, Moscow, Hong Kong and Singapore.

Table 4.3. Ranking of Prosperity.

City	Score	Ranking	City	Score	Ranking
New York	0.830	1	Singapore	0.201	30
San Jose	0.800	2	Toronto	0.194	31
Houston	0.641	3	Canberra	0.194	32
Tokyo	0.606	4	Changsha	0.194	33
San Francisco	0.554	5	Kobe	0.189	34
Seattle	0.534	6	Ottawa	0.186	35
San Diego	0.522	7	Sydney	0.186	36
Washington	0.444	8	Las Vegas	0.185	37
Los Angeles	0.440	9	Beijing	0.183	38
Seoul	0.385	10	Detroit	0.173	39
Osaka	0.381	11	Auckland, NZ	0.170	40
Chicago	0.377	12	Vancouver	0.168	41
Dallas	0.367	13	Hsinchu	0.168	42
Kyoto	0.347	14	Macau	0.162	43
Boston	0.330	15	Yokohama	0.161	44
Philadelphia	0.292	16	Sapporo	0.151	45
Shenzhen	0.283	17	Fukuoka	0.150	46
Denver	0.274	18	Brisbane	0.141	47
Shanghai	0.269	19	Taipei	0.139	48
Phoenix	0.262	20	Ningbo	0.119	49
Baltimore	0.254	21	Hangzhou	0.117	50
Melbourne	0.244	22	Incheon	0.111	51
Atlanta	0.241	23	Chengdu	0.110	52
Miami	0.239	24	Daejeon	0.110	53
Nagoya	0.236	25	Guangzhou	0.109	54
Wellington	0.227	26	Kaohsiung	0.090	55
Hiroshima	0.218	27	Tianjin	0.089	56
Moscow	0.212	28	Busan	0.089	57
Hong Kong	0.203	29	Taichung	0.087	58

(*Continued*)

Evaluation Results and Main Research Findings 77

Table 4.3. (Continued)

City	Score	Ranking	City	Score	Ranking
Daegu	0.083	59	Hohhot	0.038	80
Mexico City	0.077	60	Kuala Lumpur	0.038	81
Keelung	0.077	61	Hefei	0.034	82
Tainan	0.075	62	Nanchang	0.032	83
Bangalore	0.074	63	Shijiazhuang	0.031	84
Dalian	0.073	64	Taiyuan	0.030	85
Delhi	0.072	65	Kunming	0.026	86
Mumbai	0.072	66	Lima	0.023	87
Wuhan	0.071	67	St. Petersburg	0.023	88
Qingdao	0.068	68	Lanzhou	0.018	89
Nanjing	0.064	69	Yinchuan	0.018	90
Jinan	0.064	70	Urumqi	0.017	91
Shenyang	0.055	71	Guiyang	0.017	92
Xiamen	0.051	72	Nanning	0.015	93
Bangkok	0.051	73	Xining	0.012	94
Chongqing	0.046	74	Haikou	0.011	95
Xi'an	0.041	75	Vladivostok	0.011	96
Fuzhou	0.041	76	Jakarta	0.010	97
Harbin	0.040	77	Hanoi	0.002	98
Changchun	0.040	78	Manila	0.001	99
Zhengzhou	0.039	79	Calcutta	0.001	100

The top 31–45 cities are Toronto, Canberra, Changsha, Kobe, Ottawa, Sydney, Las Vegas, Beijing, Detroit, Auckland, Vancouver, Hsinchu, Macau, Yokohama and Sapporo.

The top 46–60 cities are Fukuoka, Brisbane, Taipei, Ningbo, Hangzhou, Incheon, Chengdu, Daejeon, Guangzhou, Kaohsiung, Tianjin, Busan, Taichung, Daegu and Mexico City.

The top 61–85 cities are Keelung, Tainan, Bangalore, Dalian, Delhi, Mumbai, Wuhan, Qingdao, Nanjing, Jinan, Shenyang, Xiamen, Bangkok, Chongqing, Xi'an, Fuzhou, Harbin, Changchun, Zhengzhou, Hohhot, Kuala Lumpur, Hefei, Nanchang, Shijiazhuang and Taiyuan.

The last 15 cities are Kunming, Lima, St. Petersburg, Lanzhou, Yinchuan, Urumqi, Guiyang, Nanning, Xining, Haikou, Vladivostok, Jakarta, Hanoi, Manila and Calcutta.

The top 10 Chinese cities are Shenzhen, Shanghai, Hong Kong, Changsha, Beijing, Hsinchu, Macau, Taipei, Ningbo and Hangzhou. Shenzhen ranks the first in China and 17th in the Asia-Pacific region. Shanghai ranks the second in China and 19th in the Asia-Pacific region. Hong Kong ranks the third in China and 29th in the Asia-Pacific region. In China, Shenzhen ranks the first in term of enterprise innovation ability, second in terms of hi-tech innovation capacity following Shanghai. The advantages of Hong Kong lie in its high resident income but Hong Kong is inferior to Shenzhen and Shanghai in enterprise innovation ability and hi-tech innovation capacity. By virtue of its powerful enterprise innovation ability, Changsha has been on the list of the top 10 Chinese cities in terms of economic affluence. Besides, among the 100 Most Innovative Companies listed by "Forbes" a famous American financial magazine, Sany Heavy Industry and Zoomlion Heavy Industry in Changsha are on the list, which also mirrors Changsha's urban innovation ability.

2. Analysis of core indexes

Urban green development requires abundant material bases with fruitful results and methods to create wealth. Through science and technology, a dynamic mechanism is formed to promote an efficient and stable growth of urban economy in an innovative manner, and get rid of economy's dependence on high emissions, high resource consumption and environmental disruption to realize innovation-driven green development. We measure a city's economic affluence by growth index, innovation index and enterprise index.

(1) **Growth index:** The top 10 cities in growth index are San Jose, San Francisco, Washington, Boston, Los Angeles, Seattle, New York, Houston, Philadelphia and Denver.

The last 10 cities in growth index are Jakarta, Guiyang, Chongqing, Bangalore, Zhengzhou, Delhi, Hanoi, Calcutta, Manila and Mumbai (see Figure 4.5). There is a distinct gap among cities in the Asia-pacific region in terms of growth index. For example, the per capita gross domestic product (GDP) of San Jose, which ranks first in growth index, totals US$77,000

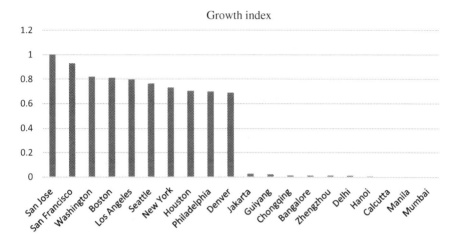

Figure 4.5. Top 10 and Bottom 10 Cities in Growth Index.

while the per capita GDP of Mumbai, which ranks last in growth index, totals less than US$1,700, a difference of over 44 times.

(2) **Innovation index:** The top 10 cities in growth index are San Jose, Seoul, New York, San Diego, Shanghai, Houston, San Francisco, Los Angeles, Chicago and Shenzhen. Among them, two Chinese cities are included, namely, Shanghai and Shenzhen. America, the biggest winner, includes 7 out of 10 and 4 cities belong to California. The last 10 cities in innovation index are Manila, Jakarta, Canberra, Ottawa, Keelung, Vladivostok, Macau, Toronto, Hanoi and Calcutta (see Figure 4.6).

(3) **Enterprise index:** The top 15 cities in enterprise index are New York, Tokyo, Houston, San Jose, Seattle, Osaka, Changsha, Kyoto, San Diego, San Francisco, Shenzhen, Washington, Melbourne, Hsinchu and Mumbai (see Figure 4.7).

(V) Ranking and analysis of inclusiveness

1. Sub-item ranking of inclusiveness index

Table 4.4 shows that the top 15 Asia-Pacific cities in the aspect of inclusiveness are Seoul, Hong Kong, Wuhan, Beijing, Nanjing,

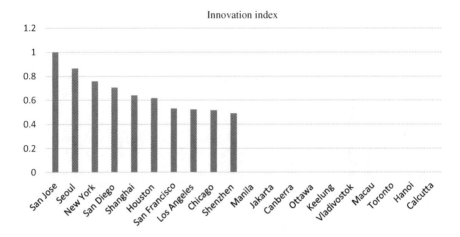

Figure 4.6. Top 10 and Bottom 10 Cities in Innovation Index.

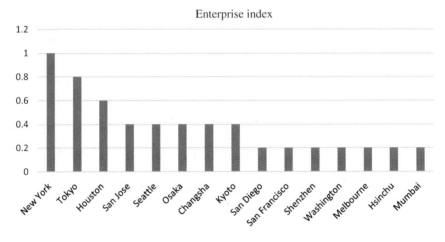

Figure 4.7. Top 15 Cities in Enterprise Index.

Nanning, Lanzhou, Hefei, Haikou, Xi'an, Chongqing, Xining, Guiyang, Hangzhou and Shanghai.

The top 16–30 cities are Shijiazhuang, Kunming, Chengdu, Harbin, Urumqi, Jakarta, Zhengzhou, Nanchang, Taiyuan, Guangzhou, Mumbai, Singapore, Yinchuan, Fuzhou and Hohhot.

Evaluation Results and Main Research Findings

Table 4.4. Ranking of Inclusiveness.

City	Score	Ranking	City	Score	Ranking
Seoul	0.765	1	Hanoi	0.548	41
Hong Kong	0.743	2	Dalian	0.543	42
Wuhan	0.673	3	Melbourne	0.542	43
Beijing	0.631	4	Lima	0.536	44
Nanjing	0.618	5	Qingdao	0.531	45
Nanning	0.607	6	Macau	0.527	46
Lanzhou	0.606	7	Ningbo	0.524	47
Hefei	0.606	8	Vladivostok	0.522	48
Haikou	0.605	9	Kuala Lumpur	0.520	49
Xi'an	0.602	10	Shenzhen	0.511	50
Chongqing	0.601	11	Daejeon	0.507	51
Xining	0.601	12	Daegu	0.505	52
Guiyang	0.598	13	Incheon	0.501	53
Hangzhou	0.597	14	Busan	0.496	54
Shanghai	0.595	15	Sydney	0.484	55
Shijiazhuang	0.594	16	Hsinchu	0.483	56
Kunming	0.594	17	Brisbane	0.478	57
Chengdu	0.594	18	Toronto	0.468	58
Harbin	0.593	19	Manila	0.462	59
Urumqi	0.593	20	St. Petersburg	0.459	60
Jakarta	0.591	21	Ottawa	0.458	61
Zhengzhou	0.591	22	Sapporo	0.457	62
Nanchang	0.590	23	Nagoya	0.452	63
Taiyuan	0.587	24	Fukuoka	0.448	64
Guangzhou	0.585	25	Tainan	0.425	65
Mumbai	0.584	26	Wellington	0.423	66
Singapore	0.583	27	Taipei	0.420	67
Yinchuan	0.579	28	Detroit	0.419	68
Fuzhou	0.578	29	Kyoto	0.418	69
Hohhot	0.578	30	Yokohama	0.417	70
Tianjin	0.575	31	Auckland, NZ	0.415	71
Changchun	0.575	32	Canberra	0.411	72
Calcutta	0.574	33	Boston	0.409	73
Bangalore	0.573	34	Hiroshima	0.407	74
Shenyang	0.572	35	Chicago	0.406	75
Xiamen	0.570	36	Atlanta	0.399	76
Delhi	0.568	37	Kobe	0.399	77
Changsha	0.567	38	Philadelphia	0.399	78
Jinan	0.566	39	New York	0.390	79
Tokyo	0.550	40	Kaohsiung	0.383	80

(Continued)

Table 4.4. (*Continued*)

City	Score	Ranking	City	Score	Ranking
Bangkok	0.381	81	Taichung	0.330	91
Houston	0.371	82	Baltimore	0.320	92
Osaka	0.370	83	Miami	0.313	93
Vancouver	0.368	84	Las Vegas	0.303	94
Keelung	0.364	85	Denver	0.302	95
San Diego	0.360	86	Dallas	0.297	96
Moscow	0.358	87	Washington	0.276	97
Los Angeles	0.357	88	San Francisco	0.275	98
Seattle	0.345	89	San Jose	0.245	99
Phoenix	0.334	90	Mexico City	0.214	100

The top 31–45 cities are Tianjin, Changchun, Calcutta, Bangalore, Shenyang, Xiamen, Delhi, Changsha, Jinan, Tokyo, Hanoi, Dalian, Melbourne, Lima and Qingdao.

The top 46–60 cities are Macau, Ningbo, Vladivostok, Kuala Lumpur, Shenzhen, Daejeon, Daegu, Incheon, Busan, Sydney, Hsinchu, Brisbane, Toronto, Manila and St. Petersburg.

The top 61–85 cities are Ottawa, Sapporo, Nagoya, Fukuoka, Tainan, Wellington, Taipei, Detroit, Kyoto, Yokohama, Auckland, Canberra, Boston, Hiroshima, Chicago, Atlanta, Kobe, Philadelphia, New York, Kaohsiung, Bangkok, Houston, Osaka, Vancouver and Keelung.

The last 15 cities are San Diego, Moscow, Los Angeles, Seattle, Phoenix, Taichung, Baltimore, Miami, Las Vegas, Denver, Dallas, Washington, San Francisco, San Jose and Mexico City.

2. Analysis of core indexes

Urban development should be inclusive. The city should have a high degree of social acceptance, which can provide a harmonious space for people with different nationalities, cultures and beliefs. Three core indexes concerning safety index, life index and education index are used for assessment of each index of social inclusion.

(1) **Safety index:** The top 10 cities in safety index are Macau, Kyoto, Yokohama, Osaka, Singapore, Sapporo, Hiroshima,

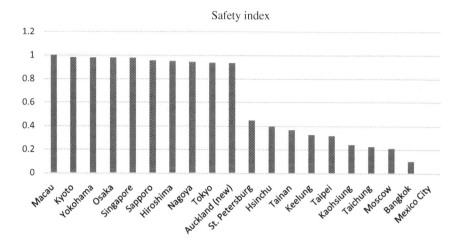

Figure 4.8. Top 10 and Bottom 10 Cities in Security Index.

Nagoya, Tokyo and Auckland (new). Most of them are cities in Japan, taking 7 of the top 10 cities.

The last 10 cities in safety index are St. Petersburg, Hsinchu, Tainan, Keelung, Taipei, Kaohsiung, Taichung, Moscow, Bangkok and Mexico City (see Figure 4.8).

(2) **Life index:** The top 10 cities in life index are Calcutta, Delhi, Bangalore, Mumbai, Vladivostok, St. Petersburg, Nanning, Lanzhou, Xi'an and Chongqing. The last 10 cities in growth index are Los Angeles, Chicago, Melbourne, Baltimore, Washington, Kyoto, Osaka, Sydney, New York and Tokyo (see Figure 4.9).

(3) **Education index:** The top 15 cities in education index are Seoul, Hong Kong, Tokyo, Melbourne, Sydney, New York, Chicago, Boston, Beijing, Brisbane, Singapore, Taipei, Hsinchu, Ottawa and Toronto (see Figure 4.10).

(VI) Ranking of governance

1. Ranking of governance index

As shown in Table 4.5, the top 15 cities in good governance are Sydney, Washington, Tokyo, Seoul, Moscow, Shanghai, Bangkok,

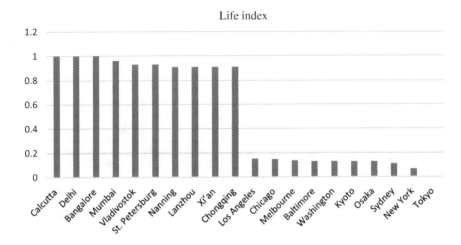

Figure 4.9. Top 10 and Bottom 10 Cities in Life Index.

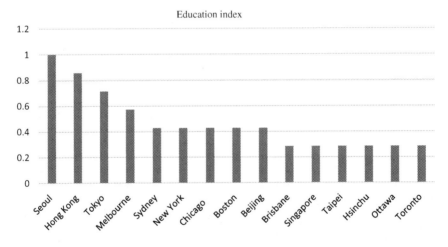

Figure 4.10. Top 15 Cities in Education Index.

Hong Kong, Beijing, Singapore, Lima, Jakarta, Kuala Lumpur, Wellington and Manila.

The top 16–30 cities are Changsha, Ottawa, Mexico City, Chengdu, New York, Delhi, Xi'an, San Francisco, Los Angeles, Changchun, Taichung, Las Vegas, Hanoi, Phoenix and Miami.

Evaluation Results and Main Research Findings

Table 4.5. Ranking of Governance.

City	Score	Ranking	City	Score	Ranking
Sydney	0.784	1	Guangzhou	0.348	41
Washington	0.781	2	San Jose	0.348	42
Tokyo	0.777	3	Vladivostok	0.346	43
Seoul	0.763	4	Tainan	0.346	44
Moscow	0.745	5	Houston	0.336	45
Shanghai	0.745	6	Seattle	0.334	46
Bangkok	0.711	7	Qingdao	0.328	47
Hong Kong	0.702	8	Denver	0.327	48
Beijing	0.699	9	Dallas	0.325	49
Singapore	0.663	10	Toronto	0.319	50
Lima	0.652	11	Kaohsiung	0.316	51
Jakarta	0.591	12	Vancouver	0.314	52
Kuala Lumpur	0.591	13	Calcutta	0.306	53
Wellington	0.585	14	Kyoto	0.304	54
Manila	0.585	15	Nagoya	0.295	55
Changsha	0.582	16	San Diego	0.294	56
Ottawa	0.581	17	Yokohama	0.290	57
Mexico City	0.577	18	Atlanta	0.272	58
Chengdu	0.556	19	Baltimore	0.269	59
New York	0.549	20	Bangalore	0.269	60
Delhi	0.526	21	Fukuoka	0.266	61
Xi'an	0.494	22	Sapporo	0.265	62
San Francisco	0.488	23	Taiyuan	0.262	63
Los Angeles	0.485	24	Boston	0.258	64
Changchun	0.475	25	Auckland, NZ	0.249	65
Taichung	0.467	26	Brisbane	0.247	66
Las Vegas	0.452	27	Detroit	0.242	67
Hanoi	0.449	28	Chongqing	0.236	68
Phoenix	0.433	29	Hsinchu	0.230	69
Miami	0.419	30	Ningbo	0.224	70
Shenzhen	0.417	31	Hiroshima	0.223	71
Mumbai	0.416	32	Busan	0.221	72
Xiamen	0.415	33	Keelung	0.217	73
Wuhan	0.413	34	Kobe	0.213	74
Taipei	0.387	35	St. Petersburg	0.211	75
Chicago	0.387	36	Hangzhou	0.206	76
Melbourne	0.370	37	Daegu	0.200	77
Osaka	0.357	38	Urumqi	0.199	78
Philadelphia	0.357	39	Canberra	0.198	79
Nanjing	0.354	40	Tianjin	0.196	80

(Continued)

Table 4.5. (Continued)

City	Score	Ranking	City	Score	Ranking
Fuzhou	0.189	81	Lanzhou	0.092	91
Daejeon	0.187	82	Macau	0.075	92
Nanchang	0.175	83	Zhengzhou	0.070	93
Kunming	0.172	84	Shenyang	0.055	94
Hefei	0.158	85	Shijiazhuang	0.053	95
Dalian	0.154	86	Hohhot	0.043	96
Haikou	0.150	87	Xining	0.029	97
Incheon	0.147	88	Harbin	0.027	98
Nanning	0.131	89	Yinchuan	0.010	99
Jinan	0.106	90	Guiyang	0.010	100

The top 31–45 cities are Shenzhen, Mumbai, Xiamen, Wuhan, Taipei, Chicago, Melbourne, Osaka, Philadelphia, Nanjing, Guangzhou, San Jose, Vladivostok, Tainan and Houston.

The top 46–60 cities are Seattle, Qingdao, Denver, Dallas, Toronto, Kaohsiung, Vancouver, Calcutta, Kyoto, Nagoya, San Diego, Yokohama, Atlanta, Baltimore and Bangalore.

The top 61–85 cities are Fukuoka, Sapporo, Taiyuan, Boston, Auckland, Brisbane, Detroit, Chongqing, Hsinchu, Ningbo, Hiroshima, Busan, Keelung, Kobe, St. Petersburg, Hangzhou, Daegu, Urumqi, Canberra, Tianjin, Fuzhou, Daejeon, Nanchang, Kunming and Hefei.

The last 15 cities are Dalian, Haikou, Incheon, Nanning, Jinan, Lanzhou, Macau, Zhengzhou, Shenyang, Shijiazhuang, Hohhot, Xining, Harbin, Yinchuan and Guiyang.

In terms of governance, the top cities are mainly national capitals. As political centers, they have special advantages in urban governance. The bottom ranking cities are Chinese cities, as the NGO development and e-government are relatively lagging behind. As Chinese government gradually encourages the development of nongovernment association, this index is expected to improve. Meanwhile, the development of e-government is also promising. With the rocketing development of information technology, Chinese government attaches great importance to the development of the

Internet, which is bound to promote the development of urban e-government.

2. Analysis of core index

Good governance is an ideal way for urban governance. The good governance of urban green development means that the realization of green development goal needs to modify diversified governance mechanism and increase the consensus and sense of identification of different stakeholders. E-government index, brand index and NGO index are three primary indexes to assess city's good governance. Here we focus on the analysis of the e-government index and brand index.

(1) **The e-government index:** This refers to the e-government management level of city-level government. Top 10 cities are Taichung, Vladivostok, Nanjing, Moscow, Taiyuan, Mumbai, Phoenix, New York, Washington and Tainan. The last 10 cities are Shenyang, Shijiazhuang, Manila, Hanoi, Hohhot, Xining, Harbin, Singapore, Yinchuan and Guiyang (see Figure 4.11).

It is not hard to know from the above rankings that e-government index is little related to the level of urban economic

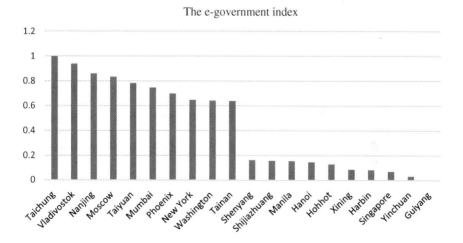

Figure 4.11. Top 10 and Bottom 10 Cities in E-government Index.

development, location and city scale. The current score of the index reflects the degree that city government focuses on e-governance as well as the resources invested into e-government construction.

(2) **Brand index:** City brand is vital for urban green development. City brand reflects how the stakeholders see the city for a long time in the past and is the "image" of city environment, economic and social, and other factors in the mind of audiences.

The top 15 cities in city brand are New York, Los Angeles, Hong Kong, Singapore, San Francisco, Las Vegas, Sydney, Tokyo, Seoul, Shenzhen, Xiamen, Shanghai, Bangkok, Beijing and Washington (see Figure 4.12), of which there are five cities of China in top 15 list, Hong Kong ranked 3rd, Shenzhen ranked 10th, Xiamen ranked 11th, Shanghai ranked 12th and Beijing ranked 14th.

(VII) Ranking of partnership

1. Sub-item ranking of partnership index

City and state are inseparable, and they should promote mutually and develop together. In terms of partnership index, it applies national-level data as a whole. Therefore, for the specific city

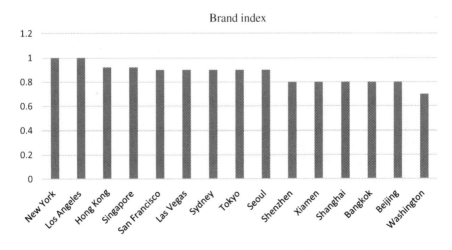

Figure 4.12. Top 15 Cities in Brand Index.

rankings, cities in same country and region almost have same score in this index.[a] Consequently, it will be more meaningful to analyze this index from the national and regional levels.

As shown in Table 4.6, with regard to the partnership index, the national and regional rankings are Macau (China), Hong Kong, Singapore, New Zealand, Japan, Korea, Canada, Taiwan (China),

Table 4.6. Ranking of Partnership.

City	Score	Ranking	City	Score	Ranking
Macau	0.915	1	Taipei	0.689	28
Hong Kong	0.908	2	Melbourne	0.685	29
Singapore	0.826	3	Brisbane	0.685	30
Wellington	0.789	4	Canberra	0.685	31
Auckland, NZ	0.789	5	Sydney	0.685	32
Nagoya	0.775	6	Washington	0.602	33
Yokohama	0.775	7	Dallas	0.602	34
Hiroshima	0.775	8	Houston	0.602	35
Kyoto	0.775	9	Atlanta	0.602	36
Tokyo	0.775	10	Miami	0.602	37
Osaka	0.775	11	San Jose	0.602	38
Fukuoka	0.775	12	Detroit	0.602	39
Kobe	0.775	13	San Diego	0.602	40
Sapporo	0.775	14	Phoenix	0.602	41
Busan	0.717	15	Philadelphia	0.602	42
Daejeon	0.717	16	Seattle	0.602	43
Daegu	0.717	17	Las Vegas	0.602	44
Seoul	0.717	18	New York	0.602	45
Incheon	0.717	19	Boston	0.602	46
Ottawa	0.698	20	Los Angeles	0.602	47
Toronto	0.698	21	Chicago	0.602	48
Vancouver	0.698	22	San Francisco	0.602	49
Taichung	0.689	23	Baltimore	0.602	50
Tainan	0.689	24	Denver	0.602	51
Hsinchu	0.689	25	Kuala Lumpur	0.601	52
Kaohsiung	0.689	26	Hanoi	0.540	53
Keelung	0.689	27	Moscow	0.510	54

(Continued)

---

[a]Part of data in Hong Kong and Macau SAR of China is different from that of Mainland China so as to more truly reflect the local development level.

90   Z. Zhao

Table 4.6. (*Continued*)

City	Score	Ranking	City	Score	Ranking
St. Petersburg	0.510	55	Ningbo	0.411	78
Vladivostok	0.510	56	Hangzhou	0.411	79
Mexico City	0.500	57	Wuhan	0.411	80
Bangkok	0.444	58	Chengdu	0.411	81
Lima	0.436	59	Zhengzhou	0.411	82
Manila	0.415	60	Qingdao	0.411	83
Guangzhou	0.411	61	Fuzhou	0.411	84
Yinchuan	0.411	62	Beijing	0.411	85
Shenzhen	0.411	63	Chongqing	0.411	86
Hohhot	0.411	64	Nanning	0.411	87
Dalian	0.411	65	Xi'an	0.411	88
Kunming	0.411	66	Changsha	0.411	89
Jinan	0.411	67	Changchun	0.411	90
Tianjin	0.411	68	Xining	0.411	91
Nanchang	0.411	69	Guiyang	0.411	92
Shijiazhuang	0.411	70	Harbin	0.411	93
Haikou	0.411	71	Lanzhou	0.411	94
Xiamen	0.411	72	Urumqi	0.411	95
Hefei	0.411	73	Bangalore	0.338	96
Shanghai	0.411	74	Calcutta	0.338	97
Nanjing	0.411	75	Delhi	0.338	98
Taiyuan	0.411	76	Mumbai	0.338	99
Shenyang	0.411	77	Jakarta	0.327	100

Note: Some data used for the analysis of China's Hong Kong, Macau and Taiwan region are different from mainland, which aims to show local development level truthfully.

Australia, USA, Malaysia, Vietnam, Russia, Mexico, Thailand, Peru, the Philippines, China, India and Indonesia.

2. Analysis of core indexes

Six indexes such as income index, information index, health index, energy consumption index, emission index and clear water index are applied to measure country prosperity. Emission index and clear water index are our key points.

(1) **Emission index:** The per capita carbon dioxide emissions situation reflects per capita carbon dioxide emissions in the Asia-Pacific countries and regions. The ranking from top to the lowest

Evaluation Results and Main Research Findings 91

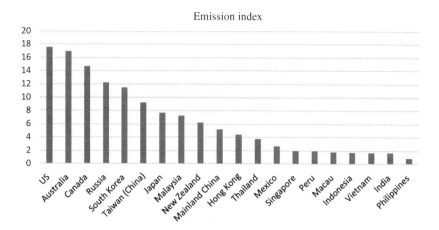

Figure 4.13. National and Regional Ranking of Per Capita Carbon Dioxide Emissions in 2010.

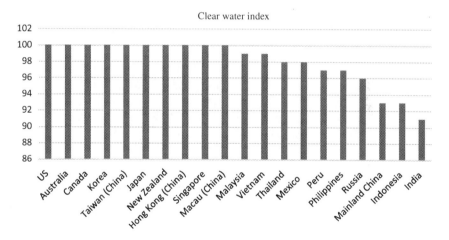

Figure 4.14. National and Regional Ranking in Water Resources Improvement Proportion.

is: the US, Australia, Canada, Russia, South Korea, Taiwan (China), Japan, Malaysia, New Zealand, mainland China, Hong Kong, Thailand, Mexico, Singapore, Peru, Macau, Indonesia, Vietnam, India and the Philippines (see Figure 4.13).

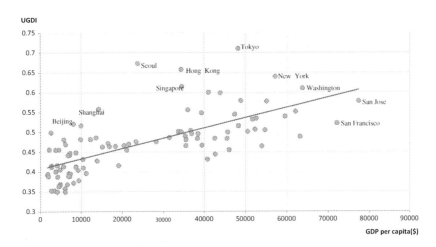

Figure 4.15. Relationship Between Asia-Pacific Urban Green Development and Per Capita GDP.

(2) **Clear water index:** Based on the proportion of urban water resource improvement in the Asia-Pacific region, the ranking from top to the lowest is the US, Australia, Canada, Korea, Taiwan (China), Japan, New Zealand, Hong Kong (China), Singapore, Macau (China), Malaysia, Vietnam, Thailand, Mexico, Peru, Philippines, Russia, Mainland China, Indonesia and India (see Figure 4.14).

II. Main Findings

(I) Economic development level determines the urban green development to a certain extent

According to our study, the Asia-Pacific urban green development index is apparently related to per capita GDP, the correlation coefficient is 0.68 (see Figure 4.15). Currently, per capita GDP of all top 15 cities in the aspect of the Asia-Pacific city green development are more than US$14,000. In the regional urban system, these cities maintain a robust growth momentum, have a reasonable and perfect industrial structure, carry out large-scale economic activity, and develop vigorously emerging industries. They are in the high value-added links of regional economic value chain and play a leading role in regional economic development and the upgrade of regional urban network system.

We can see from the study that although economic development may cause environmental pollution to a certain extent in the traditional sense, it does not necessarily mean the degradation of resource and environment. If the economic development mode is appropriate, it will be easier to increase investment in environmental protection and management. Meanwhile, accompanied by the rise of emerging industries such as information technology and Internet, light pollution industry and even pollution-free industry are becoming important driving forces for Asia-Pacific urban economic development.

(II) Income distribution is closely related to urban green development level

Based on the national standard, we averaged the green development index for all cities included in the sample and studied the relationship between green development index and GNI per capita. From the study, we found that they are significantly related and the correlation coefficient is 0.60. Then, comparing unequal income adjustment index with the Asia-Pacific urban green development index, we found that they are significantly related and the correlation coefficient is 0.72 (see Figure 4.16).

Resident income is highly relevant to green development. At the same time, with the improvement of resident income level, urban residents increasingly focus on health and quality of life, and pay more attention to environment and environmental protection. People begin to focus on environmental protection, which can be shown from the attitude and action in response to haze for residents in Beijing and other cities. However, in some underdeveloped areas, although people are also concerned about environmental issues, when faced with two tough choices of employment and environment, they often have to choose the former. In the long term, the promotion of urban green development needs to improve resident income level continuously and narrow income gap and cultivate more high-income

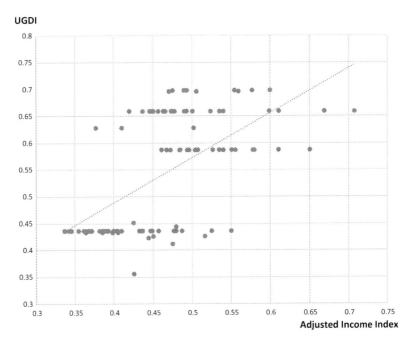

Figure 4.16. Relationship Between Asia-Pacific Urban Green Development Score and Adjusted Income Index.

and responsible citizens to improve sharing, realize co-governance and make contributions to urban green development together.

(III) Innovation is a key factor for urban green development

The importance of innovation for the city's economic and social development has been argued in a great number of academic monographs, and has also been known by many nation and city managers. Using the patent as an important index for measuring innovation level of the Asia-Pacific cities, we found that the Asia-Pacific urban green development is significantly correlated to innovation, and the correlation coefficient reaches 0.55 (see Figure 4.17). The cities with high green development level always have great innovation ability. They are usually a region's and nation's innovation center, often maintain and expand the advantage field

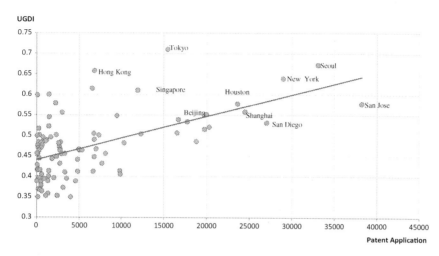

Figure 4.17. Relationship Between Asia-Pacific Urban Green Development and the Quantity of Patent Application.

through innovation, create scale economies effect by bringing their own innovation ability to full play, make use of the function of knowledge production, processing and dissemination, innovation, form radiation effects in external space of city, lead the trend of times in city's economic and social development and maintain sustainable competitiveness.

With the popularity of new generation information technology in the future, creative personal networks may be interconnected to obtain new synergy effect, and most innovations and innovation environments in the post-industrial era may appear in urban area.[1] Innovation will have a significant influence on the transformation and upgrading of traditional manufacturing industry, the improvement of labor productivity and the reduction of environmental impact. The new energy technology and green construction technology derived from innovation will play a positive role in reducing urban pollution and emission. Innovation will improve information level to help improve the level of urban governance for city managers, and ease and solve the "urban diseases". For urban green development, we should attach great importance to the value of innovation, encourage technological innovation-centered all-round innovation concerning product innovation, format innovation, mode innovation, system innovation and so on, and share the fruits of green development.

(IV) High-end service industry is the inevitable choice of urban green development

From the study, we found that almost all top 30 cities in the ranking of the Asia-Pacific Urban green development index are predominated by service industry, which even accounts for more than 80% in some cities (see Table 4.7). Moreover, the service industry in these cities is mainly predominated by high-end services such as finance, information and technology, research and development (R&D), etc. Many cities such as Tokyo, New York, Singapore and Sydney all are regional financial centers even global financial centers. Other cities such as San Jose and San Francisco are the influential R&D service center in the world.

Therefore, for urban green development, we should attach great importance to economic development of service industry, promote the transformation and upgrading of industrial structure, help the growth of service industry, especially high-end service industry, promote industry integration and industry–city integration through

Table 4.7. Proportion of Service Industry in GDP of Major Cities in the Asia-Pacific Region.

City	The Proportion of Construction Industry in City GDP (%)	The Proportion of Manufacturing Industry in City GDP (%)	The Proportion of Service Industry in City GDP (%)
Tokyo	4.66	8.67	84.9
New York	3.15	5.4	91.2
Singapore	4.3	19.0	65.4
Beijing	4.42	19.6	75.1

Notes: (1) Tokyo data were obtained in 2009 and the calculations were based on Tokyo Metropolis Statistics Yearbook 2009; (2) New York data were obtained in 2009 and the calculations were based on US Bureau of Economic Analysis, Gross Domestic Product by State, 2011; (3) Singapore data were obtained in 2010, and the calculations were based on website data of Statistics Singapore; (4) Beijing data were obtained in 2010, and the calculations were based on Beijing Statistical Yearbook 2011.

Evaluation Results and Main Research Findings 97

constructing advanced system of productive services industry and life service industry to establish reasonable and high-end urban industrial structure, and develop the city on the basis of a stable high-end industrial system.

(V) "Governance gap" is the key factor for urban green development disparity

From the study, we found that there are big gaps between city with high green development level and city with low green development level. The latter one always performs poorly on all indexes. According to the comparison of score gap of each index, the gap between indexes of governance is 0.784, closely following the index of prosperity, and is an important reason to influence urban green development (see Table 4.8).

"Governance gap" will influence the level of urban green development directly. For the city with low green development level, the realization of long-term, stable and sustained "green" progress need to further promote green production and consumption, pay attention to the construction of green development governance system, improve environment and ability of urban green development and bridge the gap with leading cities by promoting the ability of urban governance and strengthening participation of social organization and public.

(VI) The role of urban agglomerations in urban green development shall not be ignored

The study shows that the level of urban green development is closely related to the urban agglomeration it is in. For example,

Table 4.8. Comparison of Score Gap of Asia-Pacific's UGDI.

Top- and Bottom-Scoring City in Each Index	General Index Gap of Green Development	Index Gap of Prosperity	Index Gap of Inclusiveness	Index Gap of Governance	Index Gap of Partnership
	0.541	0.829	0.552	0.784	0.588

comparing with Boswah urban agglomeration (abbreviated for Boston, New York and Washington), and the Pacific rim urban agglomeration (including San Francisco, Los Angeles and San Diego), the Green development level of urban agglomeration concerning Beijing–Tianjin–Hebei, Yangtze River Delta and Pearl River Delta in China lag far behind. In the overall ranking of the Asia-Pacific urban green development index, there are five cities on the top 15 list that are included in Boswah urban agglomeration and the Pacific rim urban agglomeration. But similar situation doesn't happen in China, where the urban green development is still not "clustered", and the level of urban green development in the urban agglomeration is out of balance. For instance, Shanghai urban green development index ranked 15th in the Asia-Pacific region, Nanjing ranked 66th, and green development still doesn't generate an overall synergy effect.

It is the inexorable law for urban development to shift from a single city to urban agglomeration. It can be inferred that urban green development in the future is no longer the green development of a single city, but the green development of the metropolitan area or the urban agglomeration, which is the green development of city system featured with reasonable layout, close link and clear division of work composed by cities with different sizes and different level in a specific space. Therefore, for the urban green development, we should attach great importance to the role of urban agglomeration, co-ordinate resource allocation in a larger scope, optimize the layout and infrastructure of urban agglomeration, improve the public services of urban agglomeration and form an overall advanced urban green development network with cooperation and clear division of work.

(VII) The city and the state shall partner in green development

The study shows that the top-ranking cities in the aspect of the Asia-Pacific Urban Green Development index also take the top place in all indexes of partnership, which means that the level of

Evaluation Results and Main Research Findings 99

national green development are highly correlated to the level of urban green development. Urban green development is not isolated, and it can't be divorced from the region and state it is in. The state's green development has a significant influence and is the important foundation of urban green development.

Under the background of globalization and with the development of modern economy, society, and science and technology, the city and the state have constructed a unified, open and giant system together. The higher the overall level of urban and national development is, the stronger interaction between them will be, which will result in a mutual benefit for both the city and the state. The realization of urban green development also needs to be closely integrated with the national green development process, establish a coordinated city–state relation, rely on the state, serve national green development, and advance and retreat together in the wave of green development.

(VIII) The "Belt and Road" urban green development is confronted with infrastructure pressure

Based on the overall analysis of the Asia-Pacific green development index, we found that the infrastructure of top-ranking cities is perfect. Both the health infrastructure and a new type of Internet infrastructure are far better than that of low-ranking city. The infrastructure condition will affect the level of green development in individual cities, and is also an important factor that should be taken into consideration in major regional cooperation strategies. Main focus lies in the green development index for key cities along Maritime Silk Road — including Fuzhou, Xiamen, Hanoi, Bangkok, Manila, Jakarta, Kuala Lumpur, Singapore, Calcutta, Mumbai, etc. It can be found that most cities along Maritime Silk Road are middle and low-ranking except for Singapore (7th) and Kuala Lumpur (23rd).

We can see that the infrastructure of the "Belt and Road" urban green development is the "weak point" that restricts urban overall green development along Maritime Silk Road. Therefore, in the process of the "Belt and Road" urban green development, it is necessary to strengthen the urban infrastructure investment, especially strengthen cooperation between cities along Maritime Silk Road in the field of water supply, energy and information infrastructure, etc., work together to improve infrastructure of backward cities, and promote normal development of city along the "Belt and Road".

(IX) Urban green development in emerging market country presents obvious unbalanced characteristics

The unbalanced characteristics of urban green development in emerging market countries mainly show in two aspects: total unbalanced development and internal unbalanced development. As for the former, compared with developed countries, urban green development in emerging market countries presents a significantly unbalanced development. For example, according to comprehensive ranking of the Asia-Pacific urban green development index, the ranking of urban green development index for four Indian cities is Bangalore, Delhi, Kolkata and Mumbai. The scores of urban green development index of these four Indian cities are all lower than overall average score of the Asia-Pacific cities: Bangalore green development index ranked 74th in the Asia-Pacific region, Delhi green development index ranked 79th, the Kolkata green development index ranked 86th and Mumbai green development index ranked 93rd (Table 4.9). As for the internal development of emerging market countries, urban green development also presents a significantly unbalanced development. For example, according to the comprehensive ranking of the Asia-Pacific urban green development index, the internal ranking of urban green development index for three Russian cities is Moscow, Vladivostok and St. Petersburg, of which only the score of Moscow City green development index is higher than the overall average score of the Asia-Pacific cities, and ranked 28th in the Asia-Pacific cities, while the St. Petersburg green development index ranked 88th.

Table 4.9. Ranking of Asia-Pacific Green Development Composite Index for Major Cities in India and Russia.

Country	City	Average Score of Asia-Pacific Cities	Overall Ranking of Asia-Pacific Cities
India	Bangalore	0.466	74
	Delhi	0.466	79
	Calcutta	0.466	86
	Mumbai	0.466	93
Russia	Moscow	0.466	28
	Vladivostok	0.466	71
	St. Petersburg	0.466	88

The balance of urban green development is an urgent problem to be solved for emerging market countries. Emerging market countries should pay more attention to urban green development in the future and improve overall green development ability of city even country by playing the role of urban green growth pole to narrow the gap with the developed countries. At the same time, it should attach great importance to the "unbalance" urban green development level in the interior of country, back up leading cities of green development to maintain competitive advantage, encourage the city with low green development level to give full play to advantage of late development and promote city's overall green development through the intercity coordination mechanism.

(X) Major gap still lies between the urban green development in China and the US

According to comprehensive ranking of the Asia-Pacific urban green development index, the level of urban green development in China is far behind the US cities. There are nine cities in China whose urban green development indexes score higher than the overall average score of Asia-Pacific cities, including Hong Kong, Shanghai, Beijing, Changsha, Shenzhen, Chengdu, Taipei, Taichung and Hsinchu, which ranked 4th, 15th, 21st, 36th, 40th, 43rd, 45th, 47th and 51st,

Table 4.10. Comparison of the Ranking of Green Development Index in China and the US.

Chinese City	Ranking in China	Overall Ranking of the Asia-Pacific Cities	American City	Ranking in the US	Overall Ranking of the Asia-Pacific Cities
Hong Kong	1	4	New York	1	3
Shanghai	2	15	Washington	2	5
Beijing	3	21	San Jose	3	8
Changsha	4	36	Houston	4	9
Shenzhen	5	40	San Francisco	5	12
Chengdu	6	43	Los Angeles	6	14
Taipei	7	45	Seattle	7	16
Taichung	8	47	San Diego	8	19
Hsinchu	9	51	Chicago	9	20
Tainan	10	52	Philadelphia	10	24

respectively (Table 4.10). There are 18 cities in the US whose urban green development indexes score higher than the overall average score of the Asia-Pacific cities: New York, Washington, San Jose, Houston, San Francisco, Los Angeles, Seattle, San Diego, Chicago, Philadelphia, Dallas, Phoenix, Miami, Boston, Atlanta, Las Vegas, Denver and Detroit in turn.

As the largest developing country and the largest developed country in the world, China and the United States have made positive efforts to promote urban green development. But the green development level gap between cities in China and the United States still needs to be addressed. American cities have shown a strong competitiveness in the aspect of overall green development. Hong Kong (China), Shanghai and Beijing demonstrate high green development level, and they have been among the top in the Asia-Pacific region, but most cities still relatively lag behind. In the future, cities of China should promote wider opening up and actively learn from the experience of urban green development of the United States to enhance the level of urban green development. American cities should also strengthen cooperation with Chinese cities in resource and environmental protection, green economic development, urban governance, etc., actively share bonus of development and reform of green urbanization in China and achieve a win–win situation based on mutual benefit.

Reference

1. Tarik Fathy, *Telecity: Information Technology and its Impact on City Form*, Praeger Publishers, New York, 1991, pp. 81–101.

Part III

International Chapters

Chapter 5

Clean Technology and Sustainable Urban Solutions in Singapore

Chen Gang

Senior Researcher, The East Asian Institute,
National University of Singapore, Singapore
changang@nus.edu.sg

The galloping process of industrialization, urbanization and globalization has brought mounting environmental challenges including climate change, water pollution, acid rain, hazardous waste, smog, ozone depletion, loss of biodiversity and desertification that threaten sustainable development of our human society. Environmental considerations are assuming greater importance in the industrial and urban planning processes of an increasing number of governments around the world. While for the most part urban sustainability remained at the margins of mainstream agendas of growth and economic development espoused by global cities, international donor and policy agencies, corporations and major cities, by the 2000s, visions of low-carbon cities, resilient cities, sustainable cities and eco-cities could be found across the full range of social and economic interests concerned with urban development.[1] In this context of developing clean technology and finding sustainable urban solutions, Singapore has been an outstanding example on the global horizon that has achieved a lot in reducing carbon footprints, optimizing resource consumption and improving energy, and resource efficiency. The UN Habitat's report *State of the Worlds' Cities 2012/2013* scored the city-state highly in areas of pollution control, transport management and water treatment.[2] Besides well-designed city planning, clean technology is the key to the sustainability of urban development.

Today, Singapore is not only a "garden city" surrounded by green-belts and woodlands but also an eco-city in modern sense that enables itself to conserve water, energy and other resources through the smart use of cutting-edge clean technology and well-designed policy incentives and disincentives. Recently, Singapore announced that the city-state had dramatically reduced its carbon intensity — or the amount of carbon dioxide emissions per dollar of gross domestic product — by 30% between 2000 and 2010, compared with the global average decrease of only 0.12% over the period.[3] As most big cities are making all-out effort to fight climate change, smog and water pollution, and resource scarcity, it's time to review the main tenets of Singapore as a successful model in combining urban ecology with modern clean technology to "rebuild cities in balance with nature".[4]

I. Low-Carbon City Planning

To reduce people's heavy reliance upon privately owned vehicles and alleviate traffic congestions, Singapore's city planners have been giving preferences to pedestrianization, cycling and public transport when designing traffic systems and city layouts. Also, Singapore is not a big-sized city, it has multi-centers, with high-rise buildings being encouraged in each center areas. Dense subcenters and compact neighborhood centers are situated fairly close to the major city hub. In each center or subcenter, catering, education, medical care, sports and shopping services are available to most residents. Compact city layout and high population density, there, are necessary for a sustainable city, because it not only makes public transport feasible and reduces the per capita demand for occupied land but also cuts per capita cost of supplying piped water, sewer systems, garbage collection, postal delivery and other public services. An eco-city must provide easy access to the daily necessities and entertainment by walking, cycling and public transportation. New transportation hierarchy should be established with preference on pedestrians, cyclists, subways, buses and finally private automobiles. Roads may be narrow to make walking easy and driving difficult.

Singapore's city-planning has included the arcologies that take less land, less energy to operate and less connecting materials such as pipes and wires. In an arcological city like Singapore, major social, economic and civic activities are available within short distances, and farm production is just located outside the city gates. Individual buildings, communities and the city as a whole are to be maintained with great efficiency and little waste.

II. Wide Use of Renewable Energy, Energy-Saving Building Materials and Technology

New energy-saving (green) building materials have been widely used in the construction projects in Singapore. To achieve low emissions, local architects sometimes need to fit the buildings with solar panels to produce electricity, which will be used for lighting, office equipment and air conditioning. Better ventilation strategies need to be worked out for reducing dependence upon air-conditioning. Blinds, the opacity of windows and airflow needs to be regulated throughout the building to conserve energy for heating and for balanced natural lighting.

Singapore has been giving a big push toward green building, which refers to a structure and using process that are environmentally friendly and resource-efficient throughout a building's life-cycle with a focus on operation and maintenance. Green building emphasizes using renewable resources, e.g. using natural wind for cooling, sunlight through passive solar, active solar, and photovoltaic (PV) power generation and using plants and trees through green roofs, rain gardens, and for reduction of rainwater run-off. Many other techniques, such as using packed gravel or permeable concrete instead of conventional concrete or asphalt to enhance replenishment of ground water, should also be adopted. To reduce operating energy use, high-efficiency windows and insulation in walls, ceilings, and floors increase the efficiency of the building envelope. Effective window placement (daylighting) can provide more natural light and lessen the need for electric lighting during the day. Solar water heating further reduces energy costs.

Singapore's Building and Construction Authority (BCA) launched its Green Mark Scheme in January 2005 as an initiative to drive Singapore's construction industry toward more environment-friendly buildings. It is intended to promote sustainability in the built environment and raise environmental awareness among developers, designers and builders when they start project conceptualization and design, as well as during construction.[5] By encouraging the adoption of innovative architectural design and energy-saving technologies, Singapore has emerged as a model of green building in Asia. Singapore has been committed to green building through generous incentive schemes and a building-rating tool that encourages sun-shading exteriors, water-efficient fittings, computer modeling of energy flows and carbon emissions.

Building solar capabilities in solar PV technology is key to sustainable development, and it will provide an alternative renewable energy source for Singapore. In 2011, the Housing & Development Board (HDB) in Singapore officially awarded a tender to Sunseap Enterprises Pte Ltd, a solar system developer, to lease two mega-watt-peak (MWp) solar PV systems for 45 HDB residential blocks in Punggol.[6] This was the first solar leasing project in Singapore, which was experimented in the new town concentrated with government-subsidized (HDB) flats. Such solar leasing model helped private sectors to will design, finance, install, operate and maintain the solar PV systems in public housing projects in the city-state. The local town council reached service agreements with the company to pay for the solar power generated and consumed, at a preferential rate that was not higher than retail electricity tariff rate. The solar power generated has been used to power services in common areas such as lift operations, corridor and staircase lightings, and water pumps.

After this test-bed project, in which the housing authorities covered 30% of the initial start-up costs, the HDB continued its efforts to test-bed solar energy to promote sustainable development in residential areas. The Singapore government is envisaged that over time, the costs of solar PV will come down as PV technology improves and greater economies of scale are achieved. In 2013, the HDB awarded another tender to Sunseap, a solar system developer, to lease three MW_p PV systems for another 80 HDB residential blocks in Punggol Eco-Town. This tender attracted keen competition from the industry with a total of 13 bidders, compared with the first Solar Leasing project in 2011, which only garnered three bids.[7] Through the expansion of the solar PV installations, energy usage can be optimized with lower usage of power from the grid, in turn reducing carbon emissions in the long term. With this second Solar Leasing project, HDB moved a step closer to the ambitious goal of transforming Punggol town as a net zero energy town for these public services by 2016.

III. Conservation and Recycling of Water Resources in Urban Areas

Since water shortage a big problem for many cities in expansion, the ecologically friendly city should conserve water resources and interfere minimally with the intrinsic patterns of the water cycle in the ecological system. With a compact city layout that is necessary to reduce the footprint on the permeable soil, Singapore has been able to apply advanced water treatment technologies to its water recycle systems that make full use of creeks and reservoirs.

As a water-resource-constrained city-state, Singapore has created policies and technologies to achieve high degree of self-sufficiency of water resources and sustainability of useful and drinkable fresh water resources. Singapore's water supply comes from four different sources: local catchments, imported water, recycled water (NEWater) and desalinated water.[8] Through decades of effort and wide use of pioneering water treatment and management technologies, Singapore has successfully reduced its heavy reliance upon water imported from its neighboring country, Malaysia. Singapore's Public Utilities Board (PUB) pioneered the use of the 16-inch reverse-osmosis (RO) membrane system on a large scale. This system was first introduced in water reclamation plants in 2003. Today, this ultra-clean, high-grade recycled water is supplied primarily for nondomestic use. Branded NEWater, it contributes to about 30% of Singapore's overall water supply and will increase to 40% by 2020.

Due to Singapore's limited land size, maximizing rainwater capture from local catchments is a key priority in sustaining water security. Today, two-thirds of the island has effectively served as a clean collecting surface for harvesting and storing Singapore's 2,400 mm of annual rainfall. In recent years, Singapore successfully built a catchment area of 10,000 hectares, or one-sixth the size of Singapore, in its down town area, which is now called the Marina catchment. This Marina catchment today is not only the island's largest and most urbanized catchment but also becomes of tourism site that attracts a lot of visitors every year.

Singapore has been taking advantage of the recent advancements in technology and cheaper membrane prices that have made desalinated water viable and affordable. In September 2005, the PUB opened the SingSpring Desalination Plant in Tuas, which can produce 30 million gallons of water a day (136,000 cubic meters) and is one of the region's largest seawater RO plants.[9] During the process of desalination, sea water firstly goes through a pre-treatment process where suspended particles are removed. In the second stage, the water undergoes RO, which is the same technology used in the production of NEWater. The water produced is very pure and is remineralized in the third stage. After treatment, desalinated water is blended with treated water before it is supplied to homes and industries in Singapore. Today, desalinated water can meet up to 25% of Singapore's current water demand.

IV. Sustainable Transport

There is no doubt that the eco-city planning should put public transport in the top priority to address the air pollution and climate change issue. A variety of tools that involve policies on car parking, car access and car ownership have been used for reducing travel by private car in Singapore. Economic tools including road tolls for lorries and private cars as well as subsidies for rail and bus transport have been adopted to encourage people to choose low-carbon transport in the city-state. Eco-city designers should give preference first to the arrangement that reduces the need for transport, then to those measures that encourage travel at low speed, thirdly to public transport and mass-transit, and finally to limited use of car transport. The compact and multi-centric layout of Singapore allows most travel to take place on foot, by bike and by public transport. Only a small proportion of population drive private cars, with special tax tools in place to encourage them to buy or rent hybrid vehicles that use energy more efficiently. Yet, urban planners should bear in mind that alternatives must be of maximum quality when reducing the accessibility for the car. Otherwise, the transport inconvenience will incur public dissatisfaction or even sharp criticism.

Transport systems today have significant impacts on the urban environment, accounting for about 25% of world energy consumption and carbon emissions. Clean transport technology has to be combined with sustainable city planning. The environmental impacts of traditional transport can be reduced by improving the walking and cycling environment in cities, and by enhancing the role of public transport and green vehicles.

A rapid transit (subway, elevated railway, metro) system is an electric passenger railway in an urban area with a high capacity and frequency, and grade separation from other traffic. Service on rapid transit systems is provided on designated lines between stations using electric multiple units on rail tracks, although some systems use guided rubber tires, magnetic levitation or monorail. Today, technological improvements have allowed new driverless lines. Automated and driverless rapid transit lines in Singapore include Bukit Panjang LRT, Sengkang LRT, Punggol LRT, North East MRT Line, Circle MRT Line and Downtown MRT Line.

In Singapore, the first phase of vehicles was built by Kawasaki of Japan, the second by Siemens of Germany. Because of the capacity needed on this high-density system, the vehicles are substantially larger than conventional European underground stock. Powered at 750 V dc, the units can reach a maximum speed of 80 km/h (50 mph). The extensions to Changi Airport and the North-East Line have several state-of-the-art systems for operating ease, and passenger and staff safety. Signaling has an advanced diagnostic and monitoring system, and emergency links to the operations control center.

To reduce its carbon footprint in the climate change context, Singapore has been promoting electric cars propelled by electric motors, using electrical energy stored in batteries or another energy storage device. Currently, the Land Transport Authority (LTA) is seeking to develop a blueprint on how to bring about mass adoption of electric vehicles in Singapore. Among the things the regulator wants consultants to study are the gaps in technology, implementation issues of installing charging infrastructure, as well as an assessment of the energy savings and carbon emissions levels with the adoption of these green vehicles.[10] Electric cars bring a significant reduction of urban air pollution, as they do not emit harmful tailpipe pollutants from the onboard source of power at the point of operation; reduced carbon emissions from the onboard source of power, depending on the fuel and technology used for electricity generation to charge the batteries; and less expenditure on oil. Electric cars are much more expensive than conventional vehicles and hybrid vehicles due to the additional cost of their lithium-ion battery pack. Other unfavorable factors include the lack of public and private recharging infrastructure and the driver's fear of the batteries running out of energy before reaching their destination due to the limited range of existing electric cars.

Thus governmental subsidies are needed. The Singapore government has embarked on an electric car-sharing trial that could last up to ten years and involve as many as 1000 electric vehicles.[11] With endorsement from the government, the Clean Mobility Singapore Pte Ltd kicked off the electric-car-sharing scheme called SMOVE, which provides environmentally friendly mobility-on-demand (MOD) that can be seen as a convenient alternative to private car ownership. In Singapore, the electric cars also include the category of hybrid electric vehicles, which combine an internal combustion engine and one or more electric motors. Hybrid models include Saturn Vue, Toyota Prius, Toyota Camry Hybrid, Ford Escape Hybrid, Toyota Highlander Hybrid, Honda Insight, Honda Civic Hybrid and Lexus RX 400 h and 450 h. With low noise and zero tailpipe emissions, electric mobility will be the perfect ecologically friendly solution for city and urban driving.

Singapore has also been promoting NGVs that use compressed natural gas (CNG) as clean alternative to gasoline. CNG vehicles have lower levels of carbon emissions and lower particulate emissions per equivalent distance travelled. NG must be stored in cylinders, whether it is compressed or liquefied, and these cylinders are usually located in the vehicle's trunk, reducing the space available for other uses, particularly during long distance travel. Under the government's Green Vehicle Rebate (GVR) program offering incentives to promote green vehicles, which are more fuel efficient and emit less air pollutants than their conventional petrol or diesel equivalents, CNG and bio-fuel vehicles could have special tax exemption until 31 December 2011.[12] In addition to new vehicles, the GVR Scheme has been extended to include imported, used electric and petrol-electric hybrid vehicles registered from 1 July 2010.

V. Power Generation

Power generation is one of the major sources of carbon emissions and air-borne particulate matters (PMs). Such PMs could penetrate people's lungs and bloodstream and cause serious respiratory and heart problems. To reduce air pollution and achieve mitigation goals, since 2000, Singapore has increased the percentage of NG, a cleaner fossil fuel compared with coal or oil, used in electricity generation from 19% to 90%. Among all fossil fuels, NG produces the least amount of carbon emissions per unit of electricity. By so doing, Singapore has further improved its air quality and cut the amount of carbon released into the atmosphere. The city-state is now relying on NG piped from Malaysia and Indonesia. In order to diversify supply of NG and take advantage of global gas markets, Singapore is building a liquefied natural gas (LNG) terminal on Jurong Island. Singapore is also constructing a third LNG tank to be ready by the end of 2013 and announced plans to add a fourth storage tank to further increase the terminal's capacity.[13]

In order to achieve urban development projects with integrated sustainable solutions across all sectors, eco-city guidelines and objectives have to be woven together with local requirements.[14]

Confronted with the complexity that characterizes the real processes of the construction of the city today, urban planners need to promote cooperation in a multidisciplinary planning team as well as among all stakeholders. An eco-city should be understood as a single integrated system (holistic approach) and not as a combination or result of many sectoral developments planned in isolation.[15] As for Singapore, the idea of integrated planning is the basis for sustainable urbanism, demanding for the repeated and ongoing processes of analysis and a multidisciplinary approach to sustainability. In the city-state, those sectors related to the metabolic and environmental functions of the city (transport, energy and material flows and socio-economic aspects), which conventional planning considers as subsidiary to urban structure, are considered at the same level of importance. Priority has been given to the application of *avant garde* clean technologies with participation of various stakeholders. With active participation of different sectors and relevant stakeholders, the whole process of ecological city planning and construction is usually focused on such key areas as urban structure, transportation, energy and other resource efficiency as well as the socio-economy aspect. The main principles for the sustainable urban development, i.e. minimizing use of land, energy and materials, and minimizing the impairment of natural environment, should always be followed in the application of modern technology.

References

1. Harriet Bulkeley and Simon Marvin, Urban governance and eco-cities: Dynamics, drivers and emerging lessons, in Wilhelm Hofmeister, Patrick Rueppel and Lye Liang Fook (eds.), *Eco-cities: Sharing European and Asian Best Practices and Experiences*, Konrad-Adenauer Stiftung, Singapore, 2014, p. 1.
2. UN Habitat, State of the World's Cities 2012/2013, Prosperity of Cities, UN Habitat 2012 report, available at: http://mirror.unhabitat.org/pmss/list ItemDetails.aspx?publicationID=3387&AspxAutoDetectCookieSupport=1.
3. Singapore cut carbon intensity by 30 per cent, *Today Newspaper*, 11 December 2014, p. 1.
4. Mark Roseland, Dimensions of the eco-city, *Cities*, 1997, 14, 197–198.
5. BCA, About BCA Green Mark Scheme, available at http://www.bca.gov. sg/greenmark/green_mark_buildings.html (accessed on 12 December 2014).

6. First Solar Leasing Project in Singapore, HDB press release, 15 September 2011.
7. Another Step Closer to a Net Zero Energy Punggol Town, HDB press release, 24 January 2013.
8. Tan Say Tin *et al. Economics in Public Policies*, Marshall Cavendish Education, Singapore, 2009, p. 92.
9. PUB Desalinated Water: The 4th National Tap, available at: http://www.pub.gov.sg/water/Pages/DesalinatedWater.aspx (accessed on 1 November 2014).
10. LTA to develop a road map for electric vehicles, *Today Newspaper*, 14 March 2014, p. 1.
11. Plans for electric car-sharing trial for up to 1,000 vehicles, *The Straits Times*, 8 December 2014, available at: http://www.straitstimes.com/news/singapore/transport/story/plans-electric-car-sharing-trial-1000-vehicles-2014 1208#sthash.p7gniY6F.dpuf.
12. National Environment Agency, Green Vehicle Rebate, available at: http://app2.nea.gov.sg/grants-awards/green-technology/green-vehicle-rebate (accessed on 2 November 2014).
13. National Climate Change Secretariat (NCCS), Power Generation, available at: http://app.nccs.gov.sg/(X(1)S(4ujvw0jlrgj1lo55c0ucax55))/page.aspx?pageid=167&secid=193&AspxAutoDetectCookieSupport=1 (accessed on 5 November 2014).
14. Philine Gaffron, Ge Huismans and Franz Skala, *Ecocity Book II: How to Make it Happen*, Facultas Verlags- und Buchhandels AG, Vienna, 2008, p. 37.
15. Philine Gaffron, Ge Huismans and Franz Skala, *Ecocity Book II: How to Make it Happen*, Vienna: Facultas Verlags- und Buchhandels AG, Vienna, 2008, p. 18.

Chapter 6

Air Governance in London: Experiences and Strategies

Frank Birkin

Professor of Accounting for Sustainable Development,
Sheffield University Management School, UK
f.birkin@sheffield.ac.uk

I. A Persistent Problem

What can Asia learn from London about dealing with air pollution? There is a simple answer to this question, but it is not one that anyone wants to hear. The case of dealing with air pollution in London is historic as well as modern, technological as well as social, economic as well as natural, specific as well as generic, simple as well as complex and short-term as well as long-term. In summary, London's air has been — and still is — a complicated, intractable and deadly problem.

Hence the simple answer to the above question is: "Easy solutions do not exist". But this answer, when fully absorbed and reflected upon by everyone fighting or affected by this crippling issue, has a value. It means that we cannot place the problem in isolation, leave it to the experts or just blame governments. Everyone has a role to play and needs to be active if city dwellers are one day going to be able to breath fresh, clean and healthy air. There is no room for complacency.

Air pollution is ancient. Egyptian mummies have lungs blackened by the smoke from fires. As Seneca the ancient Roman philosopher grew old, his doctor told him to flee Rome to improve his health.

119

Seneca died in 65 AD in Rome. Anglo-Saxon villagers in ancient Britain suffered from an increasing incidence of sinusitis and inflammation of the nasal passages. This was partly due to those Anglo-Saxon architects who designed such poorly ventilated huts.

The first recorded incidence of air pollution in the UK is in 1257 when Queen Eleanor was forced to leave Nottingham because of smoke from domestic coal burning. It was her son, King Edward I, who set up the first British commission to deal with air pollution. The commission first met in 1285, but it took 31 years before a ban on burning coal fuels was introduced — and that did not have much effect.

It was left to the Black Death plague to eventually improved London's air in the Middle Ages. As many as 25% of British people died as a result of Black Death infections leaving lands uncultivated so that forests grew back. Wood then became a cheaper fuel than coal for heating homes and London's air was thereby improved.

But by the reign of Queen Elizabeth I, wood was scarce and expensive again and Londoners had returned to burning coal in their homes. Elizabeth I was "greatly grieved and annoyed with the taste and smoke" of London's air. James I succeeded Elizabeth I in 1603 and he was "moved to compassion" to learn that polluted air was eating into the stones of St Paul's Cathedral. He introduced a law banning the burning of coal within one mile of his court.

However as the city grew, London's air got worse. John Evelyn (1620–1706) described London as "eclipsed with such a cloud of sulfur as the sun itself is hardly able to penetrate". He asked, "Is there under Heaven such coughing and snuffling to be heard as in the churches and assemblies of London, where the barking and spitting is incessant and most importunate?".[1]

November 1679 witnessed the first of London's "great stinking fogs" and deaths from air pollution increased. Smogs were to continue enveloping the streets of London throughout Victorian times cloaking the nefarious deeds of the notorious serial-killer Jack the Ripper and thwarting the adventures of that great fictional detective Sherlock Holmes.

In 1952, London had the Great Smog during which an estimated 4,000 people died[a] and around 100,000 citizens had their health seriously impaired. In that smog, the Sadler's Wells opera had to abandon a performance, because the audience in the theater could not see the stage and Royal London Hospital nursing staff said they were not able to see down the length of a single ward. But even after a disaster on this scale, the then Prime Minister, Harold Macmillan, avoided taking immediate action arguing that many related economic factors had to be taken into account.

With better data, it was, however, an economic argument that did eventually bring about change. A government-initiated inquiry established that the impacts of air pollution cost £100's of millions a year — a far bigger amount than the estimated cost of cleaning London's air. As a result, the 1956 Clean Air Act was passed by the parliament.

This Act introduced smoke-controlled areas in cities where only smokeless fuels could be burned; it relocated polluting power-stations away from city centers; it had the height of some chimneys increased. It was an important milestone in dealing with air pollution in London and on its own, the act increased London's winter sunshine by as much as 70%. The age of coal burning in London was coming to an end, after causing centuries of fatal pollution.

But London was not to enjoy better air for long since just as coal burning declined, the volume of vehicular traffic on the city's streets increased. Air quality in the city is now among the worst for European capitals. In 2005, the EU established legally binding limits for air pollution on the basis of the World Health Organization's guidelines, and London has broken one or more of the limits in each subsequent year. Brixton Road, Putney High Street and other areas can be three times over the limits for the NO_2 emissions coming mainly from diesel engines.

---

[a]A recent study has estimated Great Smog deaths to be 12,000 (Bell *et al.*, 2004).

It is not surprising therefore that London is said to be in the grip of an air pollution health disaster. Government scientists estimate that air pollution coming principally from traffic is the causes 29,000 premature deaths nationally each year of which 4,200 occur in London. Studies undertaken by London Air, an initiative of the Environmental Research Group at King's College, found Oxford Street's NO_2 levels to be among the highest recorded anywhere, anywhere on Earth.[2]

In 2005, an analysis of data performed by the Massachusetts Institute of Technology revealed that emissions to the air from cars, trucks, planes and power plants in the UK was causing around 13,000 premature deaths annually. It is, however, car and truck exhausts that are the greatest cause of these premature deaths, killing about 3,300 people a year. In the UK, road accidents receive greater public attention perhaps because of their drama and higher visibility, but in 2005 there were 3,000 road accident deaths: 300 less than deaths from air pollution in the same period.[3]

Globally, air pollution's impact on humanity is overshadowed by worries about Climate Change. Air pollution is, however, one of the world's 10 greatest killers. A paper arising out of the 2013 Global Burden of Disease Study estimates that air pollution worldwide causes more than 430,000 premature deaths a year. There are of course other impacts: The final impact on human health needs to consider the total number of people disabled and suffering in their lives to the detriment of family, friends and economy.[4]

London air pollution is a serious and persistent problem. Without more and better interventions, the problem can only get worse. The UK's Office for National Statistics predicts a 13% population growth for London up to 2022, which means that the capital's population will exceed 10 million people. With ever more people wanting to get around the city, Transport for London forecast that by 2030 central London congestion will be 60% worse; an additional 350,000 cars will be added to the 2.6 million cars already running on London's streets. This dire prediction is based on the assumption that every aspect of the London Mayor's current transport strategy is implemented.

II. London's Transport Strategy

Transport for London (TfL) is the UK government organization that is responsible for most aspects of transport in London. It was created in the year 2000 and is officially part of the Greater London Authority. On the TfL website,[5] you will find diverse information relating to transport in London such as plans and strategies, investments, corporate social responsibility aspects, culture, heritage, maps, fares and travel guides.

The history of the creation of the current London Transport strategy may also be found on the TfL website. In 2008, Boris Johnson, the then Mayor of London, announced his plans to develop a new transport strategy for London. It required extensive consultation some of which was directed at the people of London themselves by means of an information leaflet and questionnaire called "Help Change London's Future".[6] London's air pollution problem was unfortunately underplayed in the consultation being mentioned most notable only under the heading of improvements to quality of life.

Boris's plan was finally published on the 10 May 2010. His proposals were far ranging and included:

- "Infrastructure investments" to transform the London Underground, enhanced rail links including the new London Overground route, improved transport interchanges, better access to transport systems, new river crossings and better use made of the Thames.
- "Changing lifestyles" with a cycling revolution and campaigns to make walking count.
- "Better management" to smooth traffic flows, improved bus services, increased information availability and improved streets.

The plan also contained actions directed at reducing air pollution notably extending the low emission zone (LEZ) and reducing carbon dioxide emissions especially by promoting electric vehicles. The LEZ aims to reduce emissions from diesel-powered commercial vehicles in London. Vehicles that fail to meet the emission standards are charged; others may enter the controlled zone without a penalty. The LEZ applies to most of Greater London 24/7.[7] It was a previous London mayor, Ken Livingstone, who established the first $980\,km^2$

London emissions zone in 2008 with costly charges and fines for polluting buses, lorries and diesel vehicles. The introduction of the zone was subject to strong opposition from vehicle manufacturers' associations and others. These groups complained that the charges and fines would badly affect owners of polluting trucks and construction machinery.

One year after the publication of the Mayor Boris's 2010 strategy, it was severely criticized by the Surface Transport Panel, a review body that was established within TfL to oversee transport issues. Critics argued that several of the plan's options to lessen congestion were insufficient and would provide only a few years of mitigation.

The panel was informed by new TfL studies of London's escalating congestion problem. The new studies highlighted opportunities to be derived from greater use of car-sharing clubs, changing freight transport policies and the provision of new tunnels. All in all, the new measures desired by the panel would require considerably more than the £30 billion estimated for implementing the Mayor's 2010 transport strategy.

Government strategies for reducing air pollution are still beset by political issues and economic considerations, and are consequentially sub-optimal from a scientific point of view. Air pollution is not that high on the UK's political agenda, though that status is changing.

III. Raising Air Pollution Awareness

It is widely recognized that people's response to many aspects of environmental deterioration is poor. Small environmental deteriorations made over long periods may be devastating — eventually — but they may simply fail to register adequately with many people. Our species has evolved to respond quickly to immediate, visible dangers such as predation. In this regard, environmentalists cite the boiled frog anecdote: A frog in cold water will not jump out as the water heats up provided that the change is slow enough. Eventually the frog will be boiled alive. This is of course not just a London problem. As a frequent visitor to Chinese cities from the UK countryside, I am sometimes exposed to poor quality in those cities and, as an asthmatic, my health can deteriorate over a short period to the surprise and concern of my hosts.

As we have seen in the long history of dealing with air pollution in London, improving air quality is no mere technical issue; it is frequently entangled with powerful economic vested interests. So to solve with the long-term problems of air pollution, it is essential to raise awareness.

There are two complementary ways of raising awareness about the quality of the air we breathe: The first is better knowledge and the second is engaging communication. The scientific understanding of air pollution and its effects is improving. Increasingly, sensitive measurement techniques invariably show that air pollution is more serious than we thought. Medical studies clearly show the deleterious effects of air pollution on health.

In the UK, air pollution information is made available by the government Department for Environment, Food and Rural Affairs (DEFRA). DEFRA publishes air pollution data and relates health advice for all regions across the UK.[8] The information is made available on a website, as well as via Twitter and Facebook accounts. It provides a Daily Air Quality Index and forecasts that can be searched by post code or location so that people are well informed about their local air quality.

IV. More Air Pollution Knowledge

(I) Nanoparticles

As technology advances, we gain more insights into our world and the many interactions we have with our environment. "Nanotechnology" was a term introduced in 1974; it refers to building or arranging matter on molecular or atomic scales. Now that we are aware of them, nanoparticles may be observed everywhere. They come from many different sources including nature and manufacturing but in city air, it is vehicles on busy roads that account for 90% of air-borne nanoparticles. Such air may hold tens of thousands of these particles and city dwellers may inhale between 10 and 80 billion nanoparticles every hour. Long exposure to such high concentrations of nanoparticles will damage lungs and cause cardio-vascular disease.

Nanoparticles are exceedingly small and measure from 1 to 100 nm.[b] This makes them around 700–70,000 times thinner than a human hair. Because of their very small size, they have very little mass. Hence mass-based, air quality regulations are ineffective in dealing with nanoparticles.

A key factor that makes nanoparticles dangerous to health is their large total surface area per unit mass that increases their chemical reactivity and absorption rates. They may pass deep into our respiratory system, react with lung tissues and enter the blood stream.

Although knowledge about nanoparticles in air pollution has increased considerably over the last decade, we do not know enough about their origins from newer sources such as biofuels. Biofuels reduce carbon emissions but evidence suggests that they increase the number of particle emissions. There is urgent need for regulation to control nanoparticle releases, but until the technology exists to accurately measure them, it is not practically possible.[9]

(II) Traffic air pollution exposure study

The Healthy Air Campaign teamed up with an environmental research group, Camden City Council and an individual London cyclist to discover the healthiest travel options between two locations in London. Six people traveled from a single starting point in Lincoln's Inn Fields to a common destination, Castlehaven Community Centre. The study was conducted during a busy rush hour one Friday afternoon in May.

Four of the volunteer travelers followed the same direct but busy London streets each using different methods of transport: Walking, cycling, bus and car. Two other volunteers took an alternative, quieter route through backstreets and along a canal footpath: One of

---

[b]The nanometer is a unit of length, which is abbreviated to "nm" and measures one billionth of a meter in length, 1×10^{-9} m.

Air Governance in London: Experiences and Strategies   127

these walked and the other cycled. Each one of the six volunteers monitored their exposure to air pollution with a personal micro-aethalometer, which measured the levels of black carbon to which they were exposed. The results were surprising.

On the direct busy-streets route, it was not the pedestrians and cyclists passing through vehicle pollution who recorded the highest levels of air pollution. It was the car driver who had the worst health experience as follows:

- The highest level of pollution on the busy streets route was experienced by the driver of the car.
- The next highest level was recorded by the person taking the bus.
- The pedestrian on the busy route was third most polluted traveler.
- The cyclist on the busy route received the least black carbon pollution.

It appears that vehicles traveling in a queue of traffic drive through streams of polluted air emitted by vehicles immediately in front. This pollution enters the car through the ventilation systems and is then trapped within the vehicles. The bus traveler had a similar experience.

But the pedestrian on the same route walked slightly to the side of the streams of vehicular pollution. So even though the pedestrian took much longer to reach the destination, this person walked through much lower concentrations of pollution and recorded overall about half the polluted air received by the car driver.

Similarly, the cyclist that took the same streets as the car driver, managed to avoid the slip streams of pollution by slipping to the sides of vehicles and having air circulating freely — not trapped — around them. In addition, the cyclist was the fastest traveler along the busy route taking 13 minutes less than the car driver to complete the journey. A shorter journey time also reduced to cyclist's exposure to black carbon in the air with the result that the cycling option recorded an eighth of the pollution received by the car driver.

As you might expect, the travelers on the quieter route recorded the lowest pollution levels of the study. The pedestrian on the quiet route received one third of the pollution received by the person

128 F. Birkin

walking the busy streets. While with regard to the two cyclists, the level of pollution encountered along the quieter route was 30% lower.

The study reveals more of the health benefits of walking and cycling; double-edged in this case since walkers and cyclists produce and receive less pollution than car drivers along the same busy routes. The option of taking quieter often more scenic routes can reduce pollution exposure for cyclists and walkers even further.[2]

V. Engaging Communication

Communication has to be clear precise and relevant but even given these desirable properties, its effectiveness may be limited. As aspect of this limitation is revealed by the gap that exists between values, attitudes and knowledge on the one hand, and action on the other. People may well know of environmental problems, and in their hearts they may want to improve the situation, but day-to-day interactions, demands and routines often mean that their actions do not follow from their best intentions. The way to bring best intentions and actions together is by using engaging communication.

Engaging communication means that people are not simply given the facts or instructed what to do; they are shown how the desired change may be woven into their day-to-day lives. Instead of simply warning about the dangers from high pollution levels of using vehicular transport on busy streets, alternative and healthier options for getting from A to B have to be provided as in the air pollution and traffic study outlined above. Instead of telling businesses that they need to be aware of the problem of air pollution across their activities, ways to change their approach to business need to be developed and implemented; such is the intent of *Improving Air Quality in the City of London: A Practical Guide for City Businesses.*[10] This guide was prepared as a result of collaboration between the City of London and the UK National Health Service.

In a clear, simple and resolutely practical document, City businesses are shown how to embed improvements to air across all their activities: From placing air quality firmly within Corporate Responsibility policies, to engaging employees and collaborations between asset owners, facility managers and tenants. The key issues, techniques and technologies are communicated and then embedded in a set of practical checklists in the appendices that deal with: Corporate Responsibility aspects; air quality monitoring and reporting; memorandum of understanding for the built environment partnerships; procedure's for retrofits; energy reviews; green roofs and walls; green travel planning; supply chain policies; and waste and recycling. This report is designed to make it as easy as possible for everyone in City businesses to implement the maxim: "whatever you're doing — think air quality".

In a similar vein but with broader objectives, the Royal London Borough of Kensington and Chelsea commissioned a report on "14 Cost Effective Actions to Cut Central London Air Pollution".[11] The immediate actions recommended by the report include the following:

- engaging with businesses as in the City Air example above,
- expansion of Car clubs to raise revenue and reduce car use,
- training taxis drivers in "eco-driving" to save both money and pollution,
- switch to competitively priced zero-emission services if available,
- enforce taxis drivers waiting at ranks to switch off engines,
- provide real-time warnings for motorists of serious road pollution on worst-case roads to discourage additional vehicles in polluted locations.

It was estimated that these actions would reduce emissions in the borough by 2% per annum. Furthermore, £248 million per annum could be saved by implementing longer-term actions as follows:

- vertical roof exhausts on buses to reduce their emissions impacts by around 90%,
- requiring all new buildings to be air quality neutral and the replacing of old gas-boilers,
- putting cycling as a top transport priority for London and extend existing cycle networks, converting cycle lanes to tracks, so that over 60% of central London journeys may be cycled,

- developing low-cost, target-location planting of vegetation to reduce pollution in their immediate vicinity.

Estimates of the cost-effective actions recommended by the Royal Borough of Kensington and Chelsea report are given in Table 6.1.

Recent years have seen the publication of several documents on air pollution in London. Insofar as they tend to reproduce a similar content to that of the Royal Boroughs of Kensington and Chelsea reviewed earlier, they represent a duplication of effort. But in reality, the documents serve different purposes and are targeted at different used groups. The "City of London Air Quality Strategy 2011 to 2015"[12] for example describes City policies on reducing air pollution through to 2015. It is an official document produced by the city's environmental services committee to fulfill statutory obligations as well as the communicating, encouraging and partnering activities.

Similarly, the London Assembly, an official, elected watchdog overseeing the capital, published an issue paper on air pollution in London in 2012.[13] This document provides a summary of the city's Health and Environment's Committees work to tackle London air pollution and considers alternative options. It is a useful resource for references and achievements. It also provides an overview of action at different levels of government from local action to the House of Commons Environmental Audit Committee and the Mayor's strategy.

It is the situation that the capital is not short of information, advice and plans regarding its air pollution. The European Commission, of course, is also working to clean Europe's air. The European Commissioner for the Environment declared 2013 to be the "Year of Air" and ordered a review of European air policy and strategies. The EU also produced a short pamphlet to state their current position and proposed action on air pollution. "Cleaner Air for All: Why it is important and what we should do?". The European Union sets air pollution standards for all member states; air quality in some of UK's cities, including London, is unlikely to meet EU standards before 2030.

Table 6.1. Cost-Effective Actions to Cut Air Pollution in Central London.

Measure	Impact Timescale from Policy Decision	Ratio of Total Benefits/ Total Costs	Benefits (NPV in 2012)	NO_x Reduction (tpa)	PM10 Reduction (tpa)	CO_2 Reduction (tpa)	Noise Improvement
Replacement of old boilers with Ultra-low NO_x devices	Years-decades	Infinite (as zero cost)	Not calculated	566.00	8.00	Not estimated	0
Business engagement (ongoing for 6 years)	Months	22.11	£4,630,096	0.07	0.01	34.92	+1
Car Clubs Expansion Programme	Months	13.58	£7,558,993	28.53	1.40	26,915.65	+1
Cycle to Work Schemes Expansion	Months	6.22	£4,567,538	3.54	0.33	2,171.49	+1
Ecodriving training for taxi drivers	Months	5.75	£7,683,700	4.14	0.36	2,023.22	+1
ZEV Last Mile deliveries	Weeks-months	5.05	£4,046	0.02	0.00	20.46	+3
Taxi Rank Idling Wardens	Months-years	4.12	£646,572	0.96	0.35	1,490.54	0
Cycle infrastructure & promotion using low cost cycle tracks	Years	2.49	£209,912,924	249.48	18.59	150,685.92	+3
Vertical exhausts at roof level on buses	Months	2.46	£24,015,078	2,667.15	21.15	—	0
Euro V requirement for Central London buses & Euro IV engine reprogramming	Months	2.41	£2,123,339	204.71	1.34	—	0
Fitting DPFs on Taxis	Months-years	2.01	£27,916,732	0.00	15.28	—	0
Campaign days	Days	2	£2,500,000	15.00	2.40	20,000.00	+1
Totals (Average for BCR)		6.2 Average BCR	£291,459,018	3,740 t.pa NO_x	69 t.pa PM	203,342 t.pa CO_2	+1 = some, +2 = significant, +3 = substantial

Source: Par Hill Research (p. 13).[11]

VI. Some Recent Proposals for Cleaning London's Air

The economic impacts of cleaning London's air have historically always been a consideration, and it is no different at the present day. Rebuilding London for cyclists, pedestrians and non-polluting transport in tandem with the construction of zero-emissions new buildings and retrofitting old ones for reduced pollution may be the ultimate solution for cleaner air, but such changes require lots of money. Besides once the major infrastructure changes have been completed, needs may change within one or two decades as they have done in times past; many cities have endured ongoing retrofitting throughout the later part of the 20th century in order to accommodate large numbers of personal car users. Hence cleaning city air requires initiatives that are big on results but not on expense.

Small-scale street-furniture changes such as fixtures that may be readily installed along London's streets are often cheap but effective attractive cleaner-air solutions. Such additions include safe parking for bikes, the creation of cycle routes separate from vehicular traffic, the provision of electric vehicle charging stations, privileged car-parking spaces for car-sharing and car club schemes, and prioritized positions at taxi-ranks for "green" taxis.

(I) Street "glue"

One recent, cost-efficient initiative was promoted by the Mayor of London, Boris Johnson, involved coating streets with "glue" (calcium magnesium acetate or CMA) to trap pollution particles and remove them from circulation in the air. In a 2012 trial, gluing dust suppressants were sprayed along 15 of London's most polluted streets. Once captured by the "glue", it was hoped that polluting particles would eventually be washed away by rain or carried away on vehicle tyres. But once spraying the streets was stopped, the beneficial effects wore off; a fact that attracted the attention of the EU since it could be construed as a temporary measure, a kind of cheating that could attract a fine. However, a close study of the glue in action found in to be incapable of "gluing" particulates from vehicle pollution. (The technique has been shown to help extract pollutants from industrially polluted air.) In short, the £1.43 m "gluing" vehicular pollution project simply did not stick.

(II) Electric vehicles

In 2012, London Transport collaborated with the Climate Group, Cenex, the Energy Saving Trust and Thomas Nationwide Transport (TNT) to prepare a guide to use electric vehicles in fleets.[14] By using a comprehensive whole-life costing approach, the report highlighted the cost efficiency of investing in a fleet of electric vehicles. The argument is that while the initial costs of an electric fleet may be higher, lower running costs, zero rate company car tax, capital allowance concessions, 100% discounts for road tax, avoidance of the congestion charge in London and fuel at a quarter of the price of that for a conventional vehicle, mean that long-term financial benefits are there for the taking.

The number of stations where electric vehicles may be recharged is growing throughout the UK and sales of electric car have topped 10,000. The use of the 170 chargers installed in motorway service stations has tripled in less than a year. However, there are over 35 million licensed vehicles on UK roads, so 10,000 electric vehicles constitute a very small percentage nonetheless some momentum is there and numbers of electric vehicle users continue to grow.

(III) Car clubs

A car is typically used for a few hours per day goes the logic behind car clubs — so why buy one?

Car Lite London[15] is operated by Zipcar (UK) limited, who claims to be the world's largest car-sharing and car club provider, estimate that for every car club introduced, some 17 individual cars are taken off the roads; car club members typically drive seven times fewer short journeys of less than 5 miles than car owners do, and car club members tend not to commute by car, since it does not make sense to pay for a car that is parked at the office all day.

In a car club scheme, cars and vans are parked in designated bays across London. They can be reserved online or by phone any time of the day or night to be used for as little as half an hour, a day or as long as needed. At the end of the reservation, vehicles are returned to the same designated bay, so final parking is not an issue. A car club member pays only for the time a vehicle is in use, which for moderate users driving 6,000 miles a year or less, there are potential savings of several thousand pounds to be taken. Because of the way that car clubs charge only for use, car club members tend to make better use of non-car means of transport such as public transport, cycling or walking.

Car Lite's vision for London car clubs in the year 2020 includes:

- Round-trip car clubs are a mainstream part of London's travel.
- Car club members have grown 2.5 times to 351,000.
- 7,900 fewer cars and 650 million fewer miles driven.
- Savings for Londoner's of £238 million per annum.
- A £120 million per annum increase in productivity for a London enjoying reduced congestion on its roads.
- Air quality improved by PM10's down by 18 tons and NO_X emission by 432 tons.

(IV) Car-sharing

Carplus is a not for profit transport non-governmental organization (NGO) that promotes environmental alternatives to traditional car use in the UK.[16] It provides online tools for potential users to calculate their car costs, find club car vehicles or join a car-sharing scheme. They argue that car-sharing must be made a more explicit part of London's transport solutions and that more actions need to be taken to motivate people to join car-sharing schemes.

Car-sharing takes place when two or more people share a car and travel together. This means they keep most of the convenience of their own car while costs are shared, congestion eased and pollution reduced. It is a low-cost scheme to implement. If done thoughtfully, car-sharing can enrich a person's lifestyle by connecting people with shared interests; it thereby adds to community cohesion.

Car-sharing brings many benefits, but it is not for everyone. However, with a range of schemes available on national or local bases, it is possible to join car-sharing schemes just for specific events-based travel, everyday commuting, services for employers on business parks or journeys to town centers. Many more people could benefit significantly from car-sharing, and it is perhaps surprising that such schemes do not get more official attention in London.

(V) Cycling

As we know, cycling provides health and air quality benefits while being a low cost, low impact means of transport. To encourage more people to take a bike, the streets of London need to be made a lot safer, preferably with separate cycle tracks — not lanes threading between lines of other traffic. The current Mayor's vision for cycling in London includes these objectives:

1. A network of high capacity, joined up cycle tracks with Dutch style segregated lanes and junctions for the exclusive use of cyclists.
2. Improvements to junctions and measure to make large vehicles less dangerous to cyclists will make London Street more cycling friendly.
3. Double the number of people cycling in London by 2020.
4. Create a village in the city of green corridors with tree planting and taking space from cars and giving it to pedestrians and cyclists.[17]

The potential for increased cycling has been measured. About 4.3 million trips a day in London by non-cycling modes of transport have been identified as being suitable for cycling instead. Of these 4.3 million potential cycle trips, 3.5 million are estimated to take a cyclist no more than 20 minutes to complete.

The London bike-sharing scheme was introduced by Mayor Boris Johnson, and it is available at over 700 docking stations equipped with a total of over 10,000 bikes. The first half hour of bike use is free — which according to the above estimates — means that around 3.5 million trips would be free. After which, there is a small charge of £2 for 24 hours worth of use. This "Boris Bike" scheme has been introduced in collaboration with Barclays bank that provides a

Barclays Cycle Hire web page and credit card facilities at the docking stations.[18]

It is not just Londoners that need to get on their bikes. The newly appointed Minister for Cycling in the British Government argues that Britain needs more everyday cyclists; those who wear ordinary clothes and pedal short distances for everyday journeys as opposed to lycra-clad cycling heroes. The minister points out that in the UK only 2% of journeys are made by bike while in the Netherlands and Denmark, the equivalent figure is more than 20%.

However, to raise the number of cyclists in the UK will cost money. The Dutch spend more than £20 per person per year on cycling and the UK equivalent spend is £2. The UK government's 2014 commitment of £375 m for cycling over 5 years is more than has been committed before. But this figure is well below investment levels in the cycling countries of the Netherlands and Denmark. To really get the British on their bikes, an estimated of at least £10 per person per year is required.

(VI)   The London village

The idea of a London village with more vegetation and space created for pedestrians and cyclists by taking it from cars is part of the Mayor's cycle strategy outlined above. But this is no mean Arcadian nostalgia. The greening of London with trees and plants offers many real advantages for creating a healthier city with less air pollution, but planting out is not limited to the streets of London.

(VII)   Green roofs

Green roofs extract polluting particles and compounds from the air and bury them not only in the plants themselves but also in their growing medium. Plants take carbon dioxide from the atmosphere and produce oxygen; in green roofs, plants reduce the heat island effect to reduce ozone production; green roofs absorb heavy metals, airborne particles and volatile organic compounds.

An individual roof will not of course have a significant effect, but large areas of green roofs in concentrated areas in cities will bring about significant change.

Livingroofs.org is the UK leader for developing green roofs and they are members of the European Federation of Green Roof Associations.[19] The Greater London Authority's Climate Change Adaptability Team have identified areas where green roofs may be retrofitted to produce a total green area more than 28 times the size of Richmond Park or over 70 square miles.

As a consequence, a distinct policy on green roofs was added to the 2008 revision of the London Plan as follows:

"The Mayor will and the boroughs should expect all major developments to incorporate living roofs and walls, where feasible and reflect this in Local Development Framework policies. It is expected that this will include roof and wall planting that delivers as many of these objectives as possible:

- Accessible roof space
- Adapting and mitigating for climate change
- Sustainable urban drainage
- Enhancing biodiversity
- Improved appearance".

It is estimated that if a green roof development policy were to be implemented in the West End of London which has a roof area of 3.2 million m^2, about £55.5 million worth of environmental benefits would be gained for an outlay of £55.5 million, i.e. an effective short-term full payback.

(VIII) Green walls

Researchers at the Universities of Birmingham and Lancaster calculate that greening the walls in our streets could provide up to 30% reduction in pollution.[20] Trees, bushes and "green walls" of grass, climbing ivy and other plants offer cost efficient ways of greatly reducing air pollution where people need it the most, within the built "canyons" of large cities.

It was once thought that pollution reductions of a mere 1% or 2% may be achieved by this method, but this study shows that real reductions of more than 10 times this magnitude are possible. With computer modeling techniques and evaluations of the effects of the hundreds of chemical reactions, the scientists identified green walls as a clear leader for air pollution control. Green walls clean the air that comes into and stays within the street "canyons" to provide a relatively easy way to improve air quality. Transport for London has installed two green walls trails and published a detailed account of their experience in the report "Delivering Vertical Green".[21]

In economically strained times, planting green roofs and walls in our cities may appear to be an unnecessary frivolity. But there is now hard scientific evidence that says otherwise, and our knowledge of the benefits of greening cities is still increasing. Green planting in cities is good for the environment, for public health, society and the economy — all for relatively low cost.

The City of London grew from the green fields of the River Thames. Now it is time for the green fields to return.

References

1. P. Brimblecombe, *The Big Smoke*, Methuen, London, 2012.
2. London Air, *Environmental Research Group*, 2014, available at: http://www.kcl.ac.uk/lsm/research/divisions/aes/research/ERG/About-us.aspx (accessed on 27 October 2014).
3. S.H.L. Yim and S.R.H. Barrett, Public health impacts of combustion emissions in the United Kingdom, *Environmental Science and Technology*, 2012, 46(8), 4291–4296.
4. R. Horton (ed), Global burden of diseases, injuries, and risk factors study 2013, *The Lancet*, 2014, available at: http://www.thelancet.com/themed/global-burden-of-disease (accessed on 27 October 2014).
5. TfL, Transport for London, *Greater London Authority*, 2014, available at: https://www.tfl.gov.uk/ (accessed on 27 October 2014).
6. HCLF, Help *Change London's Future*, Mayor of London, 2008, available at: https://www.tfl.gov.uk/cdn/static/cms/documents/mts-leaflet.pdf (accessed on 27 October 2014).
7. LEZ, *Low Emission Zone*, Transport for London, 2014, available at: https://www.tfl.gov.uk/modes/driving/low-emission-zone (accessed on 28 October 2014).
8. DEFRA, *About Air Pollution*, Department for Environment, Food and Rural Affairs, 2014, available at: http://uk-air.defra.gov.uk/air-pollution/ (accessed on 1 November 2104).
9. K. Kumar, L. Morawska, W. Birmili, P. Paasonen, M. Hu, M. Kulmala, R.M. Harrison, Norford and K. Britter, Ultrafine particles in cities, *Environment International*, 66 (May), 2014, 1–10.

Air Governance in London: Experiences and Strategies   139

10. City Air, *Improving Air Quality in the City of London*, City of London and National Health Service, 2014, available at: http://www.cityoflondon. gov.uk/business/environmental-health/environmental-protection/air-quality /Documents/improving-air-quality-city-of-london-best-practice-general.pdf (accessed on 1 November 2014).
11. Par Hill Research, *14 Cost Effective Actions to Cut Central London Air Pollution*, Royal Borough and Kensington and Chelsea, 2012, available at: http://www.rbkc.gov.uk/pdf/air_quality_cost_effective_actions_full_report.pdf (accessed on 1 November 2014).
12. City of London, *City of London Air Quality Strategy 2011-2015*, City of London, 2011, available at: http://www.cityoflondon.gov.uk/business/envir onmental-health/environmental-protection/air-quality/Documents/City%20 of%20London%20Air%20Quality%20Strategy%20Jan%2012.pdf (accessed on 1 November 2014).
13. London Assembly, *Air Pollution in London*, Issues Paper, London Assembly, 2012, available at: http://www.london.gov.uk/sites/default/files/Air %20pollution%20issues%20paper%20pdf_0.pdf (accessed on 1 November 2014).
14. Plugged in Fleets, Plugged in Fleets: A guide to deploying electric vehicles in fleets, *Transport for London,* 2012, available at: http://www. theclimategroup.org/_assets/files/EV_report_final_hi-res.pdf (accessed on 1 November 2014).
15. Car Lite London, *London's Car Conundrum*, Zipcar (UK) Ltd., 2014, available at: http://www.zipcar.co.uk/car-lite-london (accessed on 1 November 2014)].
16. Carplus, Carplus: Rethinking Car Use, Carplus UK, 2014, available at: http://www.carplus.org.uk/ (accessed on 1 November 2014).
17. Vision for Cycling, The Mayor's Vision for Cycling in London, *Transport for London*, 2014, available at: https://www.tfl.gov.uk/corporate/ about-tfl/how-we-work/planning-for-the-future/vision-for-cycling (accessed on 2 November 2014).
18. Barclays Cycle, *Barclays Cycle Hire*, Barclays Bank PLC, 2014, available at http://www.tfl.gov.uk/modes/cycling/barclays-cycle-hire?cid=fs008 (accessed on 2 November 2014).
19. Livingroofs.org, *On Green and Brown Roofs*, Livingroofs.org, 2014, available at http://livingroofs.org/ (accessed on 2 November 2014).
20. A. M. Thomas, A. Pugh, A.R. MacKenzie, J.D. Whyatt and C.N. Hewitt, Effectiveness of green infrastructure for improvement of air quality in urban street canyons, *Environmental Science and Technology*, 2012, 46(14), 7692–7699.
21. Transport for London, Delivering vertical green, *Transport for London Surface Transport*, 2012, available at: https://www.london.gov.uk/sites/default/ files/2012-10-15%20Delivering%20Vertical%20Greening.pdf (accessed on 2 November 2014).

Chapter 7

Urban Green Energy Development in Russia: Vladivostok City

Pavel Luzin
PhD in International Relations (IMEMO RAS),
Perm University, Russia
pavel.luzin@gmail.com

Usually, green energy in the cities is investigated within the dimensions of safe environment and human health. This chapter investigates green energy within the dimensions of political economy as well as the changes in the system of international relations. Using such approach helps to understand why the purposes of Rio Summit have not been achieved in Russia yet. The main focus of the research is the Russian experience in green energy and the case of the research is Vladivostok agglomeration (includes the cities Vladivostok, Ussuriysk, Artem and even Nakhodka), which is the center of the Russian Far East region and the main Russian gate in Asia-Pacific.

I. Russian Political Economy Frameworks for the Green Energy

Political economy approach allows exploring the synthesis between the economic trends of the green energy and its political consequences as well as between the changes in domestic and international affairs and political reasons for the green energy efforts.

Firstly, we need to explore the economics of green energy in comparison with the traditional power industry. In Russia, 67.9% of the power production is based on fossil fuels. This consists of electric power plants using natural gas (70%) and coal (25%). The share of nuclear energy is about 16% overall with 30% in the European part of Russia and 37% in the Northern West regions like the Leningrad and Murmansk regions.[1] The share of the hydropower plants (HPPs) is about 15.6% and the main HPPs are situated in the Kama-Volga river basins and Siberian river basins. However, the share of alternative (green) energy was about 1% in 2008, and this has not been change significantly since that time.[2]

So, the current energy balance in Russia is sustainable in the next 7–10 years. But there are a number of the economic challenges in the Russian energy sector during the long term (more than 10 years) as follows:

The Russian electric power plants using natural gas are undergoing modernization, which remains top priority for the energy companies.[3] It also means that investments in the new electric power plants will be limited during the next years.

The Russian HPPs will need investments to modernize. Equal importance will need to be given to installing safety mechanisms to avoid accidents similar to the Sayano-Shushenskaya HPP in Siberia in 2009. It is estimated that the price of modernization of 1 kW of installed HPP power generation is about US$200.[4]

Most Russian nuclear power plants will need modernization or replacement of the plants by 2020s.

Russia will need to double its per capita electric power generation capabilities in accordance with its current level of electric energy use and in comparison with the developed countries situated in the same climatic area (Canada, Finland, Norway, etc.).[5]

So, Russia will need to invest a lot of money to enhance its electric power capabilities during the next decades. And the important thing is that the cost of the installation of 1 kW of electric power produced by the electric power plants using natural gas or by HPP is comparable with the 1 kW of electric power produced by the green power stations. For example, both the cost of energy unit using natural gas and the cost of energy unit using wind are about

US\$1,000–1,500 per 1 kW.[6–9] The costs of the solar electric systems and the tidal power systems are still higher, but they will decrease due to technological developments.[10]

The bureaucratic approach to the regulation of the Russian economic life and the interests of the leading energy companies affiliated with the Russian authorities determine that the Russian political system is oriented toward the development of large electric power plants and energy systems with a high level of the centralization.[11–14] And the discourse on the diversification of the Russian energy balance is much more determined by the lobbyism of the companies in different sectors of traditional energy industry (gas, hydropower, nuclear power, coal, energy equipment) than strategic political visions.[15,a]

In the Far East regions, electric power plants using coal and heating oil are being re-equipped for natural gas after the construction of the gas pipeline from Sakhalin Island to Khabarovsk and Vladivostok and the gas pipeline to Kamchatka peninsula.[12,16] Other Russian regions went through this process in the previous decades.

At the same time, the energy system of the Russian Far East has a specific character. There exist both the low level of centralization and the high number of rural and local electric power facilities. According to the federal governmental program for the development of the Far East regions, there will be growth of green energy systems, wind and solar, especially within the hard-to-reach areas.[12,17] Nevertheless, the energy systems in the urban areas, ports and industrial facilities including the "Vostochnyi" launch site in Amur region are being developed within the traditional frameworks. These frameworks contradict Russia's national interests in economic development and in its foreign policy.

---

[a]Nevertheless, the biggest project in green energy in Russia is the development of the wind power plant in Kalmykia (the region near Caspian sea) with the power production of about 300 MW in the first stage, which has been supported by authorities. Kalmykia is the depressive agricultural region without developed industries and natural sources, so the project should build a more sustainable energy system for 280,000 citizens living there. Otherwise, the model of green energy in Kalmykia cannot be applied for Russia at all and can be compared just with African experience in green energy.

It is significant that the complex vision for Russia's prospects in green energy was developed by the International Financial Corporation of the World Bank in 2011.[18] The experts emphasized three main types of green energy, which are applicable for different Russian regions: wind, solar, biogas energy and small hydropower plants. But green energy is still a low-level priority area for the Russian government except in some special cases, as described earlier.

In the absence of private investments and liberalization in the energy market, achieving sustainable growth of GDP will be impossible in Russia. The high cost of installation of the traditional electric power plants and bureaucratic approach for energy planning mean that energy demand should be guaranteed. So, it means that industrial development and the number of population in every city and in every region should be predesigned too, but this is impossible in contemporary market economics. That's why private companies in Russia don't bring large-scale investments in the new electric power plants.

Economic liberalization will attract investments in the electric power market. Green energy will allow private investors to get the necessary flexibility and to decline the risks of economic uncertainty within the liberalized market. Such flexibility is created by green energy technologies, where the investor can install solar, wind or biogas power plants step by step and can also dismantle surplus power capabilities when the demand declines. Moreover, the flexible electric power capabilities are an essential part of the changing cities in Russia.

II. The Definition of "Flexible City"

The contemporary cities have become more and more flexible. Sure, the flexibility of every city depends on special historical and economic reasons but it seems to be a part of reality. Flexibility means the absence of predictable long-term trends or paradigm of the city's development, and it is defined by the economic and social competition between cities especially in a dynamic region like

Asia-Pacific. We use the working definition "flexible city" in our research, which consists of a number of issues.

(A) Since the collapse of the USSR, cities in Russia have begun to change, and this painful adaptation to open economics has not ended yet. In the erstwhile USSR, urban development including energy systems followed the centralized bureaucratic planning.[19] Later, the Russian bureaucracy kept its control on energy development without any control on the urban development.

There are two main trends during the adaptation, which are connected with the electric power capabilities: population change and transformation of the industry. These trends do influence dramatically on the electric power assets in Russia. The traditional electric power industry needs sustainable demand, and it cannot grow when the cities go through economic and social transformation like in Russia.

(B) The Russian regional centers have stabilized their population: the highest increment is about 40 new residents per every 1,000 residents in Tyumen in 2011. Most cities including Vladivostok and Khabarovsk in the Russian Far East have experienced increment of less than 15 new residents per every 1,000 residents and this is mostly migratory increment.[20] The sources of such migration are rural cities and towns.[21] This means that the structure of the contemporary residents' demand on the electric power is different from that in the 20th century when the demand grew up fast through growing urbanization and technological development.

Nevertheless, the demand is growing and the per capita supply of electricity in Russia still needs to be doubled in the next decades as shown above, but different strata of urban communities and different parts of the cities have different needs on the electric power.

(C) As for the Russian industry, the large machine-building factories have decreased since the Soviet era due to economic reasons and the new businesses and factories need sustainable, available and effective access to the electric power. When the energy market is monopolized in every city by the large-scale and often state-owned electric companies and moreover when the market is regulated by the bureaucracy, the businesses have limited opportunities for development.

So, the traditional electric power industry is not able to adapt well under such circumstances. Hence, the price of electricity in Russia has risen more than fourfold since 2002 and has surpassed the price of electricity in the US already. The situation may be changed in the case of countrywide development of green electric power plants, which will create market competition between the suppliers of electricity and the flexible energy environment.

(D) Also, we need to talk about the cases when the cities partly lose their economic base. We can see this process everywhere in Asia-Pacific from the Russian industrial cities to Detroit in the US. The main cause for this process is the loss of competitive positions by large-scale factories and plants, which leads to decay and restructuring of the urban areas. And the problem is the vulnerability of the traditional electric power plants behind the changing market conditions especially in the case of economic turbulence. As a result, the contemporary electric energy industry needs to be not only flexible but also sustainable for permanent adaptation to global economic changes. Green energy systems have such sustainability.[22]

(E) Moreover, the "flexible city" needs its residents to display a high degree of understanding of common responsibilities, and the green energy gives the opportunity here. Business and private activities in the creation of the wind, solar or small hydroelectric power systems increase the civil participation in urban life to make the city stronger. So we may say that it will renew the republican idea within the cities and will bring political sustainability along with economic and social development.

(F) On the competition between the cities in Asia-Pacific, the main question is: What will be the position of each city in the regional economic and political system? This is about the cities' force of attraction and their abilities for cooperation and not about domination or rigid hierarchy among them. In this context, Vladivostok (and any other Russian city) will never be able to become one of the great Asia-Pacific cities. But Vladivostok needs to be attractive for its residents, who want to be independent, to conduct their own activities in intellectual spheres or to create their own businesses with a high surplus value. The green technologies will allow Vladivostok to achieve this goal through effective electric energy systems and improving the city's environment.

At this time, it is hard to comment on "flexible city" in the Russian case where the bureaucratic and non-market approaches dominate, but this opportunity seems the only way for successful development from the current deadlock of development.

III. Vladivostok: Possible Green Energy Scenarios

Being the typical Russian city, the case of Vladivostok can be applied with some reservations in any Russian city in Siberia, Ural or in the European part of the country. At the same time, Vladivostok (and Russian Far East overall) is the only Russian gate to the Asia-Pacific region, and its development is one of the top governmental priorities although within the current political economy paradigm.[12,16,17] Moreover, the Far East is the region with the highest natural potential for the development of green energy.[6] This means that we can explore some possible scenarios for further development of green energy in Vladivostok.

(I) Intensive development of the green electric power capabilities

The scenario is based on the presumption that the current problems within the Russian political economy system will force the development of different types of green electric power plants as in Vladivostok and the Russian Far East region overall. This development will be realized by the private industrial companies and foreign investors, who will need the electric power capabilities for their business projects.

Russian authorities within the scenario will also be interested in the intensive development of green energy in Vladivostok for engaging the foreign investors in the Far East economies in order to maintain the balance between Chinese, Japanese and South Korean business interests in the region and to attract Russian businesses and citizens there. All of this will allow Russian government to maintain its competitive abilities in the Asia-Pacific.

The scenario faces the problem of poor investment climate in Russia. So, Russia will firstly need deep institutional reforms for the creation of a strong and transparent political economic system. Businesses will be ready to invest billions of dollars in the new electric power capabilities when such reforms are implemented. However, the possibility of such scenario is low in the next five years.

(II) Subsidiary development of the green electric power capabilities

This scenario presumes that the Russian government and state-affiliated energy companies will continue with the development of green electric power capabilities necessitated by technical require-ments when the traditional approach is not enough or is not effective. Also, the development of such capabilities may be defined based on their public and international image.

The green energy systems within the frameworks of the scenario will play an additional role in the local and regional energy balances. Earlier, we discussed about the prospects of green technologies in the local electric power plants in the hard-to-reach areas especially in the Russian Far East region, but the challenge of electric energy deficit exists even in Vladivostok and in some big cities in other parts of Russia. For example, there are some under-populated islands within the city district of Vladivostok where people still use the gasoline electrical generators. It is not possible to develop the islands in the absence of sustainable electric power plants, but the green systems can solve this problem.

The main problem faced in this scenario is the leading role of the bureaucracy and state-affiliated companies and the absence of private business participation. When the private (market) interests and the interests of local communities are not taken into consideration, the possibility of plan failure becomes higher. So, this way of development of green energy may lead to inefficiency. Nevertheless, it allows to eliminate some local energy problems in the near future and to sustain the idea of green development in the Russian public discourse. The possibility of such scenario is high.

(III)   Freezing of the development of the green energy capabilities

This scenario presumes that the Russian government may *de facto* freeze its efforts in green energy due to current deep economic crisis in the country. Within the scenario, the state-affiliated energy companies freeze their efforts in this way too, and the private sector doesn't have the motivation for green development due to political and economic reasons. Moreover, the Russian society's attitude is anti-modernization today, and such attitude is also contributing to freezing of the development process.

This freezing doesn't mean full rejection, but it does mean that the present inertia and sluggishness will not allow Russia to overcome its energy deadlocks and challenges. Vladivostok will not be able to integrate successfully into the Asia-Pacific economic system and to compete with other cities there. Its electric energy system as well as the electric energy system of Russia will continue to depend on traditional fossil fuel.

In such a case, the economic development of Vladivostok will need a lot of governmental investments for electric power plants and the bureaucratic and non-market model in the energy sector will be conserved. In consequence, Vladivostok, Far East region and Russia overall will remain peripheral in Asia-Pacific affairs without green energy development. The possibility of this scenario is also high.

IV.   Conclusion

We explored the influence of the Russian political economy model based on bureaucratic planning and interests of the state-affiliated corporation on the development of green energy systems in Russia.

The current Russian needs for modernization of existing electric power plants are huge, but at the same time Russia needs to double the per capita supply of electric power for its national economic development. Green technologies in the production of electric energy seem the only way out from this deadlock.

Green technologies in the production of electric energy give the necessary flexibility to businesses and urban areas. Such flexibility helps urban communities and the state adapt to the changing economic, political and social environments in the Asia-Pacific region. Moreover, the flexibility in the energy sector hedges the economic risks from private investments.

In the case of Vladivostok, which is the main Russian gate to the Asia-Pacific region, we have found three scenarios of the development of green electric power capabilities. There are also two competitive scenarios: (1) The limited optimistic scenario of the subsidiary development of the green electric power by the Russian government and state-affiliated energy companies and (2) the worst scenario of freezing such development due to economic crisis. Unfortunately, there exists low possibility for the implementation of the optimistic scenario of the development of intense, market-oriented and private-sector led production of green energy in Russia in the next years.

References

1. Proizvodstvo elektroenergii [The producing of the electricity], Rosatom, available at: http://www.rosatom.ru/aboutcorporation/activity/energy_co mplex/electricitygeneration/.
2. Vozobnovlyaemye istochniki energii [Renewable sources of energy], Ministry of Energy of the Russian Federation, available at: http://minenergo.gov.ru/ activity/vie/.
3. E.ON Russia, Godovoi otchet OAO "E.ON Rossiya" za 2013 god [Annual report of JSC "E.ON Russia" 2013], available at: http://eon-russia.ru/files /7146/.
4. Putin dal komandu na zapusk gidroagregata "odnoi iz luchshih GES v mire" [Putin commanded to start the hydro power unit on the "one of the world best HPPs"], Vedomosti, 12 November 2014, available at: http://www.vedomosti.ru/companies/news/35856381/putin-dal-koman du-na-zapusk-gidroagregata-odnoj-iz-luchshih?full#cut.

Urban Green Energy Development in Russia 151

5. Tsentr Gumanitarnyh Technologiy, Reiting stran mira po urovnju potrebleniya elektroenergii [The world ranking of the electric power concumption], available at: http://gtmarket.ru/ratings/electric-power-consumption/info.
6. Novye rynki vozobnovlyaemoi energii [The new markets of renewable energy], Polit.Ru., 16 April 2013, available at: http://polit.ru/article/2013/04/16/ps _energy/.
7. Teplovye elektrostantsii na osnove gazoturbinnyh ustanovok — sroki okupaemosti i stoimost proizvodimoi elktroenergii [Thermal electric power stations with gas turbine installation — the payback period and the cost of electricity produced], "Novaya Generatsiya" Company, available at: http://www.manbw.ru/analitycs/power_stations_basis_gas_turbine_units _paybackperiods_cost_electric_power_produced.html.
8. Tsena 1 kW na rossiiskom rynke vetroenergeticheskih ustanovok ot 15 do 215 tysyach rublei [The installation cost of 1 kW is from 15 to 215 thousand rubles on the Russian market of the wind power systems], RBC Markets Research, 23 January 2013, available at: http://marketing.rbc.ru/news_rese arch/23/01/2013/562949985572852.shtml.
9. V Permi vveden v stroi novyi energoblok Permskoi TEC-9 KES Holdinga [KES Holding started the new energy power unit on the Perm TPP-9], PROPerm.Ru., 05 February 2014, available at: http://properm.ru/busines s/news/75248/.
10. UNEP, Towards a Green Economy: Pathways to Sustainable Development and Poverty Eradication, 2011, available at: http://www.unep.org/greeneco nomy/.
11. IPEM, Analysis of the Results of Russian Electric Power Sector Reform and Proposals to Change Its Regulatory Approaches, available at: http://ipem.r u/eng/energy_studies/study_27052013.html.
12. The Government of the Russian Federation, Federalnaya tselevaya programma "Ekonomicheskoe i sotsialnoe razvitie Dalnego Vostoka i Baikalskogo regionov na period do 2018 goda" [Federal program "Economic and social development of the Far East and Baikal regions till 2018], Edition of 06 December 2013.
13. IPEM, Rost tsen i tarifov infrastruktirnyh otrasley: suschestvuet li predel? [The growth of the prices and tariffs in the infrastructure industries: Where is the limit?], available at: http://ipem.ru/news/publications/ 519.html.
14. E.ON Russia, Struktura toplivnogo balansa [The fuel balance], available at: http://eon-russia.ru/activities/fuel_balance/.
15. G. Krasnyanskiy, Khozhdenie po energeticheskim uglyam [Walking on energy coals], RBC Daily, 29 October 2012, available at: http://www.rbcdaily.ru/i ndustry/opinion/562949985021503.
16. Munitsipalnaya programma "Energosberezhenie, povyshenie enrgeticheskoi effektifnosti i razvitie gazosnabzheniya vo Vladivostokskom gorodskom okruge" na 2014 — 2018 gody [Municipal program "The energy delivery, the increase in energy efficiency and the development of the gas delivery in the city district of Vladivostok" in 2014–2018], Annex to the Order of the

Administration of Vladivostok, No. 2070, 20 September 2010, available at: http://www.vlc.ru/docs/npa/78917/.

17. JSC RAO Energy Systems of the East, Renewable Energy in Isolated Systems of the Far East of Russia, III International Conference, available at: http://www.eastrenewable.ru/en/.

18. Politika Rossii v oblasti vozobnovlyaemyh istochnikov energii: probuzhdenie zelenogo velikana [The Russian policy towards the renewable sources of energy: The waking of the green giant], International Finance Corporation, Washington, DC, 2011.

19. F. Hill and C. Gaddy, *The Siberian Curse. How Communist Planners Left Russia Out in the Cold*, The Brookings Institution, Washington, DC, 2003.

20. N. Zubarevich, "Otlichniki" i "neudachniki" rossiiskih gorodov [The "high achievers" and the "losers" among the Russian cities], Open Economy, 23 May 2013, available at: http://opec.ru/1535529.html.

21. The Federal State Statistics Service of the Russian Federation, Migration/Demography/Population, available at: http://www.gks.ru/wps/wcm/connect/rosstat_main/rosstat/ru/statistics/population/demography/#.

22. Going Green, How Cities are Leading the Next Economy, The London School of Economics and Political Science, 2013.

Chapter 8

Green Urban Development in Asia and the Pacific — Water Issues for Tourism

Susanne Becken* and Noel Scott
*Griffith Institute for Tourism, Griffith University,
Gold Coast, Australia*
*beckens@lincoln.ac.nz

I. Introduction

Global freshwater consumption has tripled over the last 50 years, and the lack of access to clean drinking water is a critical issue for many countries in the Asia-Pacific region. The Asia-Pacific region is inhabited by 60% of the world's population, but it has only 36% of global water resources.[1] Population growth is a key driver of water demand, with about two-thirds of global population growth occurring in Asia, resulting in an additional 500 million people in the next decade. Existing water stress and scarcity are likely to be exacerbated by climate change.

Water resources in the Asia-Pacific region face many complex challenges, resulting in regional hotspots. The hotspots are areas that face multiple issues, including constrained access to water and sanitation, limited water availability, poor water quality and increased exposure to climate change and disasters. The hotspots include Pakistan (due to the high risk of flooding), Cambodia, Indonesia and Lao People's Democratic Republic (PDR) (due to the exposure to natural disasters and limited access to drinking water and sanitation), India's Punjab and the North China Plain (facing falling water tables by 2–3 m a year), and also water-rich countries, because of deteriorating water quality and high levels of pollution from untreated sewage.

The dominant user of water globally, as well as in Asia-Pacific, is agriculture; however, tourism is an increasingly important water user in some regions because of its growing need for potable water.[2] Tourism will be impacted by future water scarcity and must become an active contributor to discussion and activities concerning urban water management. To date, a large proportion of the tourism-related research on sustainable development has been focused toward European and North American experience data and metrics.[3]

There is significant variation across Asia-Pacific destinations in terms of water use, with some countries consuming up to five times as much per-guest night than others. In some cities of Australia, overuse of water by tourism operators has resulted in conflicts with local communities.[4] In Bali, Indonesia, tourism reportedly consumes 65% of local water resources and conflict between the hotel industry and local communities is evident.[5]

The global challenges and geographic pressures outlined above have major implications for tourism in the Asia-Pacific Region. Building on the four issue dimensions of water, namely usage, cost, availability and quality, there are clear design, planning, procurement and development implications for the tourism industry. This chapter provides an overview of the key water-related challenges in the tourism industry, presents insights into the tourism industry's water requirements and puts forward benchmarks for "good practice" associated with water consumption in various types of tourist accommodation.

II. Water Usage

Tourism is a significant user of water. In general, tourists use more water when they are on holiday than when they are at home, which increases total global water use.[6] With over 1 billion international tourists globally, this increase is significant. Tourists use water, wastewater and solid waste services both directly and indirectly.[7] When on holiday, people consume water for drinking, washing or using the toilet, and when undertaking activities or using swimming pools. Tourism businesses also use water to maintain gardens, fill swimming pools and wash down facilities. More broadly, tourism is a generator of activities such as infrastructure development, food and fuel production and the supply and maintenance of public toilets that contributes to water use.[8]

Many forms of tourism are dependent on water both directly and indirectly. This includes golf and adventure tourism, ecotourism and leisure tourism. Changes in water supply can be detrimental to these activities. Moreover, many tourism regions are based in coastal areas or islands, which are typically extremely sensitive to water pollution.[9] Due to the transient nature of tourism, tourists create uneven water demand over time and location.[8] Tourism activity can be seasonal and often tourists arrive in the dry season when rainfall is lower and water availability is reduced. While water is a natural resource that is generally readily available, quality potable water requires infrastructure and ongoing operational expenditure. With population and tourism growth, it can be difficult to find funds to pay for the required additional infrastructure and expenditure, particularly when there is not a large or wealthy resident population.[7] While tourism businesses may pay for excess water, they generally pay the same fixed charges as other businesses, thus tourists' water use is often subsidized by the permanent population. Lastly, unlike other economic sectors, such as agriculture, there are limited water use statistics for tourism.[6,10]

Research by Gössling *et al.*[6] suggests that tourism-related water use represents an increasing share of domestic water use in many Asian countries, particularly Indonesia (8%), India (7.6%) and Thailand (6%). The United Nations Food and Agricultural Organization (UNFAO) AQUASTAT database is a global information system on water and agriculture, which collects and analyzes information on water resources and water uses (see http://www.fao.org/nr/water/aquastat/main/index.stm). EC3's EarthCheck database (http://es.earthcheck.org/) contains data on per-guest night water use in hotels in the Asia-Pacific region. A comparison of the UNFAO indicator of "municipal water withdrawal per capita" with per-guest night water

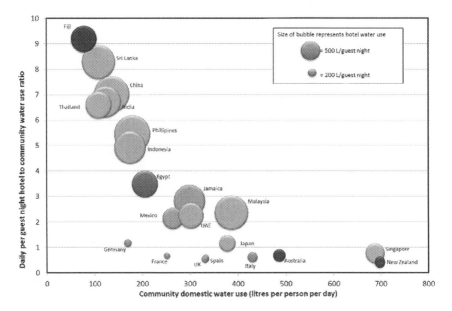

Figure 8.1. Comparison of Municipal and Tourism Water Use per Person per Day.
Source: UNFAO and EarthCheck; designed by Dr Rajan, Ecolab.

use in hotels provides an indicator of the relative impact of hotels for 21 countries, of which 12 are from the Asia-Pacific region (see Figure 8.1).

The highest per-guest night water use was found in the Philippines (981 L/guest-night), China (956 L/guest-night) and Malaysia (914 L/guest-night). Although tourism's share of municipal water use is typically quite small, it can be as high as 7.2% as in the case of Fiji.[10] At the same time, countries such as Fiji and most Asian countries are characterized by very low municipal water withdrawal per capita per day (less than 150 L), indicating greater water constraints on domestic and tourism use in developing or emerging economies.

III. The Cost of Water

Some accommodation providers can spend up to 20% of total utility expenses on water.[11] This is particularly evident in water scarce

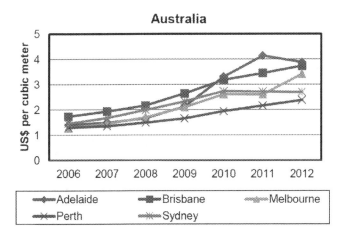

Figure 8.2. Municipal Water Tariff Rates in Selected Australian Cities.

environments, such as small island destinations that often rely on desalination or water transported in by ship. Reducing water use is not only a sustainability measure, but it is increasingly important for the financial bottom line.

Differences in water costs across destinations are considerable. Figure 8.2 shows the rates of water in five different Australian cities, ranging from US$2.40 per cubic meter ($m^3$) in Perth to US$3.88/m^3 in Adelaide. It can also be seen that water rates have climbed at an average of 14% per year in Australia's cities between 2006 and 2012 (up from US$1.43/$m^3$ to US$3.22/$m^3$).

In comparison, public utility water rates in China are considerably lower than those in Australia. The most expensive cities are Hong Kong and Tianjin at about US$0.65/$m^3$. Rates have climbed at an average of 9% per year in China's cities between 2006 and 2012 (up from US$0.29/$m^3$ to US$0.47/$m^3$), but most of this increase occurred between 2008 and 2010. Since then, water rates have been flat (Figure 8.3).

It should be noted that these costs are for municipal water supply based on a standard benchmark consumption rate of 15 m^3 per day (which is relevant to commercial enterprises and not residences). The data are sourced from the most recent global municipal water tariff survey of almost 360 utilities.[12]

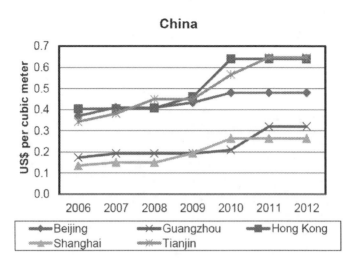

Figure 8.3. Municipal Water Tariff Rates in Selected Chinese Cities.

IV. Availability and Quality

Recent trends including the increasing intensity of agricultural production and rapid development and urbanization have resulted in increased withdrawal of freshwater resources, with mounting risks of water stress. Globally, domestic water use alone has grown on average by 2.2% every year for the last 60 years.[13] Tourism is a major global industry that is known to be a substantial contributor to local water demand.[8,14] The future availability and quality of water will also be strongly influenced by global climate change. Analyses of climatic trends in Asia-Pacific reveal a complex picture. China, for example has experienced an overall decrease in precipitation in the last 50 years, although some areas in the West and the middle and lower reaches of the Yangtze River have seen an increase in rainfall. South East Asia and the Western parts of the South Pacific have recorded an increase in precipitation, whereas Fiji, the West of Australia and the East of New Zealand have received less precipitation.[15]

(I) Benchmarking

The literature indicates that the current data available for water consumption in the accommodation sector worldwide are limited, sporadic and use varying metrics for measurement.[16–18] This highlights the need for properties to measure and report on their water usage in a consistent and timely manner.

To establish and analyze benchmarks for water consumption, it is important to distinguish between different types of accommodation types; business hotels and vacation hotels or luxury, fully serviced hotels, mid-range hotels and budget hotels. There is clearly a need to agree on the best accommodation category and definition and the methods used to measure water use. Here data from the EarthCheck database (http://es.earthcheck.org/) have been used to provide a comparison of business hotels in Asia-Pacific. The results show a wide range, from 292 L per-guest night in Australia to 956 L per-guest night in China.[2,10] Hong Kong and Japan, and to some extent the Republic of Korea and Singapore, display medium efficiency, whereas the remaining countries are characterized by high water intensities. High usages in some Asian countries may be related to extensive use of water for garden facilities, including elaborate water features both inside and outside the building.

(II) Tourism touch points

It is important to understand the key touch points for water use and management in a hotel or resort. Water is required for a range of services and the specific profile varies for each accommodation establishment. There are vast differences in the literature on how much different service components contribute,[19] but it appears that the most important areas of water consumption are as follows:

- guest rooms, with about 25–56% of consumption,
- cooling towers (air conditioning), in the order of 10–34% with higher needs in hot, tropical countries,
- swimming pools, contributing about 15–20%,
- kitchen and restaurant, with about 20% of end use.

Water usage is influenced by the presence of a cooling tower and in-house or outsourced laundry. For example, a hotel with no cooling tower and no in-house laundry is likely to have most of its water consumption in its guest rooms (56%). The second largest water use area is the kitchen. Guest rooms are still the most important area of water consumption in hotels with cooling towers and laundries, but their relative important is somewhat less.

Detailed system audits and diagnostics are needed to prescribe the best programs to maximize boiler system performance and efficiency. An effective boiler water treatment program is critical for guest rooms, kitchens, laundry and space heating. Effective mechanical, operational and chemical management of cooling towers, including makeup water treatment, is critical for space cooling. Another aspect of utility water use that can be significant in tourist destinations is associated with public spaces — pool and spa, landscaping and water features — where state-of-the-art chemistries and water-conditioning solutions can provide significant opportunities for reclaimed water use.

Effective cleaning and sanitation solutions that combine optimized chemistries, dispensers, equipment and automated controls can significantly reduce water consumption in the kitchens, restaurants and guestrooms. Resource-optimized effective chemistries for warewashing, floor care and on-premises laundry can further reduce water use in a hotel. Individual solutions for these various application platforms, when combined with either point-of-use or end-of-pipe water reclamation solutions, can significantly reduce the consumptive use of water by hotels located in water-stressed communities.

V. Measures to Reduce Water Usage

Water supplied to any tourism site or precinct may be of differing quality to coincide with its use; residential water supplies need to be potable whereas water required for usage where there is no public consumption or access (e.g. landscaping) can be gray water. As there is an energy and chemical requirement associated with producing potable and higher quality water, there are economic and environmental advantages to treat water only to the required standard. Matching water quality with its use increases sustainability.

According to Tourism Australia, water use in Australian hotels could be reduced by 20% without compromising guest experience. Addressing water consumption in a tourism accommodation business involves three key dimensions: organization/management, technology and behavior.

(I) Organizational change and management

Water demand can be reduced by the adoption of best practice water management principles. Examples include demand management, a policy for infrastructure maintenance and renewal, a management document detailing sinks and sources, and how to manage them for conservation purposes. In addition, measures can reduce potable water consumption by using treated wastewater and stormwater for non-potable usage such as for gardens and water features. This will also reduce the amount of water treatment required; thus creating a win–win situation. Further, water management needs to ensure that water distribution and irrigation systems are efficient and well maintained. Leakage need to be minimized. A proactive Leaks Maintenance and Detection Program will usually pay for itself in reduced water production costs, additional pumping costs because of pressure drops in the pipe work and reduced future repair costs. Leaks also can affect building structures and services, be a health and safety concern or detract from guest amenity. In addition to leak management, it is essential to track utility costs through a bill-monitoring program in the accounts department.

(II) Technological change

Several options exist for technological change. These include harvesting rainwater for use as a primary source of potable water. In addition, depending on the geographic context, groundwater can be extracted in such a way as to avoid drawing down the aquifer. It is important to choose technologies which are environmentally friendly and cost-effective at the same time, for example low flow showerheads or dual flush toilets.

(III) Behavioral change

Behavioral change involves both staff and tourists. As a basis, it is essential that the managers increase their own knowledge on water issues to then provide opportunity for staff to learn more about water conservation and efficiency. Particular staff programs can be developed that provide reward and recognition for excellence in water management and stewardship. These can be combined with guest education program.

VI. Conclusion

This chapter provides a starting point in discussing the global and regional context for water stewardship and water use efficiency in the tourism sector in the Asia-Pacific region. The risk of water scarcity and stress, in combination with increasingly polluted or contaminated water, has been discussed, especially against the background of increasing populations, growing industrialization, and changing hydrological cycles due to global climate change. Tourism businesses will have to consider the cost, availability, and quality of water supply for the future viability of their operations.

While not as big a water user as the agricultural sector, tourism will likely become an increasingly important player in discussions about water for several reasons. First, as the water-intensity data extracted from the EarthCheck database have demonstrated, the average use per-guest night in hotels far exceeds local levels of water consumption. A high variability between countries has been observed as well. Tourism's water intensity has not only major operational but also reputational implications, both for a business and the destination.

Tourism operations tend to be in urban areas. Tourism is also highly seasonal, putting peak demands on water systems at times when water supply (e.g. through rainwater collection) is minimal. The implications might be the need for seasonal pricing for water and wastewater services to account for these higher tourist water demands in the peak season.[7]

A brief overview of the dimensions where water consumption in a hotel could be reduced has been provided. A water audit — in addition to the increasingly employed energy audits — is an important starting point to measure and analyze businesses' consumption. This will then allow making a business case for investing in specific initiatives and technologies. Examples of efficient water technologies and practices have been provided. One key area relates to the maintenance of gardens and outdoor entertainment areas; the use of recycled water might be a viable option to reduce the usage of potable water.

Water challenges are assessed along the three dimensions of business risks: cost, availability and quality, and observations on geographic water stress are provided. Understanding the importance of cost, availability and quality of water raises important questions about design, planning, procurement and development pathways for the tourism industry. The cost of water is likely to increase and some form of "Water Footprint" estimation is inevitable in the medium term.

Overall, the aforementioned benchmark data highlight several important points. First, there is a great variety between world regions and countries. In some cases, there is almost a factor of five in terms of water consumption per-guest night. Further research on what exactly drives such significant differences would be highly beneficial. Some reasons include the type, size and style of properties typical of a region and hotel group, other reasons might include differing legislation, the quality of equipment (e.g. high water leakage rates are very common in some countries), and cultural habits and values. Second, when comparing the water consumption per-guest night with non-agricultural water intensity in different parts of the world, it becomes clear that tourism is an important consumer of water. Further research in this area is needed.

References

1. United Nations Documentation Centre on Water and Sanitation (UNDCWS), Asia and the Pacific, 2012, available at: http://www.un.org/waterforlifedecade/asia.shtml.

2. C.-l. McLennan, S. Becken and K. Stinson, A water-use model for the tourism industry in the Asia-Pacific region the impact of water-saving measures on water use, *Journal of Hospitality & Tourism Research*, 2017, 41(6), 746–767.
3. P. Bohdanowicz and I. Martinac, Determinants and benchmarking of resource consumption in hotels — Case study of Hilton International and Scandic in Europe, *Energy and Buildings*, 2007, 39, 82–95.
4. A.D. Alonso, How Australian hospitality operations view water consumption and water conservation: An exploratory study, *Journal of Hospitality & Leisure Marketing*, 2008, 17(3–4), 354–372.
5. S. Cole, A political ecology of water equity and tourism: A case study from Bali, *Annals of Tourism Research*, 2012, 39(2), 1221–1241.
6. S. Gössling, P. Peeters, C.M. Hall, J.-P. Ceron, G. Dubois, L.V. Lehmann and D. Scott, Tourism and water use: Supply, demand, and security. An international review, *Tourism Management*, 2012, 33(1), 1–15.
7. R. Cullen, A. Dakers and G. Meyer-Hubbert, Tourism, water, wastewater and waste services in small towns: TRREC Report 57, Lincoln University, New Zealand, 2004.
8. S. Gössling, The consequences of tourism for sustainable water use on a tropical island: Zanzibar, Tanzania, *Journal of Environmental Management*, 2001, 61(2), 179–191.
9. M. Kent, R. Newnham and S. Essex, Tourism and sustainable water supply in Mallorca: A geographical analysis, *Applied Geography*, 2002, 22(4), 351–374.
10. S. Becken, Water equity — Contrasting tourism water use with that of the local community, *Water Resources and Industry*, 2014, 7–8, 9–22.
11. R. Barberán, P. Egea, P. Gracia-de-Rentería and M. Salvador, Evaluation of water saving measures in hotels: A Spanish case study, *International Journal of Hospitality Management*, 2013, 34, 181–191.
12. S. Becken, R. Rajan, S. Moore, M. Watt and C.l. Mclennan, *White Paper on Tourism and Water*, EarthCheck Research Institute, Brisbane, 2013.
13. M. Flörke, E. Kynast, I. Bärlund, S. Eisner, F. Wimmer and J. Alcamo, Domestic and industrial water uses of the past 60 years as a mirror of socio-economic development: A global simulation study, *Global Environmental Change*, 2013, 23(1), 144–156.
14. C. Garcia and J. Servera, Impacts of tourism development on water demand and beach degradation on the island of Mallorca (Spain), *Geografiska Annaler: Series A, Physical Geography*, 2003, 85(3–4), 287–300.
15. M.H. Dore, Climate change and changes in global precipitation patterns: What do we know? *Environment International*, 2005, 31(8), 1167–1181.
16. N. Charara, A. Cashman, R. Bonnell and R. Gehr, Water use efficiency in the hotel sector of Barbados, *Journal of Sustainable Tourism*, 2011, 19(2), 231–245.
17. S.-M. Deng and J. Burnett, Water use in hotels in Hong Kong, *International Journal of Hospitality Management*, 2002, 21(1), 57–66.

18. B.D. Tortella and D. Tirado, Hotel water consumption at a seasonal mass tourist destination. The case of the island of Mallorca, *Journal of Environmental Management*, 2011, 92(10), 2568–2579.
19. S. Becken, N. Garofano, C.l. Mclennan, S. Moore, R. Rajan and M. Watt, *2nd White Paper on Tourism and Water: Providing the Business Case*, Griffith University, Gold Coast, 2014.

Chapter 9

Current Practice on Resource Efficiency in Southeast Asian Cities

Li Liang[*,‡] and Alice Sharp[†,§]

Department of Common and Graduate Studies,
Sirindhorn International Institute of Technology,
Thammasat University, Thailand
†*School of Bio-Chemical Engineering and Technology,*
Sirindhorn International Institute of Technology,
Thammasat University, Thailand
‡*liangli08@gmail.com*
§*alice@siit.tu.ac.th*

I. Introduction

Human settlements in the 21st century have taken place in city areas, especially in the developing countries, as these countries have a higher proportion of rural population. In 2008, the Asian Development Bank (ADB) estimated that by 2030, additional 1.1 billion people will be residing in urban cities compared with 2005. In 1950, 245 million Asians lived in urban areas and by 2010 the number had increased to 1.85 billion, and it is estimated to reach 3.3 billion people in 2050.[1] The percentage of urban population in some Southeast Asia (SEA) countries, i.e. Brunei Darussalam, Malaysia and Indonesia, has exceeded the world's average (Figure 9.1). The expansion of cities is the driver for vibrant economic growth in Asia as urban population has contributed largely to country's production. The expansion has

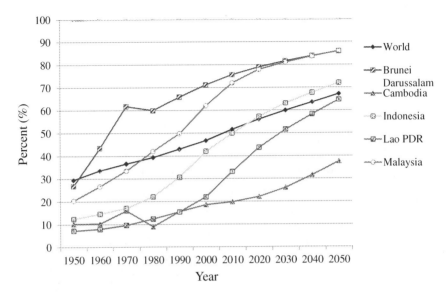

Figure 9.1. Percentage of Population Residing in Urban Areas, 1950–2050.

Source: Modified from World Urbanization Prospects.[1]

exerted more pressure on multiple sectors; such as energy, transport and waste. Together with economic growth, cities have a high level of consumption, production and waste generation, all of which hinder the process of sustainable development.

Economic growth alone does not guarantee the quality of life of its citizens. This is especially true for developing countries where many people are faced with poverty, inequity and lack of resources. Sustainability of cities, hence, depends on how cities are planned and managed as well as efficiencies in consumption and production. Recognizing the importance of moving toward sustainable consumption and production, the Global Initiative for Resource Efficiency Cities (GI-REC) was launched at the Rio+20 conference in 2012. The goal of this initiative was to ensure that resource efficiency, sustainable consumption and production are incorporated into policies and other tools enabling successful implementation of GI-REC and sustainable development at all levels.

This chapter aims to review the current situation of resource efficiency in SEA cities and link cities' resource efficiency with several key social and environmental parameters. Additionally, case studies of three cities are discussed here in order to disseminate the result of good practices from various sectors. Lessons learned from case studies will be further discussed in terms of factors influencing the successful implementation of the initiatives.

II. Trends in Resource Consumption

(I) Global resource constraints

The global initiatives will be widely accepted when constraints on resource availability can be forecasted clearly. This section provides an overview of global trends in resource utilization.

During the last century, global materials consumption increased by eightfold. In 2005, world population consumed 500 exajoules of primary energy and 60 billion tons of raw materials. Approximately, 60–80% of these materials consumption were attributed to cities.[2] Cities were believed to be responsible for using 75% of resources, and accounting for 70% of CO_2 emission.[3]

In 2008, the International Energy Agency (IEA) predicts that despite the depletion of the oil reserves worldwide, the global demand for oil will rise by 45% by the year 2030. This increase in oil demand will undoubtedly impact on transportation, industrial and food production and supply. IEA also reported in 2012 that the emerging economies demanded more oil consumption, particularly from the transportation sector.

Access to clean drinking water becomes a critical challenge due to the decrease of water resources and the diversion of water for other uses, e.g. energy production. Water demand in cities has become a key impediment of a city striving toward its sustainable development.

In addition to the demands for fossil fuels and water, a growing city also demands more food. However, most urban residents do not produce their own food; thus are more susceptible to food price increase. A strong relationship has been demonstrated in 2007–2008 in that when fuel prices rose, so did the food prices.[4]

Increase in a city's population and modern consumption patterns will also increase the generation of solid waste. In developing countries, the increase in solid waste generation leads to a higher demand for new landfills. These landfills, if inadequately managed, would become major sources of greenhouse gases emissions.

All of the aforementioned information has led us to realizing the connection between resources. Overconsumption or mismanagement of resources will also have adverse impacts on other types of resources. Solving one of the resource constraints may result in problems in other types of resources. Thus, efficient use of all resources is necessary.

(II) Economic, demographic and social change in SEA

The population of the SEA region has increased continuously due to a decline in mortality and an increase in fertility rate between the 1950s and 1960s. This resulted in an adoption of population policies that reduce the rate of population growth from 1970; thus, fertility rate declined region-wide. In countries like Singapore and Thailand, the fertility level fell below the replacement level resulting from education, industrialization, urbanization and changes in the family planning program.

Although the population growth rate has been controlled, the level of urbanization has been gradually rising from people seeking better education and job prospects in the cities (Figures 9.2 and 9.3). In terms of economic growth, the SEA economic growth is in a recovering trend after the stagnant growth in 2011 and 2012. The economic growth is projected to reach an average of 5.5% over 2013–2017. This projected growth for Asian countries has shown that some member countries: Indonesia, Cambodia and Laos, are in earlier stages of development and have room for rapid economic growth. Domestic demand growth, especially private consumption and investment, is considered the main driver for regional growth. Growing urbanization will certainly affect the structure of demand, level of consumption, and production in the region.

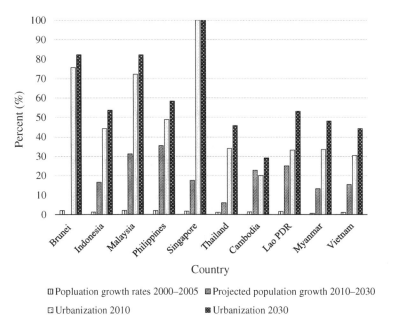

Figure 9.2. Demographic Status of SEA.
Source: The Population of Southeast Asia.[5]

(III) Trends in resource consumption for Asian countries

At the beginning of the 21st century, the Asia-Pacific region[a] was the world's largest resource consumer. This region consumed approximately 60% of the estimated 60 billion tons of annual global material use. In terms of resources required to produce one unit of gross domestic product (GDP), this region required three times the input of resources compared with other regions of the world.[7]

Figure 9.4 shows that the resource consumption patterns have changed in both quantity and quality between 1970 and 2008. In 1970, for example the resources used in this region were largely biomass-based; of which, agricultural crops, animal feed, fuel wood

---

[a]Data for Asia and the Pacific were used where data from Southeast Asia do not exist.

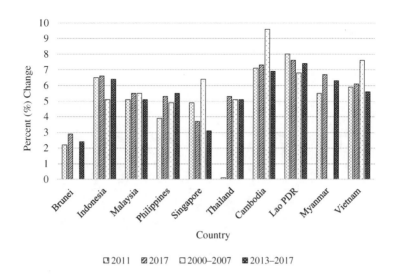

Figure 9.3. Real GDP Growth of SEA.
Source: Southeast Asia Economic Outlook 2013.[6]

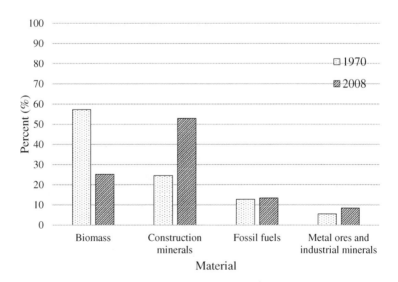

Figure 9.4. Change in Consumption Patterns in the Asia-Pacific Region between 1970 and 2008.
Source: CSIRO and UNEP Asia-Pacific Material Flow Database.[8]

and timber for construction comprised more than 50% of all the materials used. However, in 2008, there was a drastic change in the resources used in that construction minerals became one of the major resources used, representing about 50% of all the materials used in this region.

The physical trade balance (PTB = Net Import − Net Export) of the region has shown a trend toward the increase in net imports, which suggests that exploitation of the region's resources is no longer sufficient to support the fast growing economy. The net imports of fossil fuels were around 12% of the domestic extraction. When the fossil fuels are broken down into subcategories of coal, natural gas and petroleum, it shows that the petroleum net import was 140% of the domestic extraction.

In terms of efficiency, the per capita domestic material consumption (DMC) continues to grow in the Asia-Pacific. DMC for SEA continues to increase from almost 3 tons/capita in 1970 to slightly more than 6 tons/capita in 2005; however, this is still lower than that of Asia and the Pacific average at 8.6 tons/capita.[9] Material intensity (MI = DMC/GDP) of the region is increasing per unit of economic output, 2.4 kg per USD of GDP in 1970 to 3.1 kg, in 2005. This shows that the region is becoming less efficient in resource utilization. In order to stabilize the pressure on natural resources, the MI has to be decreased to the rate of increase of GDP.

As for energy demand, China, India and SEA economies have influenced the shift in global energy market to be centered in Asia due to their increasing demand. Energy use in the region increased from less than 45 exajoules in 1970 to approximately 170 exajoules in 2005. SEA's energy demand will increase by over 80% between today and 2035.[10] To meet the increasing demand, the power sector of the region relies heavily on low-efficiency (34%) coal fired power plants that also release CO_2 and other air pollutants. The energy intensity of the region reverses the decreasing trend for the rest of the world by remaining at 18 megajoules per US dollar of GDP in 2005.[7]

With a growing economy, the region has consumed significant amounts of water resources and at the same time produces a huge quantity of wastewater. Only 15–20% of the wastewater receives some level of treatment before being discharged. The remaining wastewater was directly discharged into the environment with all the toxic pollutants.[11] Most of the water resources in the region are now facing quality problems due to the aforementioned reason and the degradation of other environmental resources, poor management of watershed areas, and industrialization.

III. Resource Efficiency and Environmental Issues

Inefficient use of resources has resulted in several environmental problems. At present, various initiatives are being implemented. This section describes the current status of major environmental issues in relation to resource efficiency as well as initiatives that explicitly take this approach into practice. As most environmental issues are interlinked with one another and also contribute to climate change to a certain extent, the adaptive measures or initiatives being implemented are summarized in Table 9.2 in Section III(VIII) on climate change.

(I)   Conservation of natural resources

Demands for production and consumption in the Asia-Pacific region have surpassed the renewal capacity of the region's natural resources. While cities occupy only 3% of the land area, they consume 75% of world resources. An ecological footprint is estimated at 1.8 hectares per person. Most cities have shifted towards a much higher number. Increasing demands have resulted in a drastic change in land use patterns: declining forest area, expansion and intensification of agricultural land, and rapid urbanization. The net loss of forest in SEA has amounted to 332,000 km^2, of which, Indonesia contributed to a net loss of 241,000 km^2.

Despite the change in land use patterns, land use intensity of the region has decreased during the last few decades. This implies that less land is required per unit of economic output, or in other words, there is better efficiency in food production, but with higher pressure on land resources.

Forest resource management has shifted from forest for timber to conservation of natural ecosystems. The Philippines has effectively implemented the "participatory forestry", and in Vietnam, ownership of forestlands has been allocated to households, individuals and private entities. Legislative changes to grant ownership of forestlands are underway in several other countries.

In an attempt to handle land-use change and land-use efficiency, carbon-trading markets were formed in Asia and the Pacific. The "deforestation avoidance" carbon credits or Reduce Emission from Deforestation and forest Degradation (REDD) has received growing attention. The initiative provides better incentives to generate and maintain sustainable forests in comparison with timber production or conversion to other types of land use.

(II) Energy management

Electricity generation in the world increased by 3.4% annually from 2000 to 2008. During the same period, the electricity production in the Asia-Pacific region increased by an average of 6.1% per year. The major sub-regions in electricity generation are the East and Northeast Asia. For SEA, Indonesia and Thailand are the two countries that led with combined electricity production of 297 billion kWh or 51% of the sub-regional total produced.

The generation of electricity relies heavily on fossil fuel; e.g. natural gas and coal. Per capita energy demand in SEA has jumped by five times between 1990 and 2011 to 712 terawatt-hours (TWh). The proportion of energy consumed by industry has increased continuously, reflecting a pattern of increasing production and consumption activities. Energy intensity or the amount of energy consumed to produce one unit of GDP declined all over the region due to efficiency improvement. Despite these improvements, there is still room to improve energy efficiency. As of 2011, the region's energy intensity was more than one-third higher than the global average and more than double that of OECD.

A major factor that hinders the region to be more energy efficient is the fossil fuel subsidy policy. Subsidies, which amounted to US$51 billion in 2012, distorted the market price of energy and deterred investment for energy infrastructure, while hampering improvements in energy efficiency and development of renewable energy.

Energy efficiency policies have shown signs of improvement due to several initiatives implemented. Thailand is developing mandatory standards that will discourage the use of vehicles with low fuel economy and has introduced a 17% tax reduction for the purchase of cars with an average fuel consumption of not lower than 20 km/L, meeting at least Euro 4 emissions standards. Indonesia plans to introduce mandatory CO_2 emission standards for passenger vehicles.

(III) Human settlements

Between 240 million and 260 million people in Asia's urban areas live on less than US$1 a day, which accounts for about 70% of the world urban poor. Many of these people live under high-density conditions in degraded, informal or squatter settlements. Projections are that if nothing changes, the population of these slums will grow by an average of 110 million people a year, reaching 692 million by 2015.[12]

It is obvious that urban planning must take place in order to cope with the demographic, environmental, economic and socio-spatial challenges that lie ahead.[13] Conventional city planning does not take into account the important challenges of 21st century cities, such as climate change, oil dependence, food insecurity and involvement of stakeholders in the planning of urban areas.[13]

Innovations in city planning include the development of renewable energy in order to reduce cities' dependence on non-renewable energy sources or the development of small-scale power and water systems. Also, innovations can include increasing green spaces as part of green infrastructure development to expand renewable sources of energy, and local food production. Another initiative is the development of "cities without slums" (CWS) to ensure availability of safe drinking water and sanitation and prevent environmental degradation. Several strategies were identified during the implementation of CWS. The low-cost housing and slum upgrading strategies at

Caloocan city, the Philippines and the project to improve major infrastructures in Da Nang City, Vietnam, can be used as examples.

(IV) Transportation and mobility

Poor public transport systems in many of the cities in the region have led to an increasing number of private motor vehicles; and thus, has put more pressure on city infrastructure. Figure 9.5 shows that motorization has increased incessantly in SEA cities, especially motorized two wheelers. The motorization index is expected to be double the 2005 level (150 vehicles/1,000 people) by 2035 (327 vehicles/1,000 people).

Although road transport is a crucial element in transferring goods and people, it is also a significant consumer of liquid fossil fuels worldwide; thus, a major contributor to the increasing global greenhouse gas (GHG) emissions, especially CO_2, and air pollution. Transport energy consumption in SEA accounts for 25% of the total

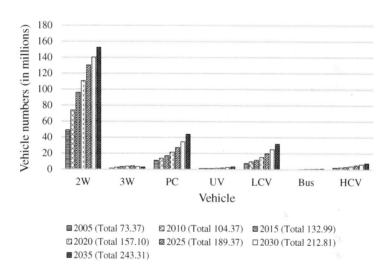

Figure 9.5. Growth of Motor Vehicles for SEA Region.

Notes: 2W = motorized two-wheeler; 3W = motorized three-wheeler; PC = personal cars; LCV = light commercial vehicles and HCV = heavy commercial vehicles.

Source: CAI-Asia Center.[14]

energy consumption in 2011. A traditional approach in tackling congestion is to provide more road capacity; however, extra capacity also induces further demand for traffic. Recently, governments have used economic tools (both incentives and penalties) in managing the transportation problems. Additionally, private sectors and citizens are encouraged to switch to cleaner cars or cleaner fuel use to make urban transport more sustainable. The Philippines has implemented several campaigns to improve public transportation. The policy on conversion of diesel-run jeepneys to clean/alternative fuels; e.g. LPG and electricity, in Manila was accompanied by an economic incentive package.

Redesign of urban public transport systems has received growing interest. The systems aim to reduce reliance on fossil fuel, traffic congestion and air pollution, and at the same time increase access and mobility of urban citizens. Countries in SEA, therefore, switched from road-based public urban transport to urban rail systems. Malaysia, Philippines, Singapore, Thailand and Vietnam have relied on rail-based public transport.

(V) Waste management

Because of rapid urbanization and life style changes, proper solid waste management has become one of the major and challenging issues in many developing countries. Landfills; though being criticized as significant sources of greenhouse gases, water and air pollution, and land degradation; are still the most preferred option in most cities of developing countries. Table 9.1 summarizes the status of waste generation, utilization and treatment facilities in some cities in SEA.

The problem related to solid waste is not only in the quantity but also in the nature of waste being discarded. Since waste separation at sources is not widely practiced in developing countries, wastes are discarded as mixed waste to include household, hazardous, industrial, and infectious wastes that can impose serious health and ecological risks. The percentage of waste utilization is still low in developing countries. Increasing utilization rate will promote efficient use of resources.

Table 9.1. Municipal Solid Waste Generation and Treatment Facilities.

Country	Annual Waste Generation (ton)	Waste Generation per Capita (kg/ca./day)	% of Municipal Solid Waste Recycled	Material Recovery Facility	No. of Open Dumpsites	No. of Controlled Landfills	No. of Sanitary Landfills
Brunei	189,000	1.4	N/A	—	6	—	—
Cambodia (Phnom Penh)	324,159	0.67	N/A	—	2	—	—
Indonesia	40,150,000	0.49	5	80	400	70	10
Lao PDR	1,204,400	0.64	N/A	—	—	—	5
Malaysia	5,781,600	0.90	4 (Kuala Lumpur)	—	—	261	10
Myanmar (Mandalay)	109,500	0.46	10	—	2	—	—
Philippines	10,539,375	0.34	28	2,361	826	273	19
Singapore	1,490,000	0.94	54	—	—	—	1
Thailand	14,640,000	0.64	22	—	—	20	91
Vietnam	12,800,000	0.41	18–22	—	49	91	17

Source: Modified from AIT/UNEP RRC.AP.[15]

Waste management initiatives being implemented in the region include the 3Rs approach to redesigning production systems by employing cleaner production technology and cleaner waste treatment technology. It is clear that no single waste management technology will deal with all problems related to solid waste management. An integrated solid waste management approach is important for sustainable development and appropriate resource utilization. To further illustrate the importance of the integration of solid waste management, a case study from Phitsanulok is presented in Section IV(III).

(VI)   Water resource management

Water is a natural resource that serves as the medium to integrate all social and economic activities as well as ecosystem components. The functioning of ecosystems and progress of all sectors depend on both the quality and quantity of available water resources. Furthermore, the importance of water should be recognized at the international level, as decisions on water use at a local level will have impacts at regional and global scales. Allocation of water requires coordination among sectors to ensure that progress made in one sector will not diminish the development opportunity in other sectors.[11]

A number of global policies have recognized the centrality of water for sustainable development and the focus on water management has been given high priority. For example, the United Nations (UN) Millennium Development Goals (MDGs) has set the target that by 2015, the proportion of world population without access to safe drinking water and sanitation be reduced by half. The UN General Assembly and the Human Rights Council also declared that access to safe drinking water and sanitation is a basic human right. As such, member states are required to guarantee this right to their population.

In order to allocate water resources among sectors effectively, it is necessary to understand drivers for water demand. The Asia-Pacific region has the highest annual water withdrawal among the world's regions. The agricultural sector plays an important role in a region's economy; hence, the sector accounts for about 60–90% of freshwater withdrawal depending on the level of economic activities. In addition, industrial sector's demand for water has increased, but water quality in the region has deteriorated due to industrial development, urbanization, and agriculture intensification.[16] Water hotspot sites have been identified for the region based on 10 categories of threats. Many countries in SEA contain compound hotspots for up to six categories. Challenges for water resource management in response to threats include: (1) water availability, (2) vulnerability and risk from water-related disaster and (3) Household water adequacy. With the challenges identified, the management of water resources in the region has slowly shifted from a supply-oriented to a more demand-oriented management approach. Governments in this region are implementing three major water management programs:

- Eco-city development — river rehabilitation, storm-water management, decentralized wastewater treatment and grey water use.
- Rural area development — modern irrigation system, rainwater harvesting and decentralized drinking water.
- Wastewater revolution — treating wastewater for reuse and low-cost wastewater processing plants.

(VII) Food security

Food security is a challenge of this region as 65% of the world's undernourished people are concentrated in seven countries; five of which, including India, Pakistan, China, Bangladesh, and Indonesia, are in this region. With population residing in cities continuing to increase, demand for food has also increased. Since urban residents do not have the ability to produce their own food or obtain locally produced food, they are vulnerable to global changes in food price. Rising fuel prices and weather fluctuations due to climate change affect agricultural production and food supplies significantly.

Cities must be directed toward food-resilience through boosting local food production and consumption. Promoting local food markets is an important measure to take, as it will reduce food carbon footprint, and build local resilience to cope with the uncertainties in global food supply.

At the regional level, the Association of Southeast Asian Nations (ASEAN) has promoted the ASEAN Integrated Food Security initiative and its corresponding Strategic Plan of Action on Food Security in the ASEAN region to achieve food security as a response to the dramatic increases in food prices in international markets. Some of the strategic action plans in the region include:

- Strengthening ASEAN food security statistical database and information to provide technical and institutional assistance for initiatives undertaken by the ASEAN Food Security Reserve Board (AFSRB) and its secretariat to compile, manage, and disseminate statistical data and information on food and food security, which will pave the way for a more effective planning of food production and trade within the region.
- Establishment of a regional food security information system for ASEAN to allow member countries to effectively forecast, plan and manage their food supplies and utilization for basic commodities using up-to-date techniques as well as to provide information for investors to undertake investments and/or joint ventures in food production in conducive areas.
- Studying long-term supply and demand prospects of major food commodities, such as rice, corn, soybeans and sugar in ASEAN.

At the country level, various types of projects are being implemented. For example, a food security project implemented in Indonesia targets not only the lack of food supplies but also the inability to access food. The Indonesian government has set policies in response to food insecurity based on local conditions. In most cities in Indonesia, authorities aim to improve transportation systems, encourage its citizenry to diversify both their food consumption and production, and generate sufficient income to purchase enough food.

(VIII) Climate change

Urban cities have significantly contributed to global climate change. Major activities; such as transportation, production and consumption; that result in GHG emissions are linked to cities. The main

Current Practice on Resource Efficiency in Southeast Asian Cities   183

Table 9.2. Summary of Specific Adaptation Measures toward Resource Efficiency by Sector.

Sector	Adaptation Measures	Examples of Implementation
Water	Rain water harvesting; water storage and conservation; water reuse; irrigation efficiency	• Singapore manages all aspects of the water cycle in an integrated manner, both in forms of supply-side and demand-side management. Activities include sourcing, collection, purification, and supply of drinking water, treatment of used water and its reclamation into NEWater, as well as the desalination of sea water
Infrastructure and settlements	Relocation; protection of natural barriers; water barriers; building design; housing programs for the poor	• Mandatory codes for building (lighting, AC, ventilation, alternative energy) in Thailand and Singapore • Voluntary codes for building in Malaysia, Philippines and Vietnam • Affordable public housing in Singapore
Human health	Safe water; improved sanitation; disaster preparedness; emergency medical services	• Disaster management policy and plans exists in several countries such as Cambodia, Indonesia, Laos and Thailand • Emergency preparedness and response programs in the Philippines include the mobilization of disaster control groups in public and private establishments
Transportation	Redesign of public transport to cope with warming and drainage; smart traffic systems; fuel subsidies, fuel taxes	• Indonesia reduced fuel subsidies scheme • Thailand, Laos, the Philippines and Vietnam have replaced fuel subsidies with fuel taxes

(Continued)

Table 9.2. (*Continued*)

Sector	Adaptation Measures	Examples of Implementation
Waste	3Rs; waste minimization; redesign of production process; cleaner production technology	• 3R's policy implementation in Thailand • Waste plastic to energy in the Philippines • Composting plants in Bangkok and Hanoi
Industry	Energy management; clean technology; product life cycle analysis	• Mandatory energy management in Malaysia Singapore, Thailand, Vietnam and Indonesia • Energy management in Cambodia and Laos
Energy	Energy efficiency; renewable energy, energy security	• Thailand aims to diversify fuel sources for electricity generation • Laos aims to become the hydropower battery of Asia • Singapore and Philippines aim to minimize wasteful energy consumption, and have achieved lowest energy intensity

sources of GHG emissions from urban areas are related to the consumption of fossil fuels in electricity supply, transportation and industry. Climate change risks in cities may include effects on water and energy supply, ecosystem services, energy provisions to the industry and disruption of local economy. Cities in developing countries are extremely vulnerable to climate change effects,[17] especially for the poor population.

As mentioned earlier, activities in cities contribute largely to climate change problems. It is, therefore, necessary to identify adaptation measures for different sectors and players in the society. Table 9.2 summarizes the adaptation measures being implemented in the region.

IV. Resource Efficiency Initiatives in South East Asian Cities

Three cities in SEA, namely Surabaya City, Indonesia; Hue City, Vietnam; and Pitsanulok City, Thailand, are chosen as study cases to demonstrate how these cities engaged in programs to lower carbon emission and to protect their respective unique environments in an integrated manner. Important elements identified in the case study to enhance resource efficiency in each of the three cities are evaluated and the results are presented in Sections IV(I)–IV(III).

(I) Low-carbon emission city: Surabaya, Indonesia

Surabaya City, Indonesia, was selected to implement one of the Japanese government initiated projects in Asian countries. Under the project, advanced Japanese technologies were adopted with a Joint Crediting Mechanism (JCM) or Bilateral Offset Credit Mechanism approach to provide crediting opportunities for implementers of the project in a measurable, reportable and verifiable manner. The project aimed to assist Surabaya city in transforming itself into a low-carbon emission city by targeting such four sectors as energy, transport and traffic, solid waste, and water and wastewater.

A workshop was co-organized by the Institute for Global Environmental Strategies (IGES) and Surabaya City under "the JCM large-scale feasibility study project for low-carbon development in Asia" in July 2013. According to IGES,[18] there were two parts in the study: (1) combining heat and power (CHP) at Surabaya Industrial Estate Rungkut (SIER) through trail calculation of CO_2 emission reduction; developing measurement, reporting, and verification methodology; and expansion of the feasibility study and (2) studying the potential of energy saving and installation of dispersion type power sources outside of industrial areas, and installation of LEDs in the highway lighting system. It is expected to reduce CO_2 emission at approximate 50,000 tons/year in the energy section by CHP installation at SIER (38,000 tons/year), energy conservation in buildings (10,000 tons/year), and installation of LEDs in the highway lighting system (630 tons/year).

In addition, the targeted total GHG emission reduction in the four sections was estimated at 130,000 tons/year, with energy sector 48,630 tons/year, transportation sector 29,000 tons/year, solid waste sector 41,000 tons/year, and water resource sector 7,060–11,960 tons/year.[18]

(II) Resource efficiency awareness campaign: Hue, Vietnam

Hue, capital city of Thua Thien Hue province, one of the most vulnerable provinces to climate change in Vietnam, was selected as one of the ten cities in a project entitled "Action towards resource-efficient and low-carbon cities in Asia" during 2009–2013 implemented by the Asian Institute of Technology. This project aimed to assist the ten cities in Asia to become a low-carbon emission society through improved resource efficiency and environmental sustainability, and to strengthen the capability of city authorities and other stakeholders in addressing climate change issues. Hue city has prioritized four sectors to improve its carbon emission: Solid waste, energy retrofitting, traveling and awareness campaign.

The outputs of the project were summarized as: (1) Initiated awareness activities related to climate change mitigation and adaptation in the city; (2) strengthened capacity of city authorities and Hue University staff related to climate change through Bilan Carbone training; (3) developed awareness materials (guidelines handbook and posters) accompanied by an official mandate of the City Mayor asking relevant units to disseminate and implement accordingly; and (4) expected reduction of GHG emission at approximate 19 tCe per year attributable to the use of efficient compact fluorescent lamps.[19]

The Hue city case demonstrated the importance of developing a city level energy plan, based on Vietnam's national guidelines, for mitigating carbon emission and minimizing the impacts of climate change. This ensured the link of "bottom up" and "top down" approaches for the development and implementation of the action plans at national and local levels. Regular technical consultation was essential to successful, smooth implementation of the plan.

(III) Zero waste initiatives: Pitsanulok city municipality, Thailand

Before implementing the zero waste management initiatives, Phitsanulok municipality, Muang District, Thailand, faced several difficulties in solid waste management. For example, a waste collection fee could not be collected effectively. The office managed to collect 600,000 Baht/year (US$20,000/year) while the municipality had an operation cost of 18,000,000 Baht/year (US$600,000/year). Local citizens did not participate in waste-reduction activities, as a result, the quantity of waste generated was as high as 142 tons/day in 1996 when 45–50% of this amount was recyclable waste. At the same time, the municipal office had neither a clear solid waste management plan nor the trained personnel to handle the complexity of solid waste management issues.

Phitsanulok municipality used a mixed policy intervention to implement their waste management policy. The main idea for the general solid waste management policy was based on the "zero waste concept". At first, it was implemented with communities to separate valuable waste from that of non-valuable. The municipality office acted as the facilitator in the implementation of the concept. Municipality executives often visited the local communities to listen to problems encountered. As a result, the city was able to reduce the waste generation at source up to 40%. In terms of policy intervention, the municipality has implemented four major policies and they are as follows:

(1) **Waste collection and disposal fee:** The municipality has implemented a fee collection, which in 1995 collected 0.6 million Baht (US$20,000). This was increased to 10 million Baht (US$333,333) in 2010.

(2) **Collection route and vehicle:** The waste collection efficiency in the Phitsanulok municipality was nearly 100% after implementing the project. The frequency of waste collection decreased from daily to weekly, reducing the collection costs by 70%. The collection was carried out at door-to-door, roadside-bins or waste stations. Citizens were informed of collection schedules and the

routes of collection were designed to minimize the transportation costs.

(3) **Waste transfer station:** Because the landfill site was 40 km away from the city, the transportation costs were high. Construction of the transfer stations effectively reduced the number of times that a waste collection truck had to drive through communities; thus creating other environmental impacts. One-third of the transportation costs have been saved from the establishment of the transfer stations.

(4) **Waste disposal:** Use of a pre-treatment method of mechanical biological waste treatment (MBT), before dumping waste at landfills, has reduced solid waste by 50%. The separation of waste piles after composting provided a supply of organic matters that can be used to produce refuse diverted fuel for gasification processes. At present, the municipality has established a pre-treatment facility using a waste-to-energy technology that will greatly reduce the quantity of waste plastic from waste piles.

V. Parameters for Gauging Resource Efficiency Implementation

From the trends of resource utilization and the aforementioned case studies, it is obvious that the utilization of resources is cross-linked with each other. City planning and management, therefore, cannot focus on a one-dimensional approach; rather an integrated approach. The social and environmental parameters for gauging the successful implementation of resource efficiency initiatives are summarized as follows:

- **Good governance and political will:** Management of city's resources requires effective multi-stakeholder participation. A top-down approach that is normally employed in developing countries has proved to be ineffective in many cases. There should be a mechanism to coordinate multi-sectors and multi-stakeholders in decision-making processes. Local governments and their political will also play a crucial role in allocating cities' resources among different socio-economic groups of citizens.

- **Holistic management approach:** Sustainable use of resource requires understanding of socio-metabolic flows.[17] This includes quantification of resources (i.e. energy and materials) consumption, degradation of ecosystems and other damages associated with the growth of a city. Both qualitative and quantitative measures should be used to monitor the changes and the sustainability of a city.
- **Urban design and planning:** Inefficient use of resources at present is partly due to inappropriate city design and planning. Originally, many cities were not prepared for rapid growth. Thus, facilities were not adequately equipped to accommodate pressure from population growth. Low-footprint design for sectors (i.e. transport sector, energy sector and construction sector) should be given high priority and incorporated into the policy formulation process.
- **Human capital development:** Human resources in some developing countries often lack appropriate skills and capacity for sustainable development. Technology transferred from developed countries requires adjustment to local conditions. Such understanding is a basis for management and maintenance of the technology. In addition, awareness of citizens on socio-metabolic flows and its implications for natural resources has not yet developed. Human development programs in response to these issues should be instituted.
- **Financing the sustainability concept:** Transition toward sustainability requires substantial amounts of investment that not all cities in developing countries can afford. Cooperation between sectors is emphasized again, as it will increase the chance of obtaining such funding and reduce the repetition and overlapping works. Economic instruments can be used as incentives or punishments to stimulate the adoption of sustainable consumption and green technologies for production processes.

VI. Conclusion

The transition of cities into resource efficient cities is a process that requires an extensive integration among sectors and stakeholders of the cities. This chapter synthesized the current state of thinking and practice on resource efficiency in SEA cities. Although resource efficiency is not fully implemented, a wide range of initiatives is being implemented in the region with some successful stories to be used as lessons learned. This includes low-carbon programs, integrated solid waste management, smart public transport, and renewable energy development. Promotion of awareness and education programs related to resource efficiency should be carried out to extend the understanding to the greater public. Without the changes in human capacity, implementation of projects is less likely to be sustained.

Acknowledgments

This work was supported by the National Research University Project of Thailand Office of Higher Education Commission, which was not responsible for or involved in the decision on designing, writing or publishing this chapter.

References

1. United Nations Economic and Social Commission for Asia and the Pacific (UNESCAP), *World Urbanization Prospects: The 2011 Revision*, CD-ROM Edition, 2012.
2. F. Krausmann, S. Gingrich, K.H. Eisenmenger, H. Haberl and M. Fischer-Kowalski, Growth in global material use, GDP, and population during the 20th century, *Ecological Economics*, 2009, 68(10), 2696–2705.
3. United Nations (UN), *Are We Building Competitive and Liveable Cities? Guidelines for Developing Eco-Efficient and Socially Inclusive Infrastructure*, Clung Wicha Press, Thailand, 2011, p. 15.
4. IEA, World Energy Outlook 2008: Executive Summary, 2008, available at: http://www.iea.org/media/weowebsite/2008-1994/WEO2008.pdf (accessed on 25 September 2013).
5. ARI, The population of Southeast Asia, 2013, available at: http://www.ari.nus.edu.sg/docs/wps/wps13_196.pdf (accessed on 28 September 2013).
6. OECD, Southeast Asia Economic Outlook 2013, 2013, available at: http://www.oecd.org/dev/asia-pacific/saeo2013.htm (accessed on 4 October 2013).
7. UNEP, Resource Efficiency: Economics and Outlook for Asia and the Pacific, Bangkok, 2011, available at: http://www.unep.org/publications/contents/pub_details_search.asp?ID=6217 (accessed on 25 September 2013).

8. CSIRO and UNEP, Asia-Pacific Material Flow Database, 2013, available at: www.csiro.au/AsiaPacificMaterialFlows (accessed on 28 September 2013).
9. UNEP, Recent trends in material flows and resource productivity in Asia and the Pacific, 2013, available at: http://www.unep.org/pdf/RecentTrend sAP(FinalFeb2013).pdf (accessed on 25 September 2013).
10. IEA, Southeast Asia Energy Outlook 2012: Executive Summary, 2013, available at: http://www.iea.org/publications/freepublications/publication/ SoutheastAsiaEnergyOutlook_WEO2013SpecialReport.pdf (accessed on 25 September 2013).
11. UN-WWAP, World Water Development Report 4; Managing water under uncertainty and risk, 2012, available at: http://unesdoc.unesco.org/images/ 0021/002171/217175E.pdf (accessed on 25 September 2013).
12. ADB, Managing Asian Cities: sustainable and inclusive urban solutions, 2008, available at: www.adb.org/sites/default/files/pub/2008/mac-report.pdf (accessed on 25 September 2013).
13. UN Habitat, Global report on human settlements 2009: Planning sustainable cities, 2009, available at: http://mirror.unhabitat.org/pmss/listItemDetails. aspx?publicationID=2831 (accessed on 25 September 2013).
14. CAI-Asia Center, Improving vehicle fuel economy in the ASEAN region, 2010, available at: http://www.globalfueleconomy.org/Documents/Publicat ions/wp1_asean_fuel_economy.pdf (accessed on 28 September 2013).
15. AIT/UNEP RRC.AP, Municipal solid waste management report: Status-Quo and issues in Southeast and East Asian countries, 2010, pp. 43.
16. APWF, Regional Document: Asia Pacific. 5th World Water Forum, Tokyo, 2009, available at: http://www.apwf.org/archive/documents/ap_regional_ document_final.pdf (accessed on 28 September 2013).
17. UNEP, Sustainable, Resource Efficient Cities — Making it happen, 2012, available at: http://www.unep.org/urban_environment/PDFs/SustainableR esourceEfficientCities.pdf (accessed on 25 September 2013).
18. IGES, Low-carbon and environmentally sustainable city planning project in Surabaya, Indonesia — inception workshop, 2013, available at: http://www. iges.or.jp/en/sustainable-city/20130710.html (accessed on 9 October 2013).
19. AIT, Action towards resource-efficient and low carbon cities in Asia: Experiences and highlights, 2013, available at: http://lcc.ait.asia/publicati on/ADEMEBOOKLET-18_Final.pdf (accessed on 13 October 2013).

Chapter 10

Case Study: Portland Urban Growth Management

Shiming Yang* and Jefferey M. Sellers
Department of Political Science,
University of Southern California,
Los Angeles, California, USA
*syang@som.umaryland.edu

Over time, American cities have been plagued by urban sprawl and the problems arising therefrom. After World War II, the automobile industry began to flourish, giving rise to a suburban culture characterized by detached houses, cul-de-sacs, scattered land use and car dependence. This has also caused environmental problems such as traffic congestion, hollowing out urban areas, reduced green land, rainwater runoff and air pollution. Although the local governments have tried to cope with the problems brought about by urban sprawl, only a few succeeded due to the tradition of American free markets and the plight of collective actions by the urban and suburban areas.

Growth management is not equivalent to "growth restriction". On the contrary, it integrates economic, social and ecological goals. At the economic level, it means to build a bustling metropolitan area with a vibrant downtown. At the social level, it means to provide affordable housing and accessible public infrastructure with less social class isolation. At the ecological level, it means natural resource protection, little environmental impact and low carbon emission. Compared with the vicious cycle of urban expansion, growth management is committed to achieving a multi-dimensional virtuous cycle of sustainable development.

The Portland Metropolitan Region (PMR) in Oregon is one of the few metropolitan areas where urban sprawl is managed. As a medium-sized region, the PMR has made solid achievements in managing urban sprawl and making public transit systems accessible, housing affordable and downtown areas vibrant. What makes the PMR different from other metropolitan regions of Los Angeles, Detroit and other cities in the US? To answer the question, this chapter deals with the development of Portland's urban growth management system from the perspectives of politics, legislations, institutions, as well as the policies and programs developed by such institutions. To figure out how policies have been developed and implemented, we shall gain an insight into the legislatures and enforcement institutions, which are exactly part of what make Portland different from many other cities.

I. Introduction

Portland is a typical American city in many ways. Like most cities on the west coast of the US, Portland thrived in the mid-19th century thanks to trade. Adjoining the Pacific Ocean on its right and along the Willamette Valley on its left surrounded by mountains, Portland had a population of 583,776 (2010). Once an all-white city without racial segregation, Portland has become more accepting of ethnic diversity since the 1980s.

In the early days, Portland's economy relied heavily on agricultural and forestry products. During World War II, as the shipbuilding industry started to boom, people from the east flocked to Portland. The population of Portland increased from 17,000 in 1880 to 373,628 in 1950. After the war, just like most other American cities, Portland was also engulfed in the wave of urban sprawl. In the 1960s, downtown Portland was confronted with the challenges in parking space, public transit systems and retail business.

By the 1960s, the history of Portland had been similar to that of most other American cities. Today, however, this city is different from other cities both economically and politically. First, Portland is the only city in the US that has retained the city commission government. Constituted of five to seven officials, the city commission is endowed with legislative and executive power. At the beginning of the 20th century, such a form of government was very popular among American cities. While it has been replaced by the mayor-council government in other cities, it was voted through in Portland by a small margin at the beginning and has been retained to this day. Second, Portland was established relatively late. Thus, its industry heritage was weak, but it had more than agriculture and forestry. These differences, driven by the intentions of the city leadership and the opportunities at the time, set the stage for Portland's urban growth management policies.

As urban and environmental crises shot up amid surging political changes in the 1960s, the baby boom generation (the generation after World War II) began to challenge the conservative politicians of the older generation. A few politicians who supported environmentalism began to take power in Oregon, including Portland. In order to revitalize downtown Portland, three "green" political leaders — Neil Goldschmidt, the Mayor of Portland, Tom McCall, the Governor of Oregon and Glen Jackson, the Chair of the Oregon Transportation Commission — proposed the Downtown Plan in 1972 and used the Highway Trust Fund to build light rail. In 1973, Oregon passed the landmark legislation — "Oregon Land Conservation and Development Act". Based on this Act, Oregon's Land Conservation and Development Commission (LCDC) was established to manage the land use of the entire state in accordance with 19 planning objectives. According to the Act, an urban growth boundary (UGB) was set in an attempt to control urban sprawl. Established in 1978 as the result of the expansion of the Metropolitan Service District built in 1970, Metro is the first regional government for the Oregon portion of the Portland metropolitan area. LCDC, UGB and Metro are the three keywords defining the differences of urban growth management between the PMR and other metropolitan regions. Political and policy changes are illustrated in Figure 10.1.

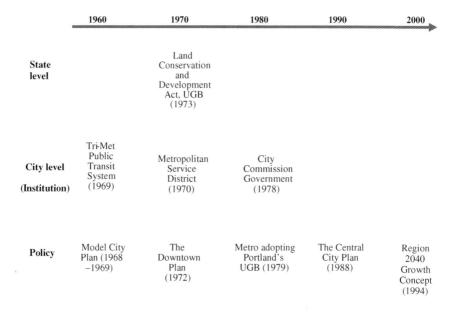

Figure 10.1. Portland's Politics and Policy Changes.

Portland's urban growth management policies were enacted based on the interests of social groups. These interest groups strove for political changes and pushed ahead with new legislation to create new institutions and procedures. To carry out the assigned tasks, these institutions have developed clear policies and projects to define land use in the metropolitan region. Therefore, to answer what makes PMR's urban growth management the way it is today, we need to understand how the management system has been established and the way it functions.

II. Politics, Institutions and Policies

(I) Political process

Covering several cities and autonomous areas, PMR's land policy involves participation at the local, regional and state levels. The land-use plan was first proposed by the state legislature. The interest groups and the political alliances organized by them promoted the state and regional legislation for PMR political management policies. The alliance between local economic growth promoters and environmentalists is a key feature of the politics of Oregon and PMR. In short, the two main sectors (agriculture and forestry) of the local economy — the urban residents who are concerned about the hollowing out of the city and the business community of the top three largest cities of PMR, along with environmentalists — jointly supported the enactment of the "Land Conservation and Development Act" so as to integrate their interests into the objectives of the whole state.

The smaller towns in the vicinity of PMR's top three largest cities, suburban developers, advocators for detached house and its ownership, and those who cannot bear the housing price increase within the UGB formed an opposing alliance but much weaker in power. Limited by the UGB, small towns were deprived of the opportunities for large-scale development. Some other organizations may benefit from suburban development, but they were limited in power. Moreover, the alliances supporting the urban growth management tried to reach a consensus with them.

Political alliances are found not only in state legislations but also in institutional policy development. The latter will be discussed in the following.

(II) Institutions

Two institutions play the most important role in the management of PMR's urban growth. At the state level, the main institution is Oregon's LCDC. Like the United States Environmental Protection Agency, LCDC was established through legislation. "Oregon's Land Conservation and Development Act" passed in 1973 gave birth to LCDC and defined its administrative duties. The Act sets out Oregon's land conservation and development goals and authorizes LCDC to manage land development and to achieve the goals. The 19 goals involve the conservation of forests, farmland and natural resources; sustainable use of land and mobilization of public participation. All counties and cities shall develop land-use plans on the basis of LCDC's standards. Therefore, LCDC plays an important interactional role in planning the use of land in the PMR and other places.

At the metropolitan region level, the main institution is Metro — the local government of PMR's part within Oregon. Managed by LCDC, Metro covers Oregon's three core counties in the PMR and is responsible for providing services and plans with regard to land use in the region in accordance with LCDC's standards. With the establishment of LCDC in 1973, Metro was established in a statewide vote in 1978. Metro is responsible for defining the UGB for PMR and implementing land management and planning. Land management involves waste disposal and a number of regional services related to public infrastructure. Metro performs its responsibilities in cooperation with Tri-Met and other public service agencies.

Metro has worked closely with LCDC on land-use planning and policy development. Their collaboration led to the enactment of urban growth management policies that brought drastic changes to PMR's urban development.

(III) Policies

The policies and projects related to the management of PMR's urban growth focus on transportation, central city planning and long-term planning tools.

1. Transportation

The drastic change in transportation policies in 1969 marked the beginning of Portland's urban growth management. Since then, urban growth management has become a major concern. In short, in accordance with PMR's transportation policies, the resources to be used to build highways would be reallocated to build public transit systems, such as light rail and bus transit. Figure 10.2 shows the timetable of PMR's transportation policies. It reveals how changes in politics and institutions have caused changes in transportation policies.

Tri-Met was established in 1969. Funded by the local government, it is the primary provider of public transit services in PMR. Having

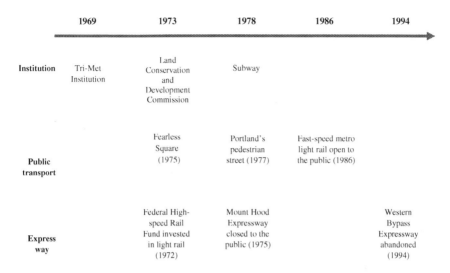

Figure 10.2. PMR's Transport Policy Changes.

taken over a private public transit company in bankruptcy, Tri-Met has renovated the public transit system for better accessibility and has built light rails. It aims to make the public transit system easily accessible in PMR's downtown by increasing parking lots and improving public transit services. As shown in Figure 10.2, Tri-Met has made it more convenient to use public transportation in PMR's downtown by building the "Fearless Square". Bus and light rail within the Fearless Square are provided for free. In addition, built in downtown Portland, the rapid transit system has the capacity to accommodate all buses traveling from the downtown to the main stations in PMR. In 1986, the first MAX light rail was put into use and new lines have been built thereafter.

PMR's transportation policies also deal with road construction. PMR believes that road construction is closely related to the urban sprawl. Therefore, it decided to limit new road projects that might disrupt local communities, natural resources or farmland. Most disputes over road construction occurred at state or interstate level, so PMR's government could not exercise full jurisdiction over such road construction projects. Therefore, it is required that institutional and political measures to be combined. In 1972, three political leaders who are environmentalist — Neil Goldschmidt, the Mayor of Portland, Tom McCall, the Governor of Oregon and Glen Jackson, the Chair of the Oregon Transportation Commission — made a joint decision to remove multi-lane expressways from Toronto's lake region so as to make space for parks to be built in the area. In addition, in the 1970s, PMR's government suspended the ongoing Mount Hood Expressway project, as it would disrupt many middle- and lower-class residential areas and had triggered fierce opposition among the local residents. In 1994, Oregon's Department of Transportation canceled the Western Bypass highway project. In PMR, resources were channeled from road construction to public transit infrastructure, making public transit system easily accessible in the downtown in a cost-effective manner and with low impact.

2. Downtown planning

The second focus closely related to PMR's urban growth management is the revitalization of PMR's downtown. If the downtown is neither useful nor beautiful in the eyes of the general public, it will not flourish even if the public transit system in the area is well established. Historically, an ideal city must have the infrastructure allowing different groups of people to communicate and exchange goods, services and ideas. A compact, multifunctional city is defined by Jane Jacobs as a vibrant one. Her definition is widely accepted around the world. Portland has embraced the idea that a city shall have multiple functions, a compact downtown and an accessible transport system. The idea has been implemented through strict downtown planning.

The downtown planning of Portland was first proposed by Neil Goldschmidt in the Downtown Plan in 1972 and adjusted in 1988 in accordance with the Central City Plan. The Downtown Plan constituted three parts, i.e. downtown planning, reconstruction of old residential areas and public transport. With regard to downtown planning, the stakeholders involved in the reconstruction of old residential areas are more diverse than those involved in public transport. This has also led to institutional innovation in urban planning, i.e. public participation on mutual voluntary basis and political alliance building.

Public participation and consensus building are nothing new. Few cities, however, were able to engage people in urban planning at that time. If urban planning failed to reach a consensus, numerous negotiations would be required. Public participation in the urban planning of PMR indicated that government influence could be effectively used to build political alliance or reach consensus.

First proposed by Neil Goldschmidt in 1972, the Downtown Plan aimed to maintain the appeal of the central metropolitan region despite the surging up of shopping malls in the suburbs and the impact of surrounding small cities. In addition to attracting people to the metropolitan region, it also satisfied the demands of different communities interested in the region.

The Downtown Plan covered downtown planning, reconstruction of old residential areas and public transport. The public participation mechanism plays a part in each of the three aspects. To increase the appeal of the downtown area, the new design included a waterfront park (rather than a highway project) and a corridor where retailers and office buildings are densely located. With regard to institutions, the Downtown Plan involves a review process for the downtown design in order to ensure public participation.

In accordance with the Downtown Plan, the old residential areas built between the 1880s and 1930s have been reconstructed. The public funds and private capital obtained through favorable policies allowed some old residential areas to be renovated. Reconstruction triggered opposition from local residents because it would cause their living costs to rise. By letting the elected residential committees participate in the negotiation, the government has managed to resolve its disagreement with the residents. Including the "well-behaved" lobbies into the decision-making group is a crucial step towards consensus based on shared interests in tough situations.

3. Long-term urban growth management tools

In addition to transportation reform and central city planning, long-term tools for urban growth management have also been used in PMR, including the UGBs and the Region 2040 Growth Concept which were proposed after the transportation and central city policies. Both were based on previous policy implementation and have been officialized in the land-use standards.

Three states in the US have UGBs, and Oregon is the first. As a policy tool, UGB aims to control unplanned land use and urban sprawl. Oregon's UGB was first introduced in 1973 in accordance with "Oregon's Land Conservation and Development Act" (LCDC was established based on this Act). To comply with the Act, the Columbia Region Association of Governments, known today as Metro, proposed the concept of the UGB for Portland in 1977. In 1978, Metro adopted the concept of UGB. In 1980, LCDC passed the UGB proposal. Since then, UGB has been expanded by 29,704 acres for additional housing and employment.

In accordance with Oregon's UGB standards, land is divided into four levels based on priority. Only after the land at a higher priority level is fully used can the land at a lower level be included into the UGBs. The four levels are reserved land, non-resource land, marginal land and farmland/woodland. Within the UGB, the burden of proof has been put on the opponents of land development. Outside the UGB, the burden of proof has been put on land developers. These developers are required to explain how to easily provide necessary services for their land and why their land has not been reserved as vacant lot or farmland. The UGB prepared for PMR serves as a land development principle for achieving the 19 urban growth management goals. In other words, UGB itself is not a planning process but an urban growth management tool for PMR development planning. Accordingly, UGB may be expanded in order to achieve new development goals.

To implement the PMR development plan, Metro began to design the "Region 2040" in an attempt to outline a framework for PMR development in the next 50 years. The PMR development framework was drafted in 1992. Not long before that, Metro had just expanded its power. The governments of the three counties and 24 cities/towns within the PMR were obliged to comply with the regulations on the division of regions based on Metro's overall planning. The draft provided four options for the development of PMR, i.e. baseline plan (not subject to LCDC's management or any planning), concept A (subject to LCDC's management but not to any planning), concept B (strong urbanization) and concept C (urbanization and satellite cities). In 1995, Metro adopted a compromised proposal between concepts B and C. This proposal involves using urban vacant lots to build multi-user dwellings, attached areas and downtown corridors, as well as to expand UGB. According to Region 2040, nearly half of the newcomers can settle in the downtown, corridor areas or on the main streets.

Whether Region 2040 can ensure PMR's sustained growth remains disputable. There are studies supporting both the positive and negative answers to the question. In any case, the consistence between the state goals, the regional development plan and the UGB prepared for specific land use is worthy of attention.

III. Conclusion

Portland is a typical American city that attempts to manage its urban growth. Like other American cities, Portland also faces urban sprawl and the problems arising therefrom, such as traffic congestion, pollution, the shrinking of green space and the hollowing out of the city. PMR attempted to control urban sprawl through a framework interconnecting the decision making at local, metropolitan region and state levels. The successful establishment of such a framework is attributed to legislation, institutional building and the establishment of efficient alliances suitable for the policy instruments. PMR's growth management system is comprehensive and consistent and the product of the system is worth analyzing.

The PMR government has made a choice between the two urban growth patterns. Following the pattern the government has chosen, the city would be developed into a compact, multifunctional one with easily accessible public transit system and multi-user dwellings. However, according to some studies, there is a price to pay for "artificial" compact cities. The rising land price within the UGB makes housing unaffordable to low-income families, thus forcing them to relocate from the downtown. Furthermore, the improvement of public transport has only contributed to a small reduction of the use of private cars, partly because the public transit system has not been so accessible to the degree that local people opt for it over private cars. In addition, growth management does not necessarily bring growth. Whether growth management will be successful depends on the integration of urban planning and real economy. It is now unclear whether PMR's growth management maintains its current goals and for how long, as the two growth patterns both have successful and unsuccessful cases.

The challenges faced by major cities in the developing world are quite different from those faced by Portland and other American cities. Cities in the developing world have higher density of population, so there is no need to attract people to the downtown areas. Besides, public transport systems are easily accessible. However, they also face increasing challenges in urban planning. For instance, urban planning and the renovation of old residential areas have gradually become normal in major cities of developing countries. The current decision-making process involves the unresolved conflicts of interests among various stakeholders. PMR's public participation mechanism provides valuable insight for making fair decisions with sufficient information. However, there is a lack of consistency between political process, institution building and policy outcomes in many cities of the developing world. Moreover, due to the lack of institutional and political support for urban planning in many cities, the effects of urban planning have fallen short of expectations.

Chapter 11

Urban Green Growth in Japan: The Case of Kitakyushu

Haibo Zhao[*] and Sho Haneda[†,‡]

[*]*China Construction Bank, Beijing, China*
[†]*The School of Economics, Nihon University, Tokyo, Japan*
[‡]*soh04ak775@gmail.com*

I. Introduction

Kitakyushu city has been facing a variety of issues such as the global crisis in 2008, the appreciation of yen and a big earthquake in Tohoku region in 2011. The city also faces depopulating society due to ageing population and higher international competition because of the growth of Asian countries and globalization of world economy. Furthermore, so as to achieve higher growth and increase the competitiveness of their industry, the city needs a new strategy that can boost economic growth and employment as well as improve the eco-system in the city.

Another aspect of Kitakyushu Green Growth project is to export its technologies and know-how to other Asian countries and cities. To do so, it is important to summarize strengths of the city regarding location, management system of waste disposal, the participation of citizens and so on. Furthermore, a variety of collaborations are essential for the success of exporting of these skills and experiences of Kitakyushu city.

The remainder of this chapter is as follows. Section II explains economic and environmental situations in Kitakyushu. Section III summarizes the Green Growth strategy regarding policies and technologies in the city. Section IV discusses the technology exporting to Asian cities and Section V concludes.

Kitakyushu city was selected by Organisation for Economic Co-operation and Development (OECD) as the city of Green Growth in 2013 (OECD 2013).[1] According to the OECD, "Green economic activities and growth can be identified primarily within three areas: recycling of residential and industrial waste, industrial energy efficiency and resource-efficient products, and emerging green technologies". So, this study is to explain the Green Growth strategy in Kitakyushu and to assess its impacts on the region. Furthermore, it will discuss the strategy of Kitakyushu regarding technology exporting to other Asian countries.

II. Economy and Environment in Kitakyushu

Kitakyushu is one of the largest cities in Kyushu region in terms of market size and the value of trade with Asian countries. The trade value of the Kitakyushu port is reported in Figure 11.1.

Although there was a huge reduction in both exports and imports in 2009 due to the financial crisis, Kitakyushu's trade volume has been gradually increasing. According to Kitakyushu Foreign Trade Association (2014),[3] top five trading countries for exporting are China, South Korea, Taiwan, US and Russia in 2013. For importing, the five largest countries are China, Russia, South Korea, Australia and Thailand in 2013. From the viewpoint of regional trade, trade values of the Kitakyushu port are dominated by ASEAN 10, China, South Korea, Taiwan and Hong Kong. Their share is 63% for exports and 56% for imports in 2013. This means that Kitakyushu city has been connecting with Asian countries through trade.

It should be noted that one of the aims of Kitakyushu Green Growth project is to increase the number of employments in the city. Although it is difficult to assess the impact of the scheme on job opportunities, it is still important to observe the condition of job applications in Kitakyushu. New job openings by industry are summarized in Table 11.1.

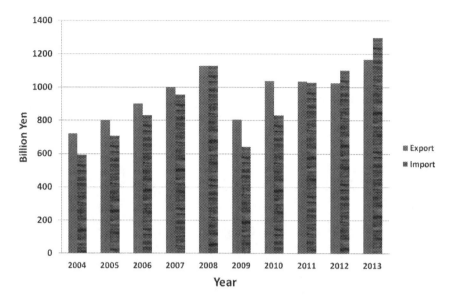

Figure 11.1. Trade Value of the Kitakyushu Port (Billion Yen).
Source: Kitakyushu Foreign Trade Association (2014).[3]

Basically, new job openings in Kitakyushu had reduced until the global crisis in 2009. After the event, this number has been gradually increasing. The top industry in 2013 is Medical and Welfare in the city, which implicitly reflects the aging population in Kitakyushu. The second industry in terms of the number of new job openings is service sector in 2013, and its number has been the largest until 2008. Again, in order to assess the effect of the Green Growth project, we need to have the number of new job openings relating to the scheme. Thus, it is useful for researchers to use those types of data on job opportunities in the city.

In the city, the amount of CO_2 emissions per person is below the average in Japan. CO_2 emissions in Kitakyushu is summarized in Table 11.2.

Although the total amount of CO_2 emission in this city has been increasing, its number in energy transformation and waste material sectors are quite low. This implies that the city can manage to produce energies with relatively low level of CO_2 emissions. The

Table 11.1. New Job Openings by Industry in Kitakyushu (Person).

Industry	Year								
	2005	2006	2007	2008	2009	2010	2011	2012	2013
Construction	7,889	9,120	7,417	6,064	3,939	4,990	5,384	5,362	5,243
Manufacturing	5,692	5,440	4,937	3,351	2,404	3,042	3,234	2,939	3,320
Information and communication	2,378	2,552	1,672	977	1,010	1,416	1,092	1,505	1,483
Traffic and postal service	6,623	6,265	6,266	5,172	4,660	6,349	5,777	4,534	3,971
Wholesale and retail trade	6,971	6,623	6,292	5,451	4,604	5,250	5,893	6,254	5,945
Lodging and food service industry	1,010	959	971	856	1,080	1,268	1,454	1,613	1,447
Medical and welfare	8,045	10,101	10,136	9,600	9,017	11,126	12,913	13,348	12,765
Service	20,006	20,698	18,622	8,368	6,993	8,535	9,298	9,564	10,377
Other	2,035	1,648	1,579	1,532	1,864	2,572	2,529	2,298	2,142
Total	60,649	63,406	57,892	41,371	35,571	44,548	47,574	47,417	46,693

Source: Kitakyushu City (2014).[2]

Table 11.2. CO_2 Emissions in Kitakyushu (1,000 tons).

	Year			
Classification	1990	2005	2010	2011
House holds	943	1,039	906	1,062
Operations division	669	1,186	1,364	1,690
Transportation	1,419	1,751	1,651	1,673
Industry	9,808	10,717	11,665	12,257
Energy transformation	347	246	336	379
Industry process	1,757	695	1,019	1,097
Waste material	252	542	364	389
Total	15,195	16,176	17,305	18,547

Source: Kitakyushu City (2011).[3]

increase in the total amount of CO_2 emissions can be explained by the big earthquake in Tohoku region in Japan and the shortage of electricity because of the disaster.

In this section, we have observed economic and environmental conditions in the city of Kitakyushu. The connections between Kitakyushu and Asian countries can be confirmed by trade data while we cannot find an obvious effect of the Green Growth project on employment so far because of the lack of data regarding job creations. The next section will discuss the strategy of Kitakyushu in terms of low-carbon energies, reuse of waste and waste water, and a variety of collaborations in the scheme.

III. Green Growth Strategy in Kitakyushu

(I) Low-carbon energies

After the big earthquake in Tohoku region in 2011, Tokyo Electric Power Co. (TEPCO) has raised the price of the electricity in Japan due to a shutdown of nuclear plants in Japan. The situation is the same in Kitakyushu, even though they were not hit by the disaster. Industries and firms in Kitakyushu have been harmed by these facts. Furthermore, policies relating to energies had been based on the decision of the central government of Japan before Kitakyushu started to design their policy in terms of energies in the region.

In order to supply low-carbon, low price and stable energies in Kitakyushu, the city has been trying to develop the hub for low-carbon energy and next-generation environmental recycling in this region.

One of the strong points of this region regarding those projects is that Hibikinada district has the port that can anchor a large-scale liquefied natural gas (LNG) tanker. Furthermore, the area is suitable for constructing electronic generating facilities. For instance, a wind condition in Hibikinada is of quite a high quality. Thus, there is a possibility for developing a wind-generated electricity facility on the ocean. For these reasons, it can be stated that Hibikinada has factors which are crucial for establishing power generation facilities. From the viewpoint of supply side, we can say this area is important for developing low-carbon societies in Kitakyushu.

However, there is another issue in terms of connections between suppliers and consumers in terms of electricity. Kitakyushu has started to promote the development of electronic generating facilities in Hibikinada in 2013 by establishing a joint working group organized by people from public administration, industry and academia. In addition, the group is divided into two groups, which are thermal power generation and wind-power generation on the ocean. According to the group, there are two issues in the agenda. First, there should be the management systems that can supply stable and cheaper energies to consumers such as companies and house holdings. Second, this system should be based on local firms in Kitakyushu in order to increase the employment in the region. The managing method is one of the key points in Kitakyushu Green Growth project. In order to achieve success in the project, the co-operation between Kitakyushu city, industry and firms should be considered carefully.

(II) Waste-to-energy and wastewater-to-energy technology (New Energy Foundation, 2010)[4]

In 2004, the weight of waste in Kitakyushu was about 168,000 tons including 59,000 tons of food scraps that were 35% of the total wastes in this region. In addition, the kitchen garbage contains 70% of moisture, which is quite problematic as we need large quantities

Urban Green Growth in Japan: The Case of Kitakyushu

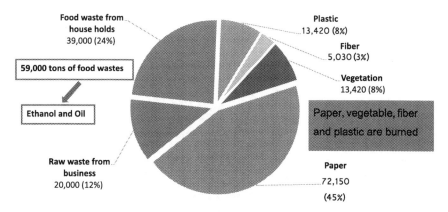

Figure 11.2. The Structure of General and Recycled Wastes in Kitakyushu.
Source: New Energy Foundation (2010).[4]

of energies to burn them. Figure 11.2 summarizes the structure of general and recycled wastes in Kitakyushu.

To solve the issue, Nippon Steel Engineering, which is now Nippon Steel and Sumikin Engineering, tried to reuse the waste to produce a fuel-ethanol. Their technology is based on three processes. First, they distinguish the waste that contains much moisture from other garbage. Second, this company produces ethanol and oil, which can be used as an alternative for Bunker A. Finally, residues that are emitted from those operations will be burned with other general wastes as usual. These skills can handle 10 tons of garbage per day and manufacture 379 kg of bioethanol and 660 kg of the oil. Using the technology in Kitakyushu, they might be able to produce 2,242 tons of ethanol per year from city's ethanol.

Because of the increase in a diffusion rate of sewer system, there has been the problem with polluted sludge. Again, to recycle the waste as the energy, Kitakyushu is trying to manufacture ethanol from the sewage sludge. Their plan is to reuse the water waste collected from Hiagari clarification center to produce fuels and to sell these energies to plants that have a coal boiler. The fuel manufactured from the sewage sludge is bio-energy, we can expect a large amount of CO_2 emission in this city.

(III) Harmonizations of many aspects in the green growth project

There is support for a business–academia collaboration regarding low-carbon energies in the city of Kitakyushu. This is monetarily supported by the Kitakyushu Foundation for the Advancement of Industry Science and Technology (FAIS). The grand funding is especially for the projects related to low-carbon technologies. However, it is difficult for small firms to conduct research and development (R&D), even if they obtain the subsidies. For this reason, Kitakyushu needs to reconsider the method to invite medium- and small-sized companies. To do so, Kitakyushu city should co-operate with other countries and cities. For example, in the United Kingdom, Knowledge Transfer Networks (KTN) has been organized so as to enhance the growth of green industry by sharing the information on R&D in the sector. According to OECD (2013),[1] 75% of firms stated that the service of KTN is effective and 50% of firms mentioned that they started to collaborate with other firms within KTN. Therefore, it is important for Kitakyushu to develop this type of networks in their region.

In the Kitakyushu Green Growth project, the participation of local people is one of the most crucial factors. Traditionally, citizens in the city of Kitakyushu have been participating in the environmental governance. Recently, Kitakyushu Clean-up Union, which is organized by 70% of local people, has been playing a key role in policy making. The organization is based on elderly people who are keen to transmit their experiences and know-how in terms of environmental issues to young people. Furthermore, people in Kitakyushu have been saving a green-point by using "Environmental Passport" and Kitakyushu Green Fund. From those systems, citizens can directly have an experience with environmental practices. Obviously, the people have had a vested interest regarding the Green Growth project. Thus, the collaboration between the government and citizens will be beneficial to both of them.

In this section, the Green Growth project in Kitakyushu has been explained. The city has many advantages such as location, technologies and local people for the success of the scheme. Nevertheless, its challenge is to export these skills and know-how to other countries and cities, especially in Asia. The next section intends to discuss this issue.

IV. Technology Exporting to Asian Cities

(I) Green growth business in Asian region

One of the aims of the Green Growth project in Kitakyushu is to target the demand in Asian countries and to export the city's technology to them. Although it is concerned that doing business in international markets might cause the hollowing out of the industry, it is also important for firms in Kitakyushu to obtain profits in other Asian counties. Furthermore, it is also essential to share their skills with other Asian cities as they might enhance the growth of Asian region regarding both environment and economic sectors.

The Kitakyushu Asian Centre for a Low-Carbon Society (KACLCS) has been discussing these strategies, especially in specific areas such as energy management, recycling and waste disposal, water business, and pollution control. They are planning to export their skills to Asian countries, e.g. Indonesia, India, Vietnam, Thailand and China. Their strong points are threefold. First, since the fact that Kitakyushu has solved problems with public disruption, the city has been seen as one of the most developed cities in terms of environment-related technologies in Japan. For this reason, the city can export their know-how regarding management systems of waste, water and energy to other Asian cities. Second, they have been supported by local and central governments. This means that these projects heavily rely on an additional policy and need supports from the government. Third, according to KACLCS, the Kitakyushu model is suitable for Asian cities. Since the model of Europe and the United States is based on zoning policies, it might not be able to fit Asian countries. These three points constitute the reason for the Kitakyushu model being appropriate for Asian region.

KACLCS states that we should think about the following points in order to export their technologies as infrastructure. First, the main player of this project is not a country, it is a city. Since this scheme is not based on the Central government, importing cities can easily enjoy advantages such as longer after care, direct access to related division of government of exporting city, etc. Second, in order to develop the environment industry in the importing city, the firms in exporting and importing cities need to co-operate with each other. To do so, the government should discuss the way to reduce barriers and promote Foreign Direct Investment (FDI) between countries.

The project has been the focus of many policy makers in Asian countries. For instance, Xi Jinping, Chinese President, visited the city of Kitakyushu in 2009. He mentioned that the Green Growth model of Kitakyushu is important for China as the city has experiences in terms of environmental protection and development of new technologies (*People's Daily*, 2009).[5] This implies that there is a possibility that Asian countries can co-operate each other, even as a country.

(II) Projects in Indonesia

The first project is the development plan of the management system of waste disposal in Surabaya city, Indonesia. Kitakyushu and Surabaya have signed an agreement, which is called Strategic Environmental Partnership, in 2009. Also, in 2012, they became a Green Sister City. Their project covers the areas such as disposal of waste, construction of sewage system, clarification of tap water, supply of drinking water and energy saving. This scheme is mainly organized by Nippon Steel and Sumikin Engineering and Fuji Electric Co., Ltd. and the expected value of investment is about 8.5 billion yen. Kitakyushu plans to establish a successful form for exporting their green technologies in Surabaya as well as use the model to export their skills to other Asian cities.

The Japan Council of Local Authorities for International Relations (CLAIR)[6] in Singapore states that the project has started to create local networks in terms of waste disposal and recycling system. In Surabaya, waste disposal system is organized as follows. First, waste material from house holdings are transferred to 170 intermediate operation points, which are called DEPO, and private firms cart all trashes from these spots to the final disposal station. In this city, waste pickers, who earn money by collecting wastes, play a key role in the process. There are about 30 waste pickers at each DEPO in Surabaya city, and their productivity is quite low as well as their working condition is poor. This project aims to develop waste collection and recycling system by employing those people, which can improve waste pickers' efficiency and condition of work. According to the calculation of KACLCS, the city of Surabaya can increase the amount of waste disposal, which is about 1,200 tons per day.

Nishihara Corporation forms a plan such that the company constructs a new type of DEPO, which can reduce 75% of total wastes in Surabaya city. Now, this company has started to employ the waste pickers to achieve their reduction target in terms of waste disposal. Additionally, TOTO Ltd. plans to introduce a water-saving equipment to Surabaya city in order to reduce CO_2 emissions. Diffusing the water-saving systems and promoting energy savings at sewage-disposal plant and filtration plant, the city can achieve the reduction of CO_2 emissions. So far, a variety of projects have been conducted by Kitakyushu and firms who have new technologies relating to environment and energy in Surabaya. However, they have just started to examine the effect of Green Growth projects on the economic and environmental conditions in this region.

(III) Projects in Vietnam and Thailand

In Vietnam, there is a similar type of Green Growth project, which is supported by Kitakyushu city. This project is based on two viewpoints. First, Green Growth is the most significant factor for sustainable economic development. Second, the reduction of CO_2 emissions and energy usage are crucial index for the development of economy. From these points of view, they institute 17 solutions regarding environmental and economic issues such as development of renewable energy, international co-operation, new rustic life model that is based on eco-system and so on. Kitakyushu and Haiphong cities in Vietnam have become sister cities in 2014. However, the last year of their projects is 2050, which means that we should recognize this scheme as a long-term work.

Japanese government has been helping Department of Industry Works (DIW), Ministry of Industry and Industrial Estate Authority in Thailand (IEAT) to construct an eco-industrial town in Rayong province. The main industry in the region is the heavy chemical industry, which implies that Kitakyushu can advise on the basis of their experiences. The key points are twofold. The first one is that plants should share energy in the town in order to decrease the loss of resources. The second one is that utility facilities should be operated by only one firm in order to unify the management systems. Combining both factors, this town can manage to improve their facilities in terms of electricity, heat power, waste disposal and sewage water.

Again, these projects are underway, which means that we need to observe their progress for a few decades. Furthermore, in order to increase the efficiency of Kitakyushu's Green Growth model and to expand its exports, feedback from importing countries and cities need to be sent to the city of Kitakyushu and the Japanese government. This may help Kitakyushu to develop a new green growth model that is specific to Asian countries and cities. In other words, Kitakyushu can contribute to the low-carbon energy society in Asia in the near future.

V. Conclusion

This chapter has discussed the Green Growth project in the city of Kitakyushu. After the big earthquake in Tohoku region in 2011, the environmental issues in Japan has changed rapidly and firms in Kitakyushu city face an unstable energy supply and the increase in the price of oil and gas. Now, it is the time for the local government to consider these problems, although the central government solved them so far. The city has already used a new technology that is planned and developed by Kitakyushu itself.

Kitakyushu is the city, which is famous for a coal quarry. For this reason, they tried to form a hub for the recycle of small electronic equipment, lithium-ion battery and solar battery in order to reuse rare metal and precious metal in the city. In addition, the town aims to become a stronghold of the next-generation environmental recycling in Asia. As part of the project, they have been trying to export technologies and know-how in terms of the Green Growth strategy to other Asian countries and cities.

In order for Kitakyushu to succeed, the city should rethink about a variety of collaborations in Japan, Asia and the world. First, there is a need for collecting the feedbacks from Asian cities regarding the impact of the Green Growth strategy of Kitakyushu so as to improve the project, which is the collaboration among Asian countries. Second, a harmonization of policies in terms of green growth and economy is needed for the success of the scheme. This implies that the project also needs to think about the collaboration between the local government and the central government. Third, although the Green Growth strategy of Kitakyushu is suitable for Asian cities, it is important to co-operate with non-Asian counties and organizations to develop better green growth approaches both for Kitakyushu and Asia. Finally, even though Kitakyushu has been conducting the Green Growth project, the effect of the task might not be obvious so far. Thus, it should be noted that we need to conduct further research on the Green Growth project in order to create a better society in the Asian region.

References

1. OECD, *Green Growth in Kitakyushu*, OECD, Japan, 2013.
2. Kitakyushu City, *Employment in Kitakyushu City*, Kitakyushu City, 2014.
3. Kitakyushu City, *CO_2 Emissions in Kitakyushu*, Kitakyushu City, 2011.
4. New Energy Foundation, *Producing Bio-ethanol from Waste Disposal*, New Energy Foundation, 2010.
5. *People's Daily*, 17 December 2009.
6. The Japan Council of Local Authorities for International Relations (CLAIR), A report on the Green Growth Project of Kitakyushu City in Surabaya City, CLAIR, Singapore, 2013.

Chapter 12

Malaysia Urban Green Development: A Case Study of Penang

Stuart MacDonald[*,‡] and Tong Yee Siong[†]

Penang Institute, Pinang, Malaysia

†*Centre of Development Studies, University of Cambridge, Cambridge, UK*

‡*stuart.mcdonald.mp@parliament.uk*

I. Introduction

A city state located in north-western Peninsular Malaysia, Penang, is the second smallest by land area among all 13 Malaysian states. It is divided into two parts — Penang Island and Seberang Perai on the mainland — which are separated by the Penang Channel. Seberang Perai is bordered by Kedah in the east and Perak in the south. With a land area that is about 1.5 times the size of Singapore, Penang has an urbanization rate of 90.5%.

Penang has long been integrated into the global economic structure, enjoys a fair degree of economic specialization and has a substantial population size. This is evident from various existing city rankings and comparisons (Table 12.1). For instance, the Globalization and World Cities (GaWC) Research Network in its 2012 ranking of cities considers Penang a "sufficiency-level city" which provides sufficient services, serves as a traditional center of manufacturing regions, and is not overtly dependent on world

Table 12.1. Penang and Selected Asian Cities at a Glance.

	Shanghai (China)	Hangzhou (China)	Xiamen (China)	Ulsan (South Korea)	Penang (Malaysia)	Zhuhai (China)	Patna (India)	Taichung (Taiwan, China)	Pekan Baru (Indonesia)
MGI classification (2011)[a]	Megacity	Large middleweight city	Midsize middleweight city	Small middleweight city	Small middleweight city	Small middleweight city	Small middleweight city	Small middleweight city	Small middleweight city
GaWC classification (2012)[b]	Alpha+ city	High sufficiency level city	Sufficiency level city	—	Sufficiency level city	—	—	—	—
Population, '000 (2010)	22,315	6,242	3,531	1,083	1,563	1,560	2,009	2,279	898
Population, '000 (2025)[c]	30,905	8,830	5,294	1,122	2,142	2,199	2,597	2,306	1,523
Total GDP, $ billion (2010)	251	71	30	49	18	18	7	43	39
Total GDP, $ billion (2025)[c]	1,112	307	180	89	41	67	31	80	32
Per capita GDP, $ '000 (2010)	19	19	15	65	20	20	8	36	16
Per capita GDP, $ '000 (2025)[c]	46	44	43	104	31	39	22	60	32

[a]MGI defines a large middleweight city as a metropolitan area with a population between 5 and 10 million, midsize middleweight city with a population between 2 and 5 million, and small middleweight city with a population between 150,000 and 2 million. A megacity is populated by 10 million people or more.

[b]GaWC divides cities into six categories: (1) "alpha++ cities", which constitute their own high level of integration (London and New York); (2) "alpha+ cities", which complement London and New York and fill in advanced service needs for the Asia Pacific region (such as Hong Kong, Paris, Singapore, Tokyo and Shanghai); (3) "alpha" and "alpha–cities", which are very important world cities in linking major economic regions and states into the world economy (such as Moscow, Brussels, Kuala Lumpur, Jakarta, Taipei, Seoul, San Francisco, Bangkok and New Delhi); (4) "beta-level cities" that are instrumental in linking their region or state into the world economy (such as Guangzhou, Bangalore, Copenhagen, Berlin, Ho Chi Minh City and Seattle); (5) "gamma-level cities" linking smaller regions or states into the world economy (such as Osaka, Tampa, Bristol, Glasgow and Tianjin) and (6) "sufficiency-level cities" (such as Chengdu, Nagoya, Wellington, Kaoshiung, Wuhan and Penang).

[c]Projections by MGI.

cities.[a] Similarly, McKinsey Global Institute (MGI) sees Penang as a "small middleweight city" alongside the likes of Ulsan, Zhuhai and Taichung.

Penang is the leader in electrical and electronic (E&E) manufacturing activities and a key growth center for Malaysia. From its early days as a British East India Company trading port, Penang has evolved into an export-oriented economy. Throughout the 1970s and 1980s, Penang set up industrial and free trade zones offering attractive fiscal incentives to Western manufacturers in the E&E sector as part of its industrialization strategy, developing the "Silicon Valley of the East". As a result, over 200 leading multinational corporations now operate in a mature E&E sector, which works closely with a universe of local firms of varying sizes and capabilities.

Capitalizing on its rich cultural heritage, historic value and scenic natural environment, Penang rapidly developed the necessary infrastructure and facilities to make tourism another key growth engine. With one of the largest collections of pre-war architecture in South East Asia, George Town, the capital of Penang, was declared as a United Nations Educational, Scientific and Cultural Organisation (UNESCO) World Heritage Site in 2008.

Penang has achieved impressive economic gains. Its gross domestic product (GDP) grew at an average of above 7% annually between 1970 and 2005, ahead of the national average. Despite being the second smallest state by land area, Penang is the second wealthiest (excluding federal territories) as measured by GDP per capita, after Sarawak, which has rich hydrocarbon and other natural resources.[1]

Economic growth and social transformation in Penang have improved the lives of many. However, rapid urbanization has also produced urban planning and governance challenges to the future livability and sustainability of Penang. Amid intensifying

---

[a] Arguing that the world of flows and competition is more city-centered than state-centered, GaWC measures cities in terms of their advanced producer services in accountancy, advertising, banking/finance and legal services, and their connectivity in the world city network. See The World According to GaWC project at http://www.lboro.ac.uk/gawc/gawcworlds.html.

regional competition for manufacturing investments, Penang has actively sought to develop higher-order functions and shift toward a knowledge-based and innovation-driven economy. This transformation cannot be achieved without the right human capital and talent, who are increasingly mobile and often prioritize where they want to live over where they want to work.[2] Therefore, livability and sustainability are key to the future economic development of Penang.

This case study examines the five thematic areas of livability and sustainability, which are most pertinent for Penang. These are: (1) physical planning, (2) transportation, (3) housing, (4) public spaces and (5) environment. For each thematic area, the existing challenges and issues faced in Penang are briefly highlighted. Key initiatives undertaken by the current Penang State Government since 2008 when it came to power are discussed. This is followed by an outline of the most significant strategies and initiatives proposed in the Penang Paradigm, a 10-year development framework adopted by the Penang State Government in February 2013. Improving livability and sustainability is one of the three inter-related objectives of the framework (the other two being restoring economic dynamism to Penang and promoting social development and inclusion).

II. Physical Planning

Historically, Penang's development planning has focused overwhelmingly on its industrial strategy. During Penang's rapid industrialization, planning for a "livable city" was not a high priority, leading to an *ad hoc* planning and mitigation approach. The emphasis was on exploring new land away from urban areas, leading to urban sprawl. Penang's population is projected to reach between 2 and 2.2 million by 2030 which will lead to increasing competition for space and higher development pressures on limited land.

The Penang State Government has in recent years encouraged greater public participation in the development planning process. Public hearings are held where planning consultants and government representatives are present to answer public queries and concerns. Plans have been developed for each of the districts on the mainland and special area plans have been produced for specific locations such as the George Town World Heritage Site.

The land-use planning and the built environment that are put in place today will be among the most important deciding factors in the future economic sustainability of Penang. The vision for Penang going forward is one where its economic potential and livability are developed simultaneously and to their fullest extent. In addition to being a prosperous place with opportunities for all, Penang should be a place where the local environment is clean and cared for — a place which is safe and characterized by accessible and affordable housing, efficient transportation systems, support for living culture and heritage, and access to the many natural features that Penang has to offer. Attendance to this "place making" should be based on Penang's unique local characteristics, it culture and its natural history.

(I) Improving the physical planning system

In order to plan effectively, institutional capacity must be strengthened. The Penang State Government will seek to develop planning experience and expertise through training and recruitment in order to institutionalize effective sustainable development policies and practices. This will also require a full and detailed review of all development control standards and guidelines, many of which have not been reviewed in years. Given the small size of Penang, which consists of only two local authority areas, significant efficiencies and scale economies may be achieved by integrating physical planning system at the state level while leaving the processing of planning applications and enforcement to local authorities. Existing planning structures and bodies should attempt to institutionalize greater participation of local residents and civil society. A Statement of Community Involvement, for example, should set out the processes for community participation and engagement from the very start.

(II) Managing growth sustainably

The Penang State Government will need to work to address the disparity between development on the island, where development pressures are high, and the mainland, which is currently much less developed. Development strategies for the island and the mainland should be integrated and complementary; land-use and transportation planning must be closely aligned. By encouraging live–work–play neighborhoods, the Penang State Government can create new mixed-use developments with a diversity of housing typologies, commercial facilities and employment opportunities to address current mismatches in the locations in which people live and work. Density should be aligned with public transport planning. This can be promoted through incentive-based zoning approaches, which offer a reward (usually in the form of reduced fees or increased density) to developers who do something extra that serves the community's interest or promotes a public goal.

(III)   Enhancing the built environment

In 2012, the Penang State Government set up the George Town Business Improvement District (George Town BID) to redevelop George Town's central shopping district through a business-led partnership. The BID model, the first to be established in Asia, is being recommended for other areas including Batu Ferringhi (a tourist beach area) and Bayan Lepas (the main industrial area) to pursue improvements in the pursue realm. Given scarce land resources, the Penang State Government, through strategies of urban regeneration and renewal, needs to further promote and incentivize redevelopment of areas that have become run down and no longer function in the way they were originally intended. This will prioritize adaptive reuse of existing urban land over high-impact development in less-developed sites. The extensive waterfronts along each side of the Penang Channel need to be revitalized and envisioned as one integrated space, which serves as a means of connection between the island and the mainland.

III.   Transportation

With more private vehicles than people,[b] Penang suffers from worsening traffic congestion. Public transport service frequency remains

---

[b]Road Transport Department data from 2009 stated that there were about 1.75 million motor vehicles in Penang, compared to an adult population of approximately 1 million.

low. Current routes are dominated by services from outlying areas into the urban centers, with few services between outlying areas. The use of ferry traversing the Penang Channel has been in decline and the service currently operates at a loss. Pedestrian access is often poor and unsafe. Penang's residents and visitors thus have few transportation options. If the trend continues, by 2030, the total number of vehicle miles on Penang's roads will increase by over 70%, average speeds at morning peak hour traffic will slow down by approximately 25%, and public transport will remain at just 3.8% of all journeys (see Footnote b).

Since 2008, the Penang State Government has set up a free Central Area Transit (CAT) bus shuttle service in George Town and the Bridge Express Shuttle Transit (BEST) park-and-ride service to bring people from the mainland to the island. Recreational cycle lanes are being developed for the island and the mainland. A bike share scheme is due to launch in 2015 and a weekly car-free zone has been established in central George Town.

The Penang State Government has also set up the Penang Transport Council with civil society involvement. A Transport Master Plan for Penang, developed jointly with the Northern Corridor Implementation Agency (NCIA), has recommended transportation improvements valued at RM27 billion, including RM15.3 billion worth of road improvements and RM9.6 billion worth of public transport improvements. In 2014, the Penang State Government issued a request for proposal (RFP) based on the recommendations of the Master Plan for implementation between 2015 and 2030.

The vision for Penang's transportation system is one that enables people to travel efficiently and safely based on the principle of "Moving People, Not Cars". Transport policy will aim to increase mobility across a range of different modes, and resources will be rebalanced to address the needs of pedestrians, cyclists, the elderly and disabled public transport users as well as private vehicle users.[3] A holistically planned public transport system is expected to increase economic efficiency and productivity, reduce negative environmental impacts and improve the quality of life in Penang.

(I) Rationalizing transport governance and management

In order to provide efficient and safe transport systems in Penang, there is first a need to streamline the governance structures that are overly complicated. For instance, four separate agencies — the Department of Works at the Federal level, the Department of Works at the State level, the Malaysian Highway Authority and the Penang Island Municipal Council — are responsible for roads on Penang Island, each with its own maintenance and funding mechanisms. The Penang State Governments needs to work with the Federal Government to decentralize power to the local level. A joint Federal–State–Local transport coordinating body for road improvements as well as rail, ferry, water taxi, bus and taxi services — with the ability to adjust fares for toll roads and bridges based on local conditions — should be considered.

(II) Building new strategic road links

Following the Transport Master Plan, the Penang State Government has commenced feasibility studies and design works in preparation for the construction of several new strategic road links that seek to connect the districts on the mainland and improve their connections to Penang Island. Creating a road hierarchy for planning and enforcement is critical. Specific rules need to be set for each type of road. Some roads will be prioritized for the rapid movement of vehicles, while others will cater to transportation of goods for businesses or shared space with pedestrian and cycle access. All roads will need clear rules and indications as to whether parking, waiting and loading will be allowed or restricted.

(III) Improving public transport

With an overall bus fleet of around 350, Penang has only one bus per 7,000 of population (compared to Singapore's 4,000 buses, or one bus per 1,325 of population). A move toward a "hub and spoke" integrated services model (with bus routes designed to connect local communities with transport "hubs" and main routes) will promote greater access to the public transport network. Smaller neighborhood shuttle buses can be utilized to bring people to the main hubs and existing larger buses can be allocated to the main routes. In the long term, a Bus Rapid Transit (BRT) and ultimately a tram system should be developed. Feasibility studies have begun, which can support an operational system by 2020. Through the introduction of dedicated travel corridors, travel times will shorten, giving public transport a competitive advantage over private vehicles. The recent double tracking of the rail network will halve the travel time from Penang to Kuala Lumpur to just 3 hours by June 2015. With the tracks completed, an extension of commuter rail services within Penang should be considered. The Penang Channel also needs to be better utilized for transportation, especially for moving people between the island and the mainland.

(IV) Improving pedestrian and cycling facilities

A lack of good pedestrian access to public transport creates a barrier to greater use of the service. All network designs, infrastructure building and future development must be built to a common design standard based on the Universal Design principles and disabled-access standards in order to take into account the needs of disabled and elderly commuters. For cyclists, the Penang Bicycle Lane Master Plan, which includes a total of 200 km of bicycle lanes for both the island and mainland, will be built in different phases. The ambition is to increase the number of cyclists in Penang from 5% in 2012 to 15% by 2015, promoting a healthy lifestyle and an alternative transportation mode.

IV. Housing

The housing market in Penang faces dual challenges: a lack of affordable property for middle-income groups and poor housing quality for lower-income groups. New housing launches increasingly cater for the rich and are skewing the supply of housing toward investment properties for the wealthy. A significant mismatch between supply and demand is evident, with not enough affordable property to local middle income groups.[c] Between 2004 and 2012,[d] the mean household income increased at an annual rate of 5.4%, while the average house price increased by 8.6% per year.[4] House prices are clearly rising faster than incomes, opening up a growing affordability gap.[5]

Existing low-cost and subsequent low-medium-cost housing policies inherited from the past impose development quotas on private development and have ensured a steady supply of housing for low-income households. But these policies are no longer sufficient because many low-cost housing units are poorly constructed, poorly maintained and inappropriately located.

Since 2008, 15,000 affordable housing units have been completed, and 20,000 more are planned in all five districts of Penang. Some 300 existing private units have been converted into social rented housing, and several abandoned housing developments have been revived. The Penang State Government has established a RM500 million affordable housing fund and has also introduced incentive-based policies, allowing increased density (87 units per acre) and reduced development charges in exchange for more affordable housing.

Penang has a vision of housing that is "Affordable for All". This requires a mixture of quality housing options distributed over a range of price levels and across locations suited to the needs and aspirations of the local population, while also supporting the needs of incoming migrants and investors.

(I) Improving housing governance

Establishing a State Housing Board or alternative governance structure is critical. Housing falls under the concurrent jurisdiction of the Federal and State Governments. The Penang State Government needs to explore how it can work with the Federal Government

---

[c]Properties priced at between RM130,000 and RM400,000.

[d]Household Income Survey, Department of Statistics, 2004 and 2012. The next survey is scheduled for 2015.

to deliver locally responsive housing solutions. These solutions include a broader range of housing requirement models as well as new standards for affordable housing by considering the economic, environmental and social factors affecting housing quality. The needs of the target groups for affordable housing (e.g. young professionals versus older adults) need to be clearly defined. Intervention is needed in housing management and maintenance. Greater support should be provided to develop an efficient, cost-effective and competent building management sector to ensure that buildings do not fall into disrepair, leading to reduced quality of life for all inhabitants.

(II)   Steering private development

The Penang State Government needs to remove the disincentives to the construction of affordable housing. This can be achieved by imposing a gross-plot-ratio ceiling on all residential properties in order to limit the size of new luxury residential developments. Residential density limits (units per acre) can be increased to allow more affordable units to be built. Penang needs to revise its current low-cost housing quotas, moving from a quota based on a percentage of units to a financial contribution based on the gross development value (GDV) of a real estate project (excluding the value of units that meet affordable-housing criteria). The system of development charges should also be revised. At present, development charges (a tax on the enhancement in land value created by density that is permitted above the development baseline) are calculated at a fixed rate per square foot and are not linked in any way to the price per square foot of the land. While this allows for simplicity in calculation, development charges should be linked to the enhancement in land value created, calculated as a percentage of GDV.

(III)   Increasing access to housing

Due to rising house prices and tightening of mortgage regulations, lower- and middle-income households face reduced borrowing capacity and are increasingly stretched by new deposit requirements. To assist these households, existing processes of applying for housing support should first be tightened to ensure that those allocated subsidized units are eligible and that the support given is appropriate for their needs. The Penang State Government should acknowledge the scale of sub-letting within the low-cost housing sector and proactively develop structures to facilitate a social rented market. Over time, greater conditions can be imposed to allow for the development of a private (long-term) affordable rented sector, in which landlords are regulated, and deposits and tenancies protected. Flexible rent-to-buy models, through which households can accumulate resources through long term rentals to facilitate an eventual move into home ownership, can be developed as an alternative path to home ownership. For those with greater resources but still priced out of the market, shared-ownership schemes are being piloted. This alternative financing model, where the Penang State Government will buy up to 30% of the property, can help low- and middle-income households gain a foot on the property ladder.

V. Public Spaces

Public spaces play a vital role in the social and economic life of communities. Penang, however, has a severe deficit of public space. According to the Penang State Structure Plan 2005–2020, public spaces totaled 449.4 hectares, equivalent to just 0.29 hectares per 1,000 population in 2010 as opposed to the Structure Plan's proposed 1.6 hectares per 1,000 population. The Malaysian Town and Country Planning Department recommends a provision of public spaces between 2.4 and 2.8 hectares per 1,000 population. There is thus an estimated shortfall of 1,000 hectares of public space for Penang Island and approximately 1,300 hectares for the mainland.[6] Since the 1980s, the lack of public space has been identified by various studies as an issue to be addressed.[7]

The Penang State Government has created a new public square at the top of Penang Hill and is developing new recreational cycle-paths and urban parks. It has also encouraged the rehabilitation of idle sites into recreational parks.

Penang's vision is to be a place where the public realm is shared by all and is clean, green and safe to enjoy. Penang's urban streetscapes and open spaces will encourage social vibrancy, promote walking, cycling and other healthy recreational activities, and be fully accessible to the elderly and disabled users. Penang's children and youth will have adequate and safe places to play and to engage in sporting activities. Its hills, beaches, rivers and parks will be connected and open for all to enjoy.

(I) Increasing the quantity and quality of public space

Penang should enhance existing spaces and create new spaces which are accessible, secured, connected, well-managed and well-maintained. Part of this will involve allocating new land for public open space. The Penang State Government needs to ensure that new public spaces feature heavily in any future land reclamation projects. A focus should be placed on converting empty and underused properties and spaces for public use. The gardens of public properties should be opened to visitors. Empty private land can be leased and turned into temporary playing fields or parks, while run-down municipal properties that have outlived their purposes can be redeveloped as community spaces.

(II) Improving accessibility and connectivity

Adopting Universal Design principles will help make the built environment both aesthetic and useable to the greatest extent possible to everyone. This can improve access for the elderly and disabled. Such principles should be embedded in all public realm improvements to ensure the creation of barrier-free, inclusive environments that encourage walking and cycling and improve connectivity and access to public transport. Investing in pedestrian and cycle infrastructure to link green spaces, river reserves, forest reserves, mangrove parks, linear coastal parks and waterfronts can create an interconnected network of public spaces that also serve as safe routes for recreational or transportation purposes. Penang can better utilize its shorelines, beaches and any remaining undeveloped land adjacent to coastal areas for public recreational spaces. The Penang State Government should also encourage both private and public institutions to open up their facilities (such as football fields, swimming pools, basketball courts and others) for public use at off-peak times, providing subsidies to cover additional maintenance costs incurred.

(III) Managing and maintaining open spaces

The iconic Penang Hill has seen significant investments to support growing numbers of tourists and visitors under a Special Area Plan. However, future development on the hill needs to be carefully balanced to ensure that its historical and ecological functions are protected. There is an opportunity to expand the Penang Botanic Gardens which skirt the base of the Penang Hill into a conservation and research center for Peninsular Malaysia. Penang needs to improve its enforcement processes and procedures to protect open spaces, ranging from pocket parks to waterfront areas, from misuse and encroachment by private users. Petty traders and street hawkers operating in recreational spaces should either be relocated or provided with designated spaces with adequate provision for hygiene and waste disposal.

VI. Environment

Once known as the "Pearl of the Orient" for its beautiful natural landscape of hills, forests and beaches, Penang's rapid development over the last half century has taken the shine off the "Pearl". Inadequate sewerage infrastructure, poor control of commercial waste disposal and primitive treatment of domestic waste have resulted in Penang having among the worst quality rivers and seas in Malaysia. In 2011, 10 out of 24 rivers in Penang were classified as polluted, with many containing industrial effluents.[8]

Public cleanliness remains an issue, and environmental awareness among Penang citizens is low. Due to limited land, development has been pushed further uphill and into the sea. This calls for environmentally sustainable solutions to hill slope development and coastal reclamation.

Since 2008, the Penang State Government has developed the "Cleaner, Greener, Safer and Healthier Penang" initiative as a central plank of state policy. Penang was the first Malaysian state to ban the giving out of free plastic bags in supermarkets. Local authorities have banned the use of polystyrene in licensed food operations. As of 2014, Penang has reached a recycling rate of 32.8%, well above the national target of 20% by 2020. Penang has set up the Penang Green Council to explore green initiatives. A new environmentally friendly solid-waste management system is being developed, with increased recycling and food-waste collection for bio-fuel and bio-fertilizer.

Together, the State Drainage and Irrigation Department and local authorities are working to rehabilitate rivers classified as Class IV (very dirty) under Malaysia's water quality index, with the aim of turning them into Class II (clean) rivers by 2020. In May 2014, the Penang State Government signed a multi-million ringgit contract to deploy an innovative quantum physics-based technology for cleaning Sungai Pinang (the main river in Penang) and its tributaries.

The vision is for Penang to become an eco-city where green lifestyles are the norm, and commercial activities coexist with nature in a sustainable manner. Penang's future sustainability requires the protection of its natural eco-systems, preservation of its biological and geological diversity, development in harmony with rural and natural areas, creation of quality urban and rural environments, and a high degree of environmental consciousness among its people and businesses.

(I) Improving environmental management

Penang should develop a state-wide Environmental Management System (EMS) to monitor environmental data in a systematic manner. The EMS can be used for evaluating the effectiveness of existing strategies and assess progress. Urban growth policies should be complemented by green-reserve policies that create protected tracts of natural habitat. The Penang State Government should plan and develop a system of national parks, state parks, marine parks, wildlife sanctuaries, bird sanctuaries, conservation areas and protected landscapes to help preserve Penang's natural heritage.

(II) Tackling waste and pollution

Penang's famous food and catering businesses are a key source of water pollution. Waste oils are improperly discharged into storm drains or sewers. Public hygiene can be improved through food-waste and used-oil collection systems, with on-site separation, collection and composting facilities encouraging proper disposal. If putrescible residual waste from households and large food-waste generators as well as animal waste from farms can be separated at source and collected, a bio-gas facility to generate electricity or other types of energy becomes feasible.

Effective pre-treatment of municipal solid waste can reduce the waste to be transferred to landfill by up to 70%. This can reduce costs of waste transportation and cut the resulting vehicle emissions. It can also significantly extend the life of the landfill site, reduce its gas generation, and generate additional value from waste.

Restoring the waterways requires significant efforts and investments to redirect commercial and industrial wastewater to proper sewerage treatment facilities. Multinational corporations should be held accountable for their entire supply chain. The Penang State Government can work with multinational corporations to establish an Environmental Business Service to help local firms better manage their pollutants and waste through improved business processes.

(III) Facing up to climate change

An environmental disaster control and mitigation plan should be developed to focus minds on the potential impact of climate change. By preventing the destruction of hill forests and water catchment areas as well as restricting hill slope cutting, soil erosion and river siltation, the worsening problems of urban flooding can be mitigated. Penang should look to protect its agricultural lands from sprawling urban development to encourage a degree of self-sustainability. Urban farming should also be promoted through allotments and the provision of spaces for rooftop farming or even micro-farming on balconies. Food waste turned into liquid fertilizers can be used in urban farming at a community level and can in turn develop greater awareness of the health impacts of diet.

Due to the abundance of rainfall in Malaysia, water is often taken for granted. Penang has the lowest water tariff for domestic consumption in the country — and among the lowest in the world. It is essential that water tariffs be restructured to reflect true costs, which includes capital investment on water-treatment facilities, operational costs of water production and water resource protection costs. A target of 20% reduction in per capita domestic water consumption should be set for 2020 to ensure Penang's future water supply is sustainable.

VII. Conclusion

Penang is striving to become a green city, with various greening efforts to tackle legacy problems and to plan for a more sustainable future set in motion. Some early results are encouraging, but a systematic and institutionalized approach is needed to deepen the gains for years to come. This requires effective governance, in which the Penang State Government has an instrumental role to play, and a suitable long-term policy framework for aligning the actions of private sector actors and society to the targeted goals and objectives.

National-level support in the form of sufficient resources, firm political commitment, competence in planning and execution at the various levels of the Penang State Government, support from the private sector as well as public acceptance count among the key success factors for achieving the goals and objectives. The ability to demonstrate positive results and their benefits to society, which is predicated upon on a transparent and credible communication platform, will reinforce these factors. On the flip side, risk factors must not be underestimated, especially in the form of resistance to change among organized interests as well as misaligned political views between the Federal and State Governments. The extent to which the Penang State Government can secure the success factors while containing the risks will directly determine the outcome of the Penang Paradigm and the attendant consequences on Penang's livability and sustainability.

References

1. Department of Statistics, Malaysia, *GDP by State 2005–2013*, The Office of Chief Statistician, Malaysia, 2014.
2. H. Kharas, A. Zeufack and H. Majeed, *Cities, People & the Economy — A Study on Repositioning Penang*, Khazanah Nasional Berhad, 2010.
3. State Secretary's Office, *The Recommended Transport Master Plan Strategy*, Penang, 2012.
4. National Property Information Centre, *Property Transaction Report*, 2004–2012.
5. Department of Statistics Malaysia, *Household Income Survey*, 2004 and 2009.
6. Y.K. Leong, *Towards a Sustainable Penang: A Report for the Penang Blueprint of SERI*, 2010.
7. Through various studies such as the Penang Environmental Conservation Strategy, Penang's first and second Strategic Development Plans.
8. Department of Environment, *Malaysia Environmental Quality Report*, Malaysia, 2011.

Chapter 13

Seoul's Experience and Inspiration from the Governance of Cheonggyecheon

Zheng Zhao

Researcher, Development Research Center
of the State Council of PRC
zz_bnu@126.com

Cheonggyecheon is a 10.84-km-long stream that runs through downtown Seoul, South Korea, with a total basin area of 59.83 square kilometers. With the rapid economic growth of Seoul in the 1850s and 1860s, Cheonggyecheon was once covered into a culvert and built into a main avenue of the city. Its water quality was severely degraded due to the discharge of industrial and domestic wastewater. Traffic congestion, noise pollution, etc. became prominent "urban diseases". Launched by the Seoul Metropolitan Government on 1 July 2003 and completed in 2005, the Cheonggyecheon Restoration Project led to the creation of a modern urban stream. This has not only improved the production and living environment for the residents in Seoul but also promoted the city image as an international green city where people and water coexist harmoniously. Moreover, it serves as good practice and provides reference for other countries in the governance of urban water environment.

I. Innovative Governance of Urban Inland Rivers

How to conduct urban river governance is a question concerning many policy makers. Before the Restoration Project started,

Cheonggyecheon had been covered by concrete paved road (50–80 m wide and 6 km long). A two-way, four-lane elevated road (16 m wide and 5.8 km long) had been built over the road and 32 types of underground pipes, such as sewer and water pipes, had been laid under it. The road and pipes served as Seoul's main artery and sewer system. Pollutions caused by sewage discharge, noise, dust and traffic congestion had become rather prominent. Restoration and renovation became imperative. Through the Cheonggyecheon Restoration Project, the elevated and the paved roads have been removed and the underground waterway has been restored to a new, natural urban stream divided into three segments: upper, middle and lower reaches. Cheonggyecheon Square is at the center of the upper reaches, surrounded by fountains and high-end office buildings. The middle reaches are mostly covered by plantations and leisure areas, serving as a modern public recreational space for tourists and local residents. The lower reaches are mostly wetland, highlighting natural sceneries. Generally, Cheonggyecheon forms an ecological urban water system that conveys the urban image and natural landscape. It has reshaped the urban image of Seoul as an environmentally friendly city where people and water coexist. Also, it has greatly reduced pollutions and improved the environment. The once covered Cheonggyecheon focused on economic efficiency and benefits. The Cheonggyecheon Restoration Project has explored new ways and methods to restore urban rivers, allowing the focus of urban development to shift from construction to restoration and from the sole pursuit of economic growth to the harmony between human and nature.

II. Inclusive Participation

The restored Cheonggyecheon is the result of joint efforts of the government, experts and citizens. At the beginning of the restoration project, Seoul Metropolitan Government set up a Cheonggyecheon Restoration Project center and a special committee of experts and ordinary citizens, responsible for collecting public opinions, convening public hearings and providing consulting services. In the Cheonggyecheon Restoration Project, the removal of the elevated and paved roads, as well as the restoration of cultural and historical relics along the stream are the results of collective intelligence of experts, the public and the government. It is particularly noteworthy that the interests of businesses in the area have been taken into full account before the Cheonggyecheon Restoration Project began. Prior to the project, the government held about 4,000 meetings in the form of project briefing, consultation and interview to collect opinions from local businesses. Based on these opinions, measures for facilitating the development of business areas have been adopted, such as reducing noise and dust through advanced construction methods; reducing parking and cargo handling charges; providing low-interest loans to small businesses in need; and developing business streets for those who intend to relocate. Respect and public participation have paved the way for the successful implementation of the Cheonggyecheon Restoration Project, which has not been hindered by conflicts of interests among various parties.

III. Integrated Renovation of Water and Transport

Before the Cheonggyecheon Restoration Project started, the average number of vehicles passing through Cheonggyecheon road and Cheonggyecheon elevated road was 168,556 per day in 2002. Many citizens had concerns that demolishing the elevated road would worsen Seoul's already severe traffic congestion. In fact, Cheonggyecheon Restoration Project had not only taken the ecological benefits brought by water management to the city into consideration but also was aimed to drive forward the development of urban public transport through water management. It was designed to shift the focus of traffic control from easing traffic flow to encouraging people to walk and use public transport. By establishing an advanced management center for public transit information in the Cheonggyecheon area, building roads suitable for pedestrians and business operations, increasing circulating bus lines, improving the underground transport capacity and centralizing commercial service facilities, the Seoul Metropolitan Government has provided local citizens with easily accessible public transportation without driving private cars or walking long distances. Through integrated governance of water and transport environment, the government has successfully shifted the focus of urban transport from vehicle to people orientation.

IV. Urban Fabrics Interwoven by Ancient Bridges

Flowing across the downtown of Seoul, Cheonggyecheon is an important river course that bridged the northern and southern parts of the city since ancient times. It is also a typical urban cultural site witnessing the daily lives of local people before World War II. The bridges over Cheonggyecheon are key embodiments of Seoul's urban culture and history. A total of nine bridges, including Guangtong Bridge, Changtong Bridge and Shuibiao Bridge, have been built over Cheonggyecheon during the past 600 years. Historically, activities such as walking on stilts and lantern festivals were held on these bridges at certain times of the year. Therefore, bridge construction was included as an important part of the Cheonggyecheon Restoration Project. As a result, Guangtong Bridge and Shuibiao Bridge have been restored. Sixteen vehicular bridges and four pedestrian bridges have been newly constructed and named after ancient ones such as Changtong Bridge and Yongdu Bridge. Traditional activities such as walking on stilts and lantern festivals have made a comeback to the Shuibiao Bridge. While demolishing the overpasses, three piers in the lower reaches were preserved on purpose. Therefore, a complete memory of Seoul can be enshrined by the city and its people today. The project allows citizens and tourists to echo with the urban spirit of Seoul. Moreover, history, water culture and modern civilization of the city are blended in Cheonggyecheon and the urban fabrics are extended in the reconstruction of inland rivers.

V. City Revitalization through Concentrated Investments

The Cheonggyecheon Restoration Project covers a length of 5.84 km and involves the restoration of 22 bridges and construction of 10 fountains, a square and a cultural center, with a total investment of around 380 billion KRW (or US$360 million). Considering the limited sources for fund raising, the Seoul Metropolitan Government reduced its annual budget. Despite the huge amount of initial investment, the short-term, concentrated investments have shown the stimulation effects on the long-term economic growth. For example, the previous Cheonggyecheon area had more than 60,000 shops and roadside stands primarily engaged in low-end wholesale and retail service. Upon completion of the Cheonggyecheon restoration project, the area has become a center of art, commerce, leisure and entertainment in South Korea. International finance, cultural and creative industries, fashion design, tourism, leisure and other high value-added industries have settled in the area, which has greatly accelerated the upgrading of industries. This has not only boosted the development momentum and vitality of the area but also laid a solid foundation for a balanced development between the south and north of Cheonggyecheon. Furthermore, the restored Cheonggyecheon has significantly improved the atmospheric environment and air quality of the city. After completion of the project, the average temperature of Cheonggyecheon's surrounding area is 2–3°C lower than the average temperature of Seoul, which makes Cheonggyecheon a livable area. In addition, the project has also enhanced the competitiveness, influence and attractiveness of Seoul as an international metropolis to draw high-end talents, innovation resources and global investments to the city.

VI. Inspirations

The Cheonggyecheon Restoration Project in Seoul can be used as a good model for the governance of water environment in modern cities. From the perspective of long-term sustainable urban development, the project is more than restoring a river course. It also represents a brand new philosophy. Through finding a balance between preservation and development, transforming the development pattern and respecting public wishes, an eco-friendly urban river area featuring economic vitality, profound history and cultural heritage where man and nature coexist harmoniously can be created while maintaining the charm of a traditional downtown. In China, during rapid urbanization over the past 30 years, many cities have pursued fast economic growth at the expense of water pollution. Such a pattern of economic growth has already brought us high price to pay. Some cities have made huge endeavors to build road infrastructure and widen lanes at the cost of turning rivers into land, disrupting green belt and building artificial wetlands and parks. However, instead of mitigating traffic congestions and improving the environment, such endeavors have led to serious waste of resources and energy. Moreover, the living quality of urban residents has not been fundamentally improved. In the new era, Chinese cities shall learn from the experience of Cheonggyecheon Restoration Project in Seoul in order to fully utilize the accumulated economic wealth and to develop a new philosophy for people-oriented urban development. To this end, Chinese cities shall combine water management with urban governance, transport system construction and historical and cultural preservation. In addition, they shall also integrate economic development with ecological conservation and combine modern urban life with environmental protection in order to develop into eco-friendly, livable, green cities where human and nature coexist harmoniously while progressing toward green urbanization.

Acknowledgments

This chapter is one of the studies that results from the South Korea Green Growth Investigation and Research Group of Beijing Normal University. Support from the following organizations is appreciated: Seoul National University, Korea Environment Corporation, Seoul Landfill Management Commune, Global Green Growth Institute (GGGI), Korea Development Institute (KDI), Samsung Electronics Co., Ltd. and Gyeonggi Urban Commune.

Chapter 14

Taiwan China: A Green City Underpinned by YouBike

Chin-Hsien Yu[*,‡] and Chin-Hsiu Ting[†]

Institute of Development, Southwestern University of Finance and Economics, Chengdu, Sichuan, China
†*Department of Public Economics,*
Xiamen University, Xiamen, Fujian, China
‡*d918404@oz.nthu.edu.tw*

According to a report of the International Energy Agency (IEA), Taiwan's total carbon dioxide emissions per year increased by about 140% from 114.59 million tons in 1990 to 274.93 million tons in 2007. Since the Kyoto Protocol, the international community has repeatedly discussed the responsibilities of different countries to reduce greenhouse gas emissions. While Taiwan is not a contracting state to the "United Nations Framework Convention on Climate Change" (UNFCCC), it approved the "Framework Policy of Sustainable Energy" on 5 June 2008 in the hope of improving energy efficiency, developing clean energy and ensuring stable energy supply. The annual carbon dioxide emission of Taiwan, on average, was 260.85 million tons during 2008–2012. The carbon dioxide emission was 256.61 million tons in 2012, equivalent to the level in 2004. This has demonstrated considerable achievements in emission reduction.

To reduce carbon dioxide emissions, the government of Taiwan has taken the initiative to develop policies for energy conservation

243

and emission reduction. In 2009, it launched the "Energy Conservation and Emission Reduction Plan". With regard to the improvement of energy efficiency and the optimization of energy mix, the government aims to make the power generated by renewable energy sources and by low-carbon natural gas account for 8% and 25%, respectively, of the general power system. It encourages industries to be high value-added, energy-efficient and green. Moreover, it strives to develop Taiwan into a low-carbon green province through the following measures: increasing the coverage of green plantations; promoting green buildings; reducing construction waste; increasing the use of recycled materials in public works; and developing low-carbon transport such as encouraging the use of alternative fuels or green transportation. There are three action plans for developing low-carbon transport: (1) building an easily accessible public transit network to prevent the increase of automobiles and to reduce the usage; (2) establishing an "intelligent transportation system" to strengthen traffic control and (3) creating an urban transport system dominated by green transportation (bike and pedestrian road/street) and oriented by people. These plans serve as guidance for the green development of cities in Taiwan. For instance, the plans promote the establishment of low-carbon or carbon-free green transport systems. Taipei's public bike rental system "YouBike" introduced in this chapter facilitates Taipei's efforts to become a low-carbon and green city.

In fact, Taiwan is not the birthplace of public bike rental concept, which has long been implemented in many European cities, such as Paris, Barcelona, Copenhagen and London. In Asia, Tokyo piloted the public bike rental program in 2009; by 2012, a total of nine public bike rental systems had been established in Japan. In May 2008, a bike-sharing system was established in Hangzhou, China. Learning from Paris, Taiwan piloted the public bike rental program in Taipei, New Taipei City and Kaohsiung in 2009[a] Taipei's public

---

[a]New Taipei City (previously Taipei County) is the first city in Taiwan that launched the manual rental of public bikes and started using the YouBike system in 2013. Kaohsiung is the second city that launched the automatic rental of public bikes, which has been operated by Kaohsiung Rapid Transit Corporation since 2011 and known as "CityBike".

bike rental system "YouBike" was put into trial in 2009 and then into official operation in 2012. By the end of 2012, the bikes rented were only slightly over 1 million man-times. However, the number exceeded 10, 20 and 30 million by the end of 2013, mid-2014, and the end of 2014, respectively. Moreover, the number of bike rental stations increased from 11 in 2009 to 163 in July 2014; and the number of bikes increased to 5,350 in July 2014, with the average turnover rate as high as 10–12 per day. This was about twice the turnover rate in Paris and almost the highest worldwide. It has been introduced to other cities in Taiwan such as New Taipei City, Taichung and Changhua. It also serves as an ideal model of green transportation for other international cities like Tokyo and Singapore. Compared to Japan and some European countries, Taipei's biking environment needs to be improved. For instance, while the total length of bike lanes in Taipei reached 323 km in 2013, most of them were shared by bikers and motor vehicles. In addition, Taipei's government failed to mobilize local people to travel by bike in the first three years since YouBike was launched. Since 2013, however, public bikes in Taipei have been rented for over 30 million man-times. How did YouBike catch on across Taiwan in two years?

Taipei has both the largest population and the most intensive motor vehicle usage in Taiwan. This has caused a lot of problems, such as traffic congestion, disrupted cityscape and air pollution. In recent decades, Taipei has made strong efforts to build public transit systems, such as Taipei Mass Rapid Transit (MRT), bus lanes and underground railways. These systems were designed to cut the use of motor vehicles in Taipei, so as to reduce energy use and carbon dioxide emissions. However, neither buses nor MRT stations could fully satisfy the demand of local citizens. Therefore, following the philosophy of targeting at the "the first and last mile to travel" and relying on the advantages as a world renowned bicycle brand, Giant, the operator of YouBike, has established and operated YouBike through the Build–Operate–Transfer (BOT). YouBike has been the only public bike rental system in the world operated by a bicycle operator.

In 2013, the annual turnover of Giant Manufacturing Co. Ltd. ("Giant" for short) reached 54.4 billion TWD. The company not only has manufacturing sites in the Netherlands, Mainland China and Taiwan China but also sales network in Europe, America, Asia and Australia. Therefore, Giant has drawn upon the experience from other countries in promoting and marketing bike rental systems and has analyzed the strengths and weaknesses of public bikes in different cities, so as to improve the design and supporting services of YouBike. The manufacturing cost of YouBike is nearly 10,000 TWD per unit. Every part of the body was carefully designed. It has the following distinctive features: tires similar to those of mountain bikes; three-phase variable speed systems commonly used in professional road bikes; covered chains; rear mudguards; adjustable seats; down tubes designed for easy bestriding; anti-rust and anti-theft functions; and distinctive appearance. All these make YouBike user-friendly and desirable.

In addition to well-designed bikes, YouBike's rental system is also super simple and user friendly. Once becoming a member of YouBike, you can rent by using credit card or EasyCard within a second. Even foreign tourists can rent a bike by using credit card through simple steps. In addition, with regard to the issue of bike shortage as complained the most by bike-sharing users in Paris, YouBike has set up a 24/7 bike coordination team to monitor bike usage through the central control center and to fill in or remove bikes in different stations based on the actual demand. This aims to ensure that the use of the bikes at every station is maximized, which has resulted in the average turnover rate as high as 10–12 per day.

YouBike not only provides the last-mile public transportation service but also promotes the idea of life experience, sports and leisure, which further enhances the influence of YouBike. YouBike rental stations are not only installed in the vicinity of MRT stations, major bus stations and residential quarters but also constructed in well-known tourist resorts such as Taipei Fine Arts Museum, Taipei Confucius Temple, Lin An Tai Historical House, Huashan Creative Park and Raohe Night Market, which not only solves the problem of traffic congestion and shortage of parking spaces but also helps with the construction of green city by improving the transportation and utilizing low-carbon and carbon-free green transportation. In addition, the Taipei City Government has constructed many bikeways for sightseeing and leisure purposes, which makes it possible for citizens and tourists without private bicycles to enjoy carbon-free trips by using YouBike rental service.

Even though the carbon emission reduction effect of YouBike has not yet been evidenced by official statistical data, YouBike's contribution in reducing the carbon emission for Taipei City remains to be substantial. For example, the YouBike rental service has been used for about 11 million times in the urban district of Taipei City in 2013, which contributed to a trip distance of about 11 million kilometers assuming that the average trip distance is calculated as 1 km. On this basis, the carbon emission reduction is equivalent to 6.89 million metric tons of carbon emissions generated by motorcycles and 27 million metric tons of carbon emissions generated by automobiles.

To some extent, public bicycles are quasi-public goods. Quasi-public goods, with characteristics of being non-rivalrous and non-excludable during the consumption process, fall in between public and private goods. Most countries will provide users with a free ride within different time limits when promoting the public bike system. For example, bicycle riders in Paris can enjoy a half-an-hour free ride; users in Copenhagen can insert a 20-krone coin into the hole on the block chain and get it back when the bicycle is returned; and in Hangzhou, people can use the public bike for free for 1 hour. Taipei City provides a 30-minute free ride service combining with a cascade rate system. After the first 30-minute, users are required to pay 10 TWD for every 30-minute ride within 4 hours, 20 TWD for every 30-minute after 4 hours and within 8 hours, and 40 TWD for every 30-minute after 8 hours. The 30-minute free ride service can encourage the public to use public bikes, while the cascade rate system can discourage users from not returning rented bikes by increasing the rental cost and thus effectively control the flow of public bikes.

The success of YouBike in Taipei City can be attributed to its concept and operation model. YouBike is the first and only public bike rental system operated by the bicycle operator — Giant Bicycles — under the BOT model in the world. Under the BOT model, Giant Bicycles, rather than the local government, is delegated to "build" the rental system, which effectively resolves the financing issue in public construction and relieves the financial pressure for the government. Then, the public bike rental system is "operated" by the private enterprise — Giant Bicycles, which contributes to a more economic and efficient allocation of public service. Furthermore, after the system improves and becomes mature, the assets and management right will be "transferred" to the government. The BOT model gives full play to the operation and management capacity of enterprises as well as the supervision and regulatory right of the government, thus achieving win–win outcomes. The YouBike project, with a total budget of 260 million TWD, has been jointly developed by Taipei City Government and Giant Bicycles under a 7-year contract. Giant Bicycles shall pay 15% of the annual operating revenue as royalty to Taipei City Government when the annual operating revenue of YouBike reaches 70 million TWD. According to statistical data provided by the Department of Transportation of Taipei City Government, the total operating revenue of YouBike was about 120 million TWD in 2013 and 18.59 million TWD was paid to Taipei City Government as royalty, which further evidenced the significant business performance of YouBike.

In addition, YouBike offers comprehensive and consumer-oriented supporting services and facilities. Firstly, a 24-hour customer service hotline is provided to handle various problems such as lost and found and abnormalities in renting and returning bicycles. Secondly, database management and software design of micro-program company have been used to analyze the utilization rate of bicycles rapidly, contributing to highly efficient allocation of bikes and reasonable selection of rental stations. Thirdly, a suitable service system has been designed to better meet consumer demands. For example, information of rental stations is provided timely to users anytime, anywhere; EasyCard has been introduced to create more convenient user experience. Fourthly, data collected by a micro-program company are utilized by the coordination team to provide round-the-clock coordination service to ensure that users can rent/return a bike within 10 minutes when there are no available bikes/spaces. Lastly, flexible rental and returning system allows users to rent in one place and return in another.

Along with the trend of global warming, green economy and sustainable development have received keen attention. The focus of transportation evaluation has shifted from the minimization of travel time and travel cost to the achievement of sustainable environmental and social development under existing economic budget. When it comes to the transportation sector, low-carbon or carbon-free green transportation means such as electric, hybrid and biofuel vehicles, and bicycles have become the preferred choice. The important role of public bicycles in developing green city and green transportation has been gradually recognized and valued by the society. The promotion of public bikes helps to alleviate traffic congestion in densely populated Asian countries. What's more, replacing motor vehicles with bicycles can reduce air pollution caused by exhaust gases to some extent, thus reducing the usage and dependency on conventional energies. YouBike has been successfully promoted in Taiwan through the concept of providing the first-and-last mile transportation service between home and public stations, which has effectively compensated the shortage of buses and MRT, alleviated traffic congestion, reduced CO_2 emissions, and promoted greener and healthier lifestyle. YouBike has also won the popularity and recognition of Taipei citizens and tourists through high-end equipment, simple registration and user experience, convenient rental and returning service, and affordable price. In the meantime, the combination of YouBike and cultural elements has facilitated the development of bike touring, which further promoted green tourism. The perception and attitude of consumers toward green city and green transportation will be changed gradually with the popularization of public bikes. Bicycles will not only be more than a green vehicle but also a way for city touring, which enables the public to explore and enjoy the place where they work and live intensively. To conclude, the promotion of YouBike will make bicycles indispensable for the green lifestyle in Taipei City.

Chapter 15

Hong Kong's Inspiring Severe Weather Pre-warning and Response Mechanism for Beijing

Chia-Kuan Han

Hong Kong General Chamber of Commerce, Hong Kong, China
hjgcuhk@gmail.com

In recent years, the air quality in Beijing has become increasingly worse due to rapid economic growth, urban sprawl and population explosion. Consequentially, the frequency of smog and haze weather in Beijing has increased significantly. What's more, Beijing is located in the high-prevalence area of sand storms, and the global climate change has also increased the frequency of extreme weather conditions such as strong wind, ice and snow, rainstorm, thunder and lightning. Influences brought by natural disasters related to those severe weather conditions on the economic growth, social development and city image of Beijing have aroused wide concern, which should not be underestimated.

Therefore, it is necessary and of practical significance to draw inspiration from Hong Kong's No. 8 Tropical Cyclone Warning System in order to develop the pre-warning mechanism for natural disasters, such as hazy weather for Beijing. The pre-warning and response system for severe weather conditions such as the tropical cyclone and rainstorm, its characteristics and successful practices in Hong Kong will be analyzed in this chapter in order to provide references for Beijing to formulate the pre-warning and response mechanism for natural disasters such as the haze weather.

I. Hong Kong's Severe Weather Pre-warning and Response Mechanism

Hong Kong is a subtropical coastal city which frequently suffers from severe weather conditions such as tropical cyclone, storm surge, extraordinary rainstorm and thunderstorm. These severe weather conditions will affect transportation and other social services seriously, and cause floods, landslips and other accidents, which may result in casualties and property losses. After long-term explorations, Hong Kong has established an effective urban management mode to cope with natural disasters effectively.

(I) Pre-warning system of Hong Kong observatory

Hong Kong Observatory is responsible for monitoring weather conditions closely, giving relevant warnings, specifying when and where the severe weather will occur, and clarifying its duration and estimated influences. Hong Kong Observatory started to issue "tropical cyclone warnings" or "typhoon warnings" since the 1970s. This warning system, also known as the "wind-ball warning system", classifies typhoons into five grades including No. 1, No. 3, No. 8, No. 9 and No. 10 in accordance with the wind strength, wind direction and distance between the typhoon and Hong Kong. In recent years, Hong Kong Observatory has also strengthened the warning of rainstorm, flood, landslip, thunderstorm and season wind. Rainstorm warning signals are classified into yellow, red and black ones according to main indicators such as rainfall to indicate the ascending order of severity.

Hong Kong Observatory also issues air pollution index on a daily basis. As influences of air quality are far less than that of natural disasters, relevant reports are simply released for the public to know about health risks. Although advices will be provided by Hong Kong Observatory as per different pollution levels, no substantial actions will be adopted in a general way.

(II) Alarm spreading and overall planning

The weather warnings of Hong Kong will be sent to all government departments, relevant institutions and the public in a timely and orderly manner through a sound and efficient comprehensive alert system. Each time when tropical cyclone, rainstorm or landslip warning signals come into effect, Hong Kong Observatory will send brief weather warnings to the media and relevant government departments hourly through Information Services Department, and will fax the brief warnings to emergency service departments, including Emergency Monitoring and Support Center, Command and Control Center of Police Headquarters, Fire Control Communication Center and Airport Authority of Hong Kong.

Information Services Department, Security Bureau/Emergency Monitoring and Support Center, Hong Kong Police Force, Fire Services Department, Transport Department, Marine Department, Airport Authority Hong Kong, Hong Kong Telecom and other institutions will then release the warnings using the established channels and ways according to the scope of responsibilities. For example, the Government Information System of Information Services Department will inform most government departments and all television and radio stations of the warnings; Transport Department will inform the bus, ferryboat, cable car and tunnel service companies by phone or fax; and Marine Department will inform the wharfs, shipyards and docks, etc. by phone and fax. In addition, the Home Affairs Department is responsible for handling with public inquiries, Information Services Department for dealing with mass media and Police Public Relations Bureau for coping with matters about actions (e.g. traffic accidents, traffic congestion, traffic diversion and road closure).

Once weather warnings are received, relevant government departments and institutions will take necessary actions in accordance with the "Natural Disaster Contingency Plan" and their detailed work instructions. For example, if a typhoon signal No. 3 or above is sent, Social Welfare Department should decide whether the social welfare institutions under its jurisdiction, including baby farms, sheltered workshops, elderly care centers, disabled child training centers and disabled social and recreational centers should be closed and when these institutions should be closed. Education Bureau should decide and announce through Information Services Department whether kindergartens, schools for mental retarded children and other schools should be closed and when these schools should be closed according to "Arrangements for Red/Black Rainstorm Warning Signals or Typhoon Signals in Force". In addition, Labor Department has formulated "Work Arrangements in Case of Typhoon and Rainstorm Warnings" to provide guidance for workshops in bad weather for enterprises and employees in Hong Kong. Highways Department should be prepared to coordinate and handle emergency projects to keep the road network unblocked according to "Arrangements for Public Road Emergencies".

(III) Natural disaster contingency plan

The Hong Kong SAR Government has a three-level Emergency Response System designed to deal with emergencies at different levels. Based on this system, the authority makes concrete contingency plans against some special accidents of important categories, stating clearly corresponding emergency response procedures and responsibilities of relevant departments. One of the examples is the "Natural Disaster Contingency Plan" made by Security Bureau for severe weather events.

It is worth mentioning that when designing the Emergency Response System, the Hong Kong SAR Government emphasizes abiding by the response policy from the bottom to the top and simplifying response actions in many ways, including restricting the number of related departments and institutions, reducing the connection levels in the emergency response system and granting necessary powers and responsibilities to relevant personnel at the emergency site, so as to take the fastest and most efficient measures for the scale and severity of events.

Hong Kong's response mechanism to bad weather mainly follows the "Natural Disaster Contingency Plan", which specifies the warnings and response action schemes in case of tropical cyclone, rainstorms, floods and other natural disasters in details and clearly state the functions of relevant responsible authorities, responsibilities of government departments and relevant non-government institutions in response to different degrees and stages of severe weathers. Besides, the Plan describes the aforementioned forecast, warning and reporting mechanism meticulously, states the operational procedures of the comprehensive alarm system and the involving institutions clearly and lists the standardized samples of various warning messages from Hong Kong Observatory and relevant departments.

According to the "Natural Disaster Contingency Plan", certain bureau or department will be appointed as "major coordinator" as required in the three stages of the emergency response system, i.e. rescue stage, rehabilitation stage and recovery stage. The major coordinator is responsible for supervising the actions of various bureaus and departments comprehensively and releasing the latest news at regular time with the help of Information Services Department, to enable citizens to know the emergency measures taken by the authorities and the progress. For example, the goal in rescue stage is to save lives, protect property, control related situations or accidents and avoid the deterioration of the situation; the rescue operation should be carried out under the direction of Fire Services Department, Hong Kong Police Force and other emergency service teams with the help of other departments and institutions. The goal in the rehabilitation stage is to recover the society to acceptable state and the key is to address the physiological, psychological and social needs of citizens; in this stage, Home Affairs Department will become the major coordinator and cooperator with Social Welfare Department, Housing Department and other departments as needed. In the recovery stage, there are many long-term maintenance works, and the departments involved in this stage are works departments mainly as well as some other departments, such as Home Affairs Department, Highways Department and Housing Department.

Besides, the "Natural Disaster Contingency Plan" also states that the Emergency Monitoring and Support Center led by the Security Bureau shall enter into operation when Hong Kong Observatory releases tropical cyclone warning signals No. 8 or above, black rainstorm warning signals or tsunami warnings. However, the center is not responsible for directing or coordinating the work of various departments but mainly for monitoring and providing liaison and necessary support for other departments.

II. Characteristics and Successful Experiences of Hong Kong's Natural Disaster Emergency Response Mechanism

(I) The alarm system features distinctive "visual management" well recognized by the public

Hong Kong Observatory has designed a set of iconic signs for different levels of typhoon, rainstorm, landslip, season wind, thunderstorm and other weather warnings. For example, a black triangle with number "8" means strong gale or storm wind No. 8 and the "NW", "SW" or other brief and clear words in Chinese or English under the sign indicate the direction of the typhoon. These signs will be displayed in a fixed position in TVs and hanged at the entrance of major public service institutions and even private estates.

The images are easy to understand and remember. This "visual management" model enables citizens to keep up to date with important information rapidly and accurately and facilitates the organizations releasing alarms to change the weather signs timely according to the instructions of Hong Kong Observatory, which helps to enhance the efficiency and penetration of alarm transmission.

(II) The alarm content focuses on predictability and facilitates all departments and institutions to respond as early as possible, which helps to prevent disasters and relieve the sudden pressure on service sectors

With improvements in weather-monitoring technology, when abnormal weather occurs, Hong Kong Observatory will increase the frequency of weather reporting and release the following forecast as far as possible, such as "Hong Kong Observatory will hoist typhoon signal No. 8 in two hours" and "The typhoon signal No. 8 will be hoisted throughout the morning", and will inform citizens of matters needing attention for disaster prevention.

These forecast information can allow emergency departments, public transportation agencies, industrial and commercial enterprises and the citizens to respond as early as possible and make preparations in advance to nip in the bud; especially, it can help reduce the sudden pressure on the transportation, supermarkets, restaurants and other service industries caused by the sudden surge in the movement of people. For example, the collective transportation system in Hong Kong must meet the public transport demand of 3.72 million working population, 0.98 million school population and the general public. So the forecast of changing trend of abnormal weather in advance can not only facilitate the subway, buses, minibuses, ships, trams and other transportation business operators to arrange the schedule but can also enable citizens to make travel arrangement according to their needs, thereby easing the flow and reducing blockage.

(III) The alarm system uses partitioned data to improve accuracy and meet citizens' demands

By establishing monitoring stations in different areas of Hong Kong, Hong Kong Observatory can record various weather data to reflect weather differences between different places due to topography, location and other factors. For example, Hong Kong Observatory has extended the reference range of typhoon signals No. 3 and No. 8 from Victoria Harbor to the network consisting of eight reference anemometer stations close to sea level and covering all harbors in Hong Kong since 2007. Also, it has strengthened the release of wind data in different areas. In addition to being a consideration factor for early warning rating, the partitioned weather data can provide more accurate, complete and practical reference data for the citizens.

(IV) Alarms are communicated at all levels, with good division of work, standardized materials and high transparency, reported to leadership and known to lower levels

In addition to Hong Kong Observatory, Hong Kong Information Services Department, Security Bureau, Hong Kong Police Force, Fire

Services Department, Transport Department, Marine Department, Airport Authority Hong Kong, Hong Kong Telecom and other institutions will release weather warnings in accordance with given procedures, forming a comprehensive alarm system network with good division of work and high coverage. The information released by Hong Kong Observatory and relevant departments must refer to standardized samples. By doing so, quick response can be achieved, risks of information inconsistency or even information disorder in different departments can be reduced and the information and content can be better grasped and understood.

In addition, one of the responsibilities of Emergency Monitoring and Support Center is to report to senior government officials in a timely manner. Meanwhile, television, radio and other mass media play an important role in the comprehensive warning system network. The government's contingency plan attaches great importance to the citizens' right to know and allows Information Services Department to set up an independent channel to issue messages to the public, so as to maintain high transparency and reassure the public to cooperate.

(V) Standardized regulations have been established and guidelines are provided to the public to ensure orderly operation of social activities

The responsibilities and contingency procedures of relevant government and public service departments under various abnormal weather conditions are specified in the "Natural Disaster Contingency Plan". Meanwhile, the Hong Kong Government has also set up standardized operating regulations and specific guidelines for the public in some key areas. For example, the *Work Arrangements under Typhoon and Rainstorm Warning* by Labor Department, *Arrangements for Red/Black Rainstorm Warning Signals or Typhoon Signals in Force* by Education Bureau, *Emergency Engineering Arrangements for Public Roads* by Highways Department and the *Work Arrangements of Emergency Traffic Coordination Center* by Transport Department. The regulations and operational guidelines in these key areas standardize the operation of public services in abnormal weather conditions, and also allow people from different walks of life to have rules to follow, which can help maintain order in social activities.

(VI) The response system offers reasonable division of labor, streamlined procedures and ensured efficiency

The Hong Kong SAR Government's Emergency Response System emphasizes the rational division of labor from the bottom to the top, and the reduction of levels of command, control and contact; the overall planning is made by the most appropriate department according to different stages, and officials at the place in emergency are empowered to perform duties. This system actually embodies the spirit of streamlined administration and institute decentralization, cross-agency collaboration and professional management, and helps to ensure efficiency.

(VII) Supporting services and social participation help promote collaboration and stabilize popular feelings

In case of bad weather and natural disasters, apart from relevant decision-making bureaus and emergency services departments, transportation, healthcare, social welfare and other departments also respond in accordance with the established regulations to provide supporting services. For example, hospital authority will strengthen emergency services and organize medical teams when necessary; Social Welfare Department will open temporary shelters for the homelessness and people in need.

At the same time, various non-governmental organizations, voluntary organizations, media, public transport and other service organizations in Hong Kong will actively participate in support and aftermath services such as contingency and relief of distress as a respond to the norms and appeals within the government's Emergency Response System and interact with the government to fully leverage the emergency mechanism. It also plays a positive role in maintaining and restoring social order before, during and after disasters.

(VIII) Meticulous and intensive communication attends to the needs of different groups, urging the public to form habits and establish a spirit of mutual support

The Hong Kong SAR Government attaches great importance to communication and education in order to enhance public's common knowledge to respond to inclement weather and the understanding of government-related services. For example, Information Services Department will broadcast announcements before wind, rain and hot weather or seasons to remind the public to be prepared. During inclement weather, the information release mechanism is even more diversified. Apart from release through television, radio, Internet and mobile phone, electronic display screen will also be set up at the main entrance of public transport, and residential management offices will be reminded to post notices and signs in the lobby of buildings, so that the information is widely spread. In addition, relevant information will be released in different languages in the ports of exit and entry of the sea, land and air to inform foreign tourists.

In addition, the government will also advocate mutual support, understanding and care during the communication, which can exercise invisible and formative influence on the reduction of losses caused by natural disasters and promotion of social harmony and integration.

III. Beijing's Existing Mechanism for Inclement Weather

In order to deal with the haze weather, Beijing has formulated the "Contingency Plan for Sandstorm Disaster in Beijing" in 2008 and the "Contingency Plan for Heavy Air Pollution Day in Beijing (Provisional)" in 2012. The former follows the principle of "Prevention First, Scientific Control, Interdepartmental Interaction and Quick

Response", and has designed a disaster emergency prevention/ control and rescue system for sandstorm with unified leadership, classified management and citywide mobilization. While it is specified in the *Contingency Plan for Heavy Air Pollution Day in Beijing* that, the municipal coordinating organization for emergency work in heavy pollution day shall be established, and the responsibility breakdown sheet of related departments shall be concluded; subarea forecast of air quality shall be carried out daily by the Municipal Environmental Monitoring Center, and corresponding healthy and compulsory measures for pollution reduction shall be formulated according to three levels: severe, serious and heavy pollution day.

Meanwhile, an Emergency Response Committee Office (Municipal Emergency Office) has been set up in Beijing for overall emergency management of major emergencies in 4 categories (natural disaster, accident disaster, public health incident and social security incident), 23 classifications and 51 types; meteorological disaster is one of the classifications. The Emergency Office has formulated measures for the implementation of emergency management in Beijing in accordance with the "Emergency Response Law of the People's Republic of China", and prepares the "Overall Contingency Plan for Emergency in Beijing" on this basis. It has defined the organizational structure and departmental division of responsibilities for emergency response, as well as the established procedures and operating standards in the whole process of monitoring and early warning, emergency handling and rescue, recovery and reconstruction, emergency support, communication, education and training. In addition, the "Emergency Plan for Traffic Guarantee on Snowy Day" and "Emergency Response Plan for Primary and Secondary Schools in Beijing on Heavy Snowy Day" have been prepared with the reference of the "Overall Contingency Plan for Emergency".

Overall, Beijing has started to set up the basic framework of early warning and emergency response mechanism for major natural disasters caused by abnormal weather. It has defined relevant organizational structure, division-cooperation system and operating procedures. However, rules and regulations dealing with abnormal weather in Beijing have been formulated only until recent years, especially after 2010. There is limited practical experience on implementation of such rules and regulations. Therefore, the content needs to be further refined and strengthened in order to improve the effectiveness and operability.

IV. Inspiration from Hong Kong's Experience for Establishing Early-warning Mechanism for Weather Crisis in Beijing

To sum up, Hong Kong has a systematic and standardized pre-warning and contingency plan for severe weather. It has also accumulated long-term experience to help itself get through many serious natural disasters. In addition, Hong Kong and Beijing are both densely populated metropolises and regional economic and trade hubs, so Hong Kong's mature contingency mechanism for severe weather is of reference significance, which can provide some enlightenment to Beijing.

Learning from the experience of Hong Kong, Beijing may consider strengthening the pre-warning and response mechanism for natural disasters like hazy weather from the following aspects:

(1) In order to cope with all kinds of meteorological disasters, a unified contingency plan shall be worked out to integrate specific emergency plans (including sandstorm, severe air pollution, drought, flood, etc.), which are now under the responsibility of different departments; it can improve the overall planning capability and efficiency, and can reserve the space to incorporate more severe weather conditions (such as thunderstorm, rainstorm and tempest) into the emergency system.

(2) On the basis of the current grading system of meteorological conditions and marking warning signals in four colors (red, orange, yellow and blue), graphical signs that are simple and easy to understand shall be designed for severe weather conditions of different kinds and grades to strengthen visual management.

(3) The release of predictive contents and sub-area data in weather reports shall be strengthened so as to facilitate early response of institutions and citizens.

(4) Relevant departments, especially the supporting public service departments, shall be urged to formulate emergency specifications within their own responsibility scope, as well as provide and spread public guidance, such as arrangements for school/office shutdown and traffic dispersion in inclement weather.

(5) The structure and settings of the existing emergency system shall be reviewed to streamline procedures and reduce intermediate links. Appropriate dedicated or competent department shall be designated to serve as the major coordinator in different disasters and phases. The onsite personnel shall be given necessary authority and responsibility to enhance cross departmental coordination, so as to improve the speed and effectiveness of responses.

(6) The grass root organizations and non-government entities shall be mobilized to take part in emergency prevention, control and rescue.

(7) The information notification under emergency circumstances shall be strengthened, reported to leadership and known to lower levels. For example, information channels within the government shall be straightened out; reminders and broadcasts in foreign languages shall be enhanced in sea, land and air ports; and the media shall be used more effectively to release information to the public, in order to improve transparency and stabilize social order.

(8) Everyday communication shall be valued to raise public awareness of disaster prevention and resistance. Public education of emergency response and the development of civilized society shall be combined. Team spirit of working together on the same boat and helping one another in crisis shall be advocated.

Chapter 16

Contributing and Creating Attractiveness through the Development of a Sustainable and Smart City District — Stockholm Royal Seaport

Emma Björner
Stockholm Business School,
Stockholm University, Stockholm, Sweden
ebj@sbs.su.se

I. Introduction

The world is changing at an ever-increasing pace, and is simultaneously facing greater socio-economic and environmental challenges.[1] At the same time, there is a global tendency that cities and regions take the lead on issues of sustainability and climate.[2] Like other cities around the globe, Sweden's capital Stockholm is trying to contend with the challenge of reconciling a rapidly growing city with a high level of environmental ambition.[3]

In Stockholm and Sweden, various sustainable city areas have been developed in recent years. One sustainable urban district currently under development is Stockholm Royal Seaport (SRS). The vision for SRS is to develop the area into a vibrant and sustainable world-class district that is able to attract the world's most highly skilled people and most successful companies.[4] The aim of this chapter is to investigate the development of SRS and to analyze it in relation to place branding research.

265

266 E. Björner

The connection between sustainable city development and place branding is interesting and relevant since places such as districts, cities and regions, increasingly are made attractive by developing images of being sustainable, smart and environmental friendly. The connection is also relevant in the light of that scholars and practitioners have put forth the idea that the attractiveness of a place is related to whether the place contributes something to humanity and the world.[4-6] The relationship between sustainable and smart cities and place branding is moreover relevant to study, since it hitherto has received limited attention in research.[7]

This chapter is structured in the following manner. First, the "sustainable and smart city" is discussed, followed by a brief discussion about the branding of a city in order to contribute. Then, the case of SRS and its development as a sustainable city area is illustrated. Finally, the conclusion brings together the various parts and elaborates on how SRS is made attractive by contributing in various ways, in line with the idea that places should contribute in order to be attractive.

II. The Sustainable, Smart City

In the past, cities have often been blamed for their exploitation of the environment. Today, cities are increasingly regarded as the source of new environmental remedies and experiments, as well as the hope for sustaining humanity.[8] Optimism about the dynamics of the city is also expressed.[9] In the last decades, we have seen the emergence of entrepreneurial and competitive styles of urban governance, and notions such as the "entrepreneurial city" have been put forth.[10,11] We have also seen a new global–local environmental politics created around ecological modernization and the partial greening of capital.[12]

Environmental sustainability is increasingly described as a growth opportunity in policy frameworks, such as "green competitiveness" and "eco-economic stimulus packages". Environmental sustainability policy frameworks also increasingly propose that sustainability and economic competitiveness are essentially mutually enhancing and interdependent. The "greening" of capitalism moreover challenges conventional thinking about economic development, and claims for green capitalism hold that environmental sustainability and economic competitiveness can be mutually enhancing.[8]

Debates about sustainability do not regard it as only an environmental concern but also incorporate economic and social dimensions.[13] It has been maintained that a heterogeneous mix of actors shape city development,[14] and that, "[...] cities represent a theatre of competing voices, each contributing to the on-going social construction of sustainability" (p. 271).

In the last 30–40 years, since the concept of sustainability was first defined, considerable literature has grown in the areas of planning, architecture and urban design. Sustainability has also become widely accepted as an important conceptual framework related to fields of urban policy and development. The "sustainable development" concept came about alongside a critical awareness in the 1980s of ecological destruction, and a realization that the retreat from social concerns resulting in urban carelessness, deprivation and poverty was untenable.[13]

Related to the idea of the "sustainable city" is the concept of the "smart city", which has been described as "a broad, integrated approach to improving the efficiency of city operations, the quality of life for its citizens, and growing the local economy".[15] Various corporations (such as IBM, Cisco, Ericsson and Siemens) have focused on smart cities and smart solutions.

"The Smart Cities Wheel" has been proposed and includes six indicators of a smart city, namely: "smart economy" (entrepreneurship and innovation, productivity, local and global interconnectedness); "smart environment" (green buildings, green energy, green urban planning); "smart government" (enabling supply and demand side policy, transparency and open data, ICT and e-governance); "smart living" (culturally vibrant and happy, safe, healthy); "smart mobility" (mixed-modal access, prioritized clean and non-motorized options, integrated ICT); "smart people" (21st century education, inclusive society, embrace creativity).[15]

III. Branding a City — to Contribute

Places and cities around the world have recognized a valuable ally in marketing theory and practice. They have adopted concepts from business, marketing and management, and paid increasing attention to city identity, brand value and city image.[16–18] Cities have also put increasing efforts into establishing the "city as a brand".[19] Branding is used in cities due to its perceived potential to increase inward investment and tourism, stimulate socio-economic development, boost residents' identification with a city, and provide a city with cultural and political significance as well as a respectable and favorable city image.[20,21]

Place branding research and practice have been criticized for including a very communication-oriented understanding being limited to the design of new logos and the development of catchy city slogans.[22,23] The large focus on visual communication has been called superficial and insufficient,[24] the reasoning being that place branding in such cases has been a pure communicative exercise not implemented in harmony with the development of the place.[25,26]

Govers also takes issue with the focus on logos and slogans, and emphasizes that branding is rather about how you contribute to the world.[5] Govers, and also Anholt (in Boland[4]) have focused this reasoning in relation to nations, and stated that: "It is not enough for a country to be successful. It must contribute something to humanity". Anholt and Govers have created the "good country index", which measures 125 countries' contribution to the world in seven categories of achievement.[4] The seven categories include science and technology; culture; international peace and security; world order; planet and climate; prosperity and equality; and health and well-being.[5] Anholt and Govers have also stated that economic growth is a good thing, but not if it is at the cost of the environment or well-being of another nation or species,[27] and that in order to be admired, you need to be admirable.[6]

Other researchers in the field of place branding have maintained that sustainable development has emerged as a distinctive marker of a place and its identity.[28] It has also been stated that certain environmental quality standards can prove to be significant in order

Contributing and Creating Attractiveness through the Development   269

to create a distinct place brand. Place branding has, moreover, been regarded as playing and important role in the sustainable development of a place, and in turn, "these sustainable developments help promote the place and thereby create stronger place brands" (p. 198).[7]

The relationship between place branding and sustainable, smart city development has, however, received limited attention in research, and there are limited studies about the branding of cities as sustainable and smart.[7] Yet, as argued by Anholt (at a conference "International City Brand Workshop" in Munich, 2014), what makes cities attractive is that they contribute.[2] The argument put forth in this chapter is that cities can contribute and build attractiveness by focusing on being sustainable and smart.

IV. Stockholm Royal Seaport: A Sustainable City Area

SRS is the largest city development area in Sweden and a sustainable urban district under construction in Sweden's capital Stockholm during 2010–2030. The area is characterized by dense, multifunctional and resource-efficient development, and is described as an urban environment with an integrated green structure and closeness to the surrounding nature.[29] The aim is that SRS shall be a sustainable city area and an international role model in sustainable city development.[30] SRS is regarded as an important part of the expanding Swedish capital city Stockholm, and resonates with the reasoning that major investments in various areas of Stockholm are needed to meet the international competition.[3] "The interest for sustainable development is large internationally, and Stockholm is on the map".[31]

The sustainability focus in SRS is steered toward energy, transportation, buildings, recycling systems, climate change adaptation and lifestyles. In SRS, the soil has been washed, and rainwater is regarded a resource. The buildings have been made sustainable, for example, by minimizing the use of hazardous substances. The target is that 80% of the area should be green, and large number of trees are being planted, one reason being to create good conditions when it is raining a lot. In the SRS district, there are limited areas for car parking and a limit of 0.5 parking lots per apartment. There are charging stations for electric cars, and priority is given to pedestrians, bicycles and public transportation. Carpooling (or car-sharing) is also available in the area in line with the notion of the "sharing economy".[2]

The location of SRS is just next to the water as well as 3.5 kilometers from Stockholm Central station and the very center of Stockholm. SRS will contain an area of 236 hectares, and include 12,000 apartments as well as 35,000 workplaces.[31] In SRS's vision document, it is stated that SRS offers good conditions for the business community to continue to grow. The emphasis is on the combination of work places, homes and leisure activities. SRS will offer a range of different opportunities for recreation and culture close to parks and green spaces. A certain focus is also on cultural activities in the area.[29]

SRS is said to offer opportunities to build a new vibrant and sustainable urban district with new jobs and homes in one of Stockholm's top locations, with proximity to business and shopping centers, nature and areas of open water.[3] People living and working in the area should also have access to advanced information and communications technology (ICT).[29]

The Information Officer at SRS[31] has stated that SRS will contribute to Stockholm's attractiveness, and maintained that this is needed since Stockholm needs to offer good services, and be attractive for companies and personnel. It has also been stated that SRS is to contribute to innovation, development and the marketing of Swedish green technology, expertise in sustainable urban development and the development of sustainable businesses with sustainable products and services.[29] Goals set for SRS are, moreover, to contribute to Stockholm's position as a leading capital city in climate work; and to contribute to the development of new technology with the aim to benefit all housing construction in Sweden.[3]

SRS has been described as a model of sustainable urban planning and said to play a key role as a source of knowledge and inspiration in

Contributing and Creating Attractiveness through the Development 271

international collaboration, exports of green technology and expertise in sustainable urban development.[29] In 2010, Stockholm was awarded "European Green City", and Stockholm is already seen as a world leader in many areas of the work to create a climate-adapted society.[3]

Yet, SRS and other city districts in Stockholm and Sweden face various challenges. Many of the challenges in creating a sustainable society for the next generation are complex and cross-boundary, and require cross-boundary solutions. ICT is also seen as playing an increasingly important part of the solutions to our common challenges. In Sweden, and SRS, four key areas have been identified, namely, "eHealth", and hence digital tools and interactive services related to health that can be handled by citizens from home; "Smart energy", and thus ICT solutions that will enable people to achieve sustainable and efficient energy production and smart consumption; "Sustainable mobility", including innovations to improve road safety and reduce environmental impact; "SME development", and hence the development of new startups and existing small- and medium-sized firms that promote a sustainable and smart society.[32]

The challenges faced in SRS are, moreover, similar to challenges experienced in other cities around the world.[33] One such challenge is financial: "To have visions is easy, to carry out in practice is harder — then money is needed".[34] Urban planners, policy makers and others involved in the development of SRS and other sustainable, smart city areas in Stockholm and Sweden regularly participate in international benchmarking consortiums in order to take home experiences and learn from other cities and regions.[35]

SRS has also drawn on experiences from "Hammarby Sjöstad" (in English, "Hammarby Sea City") in the development of a distinctive environmental profile for the area.[3] Ideas to develop Hammarby Sjöstad emerged when Stockholm was bidding for the 2004 Summer Olympics. Athens won the bid, but the plan to develop Hammarby Sjöstad was already "a fact", and the area was developed with the aim to create a sustainable city area with comfortable housing for thousands of people. Hammarby Sjöstad has come to be described

272 *E. Björner*

as an internationally recognized model of sustainable urban planning that has contributed to enhancing the Stockholm and Sweden "brands".[36]

Lessons learned from the sustainability work in "Hammarby Sjöstad" has been incorporated into the environmental profiling of SRS and includes a focus on having a comprehensive view in planning, continuous follow-up, and a clear process of rooting ideas and plans with relevant actors regarding vision and goals in the project. In order to achieve this, the city has a well-developed cooperation with the constructors; which is based on dialogue. The constructors have been offered to participate in competence enhancing seminars and workshops at an early stage of the SRS project, and have been encouraged to supply feedback and experiences that could contribute to reaching SRS's sustainability targets.[30]

In SRS, the focus has been on building city environments for children, old people and urban people, and on creating a city district where residents will enjoy living. The focus has also been on engaging citizens in dialogue, and it has been stated that SRS's vision can only be made possible by working together: "The work requires consensus, collaboration and dialogue".[3] Creating dialogue was initiated through conversations with potential residents, and continued with actual residents. It also included information meetings with various stakeholders.[31]

Related to citizen dialogue is the idea to get people living in the area involved and interested in a sustainable lifestyle: "Stockholm Royal Seaport is to be an urban district with sustainable lifestyles where 'doing the right thing is easy', and where people living and working in the area develop their knowledge and ability to live and act sustainably".[29]

V. Conclusion

This chapter has illustrated the development of a sustainable and smart city area in Sweden, namely SRS. In debates about sustainability in districts, cities and regions, environmental dimensions are not the only elements in focus, but social and economic dimensions also play important parts.[13] In the case of SRS, environmental, social, economic and technological dimensions appear to go hand in hand in the development of a sustainable, smart city area. The development of Stockholm Royal Seaport has, in this chapter, been described as contributing in various ways, in line with the idea that places should contribute in order to be attractive.[4-6]

SRS can be regarded as contributing as a source of inspiration and knowledge in international collaborations, and in housing constructions and city development projects in Sweden. SRS also contributes to the development and marketing of Swedish expertise in sustainable and smart urban development as well as businesses with sustainable products and services.[29] Incorporating smart elements into the sustainable city development, moreover, contributes to ICT solutions such as eHealth, smart energy, sustainable mobility and the development of SMEs that promote a sustainable society.[32]

Furthermore, SRS can be regarded as a contributor to a livable city environment for residents, since it offers a range of opportunities for recreation as well as green spaces and cultural activities.[29] SRS is, moreover, contributing to dialogue and collaboration regarding sustainable urban development involving residents, planners, constructors, and other key stakeholders.[3] SRS is also contributing to encouraging a sustainable lifestyle, and an environment where "doing the right thing" when it comes to the environment should be easy.[29]

These contributions can be regarded as benefiting the attractiveness of SRS, and also the attractiveness of Stockholm and Sweden. The "sharing economy" (for example discussed in Ref. 37) was referred to in SRS related to carpooling but can potentially be extended to also encapsulate the creation of sustainable, smart and attractive places, through sharing knowledge and inspiration, creating collective dialogue and collaboration, and by contributing to humanity and better urban environments.

References

1. Ericsson, Networked Society Index 2014, Brochure from Ericsson AB.
2. N. Wikholm, Presentation at lunch seminar about smart, sustainable cities and Stockholm Royal Seaport, 5 February 2015.
3. Vision 2030, Vision 2030: Stockholm Royal Seaport, City of Stockholm, 2010.

274   *E. Björner*

4. V. Boland, Ireland bags another gong: World's 'goodest' nation, *Financial Times*, 23 June 2014.
5. R. Govers, Nation brands and good countries, Presentation at "The Fifth International Conference on Destination Branding and Marketing (DBM-V)", 4 December 2014, Macau.
6. Good Country. Available at: www.goodcountry.org (accessed on 20 February 2015).
7. V. Maheshwari, I. Vandewalle and D. Bamber, Place branding's role in sustainable development, *Journal of Place Management and Development*, 2011, 4(2), 198–213.
8. C. Chang and E. Sheppard, China's eco-cities as variegated urban sustainability: Dongtan eco-city and Chongming eco-island, *Journal of Urban Technology*, 2013, 20(1), 57–75.
9. B. Hopwood and M. Mellor, Visioning the sustainable city, *Capitalism, Nature, Socialism*, 2007, 18(4), 75–91.
10. T. Hall, and P. Hubbard, *The Entrepreneurial City: Geographies of Politics, Regime and Representation*, John Wiley & Sons, Chichester, UK, 1998.
11. D. Harvey, From managerialism to entrepreneurialism: the transformation in urban governance in late capitalism, *Geografiska Annaler. Series B. Human Geography*, 1989, 71(1), 3–17.
12. A. While, A. Jonas and D. Gibbs, The environment and the entrepreneurial city: Searching for the urban 'Sustainability Fix' in Manchester and Leeds, *International Journal of Urban and Regional Research*, 2004, 28(3), 549–569.
13. N. Dempsey, G. Bramley, S. Power and C. Brown, The social dimension of sustainable development: Defining urban social sustainability, *Sustainable Development*, 2009, DOI:10.1002/sd.417.
14. S. Guy and S. Marvin, Understanding sustainable cities: Competing urban futures, *European Urban and Regional Studies*, 1999, 6(3), 268–275.
15. B. Cohen (2015). What Exactly Is A Smart City? Available at: www.fastcoexist.com/1680538/what-exactly-is-a-smart-city (accessed on 20 February 2015).
16. G.-J. Hospers, Making sense of place: from cold to warm city marketing, *Journal of Place Management and Development*, 2010, 3(3), 182–193.
17. M. Kavaratzis, Place branding: A review of trends and conceptual models, *The Marketing Review*, 2005, 5, 329–342.
18. A. W. T. Wai, Place promotion and iconography in Shanghai's Xintiandi, *Habitat International*, 2006, 30(2), 245–260.
19. S. Zenker and N. Martin, Measuring success in place marketing and branding, *Place Branding and Public Diplomacy*, 2011, 7(1), 32–41.
20. M. Balakrishnan, Strategic branding of destinations: A framework, *European Journal of Marketing*, 2009, 43(5/6), 611–629.
21. M. Kavaratzis, From city marketing to city branding: Towards a theoretical framework for developing city brands, *Place Branding*, 2004, 1(1), 58–73.
22. M. Kavaratzis and M. J. Hatch, The dynamics of place brands: An identity-based approach to place branding theory, *Marketing Theory*, (2013), 13(1), 69–86.

23. A. Therkelsen, H. Halkier, and O. Jensen, Branding Aalborg: Building community or selling place? in Ashworth G. and Kavaratzis, M. (eds.), *Towards Effective Place Brand Management: Branding European Cities and Regions*, Edward Elgar Publishing, Cheltenham, UK, 2010, pp. 136–156.

24. R. Govers and F. Go, *Place branding: Glocal, Virtual and Physical Identities, Constructed, Imagined and Experienced*, Palgrave Macmillan, Basingstoke, UK, 2009.

25. G. Ashworth and M. Kavaratzis, *Towards Effective Place Brand Management: Branding European Cities and Regions*, Edward Elgar Publishing, Cheltenham, UK, 2010.

26. M. Giovanardi, Haft and sord factors in place branding: Between functionalism and representationalism, *Place Branding and Public Diplomacy*, 2012, 8(1), 30–45.

27. Place brand observer, 2015, Available at: http://placebrandobserver.com/good-country-index-anholt-govers/ (accessed on 20 February 2015).

28. E. Gustavsson and I. Elander, Cocky and climate smart? Climate change mitigation and place-branding in three Swedish towns, *Local Environment*, 2012, 17(8), 769–782.

29. Build Stockholm, 2015, Available at: http://bygg.stockholm.se/Alla-projekt/norra-djurgardsstaden/In-English/A-sustainable-urban-district/ (accessed on 20 February 2015).

30. Sustainability report (2013). Norra Djurgårdsstaden Hållbarhetsredovisning 2013, Brochure by: *City of Stockholm*.

31. B. Hallqvist, Presentation at lunch seminar about smart, sustainable cities and Stockholm Royal Seaport, 5 February 2015.

32. Swedish ICT (2013). ICT for a sustainable and better life for everyone, Brochure by Swedish ICT.

33. K. Henriksson, Presentation at lunch seminar about smart, sustainable cities and Stockholm Royal Seaport, 5 February 2015.

34. C. Wennerholm (2015). Presentation at lunch seminar about smart, sustainable cities and Stockholm Royal Seaport, 5 February 2015.

35. T. Kikerpuu (2015). Presentation at lunch seminar about smart, sustainable cities and Stockholm Royal Seaport, 5 February 2015.

36. P. Levin and S. Pandis Iveroth, (Failed) mega-events and city transformation: The green vision for the 2004 Olympic village in Stockholm, in Berg & Björner (eds.), *Branding Chinese Mega-cities: Policies, Practices and Positioning*, Edward Elgar, Cheltenhamn, UK, 2014, pp. 155–167.

37. C. Boyd and J. Kietzmann, Ride on! Mobility business models for the sharing economy, *Organization & Environment*, 2014, 27(3), 279–296.

Part IV

China Chapters

Chapter 17

Green Space and Peoples' Leisure Life: Overseas Experience and China's Reality

Song Rui

Tourism Research Center,
Chinese Academy of Social Sciences, Beijing, China
prettysunny@126.com

I. Urban Green Space: Benefits, Classification and Standards

The important roles of social, economic, cultural and environmental aspects of sustainable development played by green spaces are recognized worldwide. Urban green spaces fulfill many functions in the urban context that benefits people's quality of life. The ecological benefits bestowed in green spaces range from protecting and maintaining the biodiversity to improving air quality through uptake of pollutant gases and particulates which are responsible for respiratory infections. Furthermore, due to their amenity and aesthetic, green spaces increase property value. However, the most sought benefits of green spaces in a city are the social and psychological benefits. Urban green spaces, especially public parks and gardens, provide resources and opportunities of relaxation, recreation and leisure for the residents. Ideally, this helps in promoting their life quality. Evidence shows a brisk walk every day, in a local green space, can reduce the risk of heart attacks, strokes and diabetes by 50%, fracture of the femur, colon and breast cancer by 30% and Alzheimer's by 25%. In addition to this, the positive impact of exposure to nature and green space on stress and mental health can be understood.

There is, therefore, a broad consensus on the importance and value of urban green spaces in cities.

The definition of urban green spaces which is agreed on by ecologists, economists, social scientists and planners is public and private open spaces in urban areas, primarily covered by vegetation, which are directly (e.g. active or passive recreation) or indirectly (e.g. positive influence on the urban environment) available for the users.[1] The management, planning, design and policy implementation of urban green spaces as the key discussion issues of sustainable environment are highly integrated and incorporated into the sustainable development at local and global levels.[2]

In order to meet the needs of citizens satisfactorily, green spaces in the city should be easily accessible, adequately optimal in quality and quantity, and uniformly distributed throughout the city area. The promotion and conservation of green space in cities is the responsibility of local authority.

In different countries, the classifications of green space are different. To get the maximum level contribution from urban green spaces, local approach and integrative approaches have focused on overcoming the challenges faced by different cities in different countries including the land allocation, size and number of green spaces based on the number of urban dwellers, accessible facilities for dwellers or tourists.[3] Most people cited getting away from daily demands of life and relieving stress as the reason for visiting green spaces.[4] To meet socio-economic, environmental, psychological needs of urban dwellers, some criteria should be developed based on the attitudes of perceived user to shape adequate uses of land and provide facilities within urban green spaces in cities.[5] Commonly used terms referring to the quantity of green spaces are green space ratio, green space coverage and green space area per capita. It is very difficult to measure the appropriate amount of required land and allocation of land, and calculate distance from residential area and especially to implement the measurement on building up urban green spaces with proper services in the highly populated countries. Table 17.1 shows the standards of minimum sizes of various types of green spaces in urban areas.[1]

Table 17.1. Minimum Standards for Urban Green Spaces.

Functional Level	Maximum Distance from Home (m)	Minimum Surface (ha)
Residential green	150	
Neighborhood green	400	1
Quarter green	800	10 (park: 5 ha)
District green	1,600	30 (park: 10 ha)
City green	3,200	60
Urban forest	5,000	>200 (smaller towns) >300 (big cities)

Source: See Ref. 1.

II. Experience of Urban Green Space from Overseas: Oxford, Britain

Oxford is famous the world over for its university and place in history. For over 800 years, it has been a home to royalty and scholars, and since the 9th century, an established town. Many businesses are located in and around the town, whether on one of the Science and Business Parks or within one of the number of residential areas. With its mix of ancient and modern, there is plenty for both the tourists and residents to do.

Oxford has an abundance of superb green spaces, which provide places where people of all ages can relax, play, enjoy nature and take part in recreation or sport. They incorporate important historic landscapes, enhance Oxford's world-famous cityscape and include nature reserves, woodland and meadows. They act as the city's lungs and are crucial for maintaining and improving people's health and well-being. The 2009 Oxford City Place Survey showed the importance people attach to their local green space by revealing that parks are the most used Council service, with 79% of respondents saying they used parks and open spaces at least once a month. They also show that parks have a high user satisfaction rate of over 80%, and all of these resulted from the efforts of local authorities and their partners.

Oxford city council has developed Green Space Strategy for a long time and updated it periodically. The latest one is named Green

Space Strategy: 2013–2027. The strategy has been produced using best practice and guidance from the Commission for Architecture and the Built Environment (CABE) and assisted by GreenSpace, the national charity which works to improve parks and green spaces.

The purposes of the Green Spaces Strategy are as follows:

- Protect and improve Oxford's accessible parks and open spaces.
- Provide clear objectives and direction for the planning and management of parks, and open spaces.
- Provide the Council with a robust basis for making development decisions and negotiating planning gain.
- Identify ways in which parks and open spaces can be improved in a coordinated way while providing value for money.

At the local level, the Oxford Green Spaces Strategy needs to be flexible enough to incorporate different plans and accommodate their objectives and priorities based on the vision for a particular area, such as the following:

- Oxford City Council's Core Strategy 2026 was adopted in March 2011 and sets out the spatial planning framework for the development of Oxford up to 2026. The Green Spaces Strategy fits in with Policy CS17 (Infrastructure and developer contributions), CS18 (Urban design, townscape character and the historic environment) CS21 (Green spaces, leisure and sport) and CS12 (Biodiversity) of the Core Strategy.
- Oxford City Council's Corporate Plan 2011–2015 vision is to remain committed to its core ambition of "building a world-class city for everyone". The City Council's corporate priorities are: CP1, A vibrant and sustainable economy; CP2, Meeting housing need; CP3, Strong and active communities; CP4, Cleaner greener Oxford; CP5, An efficient and effective Council.
- Oxford City Leisure and Parks service plan vision is to provide "World-class parks, open spaces and leisure opportunities to enhance the quality of life for everyone living, visiting or working in Oxford".

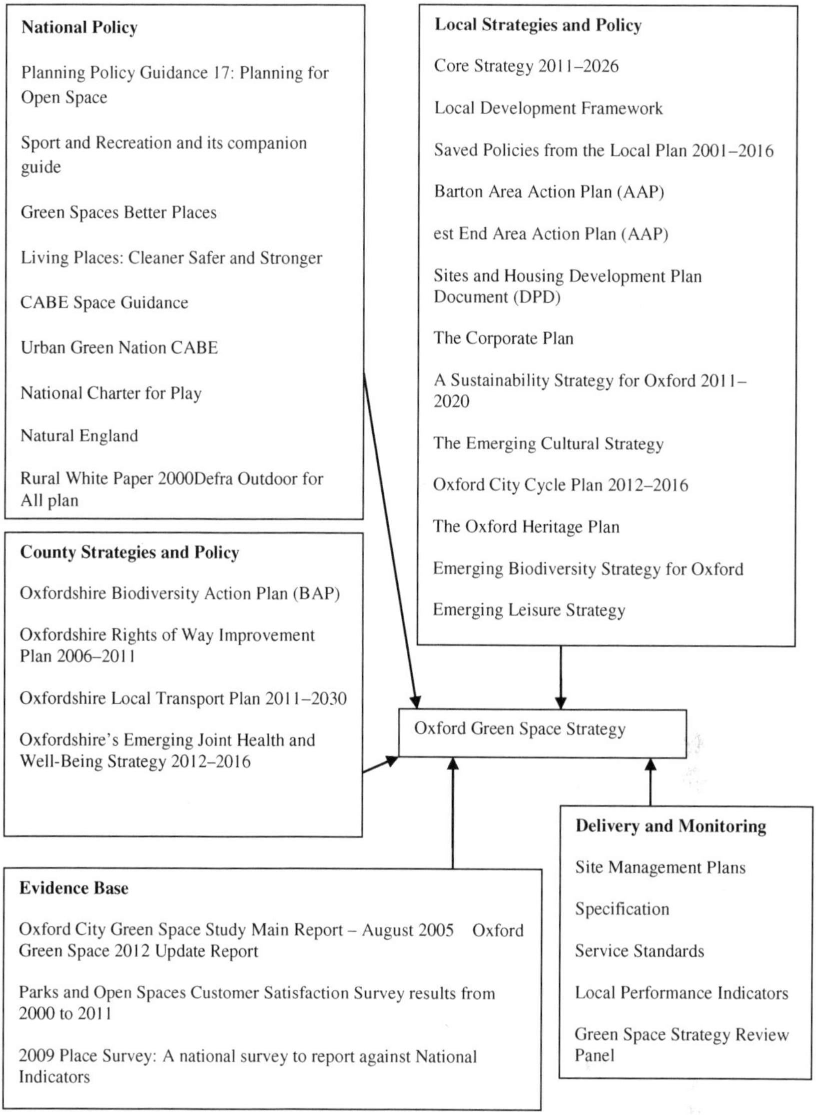

National Policy

Planning Policy Guidance 17: Planning for Open Space

Sport and Recreation and its companion guide

Green Spaces Better Places

Living Places: Cleaner Safer and Stronger

CABE Space Guidance

Urban Green Nation CABE

National Charter for Play

Natural England

Rural White Paper 2000Defra Outdoor for All plan

County Strategies and Policy

Oxfordshire Biodiversity Action Plan (BAP)

Oxfordshire Rights of Way Improvement Plan 2006–2011

Oxfordshire Local Transport Plan 2011–2030

Oxfordshire's Emerging Joint Health and Well-Being Strategy 2012–2016

Local Strategies and Policy

Core Strategy 2011–2026

Local Development Framework

Saved Policies from the Local Plan 2001–2016

Barton Area Action Plan (AAP)

est End Area Action Plan (AAP)

Sites and Housing Development Plan Document (DPD)

The Corporate Plan

A Sustainability Strategy for Oxford 2011–2020

The Emerging Cultural Strategy

Oxford City Cycle Plan 2012–2016

The Oxford Heritage Plan

Emerging Biodiversity Strategy for Oxford

Emerging Leisure Strategy

Oxford Green Space Strategy

Delivery and Monitoring

Site Management Plans

Specification

Service Standards

Local Performance Indicators

Green Space Strategy Review Panel

Evidence Base

Oxford City Green Space Study Main Report – August 2005   Oxford Green Space 2012 Update Report

Parks and Open Spaces Customer Satisfaction Survey results from 2000 to 2011

2009 Place Survey: A national survey to report against National Indicators

Figure 17.1.   Strategies and Policies of Oxford Green Space Strategy.

Source: Oxford Green Space Strategy: 2013–2027, http://www.oxford.gov.uk/ Library/Documents/Policies%20and%20Plans/Green%20Spaces%20Strategy% 202013-27.pdf.

- Parish Councils and Neighborhood Forums may, as part of their neighborhood plans, produce their own individual local Green Space Strategies.

The Green Spaces Strategy also needs to fit with other strategies and policies (Figure 17.1).

A vision statement and aims have been agreed for Oxford's green spaces: "To provide world-class parks and open spaces to enhance the quality of life of everyone living, visiting or working in Oxford". In order to achieve this vision, the following aims are proposed. The objectives to meet these aims are set out in the following six chapters.

- To establish a quantity standard of green space provision to ensure that Oxford has an agreed amount of green spaces to meet existing and future needs of residents, workers and visitors.
- To ensure everyone living in, working in and visiting Oxford has easy access to open space.
- To achieve high-quality green spaces across Oxford, including spaces that are nationally recognized for their quality and attractions.
- To promote the central role that green spaces play in contributing to the city's biodiversity, sustainability, heritage and culture
- To promote the central role that green spaces play in contributing to the city's health and well-being
- To support community cohesion and community involvement in the design and stewardship of green spaces.

III. Urban Green Space in China: Supply–Demand Imbalance and Solutions

The definition, scope and classification of green space system are still on debate. According to the Standard for Classification of Urban Green Space enacted in 2002 by the former Ministry of Construction, which was renamed as the Ministry of Housing and Construction in 2010, the urban green space is classified into five categories: parks, productive green land, protective green land, subsidiary green, land and other green land. Those five categories are further divided into

13 classes and 11 subclasses. The urban space system in China has developed gradually since 1949. At its beginning, the former Soviet Union experience was taken as the basis, the standard of service radius and average personal area at municipal, district and community levels were developed in various urban green spaces, and then, botanical gardens, public green space, orchards, plant nursery and farmland were taken as green spaces, and the urban surroundings were equipped with belt forest parks and vegetable bases and so on. Since 1970s, the green cover percentage and average green space area were required to be increased, and some measures were taken in order to make reasonable distribution of public green space and consider other functions of green space. Besides, the city greenbelt in suburbs was developed.

The insufficiency, unbalanced distribution and poor management of urban space system are reported as complaints by the citizens. For the highly populated metropolises, such as Beijing and Shanghai, the main reasons are the scarcity and competitive usages of land, and in the undeveloped regions, it may be attributed to the weakness of public financial support. However, the fact that the spatial control, construction and management of urban green space are fragmented in a complex institutional framework can't be ignored wherever. Under the extended concept, urban green space area contains the following basic elements: municipal Parks, Community Gardens, River and Streams, Costal Wet Lands, Scenic Zones, Forest Parks, Arable Lands, Timber Land and Natural Conservation zones. Different departments of a city government are in charge of the construction, maintenance and management of these elements. Over the city government, the corresponding government departments in national or provincial level issue national-/provincial-wide regulations for management of different urban green space elements and also implement direct management of the key area of some elements. The spatial boundary, land-use intentions and construction activities are under the administration of both planning control of the urban planning bureau and quantitative quota control by the land and resource bureau. The modern ecological view of urban green space requires five key principles of content, context, dynamics, heterogeneity and hierarchies to achieve its service function, which would require coordination among different governments during planning and implementation processes (Table 17.2). Whether or not such coordination is efficient will decide the result of urban green space management.[6]

The insufficiency of green space and other open spaces in China can be demonstrated as Table 17.3, which is based on a national survey I did in 2013. The question is: what do you think of the necessity to increase or improve the leisure-related space, facilities, service and environment. The answers were coded from 1 to 5, and the results shown in Table 17.3 proved Godbey's belief. Compared with balance leisure, mainly tourism, Chinese citizens attach more importance to improvement of space, service, facilities related to core leisure. It shows that the open public leisure space and facilities are most needed and expected by the respondents.

Recognizing the importance of green space, some measures are implemented in more and more cities. For example, more than 10 years ago, Guangzhou municipal government initiated an alternative approach as formulating and implementing an action plan for improving the overall environmental quality of the municipality through administrative directive. This action plan is called projects for greener mountains and green land. After the draft of the action plan was finished, it was circulated among bureaus and district governments for their comments to make sure that the task is within the capability of the responsible entity. The finalized action plan proposed to establish or upgrade $119 \, km^2$ of green space around the municipality including $33 \, km^2$ of 14 green spaces in the core urban area. The explicit plan was smoothly implemented after 2003. Under the integrated arrangement of the municipality government with administrative power and relatively sufficient investment, the tasks were successfully finished. By the end of October 2006, $131 \, km^2$ of green spaces including $36 \, km^2$ in the core urban area was established or upgraded. With the efforts of municipal governments, more and more different types of urban spaces have been developed with local features. For example, in Nanjing, due to the natural geographical conditions and historical cultural landscape in the center part, the

Table 17.2. The Institutional Hierarchy of Urban Green Space Management in China.

National	Provincial	City	Municipal Park	Community Garden	River and Stream	Costal Wet Land	Scenic Zone	Forest Park	Arable Land	Timber Land	Conversation Zone
M. of Construction	P.D. of Construction	B. of Urban Planning	o	o	o	o	o	o	o	o	o
		B. of Municipal & Landscape	*	*	*		*				
M. of Land & Resources	P.D. of Land & Resources	B. of Land & Resources	o	o	o	o	o	o	o*	o	o
M. of Water Resource	P.D. of Water Resource	B. of Water Resources			*						
State B. of Forestry	P.D. of Forestry	B. of Forestry						*		*	
M. of Agriculture	P.D. of Agriculture	B. of Agriculture, Marine & Fishery							*		
State B. of Marine	P.D. of Marine					*					
State Admin. Env. Protection	P.D. of Environmental Protection	B. of Environmental Protection									*

Notes: M. = Ministry, P.D. = Provincial Department, B. = Bureau, * = in charge of construction and conservation, o = in charge of planning.

Source: Huang *et al.*[6]

Table 17.3. Necessity of Increase or Improvement of Leisure Space, Facilities and Service.

Rank	Items	Mean
1	Open public leisure space and facilities near the neighborhood or village (outdoor)	4.16
2	Community center or villager activities center (indoor, with service)	4.12
3	Greenland/plaza/urban park/wildness park and other open space	4.11
4	Specific trails for walking/jogging/bicycling	4.10
5	Library/cultural center/art center/museum/exhibition hall/zoo and botanical gardens/science and technology museum	4.01
6	Variety of tourist attractions/rural home stay/theme parks	3.97
7	Cinema/theater/performance facilities	3.96
8	Commercial streets/shopping mall/urban complex	3.95
9	KTV/singing hall/bars/café/tea house/book bar	3.91
10	Gym/yoga club/swimming pool/ski field	3.90
11	Playgrounds for badminton/ping pang /billiards and common ball games	3.85
12	Golf course/ equestrian venue /fencing hall/tennis court	3.78
13	Internet bar/video game bar/board role-playing games club	3.76
14	Message service/healthcare center/spa/beauty salon	3.66
15	Hotels/resort/private clubs/fitness club	3.65
16	To make the gymnasium and playground of schools and units available and accessible for the public	3.63
17	To provide more amount and more convenient public information of leisure	3.60
18	To increase the NGOs related to leisure	3.58
19	To decrease or exempt the tickets price of diversified leisure resources	3.45
20	To improve the outdoor environment (air quality, afforesting)	3.42

green space system has been formed in the pattern of stripes. In Suzhou, the water network is utilized to construct the green space system, while its neighbor city, Hangzhou utilizes the surrounding mountains, water to form the green space system ringing around the downtown. In 2012, the Shanghai municipal government vowed to improve the city's environment by adding another 5,000 hectares of green open space before 2015, half of which will be allocated public space. According to official estimates, the average per person public green area in Shanghai will be increased to 13.5 m^2 within three years, up from the 13.1 m^2 by the end of 2011. Residents inside the inner ring road live no more than 500 m from an open green space larger than 3,000 m^2.

Currently, China has the world's largest urban population, with over 170 cities with populations above 1 million, of which seven have populations above 10 million Moreover, nearly 70% of China's population is expected to live in urban areas by 2025, bringing it on par with countries like Germany and Italy. By 2030, it is projected that the urbanization rate will reach 70% and 300 million people will have moved from the countryside to the cities. This demographic shift means more demands of water, electricity, land, food, housing, schools, healthcare, and also leisure spaces and facilities in the cities. It entails great improvement and even revolution of green space in urban China.

References

1. V. Herzele and T. Wiedeman, A monitoring tool for the provision for accessible and attractive green spaces, *Elsevier Sciences: Landscape and Urban Planning*, 2003, 63(2), 109–126.
2. B. Tuzin, E. Leeuwen, C. Rodenburg and N. Peter, Paper presented at the 38th *International Planning Congress on "The Pulsar Effect" Planning with Peaks*, Glifada, Athens, 21–26 September 2002.
3. Shah Md. Atiqul Haq, Urban green spaces and an integrative approach to sustainable environment, *Journal of Environmental Protection*, 2011, 2, 601–608.
4. T. Stein and M. Lee, Managing recreation resources for positive outcomes: An application of benefits based management, *Park and Recreation Administration Journal*, 1995, 13(3), 52–70.
5. S. Balram and S. Dragicevic, Attitude towards urban green spaces: Integrated questionnaire survey and collaborative GIS techniques to improve attitude measurement, *Elsevier: Landscape and Urban Planning*, 2005, 71(2–4), 147–162.
6. D. Huang, C. Lu and G. Wang, Integrated management of urban green space — The case in Guangzhou China, in *45th ISOCARP Congress 2009*.

Chapter 18

China's Regional Development Strategy and Urban Green Development Efficiency Based on Urban Data Analysis of the Silk Road Economic Belt

Zheng Zhao

Researcher, Development Research Center
of the State Council of PRC
zz_bnu@126.com

I. Introduction

About 2,100 years ago, Zhang Qian went to Central Asia from Chang'an, capital of the Western Han Dynasty, and opened up the Silk Road which connects East and West, Europe and Asia. President Xi Jinping addressed a strategic vision "to build Silk Road Economic Belt Together" during his visit to Central Asia in 2013, which gives a new meaning to the ancient Silk Road, injects new vitality to the national development strategy of Reform and Opening, and has a very important strategic significance. From a global perspective, building the Silk Road Economic Belt will help China to apply diplomacy with Chinese characteristics, to form a "community of interests" with neighboring countries, to create a better international environment for development and more favorable conditions for the country's reform and development. From the domestic perspective, building the Silk Road Economic Belt helps to construct a new opening pattern in all domains including the coastal cities, border cities and western region cities, to further narrow the regional development gap and promote balanced economic and social development of the eastern and western regions. Currently, the building of the Silk Road Economic Belt is becoming a hot issue both in theory and practice. The local governments along the Silk Road have responded positively. They have introduced development planning, trying to win more development space and opportunities through this national strategy.

However, despite the current positive progress made in research and practice, there are still two important aspects that need more attention in the building of the Silk Road Economic Belt. One is focusing more on the development of cities along the Silk Road Economic Belt. With the spatial economic theory, the development of economic belt is along the axis of transport trunk lines, and its core comprises some economically developed cities along the axis. The economic concentration and radiation functions of these cities link and drive the economic developments of cities around at different levels of scale and form an integrated economic belt. The ancient Silk Road was a trade and logistics channel consisting of all the important node cities linking Europe and Asia. Xi'an, Xianyang and Baoji in Shaanxi province; Tianshui, Lanzhou, Wuwei, Jinchang, Zhangye, Jiuquan, Jiayuguan and Yumen in Gansu province; Hami, Turpan, Urumqi, Shihezi and Yili in Xinjiang province; other cities played an important role in the development process of the ancient Silk Road. Modern society is all about cities. To achieve regional interconnection, node cities will need to be identified, and the construction of the Silk Road Economic Belt should also attach great importance to the aggregation and radiation effects of central cities along the belt, improve the city's carrying capacity and competitiveness, and build this region belt based on the urban economic belt. The other aspect is the need for more emphasis on green development.

The core of green development is to balance the environment and development, achieve sustainable use of natural resources, continuously improve ecological environment and people's quality of life, and provide sustained economic and social development within the capacity of the ecological environment and resources.

The United Nations efforts to promote the concept of green development globally since 2008 have been widely recognized. China has also attached great importance to green development and ecological civilization, and included them in their national long-term strategic development planning and new urbanization planning. The regions in the Silk Road Economic Belt have good resource endowments, cultural heritage and huge development potential, but the environmental pressure is still relatively large. There are still gaps in the national average level in some main indicators. For example, the national industrial waste water emissions per unit of gross domestic product (GDP) decreased by 61.55% from 2006 to 2012, while it only declined by 53.8% in the cities of the Silk Road Economic Belt — 7.73% lower than the national level. In 2012, the average investments of the National Urban environmental infrastructure were 16.33 billion yuan, while they were just 8.92 billion yuan in the cities in the Silk Road Economic Belt — nearly 50% lower than the national level. In the new proposal, the construction of the Silk Road Economic Belt should not be simply understood as a new round of feast of investment and construction, an extensive development relying on scale expansion, an investment-driven, vicious competition, but as a strategic opportunity to achieve regional green transformation and development through opening and exploitation.

On the basis of the national strategies and regional reality, this chapter studies about the cities in the Silk Road Economic Belt, analyzes their levels of green development, and measures the green development efficiency and its influencing factors using certain models. Then we give some policy suggestions to promote the green development of cities in the Silk Road Economic Belt, hoping to benefit from the long-term sustainable economic development of the Silk Road Economic Belt.

II. Measurement of Green Development Efficiency of Cities in the Silk Road Economic Belt

The essence of urban green development is to consume as few resources as possible, produce as much output as possible while generate as little waste as possible, which not only requires the change in quantity but also a qualitative improvement. On the basis of the analysis on the basic status of green development of cities in the Silk Road Economic Belt, we will further explore the level of green development of these cities from the green input–output efficiency point.

(I) Efficiency measurement model of urban green development

In this chapter, I use non-radial and non-oriented Slacks-Based Directional Distance Function model (SBM-DDF model), to build a measurement model of efficiency of urban green development based on productivity theory and measure green development efficiency of key cities in the Silk Road Economic Belt.

First, we treat each city as a producing and decision-making unit for green development, and construct the best practical boundary of production in each period. Suppose there are N kinds of input x, M kinds of expected outputs, y and K types of undesirable output b, and $x = (x_1 \ldots x_N) \in R_N^*$; $y = (y_1 \ldots y_M) \in R_M^*$; $b = (b_1 \ldots b_K) \in R_K^*$. (x_i^t, y_i^t, b_i^t) refers to the inputs and outputs of decision unit i in period t. (g^x, g^y, g^b) refer to direction vectors and (s_n^x, s_m^y, s_k^b) refer to slack vectors with the inputs and outputs reaching the production frontier.

Then, the best production frontier of green development of the ith city is as follows:

$$\overrightarrow{S_v^t}(x_i^t, y_i^t, b_i^t, g^x, g^y, g^b)$$

$$= MAX \left(\frac{1}{N} \sum_{n=1}^{N} (s_n^x/g_n^x) + \frac{1}{M} \sum_{m=1}^{M} (s_m^y/g_m^y) + \frac{1}{K} \sum_{k=1}^{K} (s_k^b/g_k^b) \right) \bigg/ 3$$

s.t. $x_{in}^t - s_n^x = \vec{\lambda}X, \forall n;$

$$y_{im}^t + s_m^y = \vec{\lambda}Y, \forall m;$$

$$b_{ik}^t - s_k^b = \vec{\lambda}B, \forall k;$$

$$\vec{\lambda} \geq 0,$$

$$\vec{\lambda}l = 1;$$

$$s_n^x \geq 0,$$

$$s_m^y \geq 0,$$

$$s_k^b \geq 0.$$

According to SBM-DDF model, when direction vector $g_n^x = x_n^{\max} - x_n^{\min}, \forall n$ and when $g_m^y = y_n^{\max} - y_n^{\min}, \forall m, \overrightarrow{S_v^t} \in [0,1]$, and every input, expected output and undesirable output $\in [0,1]$, we can find the degree of deviation of every input, expected output and undesirable output to the best production frontier of each city, which can measure the inefficiency level of green development of a city unit i in period $t, \overrightarrow{S_v^t}$.

Furthermore, we can obtain the efficiency of urban green development Urban Green Development Efficiency Index (UGDE).

$$\text{UGDE} = 1 - \overrightarrow{S_v^t}.$$

UGDE $\in [0,1]$ meets boundedness and monotonous tenability. If and only if all inputs and outputs slack variables are equal to zero, the objective function is equal to zero, then UGDE=1, indicating that the city is in the best practice boundary.

(II) Indicator selection

From the key city database that is monitored by the Ministry of Environmental Protection, we chose 24 key cities in five northwestern provinces (Shaanxi, Gansu, Qinghai, Ningxia, Xinjiang) and four Southwest provinces (Chongqing, Sichuan, Yunnan, Guangxi) along the Silk Road Economic Belt as research objects and used their inputs, expected outputs and undesirable output data from 2006 to 2012 to calculate their green development efficiency by the above measurement model.[a]

All data used in this paper are from "China City Statistic Yearbook", "Annual Statistic Report on Environment in China",

---

[a]We chose urban data from 2006 to 2012 for two reasons: first, the data in 2006 are not comparable with former years as a result of change in national statistic standards; second, all the cities had not released the urban energy consumption data until 2005.

"China Statistic Yearbook for Regional Economy", Data Center of the Ministry of Environmental Protection and Statistic Yearbook and Communiqué of each province and city.

1. Selection of the input variables

Considering the composing elements of urban green development, we chose capital, energy, labor and technology as four input variables.

Capital: Total capital stock of the city can properly reflect the urban green development funding in all aspects. But because there is no domestic capital stock data that can be used directly, we use the perpetual inventory method to convert. The formula is as follows:

$$\langle M \rangle K_{m,t} = K_{m,t-1}(1 - \delta_{m,t}) + (I_{m,t}/P_{m,t}),$$

where $K_{m,t}$ and $K_{m,t-1}$ refer to the estimated capital stock in year t and year $t-1$, $\delta_{m,t}$ refers to the depreciation rate of capital of year t, $I_{m,t}$ refers to the investment in fixed assets at current price of year t, $P_{m,t}$ refers to the price index of fixed assets investment in year t.

Labor: Labor is the basis for green development output. In this paper, we select an employee indicator. Employees in all industries of a city to measure the labor input for urban development green.

Technology: Technology determines the production mode and efficiency of urban green development, and is a key factor affecting urban green development. This chapter selects the indicator — city budget expenditure in science and technology — to measure the level of technical input.

Energy: It requires full consideration of the level of energy use in urban green development. According to the announced energy consumption unit GDP by each city, we calculate the total energy consumption of the whole society in each city to measure the energy input for green development.

2. Expected output variables selection

Regional GDP is sufficient to measure the actual situation of the region's economic growth. Therefore, we select the real regional GDP

China's Regional Development Strategy and Urban Green 297

with 2005 as the base period to represent the expected output of urban green development.

3. Undesirable output variable selection

Environmental pollutions of cities include waste water, waste gas and solid waste, so this chapter will consider the undesirable output of urban green development from these three aspects.

Waste water: There are two main sources of urban waste water: sewage and industrial waste water. In order to evaluate the amount of waste water generated in the whole society, we use the total emissions from municipal sewage and industrial waste water emissions to measure waste water discharge.

Waste gas: According to the monitoring data of the Ministry of Environmental Protection, a city's main waste gases are sulfur dioxide, nitrogen oxides and soot. Therefore, herein, we use the sum of sulfur dioxide emissions from urban life, nitrogen oxide emissions from urban life, soot emissions from urban life, industrial sulfur

Table 18.1. Mean and Ranks of Green Development Efficiency of Cities in Silk Road Economic Belt from 2006 to 2012.

City	Mean of Efficiency from 2006 to 2012 (%)	Rank	City	Mean of Efficiency from 2006 to 2012 (%)	Rank
Chengdu	99.22	1	Jinchuan	96.55	13
Chongqing	98.74	2	Luzhou	96.38	14
Tongchuan	97.94	3	Xining	95.85	15
Xianyang	97.56	4	Yinchuan	95.73	16
Nanning	97.28	5	Xibin	95.50	17
Beihai	97.20	6	Lanzhou	94.80	18
Yan'an	97.20	7	Liuzhou	94.47	19
Baoji	97.00	8	Shizuishan	94.22	20
Mianyang	96.93	9	Urumqi	92.31	21
Guilin	96.88	10	Qujing	91.10	22
Kelamayi	96.75	11	Kunming	90.67	23
Xi'an	96.68	12	Panzhihua	86.37	24
	Mean			95.56	

Table 18.2. Gaps in Urban Green Development Efficiency of Cities Inside Their Provinces Along the Silk Road Economic Belt.

Province	City	Mean of Efficiency from 2006 to 2012 (%)	Rank	Hugest Gap in Rank	Province	City	Mean of Efficiency from 2006 to 2012 (%)	Rank	Hugest Gap in Rank
Sichuan	Chengdu	99.22	1	23	Shaanxi	Tongchuan	97.94	3	9
	Mianyang	96.93	9			Xianyang	97.56	4	
	Luzhou	96.38	14			Yan'an	97.20	7	
	Yibin	95.50	17			Baoji	97.00	8	
	Panzhihua	86.37	24			Xi'an	96.68	12	
Guangxi	Nannning	97.28	5	14	Xinjiang	Karamay	96.75	11	10
	Beihai	97.20	6			Urumqi	92.31	21	
	Guilin	96.88	10		Gansu	Jinchang	96.55	13	5
	Liuzhou	94.47	19			Lanzhou	94.80	18	
Yunnan	Qujing	91.10	22	1	Ningxia	Shizuishan	94.22	20	4
	Kunming	90.67	23			Yinchuan	95.73	16	
Chongqing	Chongqing	98.74	2	0	Qinghai	Xining	95.85	15	0

dioxide emissions, industrial nitrogen oxide emissions and industrial soot emissions to measure emissions.

Solid waste: The sources of solid waste include the city's industrial solid waste and solid waste from urban life. However, the amount of solid waste generation from urban life data is almost negligible compared with industrial solid waste generation. Therefore, we use industrial solid waste generation to measure urban solid waste generation.

(III)   Result of analysis on efficiency measurement of urban green development

According to the above model and data, we use Matlab7.0 software to measure the green development efficiency of 24 key cities in the Silk Road Economic Belt (see Table 18.1).

We found that the overall urban green development efficiency of the Silk Road economic Belt is low, and there is a significant difference among the cities. Overall, the means of efficiencies of 24 cities are all below 1 from 2006 to 2012, indicating that none meets the best practice frontier of green development and the whole efficiency is low. In 16 cities, efficiencies are above the mean of 24 cities, and in 8 cities, the efficiencies are below the mean of 24 cities. The top five cities in efficiency are, respectively, Chengdu (99.22%), Chongqing (98.74%), Tongchuan (97.94%), Xianyang (97.56%) and Nanning (97.28%). The last five cities are Shizuishan (94.22), Urumqi (92.31%), Qujing (91.10%), Kunming (90.67%) and Panzhihua (86.37%).

Meanwhile, it is worth noting that there are gaps among cities inside the Silk Road Economic Belt, and the gap is very huge inside some provinces. The cities of Sichuan Province have the largest gap (23 in rank), followed by Guangxi (14 in rank), Xinjiang (10 in rank), Shaanxi (9 in rank), Gansu (5 in rank), Ningxia (4 in rank) and Yunnan (one in rank) (see Table 18.2).

III.   Analysis of Factors Affecting Urban Green Development Efficiency of the Silk Road Economic Belt

As can be seen from the results of the aforementioned analysis, there are significant differences in the green development efficiencies of cities along the Silk Road Economic Belt. How to understand differences in efficiency and what are the specific factors that led to these differences are questions we need to pay further attention. In this chapter, we further select factors that may affect the urban green development efficiency and perform regression analysis to explain the reasons.

Urbanization (URB): The nature of urbanization is the optimizing configuration and agglomeration of population and industries in the space, and it has internal consistency with green development. So urbanization is an important factor for urban green development. We measure the degree of urbanization of different cities from three aspects — population urbanization, spatial urbanization and economic structure urbanization. Specifically, we use the "proportion of urban non-agricultural population of the total population" as the population urbanization indicator, the "proportion of built-up area of urban municipal districts of the total area" as the spatial urbanization indicator and the "proportion of gross non-farm economic production of total gross production" as the economic structure urbanization indicator. After standardizing the three indicators, we apply the weighted average method to calculate the overall urbanization degree. In addition, to examine the nonlinear relationship between urbanization and urban green development efficiency, we added urbanization quadratic (URB2) in the regression model.

Industrial agglomeration (LQ): A city is a gathering place for industry. Industrial economy is an economy of scale and agglomeration. The gathering of industrial means of production and labor will bring the centralization of population, consumption, wealth, and politics, which is a necessary prerequisite for the formation and development of the city. Therefore, industrial agglomeration will affect the urban green development efficiency. Industrial agglomeration is usually measured by industrial location quotient (LQ). From the perspective of the city, we can examine the differences between the position of industrial i of city j in the region and the position all industries of city j in the region, the specific formula is: $\mathrm{LQ} = (sij/si)/(sj/s)$. The molecule of LQ refers to city j's share of urban industrial GDP of in the region; the denominator refers to city j's share of GDP in the region.

Regulation: Environmental regulation refers to government's directive to firms to enhance production technologies to meet the environmental standards thorough mandatory environmental institutional arrangements. Therefore, technology innovation and environmental protection can be realized. Environmental regulation will promote urban environmental protection and pollution control, and have important influence on urban green development efficiency. In this chapter, we select the removal rate of industrial sulfur dioxide to represent the strength of regulation.

Control variables: There are many other factors can affect the urban green development efficiency besides urbanization degree, industrial agglomeration and regulation. We mainly consider the impact of other four aspects and put in relevant control variables: First, the impact of the level of urban economic development (lnPerGDP) represented by per capita GDP at constant price; second, the impact of the level of foreign direct investment (FDI) represented by the share FEI accounted for the city's GDP; third, the impact of the level of urban human resource (lnHR) represented by the logarithm of the numbers of college students per 10,000 people; fourth, the impact of urban population density (lnPD) represented by the logarithm of urban population density.

Considering all these factors, we used Bootstrap method to regress. Models 1, 2 and 3, respectively, examined the influence of urbanization level, industrial agglomeration level and regulation level on urban green development efficiency with the control variables. Model 4 examined the relationship between all factors and urban green development efficiency (Table 18.3).

The results show that different factors have different impacts on urban green development efficiency.

On urbanization, in Models 1 and 4, the coefficients of URB are positive, the coefficients of URB^2 are both negative. This shows the relationship between urban green development efficiency and urbanization is U-shaped. It means that with continuous urbanization,

Table 18.3. Estimation Results of Relationships between Urban Green Development Efficiency and Each Factor.

Variable	Model 1	Model 2	Model 3	Model 4
URB	-0.068^{**}			-0.078^{**}
	(4.90)			(3.88)
URB^2	0.546^{**}			0.718^{**}
	(5.87)			(4.29)
LQ		2.609^{**}		3.757^{**}
		(0.88)		(0.84)
Regulation			-0.615^{***}	-0.579^{***}
			(0.05)	(0.06)
lnPerGDP	0.034^{***}	0.044^{***}	0.027^{***}	0.032^{***}
	(2.74)	(3.45)	(5.64)	(2.14)
FDI	0.008	0.006	-0.016	0.004
	(0.81)	(-0.55)	(0.97)	(0.65)
lnHR	-0.014	0.021	-0.026	-0.018
	(-1.34)	(2.78)	(-2.43)	(-2.01)
lnPD	-0.287^{**}	-0.378^{*}	-0.306^{**}	-0.187^{**}
	(-5.67)	(-6.34)	(-6.05)	(-3.47)
R^2	0.922	0.879	0.844	0.839

Notes: ***, **, * denote the estimated coefficient is significant at the significance level of 1%, 5%, 10%, respectively. The times of Bootstrap are 2000.

the urban green development efficiency shows a trend of "decline first and rise later". It implies that along with the acceleration of early urbanization, the rapid expansion of population and industry space may lead to significant negative influence on local ecological environment. But when high-level urbanization is reached, the agglomeration economy and radiation effects will gradually offset the negative influence, and eventually lead to an increase in urban green development efficiency.

On industrial agglomeration, the regression results show that there is a significant positive correlation between industrial agglomeration and urban green development efficiency. Industrial agglomeration can reduce the consumption of resources and pollution emissions, and increase production efficiency and urban green development efficiency.

On regulation, the regression results show that there is a significant negative correlation between regulation and urban green development efficiency, which is not consistent with our general understanding. We believe environmental regulation reflects the government's intervention in the behavior of market players. But the proper regulation intensity is not easy to control, so the negative relationship maybe attributed to excessive regulation which inhibits the role of market mechanisms.

The impacts of control variables on urban green development efficiency are different too. (1) There is significant positive correlation between urban economic development level and green development efficiency, indicating green development is a combination of green and development and economic development is still the basis of urban green development. (2) Urban FDI level is helpful for improving green development efficiency but not significantly. Urban foreign investment generally pours into those industries that have high growth potential and advanced production technologies; such investment promotes the optimization and upgrade of urban industrial structure, so enhances the urban green development efficiency indirectly. (3) There is a negative correlation between urban human resource level and green development efficiency but not significantly. This may be because most cities in the Silk Road Economic Belt are in the period of investment-driven green development, not knowledge- and innovation-driven ones. (4) The urban population density and urban green development efficiency showed a significant negative correlation, indicating that the population density is too high and will inhibit the development of urban green efficiency.

IV. Main Suggestions

First, to enhance the urban green development level and efficiency, and build urban green development belt along the Silk Road, the key is to make unified arrangement of top-level design and system design; adhere ecological bottom-line; continue to optimize the ecological environment; enrich the specific content of urban green development of the Silk Road Economic Belt; keep increasing the support to urban green development of the Silk Road Economic Belt; avoid the neglect of urban green development in order to fight for resources and policy; encourage the cities to embody green development concept in their functional positioning, industry selection and spatial layout; strengthen conservation and intensive use of resources; promote green development practices; enhance the level of urban green development of the Silk Road Economic Belt as a whole; and lead and support the building of the Silk Road Economic Belt by urban green development belt.

The second suggestion is to determine the focus of opening and development of the Silk Road Economic Belt on the basis of the non-equilibrium characteristics of urban green development. In particular, cities with higher green development efficiency such as Chengdu and Chongqing should strive to enhance the quality of urban green development; make full use of advantage of resource environment and green industries; construct the industry base of high-end manufacturing, clean energy, high-tech industries and modern service industries; create the green development pole of the Silk Road Economic Belt; and build high-end platform of international green industries and technology cooperation. While the cities with lower green development efficiency should focus on strengthening the basis of green development, increasing green infrastructure investment, accelerating the construction of green industrial systems, combining the opening and development with the transformation of the economic development pattern, and achieving the transformation and upgrade in cooperation and exchanges at home and abroad.

The third suggestion is to promote the cooperation and interaction among regional cities inside the Silk Road Economic Belt to achieve green development. The Silk Road Economic Belt is a new institutional arrangement and a new model of regional cooperation, which not only needs internal cooperation but also external cooperation. The external cooperation should be based on the internal collaboration. This requires us to face the gaps in urban green development in cities within the Silk Road Economic Belt, while promoting the interconnection network of railways, highways, aviation, telecommunications, power grids, pipelines and other energy infrastructure between the cities, to strengthen the building of green development cooperation mechanism; shape the specialization system of regional cities; improve the regional joint prevention and control system of urban ecological environment protection; establish the mechanisms of regional urban ecological compensation, carbon emissions trading, compensation for the use and trading of emission rights, and water rights trading; promote the integration of ecological environment planning, environment protection facilities, management and supervision mechanism, landscape ecology and environmental protection industry development of urban agglomeration; and form the urban "green development community" with the characteristics of equality and mutual benefit, win–win cooperation, unity and linkage.

Our fourth suggestion is to explore the main route of optimization for urban green development of the Silk Road Economic Belt. The urban green development of the Silk Road Economic Belt needs to go along the road of new urbanization and new industrialization, keep enhancing the level and quality of urbanization, improve the mechanisms for industrial agglomeration in the business parks and exit of pollution-emanating firms, maintain stable growth of urban economic development and continue the reform process. At the same time, the cities need to promote the modernization of urban green governance system and capacity, actively introduce social forces and market mechanisms to improve the green governance pattern, further transform the development pattern, optimize the human capital allocation, and achieve the transformation of green development from being investment-driven to knowledge- and innovation-driven. They also should continue to match resources and environmental carrying capacities, and the size of urban population to prevent "urban disease" caused by excessive concentration of population.

Reference

1. A. Charnes, W. Cooper and E. Rhodes, Measuring the efficiency of decision making units, *European Journal of Operational Researeh*, 1978, 2(6), 429–444.

Part V

Strategy Chapters

Chapter 19

Green Development Strategy
of Asia-Pacific Cities

Zheng Zhao
Researcher, Development Research Center
of the State Council of PRC
zz_bnu@126.com

In the past century, the city has become the main residence of mankind. According to statistics from the United Nations, 15% of the world's 1.5 billion people lived in cities in 1900. By 2000, 47% of the world's 6 billion people lived in cities. Beijing, Tokyo, Delhi and London had a population of about 1 million in 1900. By 2000, there were 100 cities with a population between 1 million and 10 million, and there were 20 metropolises with a population over 10 million. It is estimated that by 2030, 60% of the world's population will live in urban areas. Among them, the cities in the Asia-Pacific region are developing more rapidly. The world is experiencing a new round of turbulence, and the economic recovery is still a long way off. The Asia-Pacific region is the geoeconomic sector with the most growth potential and development potential, and it is also recognized as the engine of world economic growth. However, the cities in the Asia-Pacific region are also facing challenges and risks; in many cities, the task of economic transformation and upgrading and structural adjustment is arduous, and the endogenous growth momentum is insufficient, and some cities are still facing the risk of middle-income trap. It not only has important strategic significance for the Asia-Pacific region but also has a profound impact on the world's urbanization and economic development pattern for the cities in the Asia-Pacific region to choose what kind of development path and whether they can achieve green development? At present, all the countries in the world are promoting the implementation of the fair, inclusive and sustainable Post-2015 Development Agenda on the basis of summarizing the experience of the Millennium Development Goals. At a new historical starting point, although the opportunities and challenges are different, the problems of resources and environment and social equity are the common development problems faced by the Asia-Pacific cities, and no country or city can survive in global resources and environment degradation and social unrest. Green development constitutes the common development needs, development aspirations and development responsibilities of the cities in the Asia-Pacific region, and it is necessary for these cities to re-examine their own development trend, clear green development goals and form a development path, and jointly promote the green development of the region and the whole world.

I. Strategic Goals of Green Development in Cities in the Asia-Pacific Region

Green development is critical for any city in the Asia-Pacific region. The Asia-Pacific cities should work together to build a green future. They should take "green identity" as the premise, and adhere to the unity of "common destiny" and "harmony in diversity". The co-construction and sharing mechanism should be established to transform the diversity and difference of Asia-Pacific cities into potential and power of green development. The city's own interests should be combined with the common interests of other cities, so as to build a community of common destiny for green development in Asia-Pacific cities with same vision, diversified development and common progress through joint participation and cooperation.

The goal of building community of common destiny for green development in Asia-Pacific cities mainly includes three meanings:

1. **Emphasis on "green identity" of green development in Asia-Pacific cities**

   "Green identity" is the basis and premise of green development in Asia-Pacific cities. The green development of the Asia-Pacific cities is a concentrated embodiment of the relationship between man and nature, economy and society, government and market, and city and state, which reflects the progress in civilization of respecting nature, conforming to nature, protecting nature, equal development and fair development in cities. In this respect, the Asia-Pacific cities share common values and ideas, and they are common in the reflection of the traditional development path, the understanding of the realistic development path and the selection of future development path, that is, to promote the development of livability, prosperity, inclusion and good governance in cities, and build a home of green cities.

2. **Emphasis on "common destiny" of green development in Asia-Pacific cities**

   "Common destiny" is the goal and direction of green development in Asia-Pacific cities. The Asia-Pacific cities share the same sky and the same world. They are mutually inclusive, interdependent and share weal and woe. They should abandon the zero sum thinking of winner-take-all, establish the sense of community of interests and seek common ground while reserving differences, fully reflect the win–win attribute and responsibility attribute of green development, adhere to equal development, win–win cooperation and common progress, seek the greatest common divisor for the interests of all parties in common development, and build a community of destiny with co-construction and sharing, and win–win cooperation as the core.

3. **Emphasis on "harmony in diversity" of green development in Asia-Pacific cities**

   "Harmony in diversity" is the way and approach of green development in Asia-Pacific cities. The community of common destiny for green development in Asia-Pacific cities does not mean uniform development, which is not in line with the law of urban green development, nor is it practical. The green development of Asia-Pacific cities should adhere to the development of "harmony in diversity" on the basis of "common destiny", which fully embodies the multi-attribute and inclusive attribute of green development. In promoting the green development of Asia-Pacific cities, we should respect the differences in cities of different countries, development stages and cultural characteristics in the Asia-Pacific region, promote the concept and cultural exchanges of inclusive urban green development, support cities in different countries to explore green development in line with their actual conditions, and achieve the grand goal of urban green development throughout the Asia-Pacific region and even the whole world through the mutual exchanges, mutual learning and integration among the Asia-Pacific cities.

II. Strategic Path of Green Development in Asia-Pacific Cities

The strategic path of green development in Asia-Pacific cities mainly consists of one core, one emphasis and four supports. That is, in order to promote the green development of Asia-Pacific cities, it is necessary to take improvement of the green governance system in Asia-Pacific cities as the core, take promotion of green development in cities in developing countries as the emphasis, and build the support systems for green innovation, green economy, green finance and green knowledge in Asia-Pacific cities.

(I) Refining green governance system in Asia-Pacific cities

The increasingly severe natural resources and ecological environment are common problems facing the cities in the Asia-Pacific region. Seen from the current situation, although many ecological environmental risks arising from the production, consumption and trade activities of the Asia-Pacific cities are often concentrated in some cities in some countries, they have crossed national boundaries and have evolved into regional and even global problems. Whether they can benefit from these activities or not, cities in developed countries and developing countries face the common and unavoidable pressures and challenges. In the long term, the space boundaries have become blurred in terms of urban green development, so that the development of regional, national and international significance is no longer a problem of a single country or city, and the governance system for green development also needs to adapt to it. In order to promote the green development of the Asia-Pacific cities, it is necessary to improve the green governance mechanism in Asia-Pacific cities from the perspective of the development of the whole Asia-Pacific region, with the theme of open exchanges and cooperative governance.

On the one hand, the consistency of demand for the green development in Asia-Pacific cities requires an effective multilateral system. Therefore, we should focus on the integration of various bilateral and multilateral cooperation mechanisms in the Asia-Pacific region as a whole for the green development in Asia-Pacific cities, cooperate as more as possible in many cross-border, cross-continent and cross-domain governance issues, focus on the problems of basic survival of urban residents, such as poverty, health and education and realistic challenges such as climate change, energy resources security and weak economic growth, eliminate the inefficiency and fragmentation of the governance mechanism, improve multilateral mechanism, link together countries and cities on the Pacific coast, connect with emerging and developed economies, jointly build a future partnership for green development in the Asia-Pacific cities, and jointly build an open Asia-Pacific economic structure, so that the "Asia-Pacific" can evolve into a development complex affecting global green development from a geographical concept.

On the other hand, we should focus on the establishment of coordination mechanism for regional ecological environment protection in the Asia-Pacific cities, establish coordination mechanism on the core issues of cross-regional and transnational ecological environment, promote the Asia-Pacific cities to jointly carry forward and formulate the plan for cross-regional ecological environment protection, promote the common delineation of ecological protection areas in the Asia-Pacific cities and regions, delimit a common ecological control zone for trans-boundary urban agglomerations, integrate environmental factors, such as mountain, sea, forest and water, construct the urban ecological security pattern, and determine the phased job requirements and priorities and main tasks. When coping with and dealing with problems of urban ecological environment, efficient communication, quick response and joint action should be achieved. We should consider not only the particularities of specific circumstances in different countries and cities but also the common requirements of ecological environmental protection, so as to solve the common environmental problems.

(II) Promoting urban green development capability of developing countries in the Asia-Pacific region

Both developed and developing countries are faced with the problem of green development in the Asia-Pacific region. But we must realize that the short board of the wooden barrel is the most important factor affecting the overall development, and the urban green development capacity of the developing countries is of great importance. As pointed out in *Our Common Future* by the World Commission on Environment and Development (1997), cities in many industrial countries are also facing problems of the aging of public facilities, the degradation of the environment, the pollution of the city and the breakdown of neighborhood relations. However, most industrial countries have the means and funds to deal with such problems. So it is a matter of political and social choice for them. Governments of cities in developing countries often lack the capacity, funds and staff to provide the land, services and facilities needed for a decent life to the rapidly growing population. The result is the rapid emergence of illegal residential areas, where there **are** only outdated original equipments, overcrowding and rampant diseases caused by unsanitary conditions. They are facing a major urban crisis.[1] In promoting the green development of Asia-Pacific cities, we should attach great importance to the green development capability of developing countries, especially the green development of underdeveloped cities in developing countries.

First of all, in dealing with the problems of green development in the Asia-Pacific region, we must make clear the common but differentiated responsibilities. There is no doubt that coping with the ecological crisis, reducing environmental damage and promoting social equity are common responsibilities for cities in the Asian-Pacific countries. However, green development is not a problem of time point but a timing problem combining history, reality and future. Historically, unequal international economic relations have formed the imbalance of urban development. The cities in developing countries are the passive recipients of the international economic and technological situation, rather than the leaders and influencers of international economic and technological development and standards. In this case, cities in developing countries are often located downstream of the industry chain, where the export of natural resources and primary products account for a large proportion, but it cannot affect the price system of international resource products, making these cities the direct victims of the resources and environment damage. The continuation of the old international order, sharp decline in the urban economic growth rate and aggravation of debt burden of each country under the financial crisis, and the growth of protectionism in developed countries, have also exacerbated the unfavorable status of cities in developing countries. Thus, the impact of environmental degradation and resource depletion still exists and is quite severe in some places. Therefore, it is still necessary to take into account the characteristics of cities in developing countries for the green development of Asia-Pacific cities and differentiate in responsibility. Particularly in terms of goals, paths and schedules for green development, the cities in developing countries should be given more leeway and development space.

Second, cooperation between cities in developed countries and cities in developing countries should be strengthened. The cities in developed countries are encouraged to provide financial and technical support to cities in developing countries, and help them to achieve green development through various forms such as training, experience exchange, knowledge transfer and technical assistance while transforming unsustainable consumption patterns and economic structures, reducing the excessive consumption of resources and energy and the impact on the environment and ecology, and actively fulfilling the international responsibilities to which it is due.

Finally, cities in developing countries should collaborate with each other and unite for self-development to find solutions to the common urban crisis. Most cities in developing countries have similar stages of development but face similar problems and challenges of population, resources and environment. To promote the green development of the Asia-Pacific cities, we should also strengthen cooperation and coordination in terms of economy, trade, investment, technology and talent related to green development among cities in developing countries. We should broaden the scope of cooperation and improve the quality of cooperation through cooperation and exchanges on the principle of mutual respect, equality and mutual benefit, and realize the recombination of resources to compensate for losses in resources such as capital, technology and markets caused by the slowdown in the developed economies and move toward green development together.

(III) Building support system for green development in Asia-Pacific cities

The support system for green development in Asia-Pacific cities mainly includes the support system for green innovation in Asia-Pacific cities, the support system for green industry in Asia-Pacific cities, the support system for green finance in Asia-Pacific cities, and the support system for green knowledge in Asia-Pacific cities.

1. Building support system for green innovation in Asia-Pacific cities

To promote the green development of Asia-Pacific cities, efforts should be made to promote urban green development capability through scientific and technological innovation. We should jointly promote scientific and technological innovation through the joint construction of innovation carriers such as urban green science and technology parks, industrial bases, and university science and technology parks, by means of trade and technology transfer agreements, expert agreements and cooperative researches of improved equipment, focusing on energy, building, water, electricity, transportation and infrastructure in the Asia-Pacific cities. What's more, we should focus on basic research in fields including resources and environment, climate change, new energy, new materials and green building, and cultivate technology source of emerging industry, so as to lay a foundation for the urban high technology upgradation and emerging industry development in the future. In addition, we should accelerate the development of applied new products and technologies for renewable energy and pollution control, strengthen research and development and promotion of technologies for urban security design and control, accident prevention, emergency plan and damage mitigation, and continuously improve the efficiency of resource utilization, control ability of pollutant emission, and capacity for resource utilization as well as hazard prevention and control of waste in the Asia-Pacific cities.

At the same time, to promote the green development of Asia-Pacific cities, we should establish the technology transfer mechanism for cities in developed countries and developing countries, construct the multi-level, multi-channel and diversified technical assistance docking platform, technology trading market and technology transfer center, carry out systematic, supporting and engineering research and development on green technology with important application foreground, and promote demonstration applications of key technologies, including biotechnology, electronic information technology and new energy technology in fields such as pollution control, low carbon cycle, and environmental monitoring and early warning in cities in developing countries. What's more, we should promote and support the research and development, dissemination and patent transfer of scientific and technological achievements that meet the actual demand of cities in developing countries, and lower the real threshold for cities in developing countries to use technology to promote green development under the premise of protecting intellectual property rights.

2. Building support system for green economy in Asia-Pacific cities

Under the impact of global financial crisis, the common economic pressures facing the Asia-Pacific cities all exist in varying degrees in the problems, including the decline of urban income, the surge in urban expenditure, the difficulties of urban financing and the reduction of urban investment. In this case, the Asia-Pacific cities should take the development of green economy as the main measure to deal with the crisis. A high-end, innovation-driven, and green and low-carbon economic development model should be formed through the development of green economy. The development level of green economy with high-tech content, high human capital investment, high added value, high industry-driving force, low resource consumption and low environmental pollution should be raised, and the transformation and upgradation of traditional industries should be promoted to drive the green development of the industries. They should also look for new economic growth point, force the emerging green business and industry chain, expand market demand, and stimulate investment and consumption needs. At the same time, in the promotion of green development in Asia-Pacific cities, a free, open and non-discriminatory global trade system should be maintained, the liberalization and facilitation of trade and investment should be promoted, the trade and investment barriers should be eliminated, and all kinds of practical and covert protectionism borrowed from green development should be opposed and resisted. It should be noted that the urban economy tends to be the enterprise cluster economy. Thus, in the construction of the support system for green economy in Asia-Pacific cities, the transnational corporations can often exert great influence on the environment and resources of cities in other countries. Therefore, attention should be paid to the role of transnational enterprises. The transnational enterprises in fields such as energy, chemicals, metal manufacturing, papermaking, pharmacy and automobile industry should be promoted to adopt feasible and highest environmental safety and health protection standards in research and development, production, sales and service, share cutting-edge green technologies, and fulfill the corporate social responsibility for promoting green development.

3. Building support system for green finance in Asia-Pacific cities

The concept of green development should be run through the Asia-Pacific international financial institutions, especially the Asian Infrastructure Investment Bank and the Asian Development Bank. The principles and guidelines for investment and financing of environmental protection, resource utilization and social development should be established and improved to fully integrate the ecological environment and social equity into the investment and financing projects of economy, trade, energy and infrastructure, so that more transnational credit funds are used to improve the productivity in the urban environment and resources sectors, and greater consideration is given to social and environmental impact objectives broader and more long-term than stable finance. At the same time, as many environmental and social development goals are shelved due to weak urban economic growth in various countries under downward trend in the global economy, the international financial institutions should pay more attention to the fields such as urban employment, health, education, green technology research and application, public transportation and intelligent transportation, energy supply and demand management, ecological environment protection and governance, and urban–rural integration development. They should not only provide financial support for the urban green development under the depression but also inject impetus into the long-term urban green development.

4. Building support system for green knowledge in Asia-Pacific cities

The green development of Asia-Pacific cities is inseparable from the support of knowledge and intelligence. Experts and scholars often verify the apparent environmental risks and changes caused by urban activities through scientific research and academic discussion, and a large number of non-governmental organizations and social groups also play an important role in raising public awareness of the environment and applying political pressure to promote action by city governments. To build the support system for green knowledge in Asia-Pacific cities, the role of the scientific community and non-governmental organizations in Asia-Pacific cities should be emphasized, the research of urban green development by scientific research institutions, universities and academic organizations should be strengthened, and the public and private sectors of the cities should be encouraged and supported to provide advice and assistance on green development. At the same time, we should give full play to the advantages of non-governmental organizations in identifying urban ecological risks, evaluating urban environmental impacts, formulating and implementing treatment measures, and coordinating the relationship between the public and city governments; protect the right of non-governmental organizations to understand and obtain information about the environment and natural resources, the right to participate in consultations, and the right to participate in activity decisions that may have a major impact on the environment; and expand the cooperation between the city governments and non-governmental organizations in the planning, monitoring and evaluation of green development projects, to jointly provide an intellectual guarantee for urban green development.

Reference

1. World Commission on Environment and Development, *Our Common Future*, Jilin People's Press, Changchun, 1997, p. 20.

Chapter 20

Urban Green Development Strategy in China

Zheng Zhao
Researcher, Development Research Center
of the State Council of PRC
zz_bnu@126.com

China's urbanization has undergone a period of rapid expansion and quantitative growth. In 1978, China's urbanization rate was only 17.9%, and it had reached 54.7% by 2014. The urbanization rate has increased by 36.9% points in the past 36 years, with an average annual increase rate of more than 1% point. At present, China has officially entered a city-oriented society. Along with the change of urban–rural dual structure, a large number of rural population flows to the city, providing adequate and cheap labor for urban development in China, bringing a huge "demographic dividend", and strongly supporting the miracle of China's economic growth. However, despite great achievements in economic and social development, China is still a developing country. China's rapid urbanization has caused severe pressure on the environment. Due to excessive dependence on expanding the investment scale and increasing the material input, the limited natural supply capacity and carrying capacity of ecological environment have been weakened. The problem of disharmony among environment, economy and social development is becoming increasingly apparent, and the problem of uneven, uncoordinated and unsustainable development remains outstanding. "Urban diseases" such as environmental pollution, ecological damage, crowded population, traffic congestion, employment difficulties, housing shortage and polarization between the rich and the poor are becoming increasingly serious, and "rural diseases" such as economic contraction, population loss and cultural depression are also increasing. In the long run, promoting the quality, efficiency and sustainable green development of cities is not only the main direction of China's urbanization process but also an important way to promote China's economic and social development. Looking into the future, Chinese cities should adhere to the people-oriented development, realize the coordination and balance of relationship between man and nature, economy and society, government and market, and city and state, and build an urban green development system with livability, affluence, tolerance, good governance and strong state.

I. Livability Strategy

The core of the livability strategy of urban green development is to build a comprehensive urban green development system based on the rule of law to strengthen the urban environmental governance and resource conservation through comprehensive reform, to change urban industry and space development mode through the system, and to stimulate and guide urban green development.

(I) Strengthening environmental governance of air, water and soil

Serious environmental problems including air, water and soil pollution in cities that harm the health of urban residents, and affect the production and living of urban residents should be solved to build a beautiful home with blue sky, green land and clear water. (1) *Air pollution control*: The average annual concentration of PM2.5 in cities should be significantly declined. The motor vehicle pollution control project should be thoroughly implemented. The use of clean energy vehicles should be vigorously promoted, and the construction of charging facilities should be accelerated. The urban dust pollution control should be strengthened. (2) *Water pollution control*: The protection of drinking water should be strengthened, the pollution sources in water source protection area and quasi-protected area of drinking water should be comprehensively investigated, the environment remediation and recovery of water source area should be vigorously promoted, and the quality of drinking water should be constantly improved. The groundwater should be actively remediated, and source control and end restoration should be strengthened. The surface water should be vigorously controlled, and the treatment capacity of domestic sewage and discharge standard of industrial wastewater should be further improved. (3) *Soil pollution control*: Efforts should be made to control pollution sources. While paying attention to the up-to-standard discharge of the existing heavy polluting enterprises, more stringent environmental access standards should be adopted for priority areas of soil environmental protection.

(II) Promoting economical and cyclic utilization of energy and resources

Emphasis should be placed on strengthening the economy in the whole society, in the whole field and in the whole process, controlling the total amount of resources and energy consumption, and improving the efficiency and effectiveness of the utilization of resources and energy. (1) The economical and intensive utilization of energy should be promoted in cities. The application and promotion of energy-saving new technologies, new products and new equipment should be speeded up, and the application of solar thermal, geothermal and other renewable energy in urban construction should be actively promoted in industries with special focus on building materials industry and housing industry. The clean energy should be vigorously developed and used. The change of urban energy supply mode should be promoted with distributed energy, energy supply facilities for new energy vehicles and smart grid as the focus. The new energy-saving mechanisms like energy performance contracting should be vigorously implemented. (2) The recycling system of urban resources should be improved. In order to improve the utilization rate of resources, the construction of the recycling system of urban resources covering the whole process of urban production and consumption should be speeded up. The circular production mode of "source reduction, process control and end regeneration" should be promoted in the whole process of manufacturing, and energy and resources consumption and waste generation should be reduced from the source by means of green design, improvement of technological process and improvement of technical equipment level. The urban waste materials recycling network should be improved, and the sorting, processing and utilization level of waste materials should be constantly raised. The level of harmless disposal and recycling of household garbage should be improved.

(III)   Refining urban green development system

The system is of great significance to urban green development. In 1952, the London smog incident claimed 4,000 lives, so the *Clean Air Act* was enacted in Britain in 1956. The government forced people to use anthracite and moved power plants out of the city, thus London's air quality was significantly improved and London became a better place to live. The Chinese cities should also take reform and innovation as the basic impetus to promote the urban green development, create a standardized, long-term and stable urban green development system environment, form a long-term mechanism to protect green development through deepening reform, perfecting the urban green development system, and combine the "soft guidance" and "hard constraints". Emphasis should be placed on revising the local laws, regulations and normative documents that conflict with green development or are detrimental to urban green development, and on the establishment of ecological value and ecological development view of "giving priority to ecology". The red line thinking should be upheld, and the front-end system design should be completed. The institutional control of process

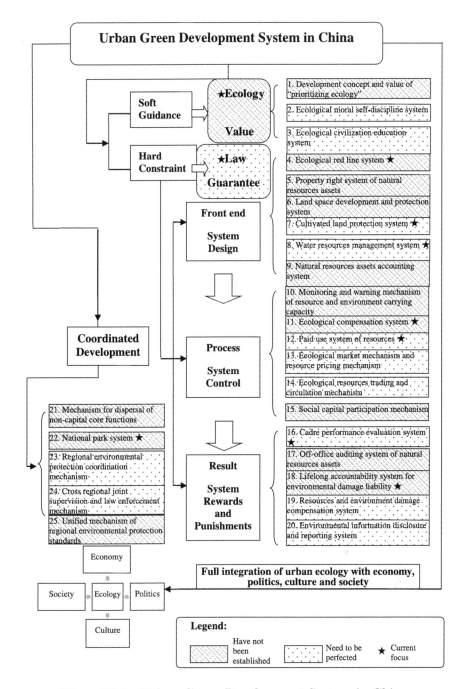

Figure 20.1. Urban Green Development System in China.

should be strengthened with the law as the guarantee. The incentive and restraint mechanism should be improved, and the complete urban green development system should be finally established with the assessment system as the guide. The five main aspects and 25 specific systems that should be established and improved for the construction of China's urban green development system are specified in Figure 20.1.

The construction of urban green development system in China is a complicated and arduous historical task. In terms of attribute, the development view and value of "prioritizing ecology" are the soft guidance and soft environment for the construction of urban green development system in China, while laws and policies about green development are the hard constraints in urban green development. The construction of urban green development system in China requires both the support of development concept and value, and the constraints and guidance of laws and policies. In terms of the process, China's urban green development system includes three basic stages, namely the front-end system design, the system constraints in the process and the system rewards and punishments for results, and a number of specific systems should be established in each stage. In terms of the content, China's urban green development system requires full integration between ecological system and economic system, political system, cultural system and social system, so as to form the five-in-one overall layout. In terms of the regional development, in the construction of green development system, the cities should also take full account of their own regional and national functional positioning to lead and promote green development in surrounding areas.

II. Prosperity Strategy

The prosperity strategy of urban green development centers on transforming urban economic development mode, promoting industrial green development and green industrialization, stimulating innovation impetus, ability and vigor of labor and enterprises and realizing green development while achieving efficient and high-quality growth under the driving force of innovation.

(I) Forming innovation-driven urban economic development model

At present, adapting and leading the development of new normal is an important part of urban green development in China. The new normal of economic development is a stage characteristic, which occurs when the economy grows at a medium-to-high speed from the growth shifting stage. Its essence is that the economy is developed into a new stage of higher level and requires green development of higher quality. Meanwhile, the scientific and technological innovation plays an increasingly important role in supporting and guiding the economic and social development of cities, and thus the innovation-driven development will be unprecedentedly important for further enhancing the capability of independent innovation and mastering the strategic initiative in the new global competition. To focus on the background of developmental stage transformation, structural adjustment and developmental method transformation of China's urbanization and economy and to promote the urban green development, the most important things are as follows: to form a dynamic mechanism different from the past, to center on improving the quality and efficiency of urban economic development, to take innovation as the fundamental driving force to improve the quality of economic growth, to optimize the arrangement of labor, capital, land, technology, management and other elements, to make overall planning to promote the vigorous development of new technologies, new industries and new operational types, to further highlight the promotion of and influence on economic development of the total innovation focusing on scientific and technological innovation, to release new demand and create new supply, to replace the traditional economic model with innovative economic model fundamentality, and to transform the urban development from original model mainly relying on labor, capital, resources, energy and other general factors into a new model mainly driven by talent, technology, information and other advanced factors.

(II) Creating domestic demand-oriented urban innovation system

China has many large cities with over 1 million people. However, compared with other metropolis at the stage of stable development around the world, cities in China are still at the stage of improving urbanization quality with great innovation demands and huge market of innovative products. The main development mode of innovative city at home and abroad is to be embedded in the global industrial chain and urban network and centered on external demands and gradually extended to high-end value chain after getting comparative advantages in some low-end links. As for China's cities, especially big cities, the huge population and economic scale itself is a potential domestic demand market, and it has a significant impact on green scientific and technological innovation and industrial application. On the one hand, a large number of green scientific and technological innovation products and services can not only create development opportunities in the external market, but also have the early advantage in the huge local market; on the other hand, megalopolises have an enormous population, diversified culture and highly developed economy, and thus they have strong demand on scientific and technological innovation, which can spawn the development of a large number of native green innovative industries and promote the green technology progress and industry transformation and upgrading. Therefore, China's cities should focus on building a domestic demand-oriented urban innovation system, further tapping their own potential, stimulating urban innovation needs, strengthening urban innovation supply, and enhancing urban green innovation competitiveness.

(III) Improving the quality of urban service economy

We shall promote large-scale, high-end, professional and international development of urban service industry, and promote the development level of modern service industry. For the city development, we shall give priority to the development of modern service industry represented by software and information, finance, e-commerce, cultural creativity, tourism and leisure, and intensive and efficient, green and low carbon productive service industry; and vigorously develop the emerging service industry spawned by the integration of network technology and communication technology, establish a cluster zone of modern service industry, foster and develop a leading enterprise in the service industry at a high level, new operation mode and excellent brand, promote the development of high-end-oriented service industry, optimize the development system, mechanism and environment of the service industry, enhance the innovative development and international level of the modern service industry, and improve the modern industrial system relying on service economy.

(IV) Promoting green transformation and upgrading of industries

We shall deploy the innovation chain centering on industry chain, develop the new energy, new materials, biotechnology and new medicine, energy saving and environmental protection and other strategic emerging industries and focus on forming the leading edge of market scale and technology in the strategically emerging industry market. We shall rely on research and development in science and technology, adhere to deep integration of industrialization and information, promote the green transformation of traditional industries with high and new technology and advanced applicable technologies, improve the clean production and pollution control, promote the transformation and upgrading of traditional competitive industries, and achieve development in the direction of being high end, green and low carbon economy. We shall constantly phase out backward production capacity, strengthen the remediation of pollution enterprises, and rationalize the industrial enterprises of severe pollution, high energy consumption and poor efficiency. We shall implement the most stringent industrial policies and standards for energy conservation and environmental protection, and strictly control industrial projects with high energy consumption and high pollution.

(V) Strengthening the competitiveness of city's green talents

Talent is the core of urban green development. According to international city development standards, the biggest resource to support the development of urban green industry may not lie in whether the natural resources and material conditions are abundant but in whether a city has irreproducible talents and knowledge advantages. To promote the development of China's urban green industry, we shall "select and use the talents from all over the world" and truly transform the comparative advantages of human resources into the competitive advantages of human capital. We shall put emphasis on the cultivation of all kinds of high-level and inter-disciplinary talents conducive to the development of urban green industry and specialized talents with relevant occupational skills, attract and gather international professional talents and outstanding entrepreneurs with global vision and strong innovative consciousness, stimulate their creative enthusiasm and innovation vigor up to the hilt, integrate the key direction of urban green industry talent cultivation, orientation of green industry with the overall planning of upgrading of industrial structure closely and enhance interaction and integration between talent structure and industrial transformation and upgrading. At the same time, we shall further promote the reform and innovation of talent evaluation system and incentive mechanism; fully respect the value pursuit of talents in enterprises, research institutions, colleges and universities; focus on the establishment of a rewarding mechanism for talents which combines short-term incentive and long-term incentive, rationally link income to performance, and fully embody the talent value and contributions; improve the talent innovation and entrepreneurship support system in order to provide solid intellectual support for the development of urban green industry.

(VI) Strengthening the competitiveness of city's green enterprises

Enterprises are the main body of green industry development, so leading green enterprises are required to enhance the competitiveness of urban green industry. The history of global industrial development in the past 100 years shows that the most effective technologies come from the leading industrial enterprises, and the innovation in major products, technology and business model almost all happens in those enterprises. The key enterprises are not only the ultimate implementer of commercial value of green technology achievements but also the main participators and executors of the whole green production and innovation activities. Hence, if a city wants to promote economic growth and achieve green development, it must enhance input competitiveness, technological achievement output, application competitiveness and market competitiveness of the key green enterprises in the urban, regional and even global green industry activities. What deserves special attention is that green small- and medium-sized enterprises (SMEs) are often the "spark" of green economic development and innovation, and the development of green SMEs is also one of the important manifestations of green economic competitiveness. In the long run, only by forming a green enterprise system with stimulation of a number of key enterprises and participation of a large number of SMEs, can a competitive urban green economic system be formed truly.

(VII) Attaching importance to the construction of innovative central cities

With the development of information technology, the global and regional scientific and technological innovation resources, elements, commodities and services flow around the world more and more conveniently and the trend of globalization of science and technology becomes obvious. This allows Chinese cities to have more opportunities and higher possibilities to participate in the division of global scientific and technological innovation at a higher level, share the achievements of global scientific and technological innovation, and play an important role in building a new global innovation governance order. Meanwhile, because of the high degree of mobility of scientific and technological innovation resources and spatial agglomeration of scientific research activities, those cities that have world-class scientific and technological innovation centers will be able to attract maximum global innovation elements, and thus obtain the strategic initiative in the international competition and the establishment of innovation governance system. At present, it is an important measure for many countries and regions to deal with the new round of scientific and technological revolution and strengthen national competitiveness by actively planning and building national and even global innovation centers. The United Kingdom selected three cities, i.e. York, Newcastle and Manchester as "Science Cities" in 2004 and selected another three cities, i.e. Birmingham, Nottingham and Bristol, aiming to develop the United Kingdom into an area mostly suitable for innovation in the world by strengthening the ties between industry and science base. The US attempted to guide the returning industry and thus reconstructed the global division system with the first mover advantage of the revolution of new science and technology and created a grand blueprint for building an "Eastern Silicon Valley" in 2012 and planned to build an applied science park in the east of Manhattan going neck and neck with the Silicon Valley in California, striving to become the "global leader of scientific and technological innovation". Under the background of globalization, to achieve innovation-driven development and build a green economic system, China's cities should actively undertake the historical mission embodied in the competitiveness of national innovation strategy, innovation ability, innovation level, innovation culture and international innovation, face the world and establish an innovation system with international influence and competitiveness and become a demonstrator and pioneer of Chinese and even global innovation-driven green development.

III. Inclusiveness Strategy

The inclusive strategy of urban green development centers more on supporting the development capacity building of vulnerable groups, further reducing the poverty, improving the welfare and strengthening the education, so that more people can participate in and enjoy the opportunities and achievements of urban green development.

(I) Reducing poverty

The green development of the cities will depend on closer cooperation with the majority of the poor in the cities, since they are often the real builders of the city. Urban poverty consists of economic poverty and dissatisfaction in realizing their social needs. The economic poverty mainly refers to shortage of food, clothing, housing and other necessities. During the urban development, attention should be paid to guaranteeing basic living standards for urban poverty-stricken population, and provide cleaner water, food and basic living facilities for them. Besides, poverty is not only a kind of physiological need but also a kind of social demand and also has social meaning. If a person lacks the resources needed to participate in social activities, then he or she is still a poverty-stricken person even if his or her physiological needs have been met.[1] Therefore, to alleviate the urban poverty, we shall shift the attention into social inclusion from economic poverty, establish the development achievement sharing mechanism based on the principles of social equality and justice, help poverty-stricken population enhance the knowledge and skills for improving economic activities and provide more opportunities for their development in the cities.

(II) Improving welfare

We shall promote paralleled improvement of urban economic growth and citizen's welfare, accelerate urban social construction emphasizing on improving people's livelihood and achieve the goal that all urban citizens can enjoy their rights to education, employment, medical and old-age care and housing. At the same time, we shall ensure that urban development is fair to all and urban mobility is adapted, and regardless of household registration and sources of the population, provide a unified, fair and inclusive basic welfare guarantee for all urban residents. We shall further improve the institutional framework of major welfare projects including education, medical treatment, pension and social assistance, establish the public service and social security equalization system, include more informal employment groups of various types, migrant farmers, poverty-stricken people and various kinds of marginal groups in the social welfare system of the city, and provide them with the same public services (including employment, children attending schools and medical services seeking) and various welfares as the citizens. Especially, we shall accelerate the renovation of shantytowns, increase the supply of low- and middle-price houses, small- and medium-sized houses and other ordinary commodity houses, regulate the development of housing market, slow the precipitous rise of housing prices, meet the housing needs of residents of different levels, and avoid the "slum" problem suffered from by western countries at early times and by some developing countries at present.

(III) Satisfying the demand for livelihood

We shall overcome the obstacle of "emphasizing on materials rather than the people" in the traditional development mode during urbanization, and promote the transformation of urban development from "urbanization of materials" to "urbanization of people". To achieve these, first, we shall promote city and industry integration, avoid urban development of marginalized people in cities, such as "empty cities" and "ghost towns", and based on urban environmental resources and conditions, promote the coordinated development of population urbanization, industrial urbanization and spatial urbanization, combine the industrial development with population concentration and urban construction, to give full consideration to the human life and development needs in the urban industry and space planning and design. Second, we should enhance the city's carrying capacity and service capacity, adjust measures to local conditions and make scientific planning, make a rational urban, intercity and urban and rural space layout, and centering on the most concerned, direct and realistic housing, transportation, education, medical treatment and other livelihood needs of urban residents, improve infrastructure and provide public services, improve the living quality in the city and enhance the quality of urban development.

(IV) Improving education quality

On the one hand, we shall strengthen the education about the value of green development. We shall change the city residents' values and attitudes toward the environment and development, strengthen the individual and collective's sense of responsibility for environment, society and for promoting the coordination between human and environment, society, and improve the overall sense of responsibility in the urban society. On the other hand, to improve the quality of education, we must strengthen the adaptability of the city to different stages of development. We shall actively improve the content and methods of education, impart knowledge on a wide range of social science, natural science and humanities concepts, increasingly use improved tools to upgrade the traditional production activities, strengthen the method of education available to improve traditional production activities, protect natural resources and promote the harmonious development of the society, make the city residents have a more profound understanding of the interaction between natural ecology and city life, economic development and resources environment and social progress. At the same time, we shall support and encourage the diversified concept innovation, idea innovation and method innovation of green development, and strive to develop the cities into important innovation cradles of new ideas, new products, new technology and new culture of green development.

(V) Strengthening social driving force of scientific and technological innovation

After the industrial revolution, cities around the world will encounter a variety of problems in the course of development and even suffer from "urban disease". The process of solving these problems is also the process of scientific and technological innovation, for example, the occurrence of rail transportation, intelligent building, social management information and other new solutions. Similarly, China's cities can't always adopt the practices of a model government or market methods including "purchase restriction", "traffic restriction", "raising prices" and "charging fees" to manage their cities, but should highlight the method of scientific and technological innovation and enable the scientific and technological innovation to play a more prominent role in the livelihood of people in their cities. We shall center on the most concerned, direct and realistic great livelihood and social development needs of urban residents, focus on promotion of research and development in technology and integration and demonstration in the key fields to cure the "urban diseases", including information infrastructure, food safety, medical care and health, scientific and technological transportation, energy saving and new energy, city security and emergency support etc., speed up the transformation and application of achievements to make the scientific and technological innovations benefit people's livelihood truly, and enhance technological support to economic and social development.

IV. Governance Strategy

For the good governance strategy of urban green development, its core is to build a sound and vibrant urban green governance system, take the common goal of urban green development as the guide, combine the urban governance capacity, governance mechanism, governance means and governance performance, and achieve "good development" through "good governance".

(I) Advancing the modernization of governance capability

First of all, we shall give full play to the role of the government in the green development of the city. (1) Establish a regulation system for the use of natural resources. Regulate the use, define the development, use and protection of various national land spaces and qualitatively classify the energy, water and mineral resources and undertake cascade utilization. (2) Establish an ecological red line system, define and maintain strictly the ecological red line. (3) Establish national land space development and protection system, and promote the development in strict accordance with the role of main functional areas. (4) Make strict access system, implement strict land use management and resource conservation management, strengthen the planning process, make strict examination and prohibit the development activities in compliance with use regulation and conservation standards. Second, we should promote the level of scientific decision-making of the city government. We should include green development in the planning of economic and social development and implement green development in the whole process of urban economic and social development. We should actively promote policy evaluation, strategy evaluation and planning evaluation, and establish a comprehensive decision-making mechanism for economic, environmental and social development. In the important decision-making process about city planning, energy resource development and utilization, industrial layout and land development process etc., we should give priority to ecological benefit and social benefit, and take the "one vote veto" measure for matters that may have severe impact on environment and society to avoid major decision-making mistakes. Finally, we shall improve the assessment system of development achievements. According to the requirements of urban green development, we shall include the indexes of resource consumption, environmental damage and social benefit in the assessment system of social economy comprehensively and attach more importance to them, and establish the target system, assessment methods and reward and punishment mechanism required by green development. We shall strengthen the comprehensive target assessment of urban leadership, pay more attention to the assessment of resource consumption, environmental damage, social benefit, and scientific and technological innovation, define the responsible body, objective and scope of urban green development and establish lifelong accountability system against damage liability.

(II) Building partnership for public–private cooperative governance

We shall encourage investment of social capital in the ecological environmental protection and social services market, and improve the supply of urban public services as well as the quality of urban public service through the cooperation model. Meanwhile, we should give full play to the role of the government policy in market incentives, accelerate the reform of natural resources and their product prices, fully reflect market supply and demand, resource scarcity, eco-environmental damage costs and repair efficiency, make the enterprises and individuals reduce the cost of resources and environment by establishing mechanisms for water right, pollution right and carbon emission permit, etc., promote technological innovation, and promote the urban green development jointly.

(III) Giving full play to social organizations

The domestic and international practices show that social organizations can mobilize resources and communication channels, and provide professional and convenient services for the general public. Besides, social organizations can also launch, organize and finance the activities to individually and jointly solve the safety problems, environmental problems, health problems and problems in the city to make up for the deficiency of competent government agencies in the city. Besides, in the process of urban green development, the city should actively guide and support the development of social organizations engaged in designing environmental protection and social people's livelihood, encourage the social organizations to provide consultation, guidance and advice for measures and methods of restoration and protection and improvement of urban green development, monitor, evaluate and report the change in urban green development at regular intervals, make scientific research on important issues affecting the urban green development, provide education and training for relevant personnel in the government and enterprises and organize and carry out specific actions and activities of urban green development.

(IV) Public participation in urban governance

The urban green development needs social understanding, support, and more public participation in the decision-making process, which will influence the natural environment and the social development. Therefore, to promote the urban green development and improve the governance mechanism, the following measures need be taken: encouraging public to take initiatives, providing legally registered public organizations, which will carry out activities with the participation rights, enabling those who truly represent the will of the people to participate in the public hearings and public consultations concerning urban development and the environmental impact, and ensuring public receives freely relevant information and technical information. We shall intensify the efforts to enable the public to participate in legal aid, establish dispute mediation and legal aid docking mechanism, guide and help the public to solve problems using law channels, and effectively safeguard the legitimate participation rights of the public. At the same time, we should explore the establishment of online solicitation and online hearings, etc., increase the citizens' participation in the regional public policy making and administrative management, allow more citizens to participate in the supervision of government policy implementation, guide the public enthusiasm for political participation, and truly promote the government's scientific decision-making, democratic decision-making and governance for the people.

(V) Strengthening e-governance

To promote the e-governance of urban green development, we shall combine the ideas and methods of e-governance on the Internet. First of all, we should fully master the characteristics of the Internet era, carry out the public service and the "citizen-oriented" concept, innovate the governance mechanisms, make the functional orientation accurate and government management humanized in a convenient, sharing, interactive and efficient governance mode, fundamentally change the traditional service mode of "citizens accept what the government provides", and improve the initiative of the content and ways of information service centering on the new mode of "the government provides what citizens need". Second, we shall use advanced big data, cloud computing, new media and other information technology tools,

340   Z. Zhao

construct a safety and reliable information network infrastructure with unified standards and complete functions, establish an efficient, fast, convenient, safe and reliable e-government application system with wide coverage, integrate the government functions and optimize the operation flows, establish a trans-department, unified, integrated and customer demand-oriented system, which support seamless integration of the foreground (government website) and background (including the government internal management information system, electronic office system, database, security platform, business platform and decision support system). Third, we shall form a mechanism to protect the smooth operation of electronic governance, get rid of the system of management by departments, and strengthen coordination among government departments, to make information freely transferred, conveniently fed back and effectively shared between different government departments, and between government departments and the public. Finally, we shall strengthen the establishment of network security system, focus on protecting the individual privacy and public security, use advanced security technology, and improve information security assurance, system security assurance, security audit, virus and harmful information control and other ancillary work systems, establish network security warning and emergency handling mechanism.

(VI)   Creating green brands

Quelch and Jocz offered five suggestions on the development of city brands in their researches: (1) clarify the city brand orientation concept, which can show various stakeholders (tourists, external customers and external investors, etc.) the declaration of excellence (how can this city be better) as well as the reason why this declaration is reliable; (2) manage the promotion of city brand orientation, especially supervise the cognition and impression of target customers on the city brands; (3) cooperate with the private sectors; (4) coordinate all links and departments; and (5) consider and include the senior leaders of the city.[2] When creating the urban green development brands, we should further clarify the orientation of urban green development, solicit the views of all parties, and thus form the orientation, promotion and evaluation schemes for urban green development brands, and based on the schemes, unite the government, enterprises and social organizations to dynamically combine city's public policies and guidelines, local planning, private and domestic investment, brand strategy, effective marketing and communication implementation and tools and other aspects by building city brands, make the stakeholders in the city change their inherent points of view, share new ideas, and consent to and be willing to make investment and efforts to make the city better.

V. Partnership Strategy

For the coordination strategy of urban green development, its core is to break the boundaries of regions and cities, and combine the national strategy, regional strategy and urban strategy and overall plan intercity relations, urban–rural relations, region relations and international relations from the perspective of globalization and regional integration to achieve mutual progress of urban and national green development.

(I) Establishing systematic green urbanization development system

Green urbanization emphasizes the comprehensive and sustainable development of urbanization, and it is a long-term and balanced development model. China shall seek the best balance between green development and urbanization growth, avoid empty talk about green concepts or blind promotion of urbanization, unify the quality and efficiency of urban green development speed and structure, take the road of green urbanization integrating greening and urbanization and enhance the ability of national urban green development on the whole based on the fact that China is still in the accelerating phase of urbanization and that people's quality of life needs to be improved. From the point of urban system layout, urban function layout, planning, construction, management and other aspects, we shall set up a green policy making, implementation and evaluation system to meet the needs of urban green development; strengthen the overall design, scientific and technological innovation, system reform and policy support; transform the urban development ideas from simply pursuing output capacity and size into improving development quality and benefit and transform the urban development goal from simply pursuing economic growth into population, resources and environment and society progress; and accomplish the comprehensive green transformation from original urban economy society.

(II) Promoting spatial balance of urban green development in China

The space development may be unbalanced due to different basic development conditions, but the balanced development can be achieved by coordinating spatial relations.[3] Hence, China's cities should narrow the difference of space levels and of the green urban development stage. The cities with leading edge should promote the coordinated development of urbanization and green development, strengthen and consolidate the development achievements, improve the quality of development, improve the strategic pattern of regional spatial urbanization taking urban agglomeration as the core, deepen the division and cooperation of cities of different scale, promote the transformation of urban agglomeration from identical development to green cooperation, grasp the commanding heights of the new round of global urban green development, and actively develop a number of world-class green cities that can participate in the global competition and embodies the national competitiveness. The cities with relatively backward development should further consolidate the foundation for the green development and take the industrial green development as the core and transform the "element-driven" model into "innovation-driven" model, lay a solid foundation for urbanization development based on green industry, and gradually narrow the gap between them with those leading green cities.

(III) Focusing on urban green development in the implementation of major regional strategies

During the implementation of key national and regional strategies such as "One Belt and One Road, Yangtze River Economic Zone, Coordinated Development of Beijing, Tianjin and Hebei Province", we shall pay attention to the role of urban green development, make unified arrangements in the planning design and implementation mechanism, take the city as the core and break the limitation of administrative divisions and overcome the system defects including separation of ecological resources, difference in administrative standards and policy mechanisms, unify regional industrial access and environmental management standards, carry out environmental information sharing, promote the establishment of eco-environment joint control and prevention system and foster an urban green development pattern. At the same time, we should enrich the specific contents of different urban green development programs, encourage the cities to embody their green development ideas in functional orientation, industry selection and space layout, realize the resource sharing and complementary advantages and avoid the phenomena where cities ignore the objectives of urban green development due to cut-throat competition in scrambling for resources and policy support.

(IV) Taking urban agglomeration as breakthrough for regional green development

Take the green development of urban agglomeration as the breakthrough for regional green development. According to the development characteristics of urban agglomeration and centered on green development, we should fully focus on resources and environmental carrying capacity of urban space, comprehensively optimize and improve the functions of urban space, adhere to the principle of "quality first", actively construct strong and market-oriented high-end industries with international competitiveness, actively develop a hierarchical and divided scientific and technological innovation system suitable for its own urban system and industry system, achieve an advantageous agglomeration of economic factors and innovation advantages, adhere to dynamic integration, positive interaction and coordinated development of industry, innovation and space, constantly enhance the comprehensiveness, coordination and sustainability of urban development, and form a number of modern green urban agglomerations with strong economic strength, innovation ability, space carrying capacity and service ability.

(V) Promoting the integration of urban and rural green development

The rural area and the city are not totally isolated and incompatible. There is a third choice, i.e. "urban–rural combination", which means harmoniously combining all the advantages and happiness of the most lively and vivid city life and pleasant rural environment, and thus creating new hopes, new life and new civilization.[4] Urban green development shall not aggravate the urban–rural segmentation but shall accelerate the urban–rural integration. We shall strengthen urban and rural planning, make scientific layout of production space, living space and ecological space, unify the promotion of rural urbanization and urban and rural ecological protection, put emphasis on strengthening the ecological construction of the city's ventilation corridors, greenways, river system, wetland and other areas with important ecological value, strengthen the construction of park green space, green buffer, urban greenways and outskirt environment, focus on promoting the green transformation of industrial parks and residential zones in the city, make the intensive and high efficiency production space, comfortable living space and beautiful ecological space, create an urban development environment suitable for living and working. Meanwhile, we shall attach great importance to the problems of rural environmental degradation, enhance regurgitation-feeding function of the city, promote rural ecological conservation and ecological restoration, enhance the service function of rural natural ecosystem, and organically combine urban and rural significant ecological function conservation areas, river system, natural mountains, ecological vegetation and industrial parks, and build the pattern of integrated green development of urban and rural areas. In the process of promoting integrated green development of urban and rural areas, we should attach great importance to the development of counties located at the end of a city and front of a village; support their active participation in the construction of multi-channel, multiform and networked coordination pattern in urban agglomeration and metropolitan areas, establish a regional development system with complementary functions and rational division of labor, receive the technology, capital, talent, information, management and other elements from large and medium-sized cities in the regional urban system, enhance the exchange and integration of research and development, production, services and sales etc., and create a channel for urban and rural development.

(VI) Increasing global influence of urban green development

We shall continue to give full play to the cities' leading role in the national green development and increase the influence of national green development by increasing the international influence of urban green development. The key point is to guide the city to maintain and develop its gathering and radiating role in gathering green resources, creating green vitality, realizing green growth and promoting green development, and to contribute more to the national green development. At the same time, we shall support and encourage the city to plan and promote green development with a global vision, fully master the development direction of global green technologies and industries, unite, combine and use the global talent and capital resources, combine the strategies of "going out" and "bringing in", create a number of hub and node cities networking the development of global green technology and industries, form a new trans-regional, interdisciplinary and interagency pattern for green technology exchange and transformation centered on Chinese cities, take the lead in green technology and industry standards around the world and make breakthroughs in promoted innovation policies and implementation mechanism, thereby highlighting the influence of national green development.

References

1. Peter A. Victor, *Managing without Growth*, China Citic Press, Beijing, 2012, pp. 194–195.
2. J. Quelch and K. Jocz, Positioning the Nation-state, *Place Branding*, 2005, 1(3), 229–237.
3. Albort Hirchman, *The Strategy of Economic Development*, Economic Science Press, Beijing, 1991, pp. 122–148.
4. Ebenezer Howard, *Garden Cities of Tomorrow*, The Commercial Press, Beijing, 2010, pp. 6–9.

Appendix I

Literature Review of Relevant Studies on Urban Green Development Evaluation

Green development is a modern trend and a core subject studied theoretically and practically. The evaluation of green development contributes to the analysis of the overall development conditions as a result of its comparison of different regions, thus allowing residents, governments and enterprises to better understand the green development, general welfare and future opportunities in their regions. Many international organizations, local governments and research institutions evaluate the level of green development by using different perspectives and different indicators and methods. As a result, a number of valuable ideas and methods for green development evaluation have formed. Here, we focus on presenting a few widely recognized studies of green development evaluation from the perspectives of various disciplines and methods, so as to provide reference for the evaluation of urban green development.

I. Green Accounting Evaluation

Green accounting refers to an integrated environmental and economic accounting system that factors the resource and environmental costs into national accounting. As a result of green accounting, data of economic activities that factors in resource consumption and environmental costs will form. The green accounting data will be used not only to indicate the change of the environment, resources

348   *Appendix I: Literature Review of Relevant Studies*

and real social wealth but also to provide bases and reference for decision-making for and the analysis and evaluation of sustainable development, including economic and social development.

Stemming from humanity's perception of environmental change and its exploration into sustainable development, green accounting has been used and improved based on the current national accounting system. Since the 1960s, amid the challenges caused by resource shortage and environmental deterioration, the sustainable development concept that features the balance between the growth of population and the development of resources and the environment has been widely recognized worldwide. The sustainable development of the economy requires countries to change their accounting systems used to evaluate national economic and social achievements, in order to effectively reflect the real gains and costs of national economic activities and motivate people to cherish resources and protect the environment, with an aim to maximize general welfare. The traditional national accounting system primarily focuses on measuring the economic effects of the national economic activities, but it does not reflect the contribution of resource consumption to economic growth or the economic losses caused by environmental deterioration. In this context, international organizations, different governments and research institutions attempt to revise and improve the traditional national accounting system and establish a feasible, effective accounting system that factors in environmental costs and can measure the real level of the development and progress of a country or a region.

The United Nations and the World Bank have undertaken great efforts in implementing the green national accounting system. In 1983, the United Nations Statistics Division officially began the environmental cost counting process. In 1989, the United Nations and other international organizations studied and defined the concept of environmental and resource accounting. In 1993, the United Nations Statistics Division and the World Bank worked together to factor the environment into the framework of the national accounting system that was being revised, forming an Systematic Environmental and Economic Accounting (SEEA). They proposed factoring the

Appendix I: Literature Review of Relevant Studies 349

environment into national accounting for the first time. Through the research and trial by the United Nations Statistics Division, the SEEA system has gradually improved. In 2003, the United Nations Statistics Division launched the newest version of the SEEA system, which is known as SEEA 2003 and used as a model for the integrated environmental and economic accounting by countries around the world.

Many countries and regions have attempted to establish their own green accounting systems that factor resources and the environment into national economy. Norway and Finland factored the consumption of natural resources into their accounting at an earlier date. As early as 1978, Norway began to establish accounting systems for energy, mineral resources, and forest resources, along with air and water pollution. The Norwegian accounting report on natural resources that was published in 1987 laid a solid foundation for the establishment of a green accounting system for national economy in Norway. Based on the general framework of the SEEA, the US has also established an integrated economic and environmental accounting system. According to this system, resources and the environment are counted as production capital; and environmental costs and resource consumption that are related to capital and inventory are counted. Based on this system, detailed economic accounting standards have been established. The Statistical Office of the European Communities (Eurostat) has designed a green accounting system for the EU's national economy. This system has also factored the costs of environmental protection activities into the national accounting. The EU's green national accounting system includes two satellite accounts (an account of environmental protection expenditures and an account of resource use and management) and one system of data collecting and processing. Based on the framework of SEEA and Canada's national conditions, Statistics Canada built an accounting system for resource consumption and environmental costs in 2006, including natural capital accounting, resource consumption accounting, and emissions/discharge accounting, along with environmental protection expenditure accounting. As the current theories and methods of green national accounting remain to be improved and environmental issues

350   *Appendix I: Literature Review of Relevant Studies*

are complex, many countries, such as France, Sweden, Germany, and Finland have adopted different systems of accounting with good results.

China started study on green national accounting very late. Under cooperation with Statistics Norway, the National Bureau of Statistics of the People's Republic of China prepared 1987, 1995 and 1997 China's energy production, accounted its usage and measured the emission volume of eight air pollutants. The National Bureau of Statistics of the People's Republic of China implemented natural resources accounting for the first time in 2001, prepared 2,000 physical scale of national land, mineral, forest and water resources and set some cities of Hainan as the pilot cities for implementation of China's green accounting system to account the loss from industrial pollution and water pollution. Subsequently, the National Bureau of Statistics successfully carried out research on "China's forest resources accounting and inclusion into green GDP" and "inclusion of environmental pollution-caused loss into green GDP". During the period, some universities also launched the green accounting research. In 2004, the Ministry of Environmental Protection of the People's Republic of China and the National Bureau of Statistics jointly prepared *China's Green National Accounting System Framework* and *China's Green National Accounting Research Report* (2004), calculated China's green gross domestic product (GDP) estimated value and accounted the water, air and solid waste pollution of 31 provinces (municipalities) and different sectors. Sustainable development research team of the Chinese Academy of Sciences put forward the accounting method of green GDP, i.e. green GDP refers to the part after deducting the imaginary numbers of natural and cultural parts. The natural imaginary part is reflected in environmental degradation due to environmental pollution; the degradation and proportional imbalance of natural resources; loss from long-term degradation of ecological quality; economic loss due to natural disasters; cost due to resources shortage; and loss from improper use of substances and energy. Research team of Beijing University brought up a set of green input and output accounting systems on the basis of the SEEA Framework of United Nations and

Appendix I: Literature Review of Relevant Studies 351

the general framework for integrated resource-economy-environment input and output accounting, designed comprehensive environment and economy accounting matrix and green social accounting matrix by combining with China's national accounting characteristics, and carried out comprehensive accounting on resource, energy, economy and environment of 1992, 1995, 1997, 2000 and 2002 and preliminary accounting analysis.

Green accounting is developed and improved on the basis of current national accounting system. It is an accounting method measuring the production activities from the perspective of sustainable development for the benefit of mankind. Green accounting that not only considers economic factors but also attaches equal importance to natural resource and ecological environment elements, reflected the relationship between resource and environment, and economic growth; it can not only strengthen and improve the function of national accounting system but is also beneficial to the sustainable development of the economic society. From the perspective of the accounting method, green accounting mainly sets up integrated resources, environment and economy accounting system, and when calculating the GDP, it deducts the cost of natural resource consumption and environmental governance by translating it into currency according to certain methods and then gets the GDP after environment adjustment. There are two prevalent green accounting methods at present: the first is a natural resource accounting method, which pays attention to accounting of the physical quantity, the balance between materials, energy and physical assets of natural resources, and uses physical units to set up physical quantity account at different levels on the basis of national economy accounting framework and accounts the generation, deduction, storage and emission of natural resources and pollutants corresponding to the economic activities; the second is a value accounting method, which mainly estimates the monetary value loss of various resource consumption, environmental pollution and iconological damages, and includes the environmental cost due to production activity into the production cost. Specifically, the value accounting method mainly includes the governance cost method and the pollution loss method.

352   *Appendix I: Literature Review of Relevant Studies*

The pollution governance method is a valuation method based on the environmental governance cost and mainly calculates the actually incurred cost for governing environmental pollution and the virtual cost for the whole governance according to the existing governance technology and levels. The pollution loss method is an assessment method based on the environmental damages and mainly calculates the damages caused by environmental pollution by means of certain technological methods and pollution loss investigation.

It shall be noted that although many international organizations and countries have had beneficial exploration on green accounting, a set of unified green accounting system has not yet been set up in the globe and the existing green accounting results cannot completely reflect the loss from environmental pollution and ecological damages due to huge difficulties in resource and environment cost valuation method and sources of basic data and information. In the long run, how to build a more scientific and feasible green accounting system is still an important topic that needs further study.

II.   Ecological Footprint Assessment

Ecological footprint is a biophysical measurement method to measure and compare the gap between the demand of human social-economic system on the natural ecosystem services and the carrying capacity of natural ecosystem. The current ecological development status in the region can be determined quantitatively by comparing the ecological footprint demand and the ecological footprint supply (i.e. carrying capacity of natural ecosystem). In 1992, the "ecological footprint" was first proposed by Rees, Professor of Planning and Resources Ecology at the University of British Columbia. The ecological footprint refers to the regional space with ecological productivity which can continuously provide resources (or reduce waste) and the regional area with ecological productivity, which is required to sustain the survival of a person, region, country or the whole world or which can reduce the wastes emitted by humans. The so-called "ecological productivity" refers to the capacity of the ecological system to absorb the materials and energy required for life process

Appendix I: Literature Review of Relevant Studies 353

from the external environment and thus to accumulate the materials and energy. It represents not only the influence of specific population on the environment under given technical conditions and at given consumption level and the ecological capacity currently occupied by the population but also the demand of persistent existence of specific population on eco-environmental resources under given technical conditions and at given consumption level as well as the ecological capacity needed by the population.

In the view of the optimum eco-economic size, the growth is achieved with certain costs instead of being free. Originally, the ecological footprint theory followed the idea as follows: Humans must consume various products, resources and services to maintain the survival; all the final consumption of products, resources and services can be traced back to the area of ecologically productive lands, which provide the raw materials and energy required for the production. Therefore, all consumption of human systems can be converted into corresponding area of ecologically productive land theoretically. Considering the per capita consumption level and technological level, the ecological footprint covers the overall and average impact of population on the environment. The ecological footprint theory is mainly based on the six assumptions as follows: (1) the production and consumption process of human society is the process of turning natural resources into waste; (2) the resources or waste streams can be converted as the production area, either producing or disposing them in such process; (3) six types of lands with ecological productivity (i.e. arable lands, grasslands, forests, building lands, waters and fossil energy lands) can be expressed in the standard unit of "global hectare" (the biological productivity per unit of global hectare is equivalent to the average biological yield on global land at the year) according to their output size; (4) the classification of land type is mutually exclusive in space without repetition or overlap; (5) ecosystem service volume and stock of tangible natural resources can be expressed in ecological production area as well and (6) the ecological footprint might be larger than ecological carrying capacity, and the ecological deficit incurred thereof relies on input resources from other areas, disposal of waste in other regions or depletion of natural capital stock in such area.

The ecological footprint is calculated based on the two facts as follows: (1) humans can determine the quantity of most of resources consumed and waste produced by them; (2) these resources and waste can be converted to the corresponding ecological productive area. The following six types of lands are mainly considered in the calculation: arable lands, grasslands, forests, buildings lands, waters and fossil energy lands; and the weighted sum of the ecological production areas of the six lands is calculated. Its calculation formula is:

$$\text{EF} = N \times ef = N \times r_j \times \sum (aa_i) = N \times r_j \times \sum (c_i/p_i).$$

In the formula, EF is the total ecological footprint, N is the number of population, ef is the per capita ecological footprint, aa_i is the biological productive land area converted from per capita trading goods i, i is the type of consumed commodity and inputs, and r_j is the equivalence factor. The biological productivity per unit area of arable lands, grasslands, forests, building lands, waters and fossil energy lands varies greatly, so, in order to make the calculation results comparable, it is necessary to multiply the biologically productive area of every land type by an equivalence factor (weight) to convert it to a uniform and comparable biologically productive area; j is a type of biological productive land; c_i is per capita consumption of commodity i; p_i is average productive capacity of consumed commodity i.[1]

The methods and ideas of ecological footprint assessment and analysis are also applicable to the study of a single ecological object. From the perspective of the ecological system, apart from the lands, water, air, energy, etc., are basic ecological objects as well. Meanwhile, the carbon footprint research is also a focus point at present, where attention has been paid to the issues of carbon emissions and global climate change. The World Wide Fund for Nature (WWF), Global Footprint Network (GFN) and other organizations have separately assessed the carbon footprint and water footprint. China Council for International Cooperation on

Environment and Development (CCICED) and other organizations have published the China Ecological Footprint Reports with WWF simultaneously. Among them, the *China Ecological Footprint Report 2010 — Biocapacity, Cities and Development* published in 2010 points out that, similar to the composition of the global ecological footprint, China's carbon footprint in 2007 accounts for 54% of the ecological footprint. Apart from the expansion of ecological footprint research contents and problem analysis, some scholars have carried out ecological footprint research concerning mining industry, transportation industry, schools, land planning, desertification, and other small and specific industries or sectors and even specific projects.

Of course, there also some controversies for the ecological footprint assessment: (1) in the ecological footprint theory, it's assumed that ecological productive lands are used for one purpose only and the lands are mutually exclusive in space, which may result in deviations of calculation results of ecological footprint; (2) the ecological footprint emphasizes the impact of human development on the environment and resource system and its sustainability but fails to fully consider the economic and social sustainability, especially the impact of technological progress on the development and ecological footprint and (3) human welfare is reflected in many fields and shall not be represented with single index, and according to research results, when ecological footprint is used for assessment of sustainable development at national or regional level, it is often the case that the less developed the economy in a region is, the lower people's living standard is, the stronger the sustainability is, which goes against the idea of sustainability that everyone has the development right.[2]

III. Green Economic Assessment

In recent years, green economy has become an important concept and way of economic transformation and development. In 2009, the Organization of Economic Cooperation Development (OECD) developed a green growth strategy, established a comprehensive analysis framework of economic, environmental and social problems

356   *Appendix I: Literature Review of Relevant Studies*

for all countries, and put forward the solution to environmental pollution and destruction, climate change and other problems by developing economy. In order to guide and evaluate green growth, the OECD has released a report *Toward Green Growth: Monitoring Progress* and built a complete indicator system covering economy, environment human welfare, etc. This system takes the core elements such as environment and resource productivity in the economic activities, natural asset base, environmental factors of living quality, economic opportunity and policy response, social background and economic growth characteristics as first-level indicators. Overall, the OECD green growth strategy framework focuses on economic growth, emphasizing the realization of resource and environment protection through economic activities (Table AI.1).

The United Nations Environment Programme (UNEP) has also been exploring green economy measurement framework, and has finished the *Measuring Progress Towards a Green Economy and Green Economy Indicators: An Operational Manual* and can provide timely and useful guidance on the development of green economy for policy makers of various countries. The UNEP green economy measurement framework mainly covers the contents in three aspects as follows: agenda setting indicators (environmental issues and targets, policy making indicators (policy intervention, cost and effectiveness) and policy evaluation indicators (impact on welfare and equity), including the economic transformation, resource efficiency, social progress and well-being of humans. Among them, the economic transformation is the core of the green economy. The current investments are mostly concentrated in the industries with high consumption, high pollution and high emission. The green economy is aimed at transferring the investments to low-carbon, clean and resource saving industries. One of the remarkable sign of successful economic transformation is the improved resource utilization efficiency. The most important goal of green economy development is the social progress and well-being of humans (Table AI.2).

In addition, Dual Citizen, an international consulting company, has developed the global green economy index (GGEI), established four indicators including leadership, policy, clean technology

Appendix I: Literature Review of Relevant Studies 357

Table AI.1. OECD Measurement Indicators of Green Economic Growth.

Core Indicators	Specific Indicators
Environment and resource productivity	Carbon and energy productivity Resource productivity: Materials, nutrients, water, waste Total factor productivity after environmental adjustment
Natural asset base	Stocks of renewable natural resources: Water, forest and fishery resources Stocks of non-renewable natural resources: Mineral resources Biodiversity and ecological system
Environmental dimensions of living quality	Environmental health and risk Environmental services and facilities
Economic opportunity and policy response	Technology and innovation International financial flows: FDI and aid, etc. Taxes, prices and transfers Regulation and management measures Skills and training Environmental goods and services
Socio-economic background and growth characteristics	Economic growth and structure Productivity and trade Labor market, education and income Social-demographic model

investment and sustainable tourism, and evaluated the national policy implementation and performance concerning the development of green economy. Currently, the GGEI (3rd edition) covers 27 countries and their cities and mainly adopts the satisfaction survey method in the evaluation based on 1,440 survey samples (Table AI.3).

Generally, the UNEP's design concept of green economy measurement framework is similar to the OECD green growth strategy framework. These two frameworks cover economic, social and environmental issues and are aimed at reducing environmental pressure. However, they have many differences, for example the OECD focuses more on economic growth, emphasizing protecting resources and

358   *Appendix I: Literature Review of Relevant Studies*

Table AI.2. Framework of UNEP Green Economic Indicators.

Agenda setting indicator	Climate change	Carbon emissions/renewable energy sources (its proportion in energy supply)/per capita energy consumption
	Ecosystem management	Forest area/water resources pressure/land and marine reserves
	Resource efficiency	Energy productivity/material resource productivity/water resource productivity/CO_2 emissions
	Chemicals and waste management	Waste collection/recycling and reuse rate/waste production or burial capacity
Policy making indicators	Green investment	R&D investment/EGSS investment
	Fiscal reform	Fossil fuels, water and fishery subsidies/fossil fuel taxes/renewable energy subsidies
	Pricing	Carbon price/ecosystem service value (e.g. water supply)
	Green purchasing	Expenditure of sustainable procurement/ government operational productivity
	Green working skill training	Training cost/the number of trainees
Policy evaluation indicators	Employment	Construction industry/operation and management/income creating/Gini coefficient
	Environmental goods and services sector performance	Value added/employment/material productivity
	Total wealth	Value of natural resources stock/annual average net worth/literacy rate
	Resource availability	Modern energy/water resources/sanitary fittings/medical treatment
	Health	Proportion of harmful substances in drinking water/number of the sick due to air pollution/ number of traffic casualties

environment through economic activities, but the UNEP pays more attention to environmental protection and invests more funds in the environmental fields. Moreover, the UNEP embodies social progress and human welfare in the frame design and index construction, while the OECD pays less attention to this and pays more attention to

Appendix I: Literature Review of Relevant Studies 359

Table AI.3. GGEI of Dual Citizen, an International Consulting Company.

Category	Indicator	Proportion (%)
Leadership	Head of state	15
	Media reports	10
	International forum	55
	International aids	20
Policy	Commitment on renewable energy sources	20
	Clean energy policy	25
	Emissions	40
	Renewable energy target	15
Clean technology investment	Amount of investment	30
	Commercialization of clean technology	30
	Innovation of clean technology	30
	Investment facilitation	10
Sustainable tourism	Tourism competitiveness	45
	Certification scheme	45
	Evaluation of the Ministry of Education	10

the influence of policy on economic activities. The GGEI of Dual Citizen is not evaluated with objective statistical data but evaluated subjectively. It has certain value in the evaluation of green economy effect, but its evaluation structure is more likely to be restricted by sample size and sample coverage.

IV. Green Index Evaluation

At present, there are two influential green indexes mainly, i.e. the "green index" of environmental quality put forward state by state by American scholars B. Hall and M.L. Kerr in 1991, and the "green index" of consumer environment protection proposed by *National Geographic* and GlobeScan jointly in 2008.

In 1991, the American scholar Bob Hall clearly put forward the "green index", evaluated and ranked the environmental quality in 50 states by using a comprehensive method of measuring environmental health and finally put forward the policies and guidelines to improve the environment in the book *1991–1992*

360   *Appendix I: Literature Review of Relevant Studies*

Green Index: A State-By-State Guide to the Nation's Environmental Health. The green index evaluation index system has first-level indicators, second-level indicators and third-level indicators, totaling 256 indexes. Thereinto, the first-level indicators are divided into two categories: green state indicators and green policy indicators. The green state indicators consist of seven second-level indicators (including 1. air pollution, 2. water pollution, 3. energy consumption and transportation, 4. toxic substances, 5. hazardous and solid waste, 6. community health and working environment, 7. agriculture, forestry and fisheries and entertainment), which comprise 179 third-level indicators. The green policy indicators consist of two second-level indicators, i.e. government guidance and policy promotion, totaling 77 third-level indicators, which highlight the role of government in improving environmental quality. The green index will convert the raw data of each indicator into data per capita, data per area or correlation ratio, so as to minimize the impact of difference in the area or population size of states. For weighting selection, every indicator in the green index is provided with the same weight, and the missing value is replaced by an appropriate numerical value. The ranking is made in following steps: Calculate all the indicators and rank the indicators separately, and then add up the indicators in same category to get the integrated ranking correspondingly. The results of green index indicate that there is an important relationship among economic justice, public health and the overall environment. The society will be faced with the risk of crisis if any of the three parts is lost.[3]

In 2008, *National Geographic* and *GlobeScan*, a famous Canadian polling company jointly launched a global survey of "green index", which focused on the consumer behavior that is closely related to the environment. The survey builds a green index from the perspective of consumers. It covers four parts of housing, transportation, food and other commodities, which are weighted by 30%, 30%, 20% and 20%, respectively. In 2008, it investigated 14,000 consumers from 14 countries for the first time. In 2009, the survey was extended to 17 countries. For the green index ranking, India, Brazil, China and

Appendix I: Literature Review of Relevant Studies 361

Argentina ranked in the top four, but the US, Canada, Japan and Britain ranked behind.

V. Governance Performance Evaluation

A representative research achievement based on environmental governance performance evaluation is the environmental sustainability index (ESI) (renamed as the environmental performance index, EPI) jointly developed by Yale University and Columbia University in 2000. The index system can measure the sustainable development degree in different countries on the basis of environmental protection. In 2006, the team released the EPI (including 16 basic indicators) to replace the ESI for the first time, and improved and published 2008EPI, 2010EPI and 2012EPI (including two goals, 10 policy categories and 25 basic indicators) successively. Thereinto, the two goals are environmental health and ecosystem vitality. Ten policy categories include impact of air pollution on human health, impact of water on human health, environmental burden of disease, impact of air pollution on ecosystems, impact of water on ecosystems, biodiversity and habitats, forest, fisheries, agriculture and climate change. Six of 25 basic indicators (i.e. per capita emissions of sulfur dioxide, per capita emissions of nitrogen oxide, per capita emissions of volatile organic compounds, per capita emissions of carbon dioxide, carbon dioxide emissions per unit GDP, carbon dioxide emissions per unit generating capacity), reflect the efficiency of energy saving and emission reduction of different countries. In EPI, the weights of indicators are usually determined through the principal component analysis, equal weight method and Delphi method. But the weights of indicators are constantly adjusted and changed every year since the standard is not uniform (Table AI.4).

VI. Comprehensive Welfare Assessment

(I) Human Development Index

Human Development Index (HDI) is an index proposed by the United Nations Development Programme (UNDP) in the "Human Development Report 1990" to measure the economic and social

Appendix I: Literature Review of Relevant Studies

Table AI.4. EPI Indicator Framework.

Goal	Category	Basic Indicator	
Environmental health	Impact of air pollution on human health	Indoor air pollution	PM2.5
	Impact of water on human health	Availability of drinking water	Availability of healthcare
	Environmental burden of disease	Infant mortality rate	
Ecosystem vitality	Impact of air pollution on ecosystem	Per capita emissions of sulfur dioxide	Emission intensity of sulfur dioxide
	Impact of water on ecosystem	Change in total water	
	Biodiversity and habitats	Biome reserves	Marine reserves
		Important habitat reserves	
	Forest	Forest destruction and damage	Change in forest coverage
		Change in forest reserves	
	Fisheries	Fishing pressure in the coastal shelf	Overexploitation of fish resources
	Agriculture	Agricultural subsidies	Pesticide regulation
	Climate change and energy	Per capita emissions of carbon dioxide	Emission intensity of carbon dioxide
		Carbon dioxide emissions per unit generating capacity	Renewable energy generation

development levels of the United Nations member states, which is the result of a challenge to the traditional gross national product (GNP) index. In 1990, the UNDP created the HDI, which is a comprehensive index obtained according to certain calculation methods with three basic variables "life expectancy, education level and quality of life", and published in the "Human Development Report" of that year. The characteristics of HDI include: Firstly, it

Appendix I: Literature Review of Relevant Studies 363

can measure the basic connotation of human development; secondly, it only includes limited variables, which is easy to calculate and manage; thirdly, it's a comprehensive index instead of including many independent indicators; fourthly, it includes both the economic and social choices; fifthly, it maintains the flexibility of index range and theory.

(II) Inclusive Wealth Index

The Inclusive Wealth Index (IWI) is primarily proposed by the UNEP to calculate wealth based on the value of manufacturing capital, human capital and natural capital stocks. Among them, the natural capital includes farmland, forest resources, fishery resources, fossil fuel resources, metal and mineral resources, etc., and it's adjusted according to some indicators, such as carbon losses, oil capital gains and total factor productivity (Table AI.5).

From the perspective of indicator, the IWI emphasizes the role of natural capital in the creation of wealth. At present, the IWI has been covered in countries including Australia, Brazil, Canada, Chile,

Table AI.5. Indicator System of Inclusive Wealth Index.

Natural Capital	Indicator
Farmland	Crop yield and price, rental rate, crop harvest area, long-term crop land area and permanent pasture land area
Forest resources	Forest reserves, forest commercial accumulation, timber production, timber production value, rental rate, forest area, non-timber forest benefits (NTFB) value, percentage of forest area used to extract NTFB and discount rate
Fishery resources	Fishery stocks, capture fishery's value, fishing quantity, occupancy rate
Fossil fuel resources	Reserve, output, price, rental rate
Metal and mineral resources	Reserve, output, price, rental rate

364   *Appendix I: Literature Review of Relevant Studies*

China, Columbia, Ecuador, France, Germany, India, Japan, Kenya, Nigeria, Norway, Russian Federation, Saudi Arabia, South Africa, the US, the UK and Venezuela.

(III)   Genuine Progress Indicator

The Genuine Progress Indicator (GPI) was proposed by Cobb and others of Redefining Progress in 1995. The GPI is designed to measure the genuine economic welfare of a region. The indicator extends the traditional national economic accounting framework, which includes three accounts of society, economy and environment, and was first applied in the US, Canada and the UK.

GPI and GDP have the same study model, and some important differences. For example, all "expenses" for social disorder and backward development caused by crimes, natural disasters and family disintegration are regarded as social wealth in GDP without distinguishing economic activities that increase welfare and reduce welfare, and ignoring the contribution of non-market transaction activities, such as family and community, natural environment, etc. The GPI estimates more than 20 aspects that have been neglected in GDP, which increases family and volunteer work's contribution to the economy, monetizes the non-market services such as family work and voluntary activities, measures the national welfare from an economic perspective, considers the depletion of natural and social capital, and calculates the values of services and products consumed in economic activities. Specifically, the GPI's adjustment to GDP is mainly reflected in the expenditure deduction of three aspects, that is, defense expenditures, social costs and environmental assets and natural resources consumption.

GPI estimates more than 20 economic factors that have been neglected in GDP, which helps to measure the level of good living and to better understand whether economic growth has actually made progress. It has made up for the deficiencies in GDP to a certain extent and incorporates the value of both market and non-market activities in a concise and comprehensive framework. At the same time, since it's difficult to measure the non-market goods and

Appendix I: Literature Review of Relevant Studies 365

services, a revised accounting system is needed. In addition, it is often subjective to determine whether a certain factor in GPI adjusts GDP in positive or negative direction, which has great influence on the accuracy of measurement results.

(IV) Your Better Life Index

Your Better Life Index is created by the OECD, which mainly evaluates the quality of personal life from the perspective of welfare. Your Better Life Index includes four categories, i.e. natural capital, economic capital, human capital and social capital. It includes 11 specific

Table AI.6. Indicator System of Your Better Life Index.

Category	Indicator
Housing	Per-capital housing
	Housing expenditure
	Infrastructure
Income	Household disposable income
	Household financial assets
Employment	Employment rate
	Long-term unemployment rate
	Personal income
	Work safety
Community	Support network quality
Education	Education level
	Years of schooling
	Student's math, reading and natural science skills
Environment	Air pollution
	Water quality
Public participation	Voter turnout
	Rulemaking consultation
Health	Life expectancy
	Self-reported health
Life satisfaction	Subjective life satisfaction
Safety	Murder rate
	Attack rate
Work–life balance	Long duration working staff
	Leisure and personal care time

366   *Appendix I: Literature Review of Relevant Studies*

indicators, namely work–life balance, health, education and skills, social contact, public participation and governance, environmental quality, personal safety, subjective satisfaction, income and wealth, employment and income, and housing. At present, Your Better Life Index is used to calculate the index of 36 countries, including the member states of the Economic Cooperation Organization, Brazil and Russia (Table AI.6).

VII. Green City Assessment

Dr. Rashmi Mayur of India emphasized in the book *Green City* in 1990 that the green city should be the fundamental principle of city planning, which was a natural reaction to the deformed, ugly, diseased and uninhabitable city we created. It not only paid attention to ecological balance and natural protection but also to human health and cultural development. He clarified the essence of green city, and thought that the green city should surpass the coordination between urban construction and natural environment, which should not only emphasize ecological balance and natural protection but also emphasize human health and cultural development. He also emphasized that the essential conditions for a green city were as follows: The biological materials and cultural resources shall be connected in the most harmonious relationship, and they shall be full of vitality and self-supporting and maintain ecological balance. The natural environment shall have full survivability and energy balance, and even output the surplus energy to produce value. The natural resources shall be protected, waste shall be eliminated or reduced as far as possible, and waste materials shall be recycled. The natural space shall be vast, and other species coexisting with human beings shall be rich and varied. Human health shall be maintained and a healthy lifestyle shall be encouraged. Each component shall be arranged according to the aesthetic relationship; the habitation shall be graceful and rhythmic, and the culture shall be comprehensive, and full of joy and progress. Human habitat and new space for future civilization process shall be provided.

Appendix I: Literature Review of Relevant Studies 367

Matthew Kahn, an American economist, believes that green cities should have clean air and water, clean streets and parks. In the face of natural disasters, green cities have the capacity to recover themselves, and the morbidity of infectious diseases in these cities is also low. Green cities also encourage green behavior, such as encouraging people to use less polluting public transport. Matthew Kahn constructs a green city index, and defines green city as a city that can get high marks no matter evaluating locally or globally, i.e. residents of green cities should also avoid bringing negative externalities to residents in other regions, while enjoying the local fresh air and clean water.

Green city index $= (b1X$ environment-related morbidity$)$

$+ (b2X$ environment-related mortality$)$

$+ (b3X$ pollution avoidance expenditure$)$

$+ (b4X$ local discomfort$)$

$+ (b5X$ ecological footprint$)$,

wherein, "b" stands for the weight of index. The city with low index is "green city", and the city with high index is called "brown city". The environment-related morbidity in the equation refers to the number of sick days per capita of urban residents due to the pollution of the urban environment. Similarly, the environment-related mortality refers to the increased risk of death per capita among urban residents due to environmental threats. Pollution avoidance expenditure refers to per capita protection investment, such as bottled water, which increases with the aggravation of pollution. Local discomfort refers to factors that reduce the quality of the local environment but do not necessarily increase the environment-related morbidity and mortality. Finally, ecological footprint refers to the amount of per capita carbon dioxide emissions (in ton).[4] Although a lot of data of the green city index are subjective and not easy to obtain, it provides a standard for us to judge whether the city is green or not.

Some other scholars have established the evaluation index system from the perspective of urban green policy. Kent Portney has constructed green policy indicators for more than 30 cities, and summarized the achievements of some cities in countering the spread of the city and its impact on the environment through the "smart growth" policy. These indicators include whether the brownfields will be redeveloped, whether environmental sensitive areas will be determined through zoning, whether tax incentives will be given to transportation favorable to the environment, whether the parking area will be limited and whether the energy-saving automobiles will be purchased and leased. Portney has calculated the sustainability scores of 24 cities on the basis of these indicators. For example, if a city performs well in 17 indicators of 30 indicators, the score is 17 points. Portney has identified the seven cities with the greatest potential for sustainable development through this method: Seattle, Scottsdale, San Jose, Boulder, Santa Monica, Portland and San Francisco. The scores of the seven cities are over 23.[5]

At the practical level, the US has been leading the world in the assessment of green cities, and the United States Environmental Protection Agency (EPA) has begun the selection since 2005. The data in green guide of the United States Census Bureau and the National Geographic Society are uniformly adopted, which cover more than 30 categories (a total of four classes), such as air quality, energy and transportation. Each category is given a certain weight. The sum of the scores for the four classes obtained by each city determines the level of the green city index. The four classes are: (1) *Energy*: Here, it will be mainly measured whether the city uses renewable energy such as wind energy, solar energy, bio-energy and hydropower. At the same time, it will also be examined whether the city implements policies to encourage residents to use renewable energy. (2) *Transportation*: The air quality, trip proportion of urban public transport mode and whether residents are encouraged to carpool will be evaluated. (3) *Green lifestyle*: The number of green buildings approved by the US Green Building Council, and the areas of public parks and natural reserve in the city will be mainly evaluated. (4) *Coverage of recycling and green strategy*: The implementation of the city's recycling plan and how the city residents view the environmental issues will be mainly evaluated.

VIII. Green Development Evaluation in China

In order to promote the green development in China, form a resource-conserving and environment-friendly spatial pattern, production mode, industrial structure and lifestyle within the region, and construct ecological civilization. Beijing Normal University, the National Bureau of Statistics and other units have started to put forward China's green development index for 6 consecutive years under constant improvement and correction to measure the green development of provinces and cities in China since 2010. China's green development index is composed of three first-class indicators (green degree of economic growth, policy support of government, and potential carrying capacity of resources and environment), nine second-class indicators (green growth efficiency indicator, primary industry indicator, secondary industry indicator, tertiary industry indicator, environmental pressure and climate change indicator, resource abundance and ecological protection indicator, green investment indicator, infrastructure indicator and environmental governance indicator) and 60 third-class indicators, and it evaluates the green development of China's 30 provinces (districts and cities) and 100 key cities. China's green development index has highlighted the combination of green and development, stressed the government's guiding role in green management and strengthened the importance of green production (Table AI.7).

In general, international organizations, government agencies and academic institutions have carried out a lot of valuable studies on green development; the green development evaluation indicator system is developing and improving constantly; and the theoretical framework and method system have been gradually formed. Each indicator system is trying to fully capture and reflect the green development, which has positive significance to both theory and practice. However, there are still some problems to be solved in the present study. For example, in terms of content, most of the indicators in the existing evaluation system put more emphasis on resource and environment content, and lack the comprehensive evaluation on resources and environment, economic development and social welfare.

370   *Appendix I: Literature Review of Relevant Studies*

Table AI.7. Indicator System of Urban Green Development Index in China.

First-Class Indicator	Proportion (%)	Second-Class Indicator	Proportion (in First-Class Indicator) (%)
Green degree of economic growth	33	Green growth efficiency indicator	50
		Primary industry indicator	5
		Secondary industry indicator	30
		Tertiary industry indicator	10
Potential carrying capacity of resources and environment	34	Resource abundance and ecological protection indicator	5
		Environmental pressure and climate change indicator	95
Policy support of government	33	Green investment indicator	25
		Infrastructure indicator	45
		Environmental governance indicator	30

In terms of national economic accounting evaluation, emphasis is put on green GDP accounting, net economic welfare indicators, extended wealth and so on. In terms of ecological environment, more emphasis is placed on the evaluation of environmental quality or "green index" of environmental sustainability. In terms of resources and energy, the global alternative energy index is emphasized. In terms of the evaluation object, most of the indicators are mainly adapted to the state, while relatively few studies are specifically for cities. In the future, how to define the urban green development, how to measure the urban green development, how to better establish the evaluation indicator system that reflects the nature, economy, society, governance and relationship between city and state, and how to guide decision-making and management practice more effectively through the urban green development evaluation indicator system, are issues that need further exploration and research.

References

1. M. Wackernagel and W.E. Rees, *Our Ecological Footprint: Reducing Human Impact on the Earth*, New Society Publishers, Gabriola Island, 1996.
2. F. Nathan, Measuring sustainability: Why the ecological footprint is bad economics and bad environmental science, *Ecological Economics*, 2008, 67, 519–525.
3. Bob Hall and Mary Lee Kerr, *Green Index: A State-By-State Guide to the Nation's Environmental Health*, Normal University Press, Beijing, 2011.
4. Matthew Kahn, *Green City*, Citic Press, Beijing, 2008, 29–33.
5. Portney, Kent E. *Taking Sustainable Cities Seriously: Economic Development, the Environment, and Quality of Life in American Cities*, Cambridge, Mass. The MIT Press, 2003.

Appendix II

Interpretation and Data Sources of Urban Green Development Indexes

Index	Explanation on the Index	Source of Data
Climate	Consists of air temperature index, humidity index and sunny days index	Official websites of cities
Environmental	PM10 (mg/m^3)	World Health Organization
Population	Population density (population per km^2)	Official websites of cities
Growth	Per capita GDP (US dollars)	Official websites of cities
Innovation	Patents	World Intellectual Property Organization
Enterprise	List of Forbes innovation enterprise	Forbes

(*Continued*)

374 *Appendix II: Interpretation and Data Sources*

(*Continued*)

Index	Explanation on the Index	Source of Data
Safety	Crime rate	Official websites of cities and statistical yearbook of the country
Living	Living cost of the local residents	Research Report of Singapore Nanyang Technological University and Mercer Management Consulting
Education	Times 400 universities	Times
E-government	Visits on the government websites	Alexa website
Brand	City brand	Expert scoring
NGO	The seat of offices of the main international environmental protection organizations	Websites of the main international environmental protection organizations
Income	Income index after the adjustment of disproportion	United Nations Programme on International Development
Information	International Internet access rate	World Bank

(*Continued*)

Appendix II: Interpretation and Data Sources 375

(*Continued*)

Index	Explanation on the Index	Source of Data
Health	A percentage of the population who have received improved health facilities to the total population	World Health Organization
Energy consumption	Energy consumption per unit of GDP	World Bank
Emission	Per capita carbon dioxide emissions	World Bank
Purified water	A percentage of the urban population who have received improved water to the total population	World Health Organization

Appendix III

Analysis on Urban Green Development Index Rankings of Main Cities in Asia-Pacific Region

I. China

In light of the comprehensive ranking of urban green development index of cities in the Asia-Pacific Region, the rankings of 43 cities in China are as follows: Hong Kong, Shanghai, Beijing, Changsha, Shenzhen, Chengdu, Taipei, Taichung, Hsinchu, Tainan, Wuhan, Macau, Guangzhou, Kaohsiung, Xi'an, Xiamen, Nanjing, Changchun, Keelung, Qingdao, Hangzhou, Tianjin, Taiyuan, Ningbo, Chongqing, Kunming, Nanchang, Hefei, Dalian, Fuzhou, Haikou, Jinan, Nanning, Huhehot, Shijiazhuang, Zhengzhou, Shenyang, Yinchuan, Urumqi, Lanzhou, Xining, Harbin and Guiyang.

Among them, nine cities of China have higher scores of urban green development index than the overall average score of Asia-Pacific cities. They are: Hongkong, Shanghai, Beijing, Changsha, Shenzhen, Chengdu, Taipei, Taichung and Hsinchu and they are ranked at 4th, 15th, 21st, 36th, 40th, 43rd, 45th, 47th and 51st place, respectively (Table AIII.1).

II. United States

In light of comprehensive ranking of urban green development index in the Asia-Pacific Region, rankings of 19 cities of US are as

378   *Appendix III: Analysis on Urban Green Development Index Rankings*

Table AIII.1. Ranking of Green Development Composite Index of Main Cities of China.

City	Score	Domestic Ranking	Average Score of Asia-Pacific Cities	Overall Ranking in Asia-Pacific Region
Hong Kong	0.611	1	0.466	4
Shanghai	0.550	2	0.466	15
Beijing	0.526	3	0.466	21
Changsha	0.487	4	0.466	36
Shenzhen	0.480	5	0.466	40
Chengdu	0.477	6	0.466	43
Taipei	0.475	7	0.466	45
Taichung	0.474	8	0.466	47
Hsinchu	0.466	9	0.466	51
Tainan	0.463	10	0.466	52
Wuhan	0.457	11	0.466	54
Macau	0.451	12	0.466	56
Guangzhou	0.449	13	0.466	59
Kaohsiung	0.448	14	0.466	60
Xi'an	0.447	15	0.466	61
Xiamen	0.437	16	0.466	65
Nanjing	0.436	17	0.466	66
Changchun	0.432	18	0.466	67
Keelung	0.420	19	0.466	70
Qingdao	0.410	20	0.466	72
Hangzhou	0.410	21	0.466	73
Tianjin	0.405	22	0.466	75
Taiyuan	0.403	23	0.466	76
Ningbo	0.400	24	0.466	77
Chongqing	0.399	25	0.466	78
Kunming	0.393	26	0.466	80
Nanchang	0.392	27	0.466	81
Hefei	0.389	28	0.466	82
Dalian	0.388	29	0.466	83
Fuzhou	0.386	30	0.466	84
Haikou	0.385	31	0.466	85
Ji'nan	0.381	32	0.466	87
Nanning	0.372	33	0.466	89
Huhehot	0.370	34	0.466	90
Shijiazhuang	0.368	35	0.466	91
Zhengzhou	0.365	36	0.466	92

(Continued)

Appendix III: *Analysis on Urban Green Development Index Rankings* 379

Table AIII.1. (*Continued*)

City	Score	Domestic Ranking	Average Score of Asia-Pacific Cities	Overall Ranking in Asia-Pacific Region
Shenyang	0.364	37	0.466	94
Yinchuan	0.361	38	0.466	95
Urumqi	0.355	39	0.466	96
Lanzhou	0.346	40	0.466	97
Xining	0.343	41	0.466	98
Harbin	0.337	42	0.466	99
Guiyang	0.337	43	0.466	100

follows: New York, Washington, San Jose, Houston, San Francisco, Los Angeles, Seattle, San Diego, Chicago, Philadelphia, Dallas, Phoenix, Miami, Boston, Atlanta, Las Vegas, Denver, Detroit and Baltimore.

Among them, 18 cities of the US have higher scores of urban green development index than the overall average score of Asia-Pacific cities and only one city, namely Baltimore, has lower score. This indicates that the US has overall strong strength in green development (Table AIII.2).

III. Japan

In light of comprehensive ranking of urban green development index in the Asia-Pacific Region, rankings of nine cities of Japan are as follows: Tokyo, Osaka, Kyoto, Nagoya, Yokohama, Hiroshima, Fukuoka, Sapporo and Kobe.

All of the nine cities of Japan have higher scores of urban green development index than the overall average score of Asia-Pacific cities, indicating that Japan has overall strong strength in green development. However, the urban green development level of Japan is not evenly distributed and the urban green development index of Tokyo is far higher than that of other cities in Japan (Table AIII.3).

380   *Appendix III: Analysis on Urban Green Development Index Rankings*

Table AIII.2.   Ranking of Green Development Composite Index of Main Cities of the US.

City	Score	Domestic Ranking	Average Score of Asia-Pacific Cities	Overall Ranking in Asia-Pacific Region
New York	0.650	1	0.466	3
Washington	0.611	2	0.466	5
San Jose	0.580	3	0.466	8
Houston	0.578	4	0.466	9
San Francisco	0.556	5	0.466	12
Los Angeles	0.551	6	0.466	14
Seattle	0.540	7	0.466	16
San Diego	0.535	8	0.466	19
Chicago	0.527	9	0.466	20
Philadelphia	0.507	10	0.466	24
Dallas	0.506	11	0.466	25
Phoenix	0.504	12	0.466	27
Miami	0.496	13	0.466	30
Boston	0.494	14	0.466	31
Atlanta	0.485	15	0.466	37
Las Vegas	0.484	16	0.466	38
Denver	0.473	17	0.466	48
Detroit	0.468	18	0.466	50
Baltimore	0.461	19	0.466	53

Table AIII.3.   Ranking of Green Development Composite Index of Main Cities of Japan.

City	Score	Domestic Ranking	Average Score of Asia-Pacific Cities	Overall Ranking in Asia-Pacific Region
Tokyo	0.707	1	0.466	1
Osaka	0.540	2	0.466	17
Kyoto	0.536	3	0.466	18
Nagoya	0.524	4	0.466	22
Yokohama	0.501	5	0.466	29
Hiroshima	0.493	6	0.466	33
Fukuoka	0.490	7	0.466	34
Sapporo	0.478	8	0.466	41
Kobe	0.478	9	0.466	42

Appendix III: Analysis on Urban Green Development Index Rankings 381

Table AIII.4. Ranking of Green Development Composite Index of Main Cities of South Korea.

City	Score	Domestic Ranking	Average Score of Asia-Pacific Cities	Overall Ranking in Asia-Pacific Region
Seoul	0.669	1	0.466	2
Busan	0.457	2	0.466	55
Daejeon	0.450	3	0.466	58
Daegu	0.446	4	0.466	62
Inchon	0.437	5	0.466	64

IV. South Korea

In light of comprehensive ranking of urban green development index in Asia-Pacific Region, rankings of five cities of South Korea are as follows: Seoul, Busan, Daejeon, Daegu and Incheon.

Among them, only Seoul has a higher score of urban green development index than the overall average score of Asia-Pacific cities. Urban green development of South Korea is unbalanced. Seoul's urban green development index ranked second in overall rankings of Asia-Pacific cities, but that of other cities ranked out of the top 50 (Table AIII.4).

V. Australia

In light of comprehensive ranking of urban green development index in Asia-Pacific Region, rankings of four cities of Australia are as follows: Sydney, Melbourne, Brisbane and Canberra.

All these four cities have higher scores of urban green development index than the overall average score of Asia-Pacific cities. The cities have relatively balanced urban green development. Sydney and Melbourne are slightly ahead of others, with the green development index ranking 6th and 13th in the overall ranking of Asia-Pacific Region. Brisbane and Canberra slightly lag behind, with the green development index ranking at 35th and 44th place in overall ranking of Asia-Pacific cities, respectively (Table AIII.5).

382   *Appendix III: Analysis on Urban Green Development Index Rankings*

Table AIII.5. Ranking of Green Development Composite Index of Main Cities of Australia.

City	Score	Domestic Ranking	Average Score of Asia-Pacific Cities	Overall Ranking in Asia-Pacific Region
Sydney	0.600	1	0.466	6
Melbourne	0.555	2	0.466	13
Brisbane	0.490	3	0.466	35
Canberra	0.475	4	0.466	44

Table AIII.6. Ranking of Green Development Composite Index of Main Cities of Canada.

City	Score	Domestic Ranking	Average Score of Asia-Pacific Cities	Overall Ranking in Asia-Pacific Region
Ottawa	0.560	1	0.466	11
Toronto	0.506	2	0.466	26
Vancouver	0.471	3	0.466	49

VI. Canada

In light of comprehensive ranking of urban green development index in Asia-Pacific Region, rankings of three cities of Canada are as follows: Ottawa, Toronto and Vancouver.

All these cities have higher scores of urban green development index than the overall average score of Asia-Pacific cities. The cities have relatively balanced urban green development. In light of urban green development index, Ottawa ranked 11th, Toronto ranked 26th and Vancouver ranked 49th in the overall ranking of Asia-Pacific cities (Table AIII.6).

VII. Russia

In light of comprehensive ranking of urban green development index in Asia-Pacific Region, rankings of three cities of Russia are as follows: Moscow, Vladivostok and Saint Petersburg.

Appendix III: Analysis on Urban Green Development Index Rankings 383

Table AIII.7. Ranking of Green Development Composite Index of Main Cities of Russia.

City	Score	Domestic Ranking	Average Score of Asia-Pacific Cities	Overall Ranking in Asia-Pacific Region
Moscow	0.502	1	0.466	28
Vladivostok	0.410	2	0.466	71
Saint Petersburg	0.377	3	0.466	88

Table AIII.8. Ranking of Green Development Composite Index of Main Cities of India.

City	Score	Domestic Ranking	Average Score of Asia-Pacific Cities	Overall Ranking in Asia-Pacific Region
Bangalore	0.405	1	0.466	74
Delhi	0.398	2	0.466	79
Calcutta	0.385	3	0.466	86
Mumbai	0.364	4	0.466	93

Among them, only Moscow has a higher score of urban green development index than the overall average score of Asia-Pacific cities. The green development levels in different cities are uneven. In light of urban green development index, Moscow ranked 28th, Vladivostok ranked 71st and Saint Petersburg ranked 88th in the overall ranking of Asia-Pacific cities (Table AIII.7).

VIII. India

In light of comprehensive ranking of urban green development index in Asia-Pacific Region, rankings of four cities of India are as follows: Bangalore, Delhi, Calcutta and Mumbai.

All these four cities have lower scores of urban green development index than the overall average score of Asia-Pacific cities, indicating that the overall urban green development of India lags behind. In light of urban green development index, Bangalore ranked 74th, Delhi

384   *Appendix III: Analysis on Urban Green Development Index Rankings*

Table AIII.9. Ranking of Green Development Composite Index of Main Cities of New Zealand.

City	Score	Domestic Ranking	Average Score of Asia-Pacific Cities	Overall Ranking in Asia-Pacific Region
Wellington	0.577	1	0.466	10
Auckland, NZ	0.494	2	0.466	32

ranked 79th, Calcutta ranked 86th and Mumbai ranked 93th in the overall ranking of Asia-Pacific cities (Table AIII.8).

IX. New Zealand

In light of comprehensive ranking of urban green development index in Asia-Pacific Region, rankings of two cities of New Zealand are as follows: Wellington and Auckland, NZ. Both these cities have higher scores of green development index than the overall average score of the Asia-Pacific cities and ranked 10th and 32nd, respectively (Table AIII.9).

Index

A

2030 Agenda for Sustainable Development, 5–6, 11, 14
Affordable for All, 228
Agenda 21, 4
Analysis of Core Indexes, 73, 78, 82, 90
Analytic Hierarchy Process (*see also* AHP), 63
Annual Statistic Report on Environment in China, 295
Anti-Smoking Law, 42
Arrangements for Public Road Emergencies, 254
Arrangements for Red/Black Rainstorm Warning Signals, 254, 258
Artificial Compact Cities, 203
ASEAN Food Security Reserve Board (*see also* AFSRB), 182
Asian Development Bank (*see also* ADB), 167, 319
Athens Charter, 42

B

Baseline Plan, 202
Belt and Road, 99–100
Bertalanffy Equation, 16–17

Better Management, 123
Black Death Plague, 120
Boris Bike Scheme, 135
Brand Index, 87–88
Bridge Express Shuttle Transit (*see also* BEST), 225
British East India Company Trading Port, 221
Brixton Road, 121
Brown City, 367
Brunei Darussalam, 167–168
Building and Construction Authority (*see also* BCA), 110
Build–Operate–Transfer (*see also* BOT), 245
Bukit Panjang LRT Line, 113
Bus Rapid Transit (*see also* BRT), 227
Business–Academia Collaboration, 212

C

$1 + 1 > 2$ Concept, 15
14 Cost Effective Actions to Cut Central London Air Pollution, 129
1956 Clean Air Act, 121
Capital Utility Function, 15

385

386   *Index*

Car-Sharing, 114, 124, 132, 134–135, 270

Carpooling, 270, 273

Central Area Transit (*see also* CAT), 225

Change in Consumption Patterns in the Asia-Pacific Region, 172

Changing Lifestyles, 123

Charging Fees, 336

Cheonggyecheon Restoration Project, 237–242

Cheonggyecheon Square, 238

China City Statistic Yearbook, 295

China Ecological Footprint Report 2010, 355

China Statistic Yearbook for Regional Economy, 296

Circle MRT Line, 113

Cities Without Slums (*see also* CWS), 176

Clean Air Act, 324

Cleaner Air for All: Why it is Important and What We Should Do?, 130

"Cleaner, Greener, Safer and Healthier Penang" Initiative, 232

Clear Water Index, 90–92

Climate Index, 73–74

Combining Heat and Power (*see also* CHP), 185

Commission for Architecture and the Built Environment (*see also* CABE), 282–283

Common Destiny, 310–312

Community of Interests, 291, 311

Comparison of Municipal and Tourism Water Use, 156

Comparison of Score Gap of Asia-Pacific's UGDI, 97

Comparison of the Ranking of Green Development Index, 102

Compressed Natural Gas (*see also* CNG), 115

Concept A, 202

Concept B, 203

Concept C, 203

Contingency Plan for Heavy Air Pollution Day in Beijing, 260–261

Contingency Plan for Sandstorm Disaster in Beijing, 260

Cost of Economic Growth, 26

Cost-Effective Actions, 130–131

D

Daily Air Quality Index, 125

Daylighting, 109

Declaration of the United Nations Conference on the Human Environment, 4

Declaration on Green Growth, 7

Deforestation Avoidance, 175

Delivering Vertical Green, 138

Demographic Dividend, 321

Demographic Status of SEA, 171

Department for Environment, Food and Rural Affairs (*see also* DEFRA), 125

Department of Industry Works (*see also* DIW), 216

DEPO, 215

Distribution of Evaluated City Samples in Asia-Pacific UGDI, 62

Domestic Material Consumption (*see also* DMC), 173

Downtown MRT Line, 113

Downtown Plan, 175, 196, 200–201

Dual Citizen, 356, 359

E

Eastern Silicon Valley, 332

Eco-City Designers, 112

Eco-City Development, 181

Eco-Driving, 129

Eco-Economic Stimulus Packages, 266

Ecological Footprint, 174, 352–355, 367

Ecological Productivity, 352–353

Ecology–Technology System, 35

Economic Liberalization, 144

Education Improvement, 41

Education Index, 82–84

Index

387

E-Governance, 48–49, 60, 267, 339

E-Government Index, 87

Ehealth, 271, 273

Electrical and Electronic (*see also* E&E) Manufacturing, 221

Element-Driven Model, 342

Emergency Engineering Arrangements for Public Roads, 258

Emergency Monitoring and Support Center, 255, 258

Emergency Plan for Traffic Guarantee on Snowy Day, 261

Emergency Response Plan for Schools in Beijing, 261

Emergency Response Committee Office, 261

Emergency Response Law of the People's Republic of China, 261

Emission Index, 90

Empty Cities, 334

Energy Conservation and Emission Reduction Plan, 244

Energy Consumption Index, 90

Enterprise Index, 78–80

Entrepreneurial City, 266

Environment Index, 75

Environment Utility Function, 15

Environmental Business Service, 234

Environmental Management System (*see also* EMS), 233

Environmental Passport, 212

Environmental Regulation, 301, 303

Environmental Sustainability Index (*see also* ESI), 361

Environmental Sustainability, 186, 266–267, 370

EPI Indicator Framework, 362

Estimation Results of Relationships Between Urban Green Development Efficiency and Each Factor, 302

Europe 2020 Strategy, 7

European Green City, 271

Evelyn, John, 120

F

Fearless Square, 199

Fire Services Department, 253

First and Last Mile to Travel, 245

Five-Dimensional Analysis Framework of Urban Green Development, 30–31

Flexible City, 144–147

Foreign Direct Investment (*see also* FDI), 214, 301

Four Stages of Urban Development, 19–20

Framework of UNEP Green Economic Indicators, 358

Framework Policy of Sustainable Energy, 243

G

2013 Global Burden of Disease Study, 122

Gaps in Urban Green Development Efficiency of Cities inside their Provinces, 298

Garden City, 108

Genuine Progress Indicator (*see also* GPI), 364

George Town World Heritage Site, 222

GGEI of Dual Citizen, 359

Ghost Towns, 334

Global Footprint Network (*see also* GFN), 354

Global Goals, 5

Global Green Economy Index (*see also* GGEI), 356–357, 359

Global Green New Deal, 7

Global Greenhouse Gas (*see also* GHG) Emissions, 177, 182, 184, 186

Global Initiative for Resource Efficiency Cities (*see also* GI-REC), 168

Global Leader of Scientific and Technological Innovation, 332

Index

Globalization and World Cities (*see also* GAWC) Research Network, 219

Global–Local Environmental Politics, 266

Godbey's Belief, 286

Goldschmidt, Neil, 195, 200–201

"Going Out" and "Bringing In" Strategies, 345

Good Country Index, 268

Good Development, 45, 336

Good Governance, 38, 44–45, 49–50, 65, 83, 87, 188, 311, 322, 336

Governance Gap, 97

Governance Performance Evaluation, 361

Government–Enterprise–Public Interconnected Network, 49

"Greening" of Capitalism, 267

Green Accounting, 347–352

Green City Assessment, 366

Green City, 235, 237, 244, 249, 366–367

Green Competitiveness, 266

Green Development Community, 305

Green Development Index, 57, 70, 92–93, 98, 100, 102, 369–370

Green Economy, 7, 249, 312, 318, 356, 359

Green Governance System, 305, 312, 336

Green Growth, 206, 215, 356

Green Identity, 310–311

Green Index, 359–360, 370

Green Taxis, 132

Green Transformation, 27, 293, 329, 342, 344

Green Transportation, 244–245, 247, 249

Green Urbanization, 103, 242, 341

Green Vehicle Rebate (*see also* GVR), 115

Green Walls of Grass, 137

Gross Development Value (*see also* GDV), 229

Gross Domestic Product (*see also* GDP), 64, 78, 92, 171, 173, 221, 236, 293, 296, 301, 351, 364

Gross National Product (*see also* GNP), 26, 362

Gross-Plot-Ratio, 229

Growth Index, 78–79, 83

Growth Machine, 50

Growth of Motor Vehicles for SEA Region, 177

Growth Restriction, 193

Growth Trumps All, 25

Growthmania, 26

Guiding Factors, 18, 20

H

Hall, Bob, 359

Hammarby Sea City, 271

Hard Constraints, 324, 326

Harmony in Diversity, 310–312

Health Index, 90

Healthy Air Campaign, 126

Hierarchical Spreading, 29

Higher-End Talents, 33

Highways Department, 254–255, 258

Histogram of Score of Green Development Index of Asia-Pacific Cities, 70

Home Affairs Department, 253, 255

Hong Kong Police Force, 253, 255, 257

Hong Kong's No. 8 Tropical Cyclone Warning System, 251

Housing & Development Board (*see also* HDB), 110–111

Housing Department, 255

Hub and Spoke, 226

Human Development Report, 361–362

Human Development Index (*see also* HDI), 361

Hydropower Plants (*see also* HPPS), 142, 144

Index

I

Inclusive Wealth Index (*see also* IWI), 363
Inclusiveness Strategy, 332
Income Index, 90, 94, 374
Index System of Asia-Pacific's UGDI, 60
Indicator System of Inclusive Wealth Index, 363
Indicator System of Urban Green Development Index in China, 370
Indicator System of Your Better Life Index, 365
Industrial Agglomeration, 300–302, 305
Industrial Civilization, 4, 8, 14
Industrial Revolutions, 12–13
Industrialization, 4, 6, 72, 75, 107, 162, 170, 174, 221–222, 305, 329
Information and Communications Technology (*see also* ICT), 267, 270–271, 273
Information Index, 90
Information Services Department, 253–254, 258, 260
Infrastructure Investments, 123
Inland Spreading, 29
Innovation Index, 78–80
Innovation-Driven Model, 342
Institute for Global Environmental Strategies (*see also* IGES), 185
Institutional Hierarchy of Urban Green Space Management in China, 287
Intelligent Transportation System, 244
International City Brand Workshop, 269
International Energy Agency (*see also* IEA), 169, 243

J

Jack the Ripper, 120
Jackson, Glen, 195, 200
Jacobs, Jane, 200

James I, 120
Japan Council of Local Authorities for International Relations (*see also* CLAIR), 214
Johnson, Boris, 123, 132, 135
Joint Crediting Mechanism (*see also* JCM), 185

K

Kahn, Matthew, 367
King Edward I, 120
Kitakyushu Asian Centre for a Low-Carbon Society (*see also* KACLCS), 213–215
Kitakyushu Foundation for the Advancement of Industry Science and Technology (*see also* FAIS), 212
Kitakyushu Green Growth Project, 205–207, 209–210, 212–213
Knowledge Transfer Networks (*see also* KTN), 212

L

Labor Utility Function, 15
Land Transport Authority (*see also* LTA), 114
Lao People's Democratic Republic (*see also* PDR), 153, 168, 179
Leisure Time, 42
Life Expectancy, Education Level and Quality of Life, 362
Life Index, 82–84
Limiting Factors, 18–20
Liquefied Natural Gas (*see also* LNG), 115, 210
Livable City, 222, 273
London Smog Incident, 324
Low Emission Zone (*see also* LEZ), 123

M

Macmillan, Harold, 121
Malaysian Town and Country Planning Department, 230

390   *Index*

Maritime Silk Road, 99–100
Market Competitiveness, 27, 331
Market-Based Economic Efficiency, 26
Mass Rapid Transit (*see also* MRT), 113, 245–246, 249
Mccall, Tom, 195, 200
Mckinsey Global Institute (*see also* MGI), 221
Mean and Ranks of Green Development Efficiency of Cities, 297
Mechanical Biological Waste Treatment (*see also* MBT), 188
Millennium Development Goals (*see also* MDGs), 5, 180, 310
Minimum Standards for Urban Green Spaces, 281
Ministry of Industry and Industrial Estate Authority in Thailand (*see also* IEAT), 216
Mobility-on-Demand (*see also* MOD), 114
Moving People, Not Cars, 225
Municipal Environmental Monitoring Center, 261
Municipal Solid Waste Generation and Treatment Facilities, 179
Municipal Water Tariff Rates in Selected Australian Cities, 157
Municipal Water Tariff Rates in Selected Chinese Cities, 158
Municipal Water Withdrawal Per Capita, 155–156

N

Nanotechnology, 125
National and Regional Ranking in Water Resources Improvement Proportion, 91
National and Regional Ranking of Per Capita Carbon Dioxide Emissions, 91
Natural Disaster Contingency Plan, 253–255, 258

Necessity of Increase or Improvement of Leisure Space, Facilities and Service, 288
New Job Openings by Industry, Kitakyushu, 208
Nippon Steel Engineering, 211
Non-Governmental Organization (*see also* NGO), 47, 134, 259, 319–320
Non-Timber Forest Benefits (*see also* NTFB) Value, 363
Normalization, 64
North East MRT Line, 113
Northern Corridor Implementation Agency (*see also* NCIA), 225

O

2009 Oxford City Place Survey, 281
OECD Measurement Indicators of Green Economic Growth, 357
One Belt and One Road, 343
Only One Earth, 4
Oregon's Land Conservation and Development Act, 195, 197, 202
Organisation for Economic Co-operation and Development (*see also* OECD), 7, 63, 175, 206, 212, 355–358, 365
Our Global Neighborhood, 44
Overall Contingency Plan for Emergency in Beijing, 261
Overall Ranking of Asia-Pacific's UGDI, 68
Oxford City Council's Corporate Plan 2011–2015, 282

P

Participatory Forestry, 175
Particulate Matters (*see also* PMs), 115
Partnership Strategy, 341
Pearce, David, 7
Pearl of the Orient, 232
Penang and Selected Asian Cities at a Glance, 220

Index

Penang Bicycle Lane Master Plan, 227
Penang Botanic Gardens, 232
Penang Hill, 230, 232
Penang State Structure Plan 2005–2020, 230
Percentage of Population Residing in Urban Areas, 1950–2050, 168
Photovoltaic (*see also* PV) Power Generation, 109–111
Place Making, 223
PMR's Transport Policy Changes, 199
Population Index, 73–74
Portland Metropolitan Region (*see also* PMR), 194
Portland's Politics and Policy Changes, 196
Portney, Kent, 367
Poverty Relief, 40
Principle of "Quality First", 343
Proportion of Service Industry in GDP, 96
Public Participation in Governance, 47
Public Transit Services, 198–199
Public Transportation, 42, 108, 178, 199, 239, 246, 257, 270, 319
Public–Private Cooperative Governance, 46, 337
Punggol LRT Line, 113
Purchase Restriction, 336

Q

Queen Eleanor, 120
Queen Elizabeth I, 120

R

Raising Prices, 336
Ranking of Asia-Pacific Green Development Composite Index, 101
Ranking of Governance, 83, 85
Ranking of Green Development Composite Index, 378, 380–384
Ranking of Inclusiveness, 79, 81

Ranking of Livability, 71
Ranking of Partnership, 88–89
Ranking of Prosperity, 76
Rashmi Mayur, 366
Real GDP Growth of SEA, 172
Realization Mechanism of Urban Green Development, 14, 21
Reduce Emission from Deforestation and Forest Degradation (*see also* REDD), 175
Reduction of CO_2 Emissions, 215
Rees, 352
Region 2040 Growth Concept, 196, 201–203
Relationship Between Asia-Pacific Urban Green Development and Per Capita GDP, 92
Relationship Between Asia-Pacific Urban Green Development and the Quantity of Patent Application, 95
Relationship Between Asia-Pacific Urban Green Development Score and Adjusted Income Index, 94
Request for Proposal (*see also* RFP), 225
Resource Utility Function, 15
Reverse-Osmosis (*see also* RO), 111–112
Rural Area Development, 181
Rural Diseases, 322

S

Schools in Beijing on Heavy Snowy Day, 261
Science Cities, 332
Security Index, 83
Self-Correcting Ability of Democratic Government, 26
Sengkang LRT Line, 113
Sharing Economy, 270–273
Sherlock Holmes, 120
Silent Spring, 4
Silicon Valley of the East, 221

Index

Silk Road Economic Belt, 292–293, 295, 303, 305
Singapore's Public Utilities Board (*see also* PUB), 111–112
Singspring Desalination Plant, 112
Slacks-Based Directional Distance Function Model (*see also* SBM-DDF Model), 294–295
Small- and Medium-Sized Enterprises (*see also* SMEs), 331
Small Middleweight City, 220–221
Smart Cities Wheel, 267
Smart City, 266–267
Smart Economy, 267
Smart Energy, 271, 273
Smart Environment, 267
Smart Government, 267
Smart Growth Policy, 368
Smart Living, 267
Smart Mobility, 267
Smart People, 267
SMOVE, 114
Social Welfare Department, 253, 255, 259
Soft Guidance, 324, 326
Soil Pollution Control, 323
Solar Leasing Project, 110–111
Special Area Plan, 222, 232
Spengler, Oswald, 9
Spreading Effect, 28
Stability and Safety, 43
State of the Worlds' Cities 2012/2013, 107
Statistical Office of the European Communities (*see also* Eurostat), 349
Stockholm Royal Seaport (*see also* SRS), 265–266, 269–273
Strategic Environmental Partnership, 214
Strategies and Policies of Oxford Green Space Strategy, 283
Street "Glue", 132
Structure of General and Recycled Wastes in Kitakyushu, 211
Sufficiency-Level City, 219

Summary of Specific Adaptation Measures toward Resource Efficiency by Sector, 183
Sustainable and Smart City, 265–266, 272
Sustainable Development Goals (*see also* SDGs), 5–6
Sustainable Mobility, 271, 273
Sustainable Economic Growth Benefits based on Fossil Fuel, 26
Sustainable Welfare, 26
Systematic Environmental and Economic Accounting (*see also* SEEA), 348

T

Technology Utility Function, 15
The Limits to Growth, 4
Theory of "Unity of Nature and Man", 24
Thomas Nationwide Transport (*see also* TNT), 133
Tokyo Electric Power Co. (*see also* TEPCO), 209
Tourism Businesses, 155, 162
Traffic Restriction, 336
Transport for London (*see also* TFL), 122–123, 138
Tri-Met, 196, 198–199
Tropical Cyclone Warnings, 252
Typhoon Signals in Force by Education Bureau, 258
Typhoon Warnings, 252

U

UK's Office for National Statistics, 122
Unbalance, 101
United Nations Center for Human Settlements (*see also* UNCHS), 13
United Nations Development Programme (*see also* UNDP), 361–362
United Nations Educational, Scientific and Cultural

Organisation (*see also* UNESCO), 221

United Nations Environment Programme (*see also* UNEP), 7, 356

United Nations Food and Agricultural Organization (*see also* UNFAO), 155

United Nations Framework Convention on Climate Change (*see also* UNFCCC), 243

United States Environmental Protection Agency (*see also* EPA), 197, 368

Universal Design Principles, 227

Urban Community Governance, 48

Urban Disease, 11, 95, 237, 322, 305, 335–336

Urban Ecological Security Pattern, 314

Urban Economic Theory, 18

Urban Green Development Efficiency Index (*see also* UGDE), 295

Urban Green Development Index (*see also* UGDI), 57, 67, 92, 100, 102, 370, 373, 377, 379, 381, 383

Urban Green Development System, 14–15, 322, 325–326

Urban Green Space Area, 285

Urban Growth Boundary (*see also* UGB), 195–197, 201–203

Urbanization (*see also* URB), 3, 9, 51, 145, 170, 178, 181, 203, 219, 242, 289, 293, 300–301, 305, 321, 334, 341, 344

Urban–Rural Combination, 344

Urban–Rural Development, 30

Urban–Rural Dual Structure, 11, 321

Urban–Rural Integration, 319, 344

Urban–Rural Relations, 341

Urban–Rural Segmentation, 344

V

Visual Management, 256, 262

Vostochnyi, 143

W

Wastewater Revolution, 181

Wastewater-To-Energy Technology, 210

Water Footprint, 163, 354

Water Pollution Control, 323

Welfare Enhancement, 40

Welfare Improved Through Free Trade and Globalization, 26

Well-Behaved Lobbies, 201

Wind-Ball Warning System, 252

Wirth, Louis, 48

Work Arrangements in Case of Typhoon and Rainstorm Warnings, 254

Work Arrangements of Emergency Traffic Coordination Center, 258

Work Arrangements under Typhoon and Rainstorm Warning, 258

World Health Organization, 121, 373, 375

World Wide Fund for Nature (*see also* WWF), 354–355

X

Xi Jinping, 214, 291

Y

Youbike, 244–249

Your Better Life Index, 365–366

Z

Zero Growth Strategy, 4, 25

Zero Waste Concept, 187